T0289860

# *Exploring Creativity*

Under the guidance of Moeran and Christensen, the authors in this volume examine evaluative practices in the creative industries by exploring the processes surrounding the conception, design, manufacture, appraisal, and use of creative goods. They describe the editorial choices made by different participants in a 'creative world', as they go about conceiving, composing or designing, performing or making, selling and assessing a range of cultural products. Their study draws upon ethnographically rich case studies from companies as varied as Bang & Olufsen, Hugo Boss, and Lonely Planet, in order to reveal the broad range of factors guiding and inhibiting creative processes. Some of these constraints are material and technical; others are social or defined by aesthetic norms. The authors explore how these various constraints affect creative work, and how ultimately they contribute to the development of creativity.

BRIAN MOERAN is Professor of Business Anthropology at the Copenhagen Business School, and founding editor of the Open Access *Journal of Business Anthropology*.

BO T. CHRISTENSEN is Associate Professor in the Department of Marketing at Copenhagen Business School.

# Exploring Creativity

Evaluative Practices in Innovation,
Design, and the Arts

Edited by

BRIAN MOERAN
BO T. CHRISTENSEN

CAMBRIDGE
UNIVERSITY PRESS

CAMBRIDGE
UNIVERSITY PRESS

University Printing House, Cambridge CB2 8BS, United Kingdom

Published in the United States of America by Cambridge University Press, New York

Cambridge University Press is part of the University of Cambridge.

It furthers the University's mission by disseminating knowledge in the pursuit of
education, learning and research at the highest international levels of excellence.

www.cambridge.org
Information on this title: www.cambridge.org/9781107033436

© Cambridge University Press 2013

First published 2011, 2013
Second Edition 2012
Reprinted 2013

*A catalogue record for this publication is available from the British Library*

*Library of Congress Cataloguing in Publication data*
Exploring creativity : evaluative practices in innovation, design, and the arts / edited by
Brian Moeran, Bo T. Christensen.
    pages    cm
ISBN 978-1-107-03343-6 (hardback)
1.    Creative ability in business.    2. Technological innovations.    3. Design.
4.    Organizational behavior.    I. Moeran, Brian, 1944– editor of compilation.
II.    Christensen, Bo T., editor of compilation.
HD53.E99 2013
658.4′0094–dc23

                                                                        2012036007

ISBN  978-1-107-03343-6  Hardback

# Contents

# Figures and tables

# Contributors

ANA ALAČOVSKA is completing a PhD thesis on cultural production and autonomy in the Department of Intercultural Communication and Management at the Copenhagen Business School, Denmark. Her interests include media and cultural production, creative and media work, new media and digitization, authorship, and creativity. Together with Brian Moeran, she has edited the four-volume reader *Creative Industries: Critical Readings* (2012) and has published in *Communication, Culture and Critique*.

MARIANNE BERTELSEN is a Ph.D. Scholar at the Department of International Economics & Management at Copenhagen Business School, Denmark. She is completing her Ph.D. thesis on professionalization and identity formation at institutions of higher arts education, based on a comparative study of Danish and Chinese academies of fine arts. Additional research areas include artistic work and careers in the cultural industries.

C. CLAYTON CHILDRESS is a Postdoctoral Fellow at the Center for the Study of Social Organization at Princeton University, and an Assistant Professor in the Department of Sociology at the University of Toronto-Scarborough. He has recently published in *American Sociological Review* and the *European Journal of Cultural Studies* and is currently working on a book manuscript on the creation, production, and consumption of Jarretsville, as well as on the Man Booker Prize for Fiction (with Brian Moeran).

BO T. CHRISTENSEN, PhD is Associate Professor at Copenhagen Business School, where he studies creative processes. A cognitive psychologist by training, his research interests focus on creative cognitive processes such as analogy and mental simulation in a variety of the creative industries (design, engineering, cuisine, architecture). Notably, he uses ethnographic methods (including audio and video recordings) to study professionals performing creative tasks in their normal work environment, and subsequently analyzes the transcribed conversations for cognitive operations. Furthermore, he studies how consumers come to perceive creativity in objects. He has published in such international journals as *Memory and Cognition*, *Creativity Research Journal*, *Journal of Applied Cognitive Psychology*, *Journal of Engineering Design*, and *Design Studies*.

FABIAN FAURHOLT CSABA is Associate Professor of Corporate Communication and Branding at the Department of Intercultural Communication and Management at the Copenhagen Business School, where he was a member of the ©*reative Encounters* research program on the socio-economic organization of creative industries from 2006–2010. He received his PhD (Marketing and Consumer Theory, American Studies) from Southern Denmark University in 2000. He was Fulbright visiting doctoral candidate at the University of Minnesota and Assistant Professor at Bilkent University in Ankara, Turkey. He has published in journals such as *Culture Unbound* and *Advances in Consumer Research*, as well as in edited books on marketing. His current research includes food culture and experience, children's fashion, and luxury consumption and branding.

GÜLIZ GER is Professor of Marketing and Director of the Center for Research in Transitional Societies at Bilkent University, Turkey. She obtained her PhD (1985) in Marketing from Northwestern University (USA), MBA (1977) from Middle East Technical University (Turkey), and BS (cum Laude) (1974) in Psychology from the University of Illinois at Champaign-Urbana (USA). She has published in such journals as the *Journal of Consumer Research*, *California Management Review*, *Journal of Economic Psychology*, *Journal of Public Policy and Marketing*, and *Journal of Material Culture*, as well as in a number of books on consumption and marketing. She is currently working on consumption among immigrants, production and consumption of cultural products, historical foundations of consumer culture, and temporality and materiality of consumption practices.

JAKOB KRAUSE-JENSEN is Associate Professor at the Institute of Education, Aarhus University, Denmark. His research and teaching focus on the ways ethnographic research strategies and anthropological theory can be used to understand organizations and the life within them from fresh perspectives. He has done fieldwork in both private and public organizations, and has written a book, *Flexible Firm. The Design of Culture in Bang & Olufsen* (2010) based on his fieldwork among human resource consultants in Bang & Olufsen.

TIMOTHY DE WAAL MALEFYT is Visiting Associate Professor at the Center for Positive Marketing, Fordham University Business School in NYC. Previously Vice President Director of Cultural Discoveries at BBDO Worldwide in NYC, he led an in-agency ethnographic group which uncovered insights for AT&T, Campbell's soup, eBay, FedEx, GE, Gillette, HBO, J&J, Master Foods, New Balance, P&G, and PepsiCo, among other brands. Before this, he generated insights at D'Arcy advertising in Detroit, which led to the successful 'breakthrough' campaign for the Cadillac automobile brand. He holds a PhD in anthropology from Brown University, and is co-editor of *Advertising Cultures* (2003) and co-author of *Advertising and Anthropology* (2012). He is frequently cited in *Business Week*, *The New York Times*, *USA TODAY*, *BrandWeek*, among other media.

CHRIS MATHIEU is Associate Professor of Sociology of Work and Organization at Lund University, Sweden. His research focuses primarily on creativity, evaluation, inter-professional collaboration, gender, and occupational meaning and satisfaction in work contexts. Empirically he has studied the IT industry, and most recently the Danish film industry. He has recently edited the book *Careers in Creative Industries* (2012).

BRIAN MOERAN is Professor of Business Anthropology at the Copenhagen Business School, Denmark, and Director of ©reative Encounters, the program that funded the research of many contributors to this book. A social anthropologist specializing in Japan, he has conducted research over a thirty-year period on different forms of cultural production, including ceramics, advertising, women's fashion magazines, publishing, and incense. He has published several monographs and edited volumes, including *A Japanese Advertising Agency* (1996), *The Business of Ethnography* (2005), and *Negotiating Values in the Creative Industries* (2011, co-edited with Jesper Strandgaard Pedersen).

SHANNON O'DONNELL is Assistant Professor in the Department of Management, Politics and Philosophy at the Copenhagen Business School, Denmark. Her research focuses on innovation processes that involve or are heavily informed by artistic processes, often enabled by technology, and she has co-developed a number of Harvard Business School teaching cases on this topic. She is co-author of two books, *Harder Than I Thought: Adventures of a twenty-first century leader* (2011) and *The Adventures of an IT Leader* (2009), along with articles related to the special pedagogical approach developed for the latter book. Prior to beginning research in the arts and business field, she worked as a professional theater director and dramaturg.

KEITH SAWYER is Associate Professor of Psychology, Education, and Business at Washington University in St Louis. He studies creativity and learning in collaborating groups. He is the author or editor of twelve books, including *Explaining Creativity* (2012) and *Group Genius* (2007). His approach is inspired by his early empirical studies of the interactional processes in jazz ensembles, improvisational theater groups, and children at play. Sawyer analyzes these phenomena within a theoretical framework that he has called 'collaborative emergence.' In his current research, he is studying how teaching and learning are organized in professional schools of art and design, with the goal of identifying a core set of features that can be used to design learning environments that foster creativity.

JESPER STRANDGAARD PEDERSEN, PhD is a Professor at Copenhagen Business School, where he serves as Director of '*Imagine...* Creative Industries Research Center.' His research interests focus on organizational and institutional change, institutional action and agency, industry emergence and field structuring, and organizational identity construction and legitimacy. Studies include cultural transformation processes in innovative firms, mergers and acquisitions in high-tech firms, diffusion and institutionalization of managerial ideas and practices in creative and knowledge-intensive firms. Recent research on changes and strategies for organizing and managing creative enterprises in the film and media field is published in international journals and in *The Negotiation of Values in the Creative Industries: Fairs, Festivals and Competitive Events* (2011, co-edited with Brian Moeran).

KASPER T. VANGKILDE is a PhD Scholar at the Department of Anthropology, University of Copenhagen, Denmark. He is currently completing his doctoral dissertation on creativity in fashion based on ethnographic fieldwork in HUGO BOSS.

# Foreword

HOWARD S. BECKER

Managers like to – well, manage. They like to know that if they do X, they will get Y result. And if all that can be expressed in hard numbers, so much the better. Not surprisingly, they find it harder to do than they would like. And no wonder. The inputs to the equations that might be thought to give the solutions to such problems are difficult to construct, and the actual numbers that would replace the Xs and Ys in them prove themselves difficult to come by. Nowhere is this more evident than in the problem of creativity and the corollary problem of innovation, where definition of the key terms and the discovery of viable metrics have long eluded all the interested parties.

This should not be surprising. Anyone who has actually watched the processes that we like to encapsulate in words like 'innovation' and 'creativity' knows that the people involved in doing these things and managing their being done have great difficulty settling on what the words mean and what indices might be used to measure their presence. The chapters in this volume report the results of close investigation of these slippery variables. The researchers went to organizations which consciously sought to create new and different results, to find innovative ways of producing heretofore unseen products which would appear to the ultimate users. They watched the people who spent their time producing these innovative results and then watched what happened when the rest of the organization had the opportunity to respond to what the innovators had innovated. They followed innovations through the entrails of the organizations in which they occurred and met their fate.

I won't try to summarize the results of this remarkable set of investigations here. The results – no surprise – varied considerably. The industries and organizations involved in creating these hubs of innovation varied in all sorts of ways – size, kind of product, forms of authority, and all the other things students of organizations know so well. Because serious investigation of such processes in depth takes a lot of time and many investigators to do properly, these studies could not produce the numbers of cases standard forms of statistical analysis require. So the results presented here are, in the best sense, exploratory, designed to alert researchers and managers to some, at least, of the things that need to be taken into account when we try to understand how and when new ideas take shape and make their way through a complex business organization.

I take a few lessons from the case studies in this volume. The first is that the crucial thing to understand is that innovation and creativity are not *things* but rather *processes*. They don't happen all at once, as the result of the coming together of an appropriate mix of the right ingredients in the right proportions: so much careful selection of properly trained personnel, so much managerial input, so much in the way of resources of money and time, etc. Innovation is not a 'thing' that comes out of a machine fed the right ingredients. Instead, innovation is a shorthand term for a long story.

The story includes a lot of twists and turns and byways, all explored in the chapters that follow. The story line includes things such as 'new ideas,' 'managerial initiatives,' and 'assessments of marketability.' It is punctuated by events like 'managerial careers' and their stages and steps, 'invocations of company policy,' 'invocations of "the brand,"' 'meetings,' and 'reviews of results.' The story concludes with the outcome with which managerial science generally concerns itself: 'decisions.'

The chapters in this book focus, in large measure, on practices of evaluation. They ask who evaluated the proposed innovations at every step of their progress through an organization, and what the consequences of those evaluations were for the proposed product, for the organization, and for the careers of those involved.

The story-like character of innovation means, most crucially, that appropriate mixtures of inputs never guarantee desired outputs. Each step of a story has several possible next steps, each one leading to a somewhat different outcome, perhaps involving different people. As the number of steps multiplies, the number of possible outcomes multiplies as well. In the end, we can account for the outcome only by telling the story of how it came out that way: who took what steps and then what happened, which possibilities opened up as a result, and which disappeared from view. The chapters in this volume propose – implicitly for the most part, but the implication is there – that the equations for estimating the likelihood of innovation and creativity in organizations lie a long way down the road.

I take a second lesson from these chapters. It takes a lot of people to create 'innovation' and 'creativity.' I put the words in quotation marks because one of the key events in the process we're concerned with here occurs when someone in an organization who is empowered to make that sort of judgment decides that a particular product or idea is, after all, innovative and creative and therefore just what our organization needs or, conversely, that it is not after all either of those things and instead is something that, after all, doesn't 'fit with the image of our brand' or will 'disrupt the way our organization works' or any of the many other things that might lead to a negative evaluation.

The key term is 'someone in an organization who is empowered to make that sort of judgment.' If we make a list of all the people whose inputs to the process affect the result, people who fit that description have perhaps the most influence. They sit at the end of the production line, doing what we might call quality control, and make the final judgment that sends the idea on to full implementation or instead throws it into the bin of rejects. Who sits in that position may well be the CEO or some other highly placed person in the organization chart, but that isn't sure. Only close-up investigation of the organization as it goes about its daily work can reveal who actually makes such decisions. It's never sure who is the crucial decider until you can follow what happens as it happens.

The generalization of that observation says that every person in the organization (and others outside it) has a potential effect on what the organization does. We won't know how innovative and creative acts and results occur until we know what everyone involved (reckoned broadly, I'd better repeat) has done or not done to make things happen just as they finally did happen.

The more easily understood cases in this book describe situations of conflict, in which one party – a designer, perhaps, or the members of a 'creative team' – produces something 'innovative' and another party says 'No.' Saying 'No' doesn't always result from a judgment that the new idea is not a good one but because it runs afoul of something else already in place in the organization: a brand's image, someone's prerogatives which will be infringed on by the consequences of the new idea, perhaps the judgments (real or anticipated) of someone else farther down the line – customers, dealers, etc.

The more complicated stories involve complicated interactions among several categories of people, each group or perhaps each individual pursuing their own interests and not worried that much about the interests of others.

If we combine the possibilities of stages in the story and the possibilities of the conflicting interests of the many groups and individuals who take part or are implicated in all these stories, logic tells us that the number of combinations is very large and the possibility of planning for the desired outcome will be correspondingly difficult, and may be in any practical sense not possible.

A final thought. All the cases in this book started out with the knowing and willing cooperation of the management of the organizations involved. What would they look like if they had been done in some different way that didn't require that cooperation? Would the investigators have seen other things? Would they have glimpsed a different approach to these phenomena which didn't take as given the problem that management presented them with? There's no way to know that until such approaches are tried.

# Acknowledgments

This edited volume is the result of two intensive workshops organized by Brian Moeran and Bo T. Christensen in May and September 2011 under the title of *Creative Encounters: Evaluative practices in the creative industries*. These were two of a number of similar workshops taking place under the auspices of ©*reative Encounters*, an interdisciplinary research program focusing on the socio-economic organization of creative industries. It was funded by the Strategic Research Council of Denmark (2007–2011), and based at the Copenhagen Business School. We are very grateful to both organizations for enabling us to engage in such exciting research.

As organizers, we would like to thank Carsten Yssing, program administrator of ©*reative Encounters*, for the hard work he put into organizing the two workshops. We would also like to thank Associate Professor Keith Sawyer for serving as an excellent discussant at the first workshop, and Professor Howard S. Becker for mentoring and providing inspiration during the second workshop. And finally, of course, thanks to the authors, who accepted our invitation to carry out ethnographies in a string of creative industries, probably without realizing the scope of the journey and the mass of work involved.

The venture of writing this book mirrors many of the topics covered in it. We've negotiated multiple opinions of what the vision for the book was supposed to be, and battled with authors and publishers about the how and why. Was this to be a book situated in the genre of anthropology, business, psychology, of some interdisciplinary mix? Ideas have surfaced, and been killed along the way, where we as editors have also experienced that some of our pet ideas had to be slain. Chapters have been written, rewritten, retracted, failed to meet deadlines, and cut, before we finally arrived at this particular set of chapters. A mysterious syndicate at Cambridge University Press made the decision to support the project, and we wish to extend our gratitude to Paula Parish at Cambridge University Press for nursing this manuscript to book form.

At this point our editorial thumbs are pointing upwards, and now it's over to our readers, critics, and reviewers to make up their minds about whether all this exploring, evaluating, negotiating, and deciding was worthwhile. All we can do now is await their decisions, and contemplate who else we might wish to thank in the obligatory thank-you speeches.

# Introduction

BRIAN MOERAN AND BO T. CHRISTENSEN

This book explores creative processes surrounding the conception, design, manufacture, appraisal, and use of creative goods. In short, it explores creativity. More specifically, it is about evaluative practices in the creative industries: about the choices made by different participants in a 'creative world', as they go about conceiving, composing or designing, performing or making, selling and assessing a variety of creative products. Consisting of ten case studies focusing on a novel, a travel guidebook, performances of a piece of classical music, an advertising campaign, a line of faience tableware, an oriental carpets auction, new Nordic cuisine, film juries, design, and fashion design, this book reveals a broad range of material, stylistic, aesthetic, organizational, situational, and financial factors by which different actors are guided and constrained during the course of their work.

As a general rule, creative work moves through many hands before it finally passes from producer to consumer. In so doing, it is subject to all sorts of judgements by a long series of intermediaries (professional colleagues, clients, performers, managerial staff, and so on) before some sort of evaluative standard of what constitutes creativity is arrived at in relation to work whose quality has yet to be determined by those consumers at whom it is directed (Hauser 1982: 431). The studies presented here show that, to understand the meaning of 'creativity,' we have to explore what choices are made by those involved and from what range of possibilities they are selected (Becker 2006: 26). In short, they take creativity out of the crypt and air it in the alley.

Creativity is a word much used and abused – by politicians, civil servants, policy makers, administrators, and academics, among others. The majority of books with 'creativity' in their titles are in the fields of business and organizational management, which – like politicians, civil servants, and policy makers – see creativity as a – sometimes *the* – key to commercial success. We also find them in the field of education, 'which is supposed to produce the kinds of creative individuals who will go on to

1

succeed in a knowledge-based economy' (Ingold and Hallam 2007: 2). In other words, creativity is celebrated entirely in economic terms as education feeds into the organization of capitalism and business.

And yet creative *processes* are rarely examined in depth in the manner of the case studies presented in this book. This is not to say that *Exploring Creativity* is the only volume of its kind; far from it. Anthropologists, artists, authors, business and management gurus, consumer and cultural studies scholars, linguists, poets, psychologists, philosophers, sociologists, and many, many more have had a lot to say about creativity over the years. But this is the only volume that we are aware of which systematically uncovers the creative processes at work in different forms of cultural production: the (re-)writing, editing, and marketing of an historical novel; the creation of a 'funky-formal' fashion line for HUGO BOSS; preparations for the first performances of a piece of classical music written for not one but four string quartets; the design of electronic goods at Bang & Olufsen; the introduction of a faience tableware range at Royal Copenhagen; the concept of 'good work' for travel guidebook writers in the face of digitization and the Internet; the play-off between age and novelty in the evaluation of the quality and value of oriental carpets; the struggle by different actors for recognition of their role in an advertising campaign that won prizes for its 'creativity'; the processes by which prizes are themselves awarded at film festivals; and the awards systems developed by Michelin and San Pellegrino in the rating of *haute cuisine*.

This in itself invites us to say here and now what the book is *not* about. It is not about the study of consumption practices as cultural or symbolic creativity (Willis 1990). Nor is it about cultural creativity and resistance (Fiske 1989), the aestheticization of everyday life (Featherstone 1991), or cultural intermediaries (e.g. Bourdieu 1984). It does not consider creativity as a 'weapon of the weak': 'the underdogs of the modern world: consumers, workers, women, teenagers, colonial and post-colonial subjects' (Löfgren 2001: 97). It does *not* 'celebrate' creativity (Liep 2001: 1); it merely explores it (Boden 1994).

## Creativity, innovation, and improvisation

This volume provides ethnographies of creativity at work, although only some of those whose stories are told use the word 'creativity' themselves to describe what they are doing. Fashion designers and advertising creatives do, but generally not musicians, writers, designers, or potters. 'Innovation' is another word that may or may not be used. It is important in Bang & Olufsen design, where it implies an ability to produce something that appeals to consumers at a relatively affordable price (Krause-Jensen). It is not important so far as inspectors for the *Michelin Guide* are concerned, but is so for its rival, the San Pellegrino list of the world's '50 best restaurants', under the headings of 'novelty' and 'originality' (Christensen and Strandgaard Pedersen). All these words – creativity, innovation, originality, quality, and so on – are semantically dense 'keywords' (Williams 1976) that allow different constituents in a creative field to propose, negotiate, argue over, and, provisionally at least, sometimes agree on a particular meaning or set of meanings (Moeran 1984). That such negotiations do not always end in a positive result may be seen in the argument that took place between a digital shop and the advertising agency which employed it to help produce an award-winning campaign: each claimed, and refuted the other's claim to, 'originality.' What matters to all concerned is who takes credit for things such as 'originality,' where creative ideas are generated, how they develop, who contributes what, and to what ends they do so: in short, who defines a creative narrative (Malefyt). Those who are publicly recognized for their 'creativity' – an advertising agency or well-known design company, for example – are not necessarily those who create winning concepts; others – a digital shop or independent designer – may be the driving forces behind them. Legitimacy is everything.

One word that illustrates the social processes described in many of the chapters that follow is 'improvisation.' It is how different people decide on and evaluate improvisations made along the way that is of interest, and not just the final product. The argument put forward here rests on two contrasting theories of creativity proposed by anthropologists John Liep (2001) and Timothy Ingold, with Elizabeth Hallam (2007). While the former equates creativity with innovation (Liep 2001: 2), the latter counter-argue that innovation can be gauged only by looking backwards at past products (which is basically how politicians and administrators function because it provides them with a means of *measurement*). What is required, they propose, is a focus on *processes* of 'in-the-making', rather than on the *products* made. At the heart of such processes is improvisation, and it is improvisation, not innovation, which explains 'creativity' because it is *forward-* not backward-looking (Ingold and Hallam 2007: 2–3).

This is a neat distinction, but alas, it doesn't quite work in practice, for it is often hard for those working together in creative situations to detach improvisation from innovation, process from product. Perhaps this is a characteristic particular to cultural production in the 'creative' industries, which are always conceptualizing and manufacturing new products on the basis of past products and experiences. For them, primarily because they are working for the most part with defined genres and brands, the present *is* the past.[1] This is made very clear in how travel guidebook writers improvise with novel descriptive language in their otherwise formulaic tasks, determined by previous guidebooks (Alačovska); and in how a team of young fashion designers must first comprehensively understand and then 'tweak' the BOSS Orange brand in such a way that their collection is 'true' to the brand's image but also advances it onto new symbolic territory (Vangkilde).

Contributors to this book for the most part follow the line that creativity is *product-as-process*, neither one, nor the other, but both together. Take, for example, Clayton Childress's account of the making of the novel *Jarrettsville*, which elicits so many different reactions at different stages in its production and reception that it is more a 'multiplicity of novels' than a single work of fiction. Its author, Cornelia Nixon, first heard the basic plot from her mother at the age of sixteen on an airplane: one of her ancestors had shot and killed her fiancé while pregnant with his child, in front of fifty witnesses during a parade celebrating the fourth anniversary of the surrender at Appomattox in a border town in Northern Maryland following the Civil War. This, together with a family photograph, a single line in a court transcript, a memory of an old backyard, and other details, she gradually turned into a full-blown manuscript that was then rejected by one publisher after another because it didn't fit neatly into any single publishing genre. Was it 'literary' or 'popular,' 'romantic' or 'historical' fiction?

One comment from an editor spurred Nixon to rewrite her novel in such a way that a story about a person (*Martha's Version*) became a story about a place (*Jarrettsville*) and its structural effects upon the characters in the novel. Accepted for publication by an independent publisher called Counterpoint, the revised manuscript was subjected to further evaluation of two different kinds: one related to the image of the

---

[1] In this respect, we might note that creative industries do not even begin to materialize over Ingold and Hallam's intellectual horizon.

publisher; the other to the genre in which the novel needed to be marketed. How was *Jarrettsville* to become a 'Counterpoint book'? The fact that it spanned genres by being both 'literary' *and* 'popular' was good, as was Cornelia Nixon's established reputation as a novelist: both fitted the Counterpoint image. But the novel's opening, with its focus on Martha's love affair, might lead readers to think of it as a 'romantic' novel – and romantic novel it was not, given its unhappy ending. So the author engaged in a further rewrite and reorganization of her material, until the publisher was able to classify and market *Jarrettsville* as a readily recognizable example of 'historical fiction' (even though it wasn't!).

This case study, like many others in this book, elegantly illustrates the processes involved in conceptualizing, making, marketing, and using cultural products, and how different people (writer, editor, publisher, cover designer) are obliged to improvise along the way in order to meet certain established preconditions of the product with which they are engaged. In their edited volume, Ingold and Hallam (2007) posit four characteristics of cultural improvisation which we outline here with examples from other chapters in *Exploring Creativity*. But what we wish to emphasize from our ethnographic experiences is that improvisation is never *only* generative or temporal, never *only* relational or in the way people work. Rather, creative people make use of different forms of improvisation sequentially and/or simultaneously as circumstance requires.

The first characteristic of improvisation is *generative*. Kasper Vangkilde recounts how five young designers, who form a 'Talent Pool' at HUGO BOSS, Ticino, are told by the Creative Director to come up with something 'truly innovative and creative' and present a 'funky-formal' collection for the BOSS Orange brand. The young designers first have to get to know the brand, then seek to be *inspired* as they transform it into a compelling and valuable *concept*. This generates a whole string of ideas – such as Double Life, Surface and Soul, Liquid Cut – that they transform into designs situated between newness and continuity of the brand. But which is 'better' than which? They battle their ideas out among themselves in a series of strategic exchanges, as each tries to convert inspiration into a compelling concept and so justify their status as a *designer*. But in order not to create winners and losers among themselves, they avoid singling out any one concept and, instead, present several in the final round, since it is the

Creative Director who is the ultimate arbiter of BOSS Orange taste. They work, then, in a 'creativity of uncertainty,' guided only by a vague knowledge of and feeling for 'the time' (or *zeitgeist*), and it is such uncertainty that allows the unexpected to emerge: funky-formal as 'ergonomic', 'energetic,' and somehow 'twisted'!

The second characteristic of improvisation is *relational*. In many of the chapters that follow, we see how mutually constitutive relationships are forged – and, in the case of an advertising campaign discussed by Timothy de Waal Malefyt, occasionally questioned – by people working together. Through a concatenation of circumstances, the Danish potter, Ursula Munch-Petersen, for example, found herself attached to Royal Copenhagen's porcelain factory. There, as Brian Moeran relates, she set about developing a new line of faience tableware. To do so successfully, she needed the assistance of Royal Copenhagen's glaze expert, with whom she tested, discarded, and eventually selected a number of different coloured glazes for her pots. At the same time, though, she had to gain the respect of the product manager, with whom she worked to develop suitable forms, and who liaised between her and the company's board of directors, advising her about what to do when, and where to draw the line regarding her craft ideals. She also had to enlist the willing cooperation of other specialists who made mock-ups of her pottery forms, as well as final moulds for casting them. It was the combined abilities of potter, glaze specialist, product manager, and various different factory workers to improvise as they went along, and so to overcome the technical and managerial difficulties that emerged, that enabled the famed *Ursula* line to be mass produced, in spite of reservations on the part of senior management.

Third, improvisation is *temporal*. A piece of music written for four string quartets may have existed first as a composition on paper, but it then had to be played for Sir John Tavener's musical vision to be realized. Yet, getting four string quartets to play *together* – or 'ensemble', in Shannon O'Donnell's phrase – did not involve a simple conversion of written notes to sound. The layout of the venue for the premiere performance – the Rubin Museum of Art in New York – necessitated each quartet being placed on a different level of a spiral staircase. As a result, players in one quartet could not see other players in other quartets. Yet visibility is crucial to communication between musicians, who need gestured cues to maintain a musical rhythm and so 'ensemble.' The resolution of timing thus became central to performance and different options were tried. A lead violinist, for example, stood up to enable others to see and follow her, but she was visible only to some and not to all others. In the end, the issue was resolved – unwillingly on the part of some of the musicians – by use of a 'click-track,' a metronome heard only by the lead player in each quartet, which enabled her to keep in time with the others. Temporal improvisation allowed a musical piece to be successfully performed.

Finally, improvisation is in the *ways we work*. Ana Alačovska's account of travel guidebook writers nicely illustrates this characteristic. Guidebook writers are committed to doing as good a job as possible within the limits imposed upon them by their publishers in what is known as 'the editorial brief.' Constrained by stringent rules about word length, detailed stylistic guidelines, extensive product manuals, and meticulous instructions that characterize both the genre of the travel guidebook and the brief given to each writer by the publisher, guidebook writers take pride in meticulously following instructions (since this may lead to repeat commissions), while at the same time providing work that is 'atmospheric,' that has 'an angle,' and that gives a sense of 'being there' for an imagined audience. Because they care about the products they create, guidebook writers constantly employ craft standards, or inner criteria of excellence, by which they judge good or bad performance.

It seems fair to say that the vast majority of creativity research, especially in psychology, has focused mainly on generative processes: on how creative ideas and products come to surface through more or less 'special' processes such as insight, which arrives seemingly '*ex nihilo*.' Part of the reason may be that a lot of the playfulness and fun in creativity comes from these generative aspects; it was always more fun to follow wild ideas than it was to sort the Post-its and make a plan for action in a brainstorming session. Much of the romantic feel of creativity comes from closely tying it to such specialized, seemingly magical, processes that bring it into being. In this book, we shift the emphasis to the equally important processes of being able to 'explore ideas,' and to 'recognize creativity when you see it,' in order to guide the creative process ever onwards, or to select the uniquely valuable among a pool of ordinaries. The overwhelming focus on generative processes in past research, at the expense of evaluation or exploration, seems unjustified since it does not matter whether someone generates five potentially creative ideas if they are not picked out for further development and brought to completion in the creative process. Creativity involves a heavy dose of both generative and evaluative practices (Finke, *et al.* 1992). This book, then, focuses on the much overlooked judging, picking, choosing, guiding, and directing of creativity. Importantly, we do not intend to replace one romantic set of (generative) processes with another romantic set of (evaluative) processes. By focusing on evaluative practices across a broad range of creative domains, this book uncovers everyday evaluation in the creative industries, and shows it to be much more about bitter quarrels, negotiations, compromises, and 'books by many authors' than a matter of having magical abilities to 'pick the winners.'

## Editorial moments

If we accept that creativity emerges out of a series of different kinds of improvisations made during the *processes* of engaging in cultural production, and that 'innovation' can be recognized and measured only by looking back at past *products*, then we need to ask ourselves why and for what purposes people *evaluate* the work that they do in creative industries. Evaluative practices are what Howard Becker (1982: 198) calls 'editorial moments' – the actual choices made by different people at different stages during the performance of a creative work: a potter's decision to use faience, rather than porcelain, clay for a line of ceramics; an editor's decision to opt for one literary genre rather than another; a composer's decision to write a piece for not one but four string quartets; an audio-visual home electronics company's decision to separate the functions of design and engineering, rather than to make them joint activities. Such decisions tend to have their knock-on effects: the choice of a particular kind of clay affects the kinds of glazes used and thus the finished tableware; a genre change involves writing changes on the part of the author who makes adaptations to the plot of her novel accordingly; compositional style brings in its wake numerous technical difficulties for those asked to perform the piece in question; an organizational decision leads to designs being created first in a 'cloud', then in the more customary 'tube.' During the course of such developments, we find different critical observations about the same product – a dish, a novel, a piece of classical music, or an audio player. These should be seen not as competing solutions to particular problems so much as variations that are in one way or another related (Hauser 1982: 478).

Above all, then, editorial moments confirm that creative work is a cooperative venture (Becker 1982: 201) and it is creative professionals' involvement with and dependence on such cooperative links that necessarily constrain the kind of work they produce (Becker 1982: 26).

Editorial moments constitute a kind of evaluative practice taking place throughout the production–consumption chain. It is easy to assume, mistakenly, that *production* primarily makes use of generative creative processes, whereas the *consumption* side mainly constitutes evaluations by critics, reviewers, and consumers. However, such a close association between production and generative processes on the one hand, and consumption and evaluative processes on the other, is unwarranted. The chapters included here show that evaluative practices in the form of editorial moments are not just something that takes place after the creative outcome is finished, but rather something that occurs throughout the production–consumption chain. One overarching theme in the book is precisely that evaluative practices abound both during the production of cultural goods (typically by the creator or co-creators) and in the consumption thereof (for example, by critics, reviewers, and consumers) subsequent to their making. As such, editorial moments may be separated into two important forms. In the first place, they embrace the internal evaluations made by producers and stakeholders during the creative (and managerial) processes of conceptualizing, designing, and finally making new products. Second, they refer to external, 'post-production' evaluations that seek to compare and rank cultural producers and goods in a particular domain, such as film and food. Some of these are then picked out and given prizes or awards at regular intervals. The ordering of the chapters follows this distinction, in that the primary focus of Chapters 1–7 is on evaluative practices on objects in-the-making, while that of Chapters 8–10 is mainly on editorial moments post-production, with external systems evaluating creative products.

In the first form, we find all the nitty-gritty detail of evaluating practices that, constantly and continuously, take place as those involved in creative work go about their work and search for 'novelty' – that small difference distinguishing this particular product from all others that have gone before or are currently on the market. In order to make such an assessment, those concerned take into account how the current state of the work-in-progress compares with the artist's (composer's, designer's, film director's, potter's, writer's) vision, the criteria and constraints of the task at hand, the norms of the categories and genres in question, and the standards and canons of the domain in which they find themselves. When managers are involved, we find that important editorial moments may be put in the hands of people with a financial, technical, or administrative background – people who are neither trend-spotters nor designers, and probably know little about creative processes. This can lead to 'social dramas' (Krause-Jensen). In organizational contexts, what seems evident from these chapters is that it is less a matter of the creator 'having a vision' than it is a 'struggle for which vision to pursue.' Work-in-progress assessments can be more or less formalized. Product development funnels and stage-gate models explicitly dictate exactly who, when, and how decisions are to be reached when killing ideas. Less visible, but perhaps more common, is the informal on-going conversation among co-creators in trying to make sense of what is good or bad; what holds promise and what is a dead end; what 'sparkles' and what 'stinks.'

The main purpose of this form of editorial moment is to guide the 'creative process' ever onwards in fruitful directions in order to arrive finally at 'valuable novelty.' Progress, however, tends to be characterized by fits and starts rather than by a smooth, continuous flow. Considerable disagreement can arise when key actors make use of differing standards or criteria in their judgements about what is, or is not, 'good.' This then leads to different takes on what the object-in-the-making should be, as well as on whether it will succeed or fail. Several of the case studies in this volume highlight such disagreements. At Bang & Olufsen, a disagreement over the criteria to be used to evaluate good design – one aesthetic, the other functional – led to the establishment of two different departments within the company's organizational structure (Krause-Jensen). Different interpretations of the composer's vision and intention led to disagreement about what criteria should be used to evaluate procedures in performing a piece of his music (O'Donnell). Young fashion designers at HUGO BOSS, exposed to vague and uncertain criteria about what constitutes a particular product line, end up with distinct interpretations of how best to go about the work at hand (Vangkilde).

The second kind of editorial moment concerns the practice of evaluating and making decisions in institutions and systems that are external to the actual production of a cultural good. An art world of any kind devotes much of its time to discussing the relative quality and value of individual artworks, which it then compares, ranks, selects, and rewards. But, as the last three chapters in this book show, the same is true of the worlds of advertising, film, and cuisine, as well as of many other forms of cultural production. In their account of how *Michelin Guide* inspectors arrive at decisions about the quality of the restaurants that they visit, for example, Bo Christensen and Jesper Strandgaard Pedersen highlight a series of editorial moments that leads to their final evaluations: on the one hand, they consider the 'pavillion' – the external impression of the restaurant, telephone enquiries service, reception, quality of overall service, a kitchen visit, and so on. On the other, they turn their attention to the more important 'fork and spoon' or food and wine. Each course – appetizer, entrée, cheese, and dessert – receives its own rating (ranging from very bad, bad, and average, to one, two, or three stars). Each of these editorial moments is designed to answer the question: is there a match between the quality of the food and the bill that is paid? Does a restaurant offer value for money?

Evaluations such as these typically focus on a variety of criteria: 'classical virtues' in the case of the *Michelin Guide*, 'patina' and 'authenticity' in oriental carpets, 'funky formality' in a fashion brand, an ability to 'cross media' in an advertising campaign. Most often, however, it is 'originality' and 'novelty' that cause the most discussion and thus are of value in different domains (such as advertising, art and design, fashion, film, and publishing), even though exceptions (such as the *Michelin Guide*) occur. If such originality is accepted by critics and other gatekeepers, both product and producer may then be assured of a place in the longer-term history of that domain, as novelty is transformed into 'innovation.' Some systems, like the *Michelin Guide*, utilize ratings according to stable and explicitly formulated criteria in coming up with their overall assessment of a restaurant. But in other systems, the weight and selection of criteria are up for discussion and negotiation, as when a film jury has to decide whether this time an excellent cast performance, or a film with a 'a lot at stake,' or the most aesthetically pleasing production, is to be nominated as 'best' film. Yet other systems refuse to rely on explicit criteria, and gain legitimacy instead from the expertise of the judges, as is the case in the San Pellegrino World's 50 Best Restaurants list, which leaves it entirely to each individual judge to work out for themselves what 'best' restaurant actually means when casting their votes.

Precisely because they are in many ways repetitive and routine, as well as innovative, and because they involve reflection on past practice as well as creative solutions to present problems, editorial moments 'embody an interesting and difficult dilemma' for creative professionals. To paraphrase Becker (1982: 204): to produce creative products (including performances) that will be of interest to their target audiences, creative workers need ideally to unlearn some of what they have learned as the conventionally 'right' way of doing things. Totally conventional pieces appeal to nobody; in the lingo of the market, they become 'product failures' or flops. For a product to be successful, therefore, creative professionals should, to some extent at least, transgress standards and expectations that have been more or less deeply internalized. To this end, they enter into an inner dialog, within and among themselves, that evaluates not just the materials, forms, and colours of their designs but the whole world of competing products and organizations.

## Creativity and constraints

One question that we need to ask ourselves, therefore, when considering such editorial moments, or evaluating practices in the contexts of creativity and innovation, is: what choices are being made, by whom, and from what range of possibilities, in the conception, design, production, marketing, sale, and reception of a particular cultural good? As Chris Mathieu and Marianne Bertelsen point out, jury members thrown together to award prizes at a film festival have to start their deliberations by discerning the rules of the context in which they find themselves. They need to learn first how to operate, by establishing the facts of matters at hand and respectfully listening to and considering the perspectives and opinions of all jury members in an effort to come to a collective decision. Only thus will they arrive at a reasoned assessment of what is 'best' (director, screenplay, music, male or female lead, and so on). Operation, then, precedes cooperation, which can end up as a mutual 'back-slapping society' as players bestow upon each other awards (Malefyt). This in itself raises another challenge: is it possible to follow *systematically* 'the invention and testing of multiple possibilities' that are 'the signature of creative activity' (Menger 2006: 63)?

One way to go about answering these questions is by looking at what has been called 'the iron cage' of creativity (Friedman 2001): at the various ways in which artists and craftsmen, designers and engineers, writers and editors, composers and musicians, copywriters, art directors, and account planners, and others in the creative industries, are constrained by material, technological, financial, social, aesthetic, and other forces around them. In the creative industries, there is a continuous, often unresolved, tension between creativity, which we may provisionally define as the ability to push boundaries, and constraints, which uphold them. Just how strong or weak these boundaries are sometimes depends on organizational rules: in Bang & Olufsen's design, liquid that runs in a 'tube' can be controlled and directed, whereas the molecular movements in its alternative 'cloud' are turbulent and unpredictable (Krause-Jensen). In general, though, we make what we make and do what we do because of, and in spite of, the materials and technologies available to us; the people and organizations with which we are, either voluntarily or involuntarily, caught up; and the other, broadly similar, things that others like us have already made or done with the materials and technologies available to them among people and organizations by which they, too, have been surrounded. And all the time we ignore at our peril what it costs us to make what we make, and for whom, and the financial rewards that accrue from the things that we have already made.

## Material conditions

In all creative industries, people tend to rely on established conventions (about how a film should be made, a fashion collection shown, or string quartet perform) in order to go about their work. They all make use of standard equipment and materials, which affect – or, in Gibson's (1977) phrase, 'afford' – both how they work and the finished forms of that work. It is convention that dictates what materials are used; what abstractions are best suited to convey ideas or experiences; and the form in which materials and abstractions are combined (Becker 1982: 29).

The emergence of a set of conventions may depend upon the introduction, or lack, of particular materials. In the early days of film making, for example, when the film camera was not what it is today, electric light was not strong enough to substitute for natural light. As a result, production companies based in New York and Chicago began to seek out sunny locations during the winter season. This led to the establishment of motion picture companies in southern California, where there was a stable climate, a constant supply of natural light, a wide variety of landscape settings, and low wages. As a result, the number of outdoor shootings increased. This in itself encouraged directors to position their cameras more freely, to split camera 'takes' into more frequent and shorter shots, and to introduce long shots as they moved actors and animals deeper into space. From such developments emerged the idea of film as spectacle and the particular genre of the Western (Hutter 2008: 67–69), which quickly developed its conventions of chases, battles, gunfights, rugged cowboys, and so on, which themselves were transferred to the later genre of police detective films.

Given materials, and the techniques afforded for their use, tend to condition cultural forms. A potter, for example, uses clay and glaze materials to form and decorate her pots. Nowadays, as in the case of *Ursula* tableware, the commercial preparation of clays and glazes has advanced to a level where there are virtually no differences between batches of materials. Adjustments do not need to be made every time a new sack of quartz or feldspar is opened and used. Nevertheless, at Royal Copenhagen, workers tend to mix the new with the old, to make absolutely sure that there is a continuity of the ingredients that go into the glazes which, when fired, give pots a standardized finish (Moeran).

In a less industrialized environment, however, neither clays nor glazes are as malleable to production; nor are they as uniform over time. In one particular style of hand-made pottery, for example, there is inconsistency in both clay and glaze materials, depending on where they are dug by potters from the surrounding land. Also, the nature of the clay – in particular, its plasticity – determines in large part what forms potters can throw on the wheel. Clay containing a high degree of iron oxide prevents the throwing of flat plates (because it collapses beyond a certain vertical angle); it also tends to crack at the base if a potter makes it too broad in proportion to the outer rim of the pot. Glaze materials have to be prepared and mixed in such a way that they adhere to the clay and do not fly away during firing. Moreover, since different glaze recipes tend to melt at different temperatures (brown more quickly than green, for example) because of the different ingredients they contain, a potter has to know which parts of his traditional climbing kiln are hotter or cooler than other parts during firing, so that he can fire different glazes to the same overall temperature without risk of excessive breakage (Moeran 1997). All this would change if he decided to use a different kind of clay, synthetic rather than natural materials for his glazes, and a gas- as opposed to wood-fired kiln – in the way done by other craft potters, as well as by Royal Copenhagen.

Similarly, in Fabian Csaba and Güliz Ger's account of oriental carpets, we learn about how the introduction and rapid spread of synthetic dyes and machine-spun yarn in the late nineteenth century led to a decline in both aesthetic and technical quality, as well as to a loss of 'authenticity.' While this development arose from producers' attempts to meet increased (Western) demand, it also led to less variation in the colours used, as well as in the texture of carpets. Structure, surface, and colour may have become regularized as a result, but they put off discerning collectors. Moreover, synthetic dyes faded unsatisfactorily; yet the fade is an important aesthetic dimension of oriental carpets. As a result, note the authors, synthetic dyes and machine-spun yarn 'represent one of the rare examples in which modern science has, at least so far, failed to match traditional standards.'

In their attention to material properties of oriental rugs, Csaba and Ger outline an aesthetic of patina that goes totally against the idea of novelty, generally linked with creative products. They point out that the appearance of a carpet and the manner in which it ages are largely dependent on the dyes that have been used. Dyes differ in their colour fastness and the long-term effect on the wool. Colours tend to fade or otherwise change with exposure to light or abrasion. They may bleed when exposed to moisture, while the dyestuff or processes required to achieve certain hues weaken the wool fibers. Although the bleeding of colours and rapid fading are considered undesirable, since they upset the harmony of the colours or obscure design through loss of contrast, the aging processes through which colours settle, mellow, or soften are generally highly sought-after aesthetic effects. These and other material properties contribute to an oriental carpet's patina. It is *ageing* processes, and not novelty, that are valued.

Other material conditions abound. In the advertising industry, for example, copywriters use particular forms of punctuation and font size for headlines, while selecting from among different typefaces for a 'look' that they feel is best suited to the product advertised. For their part, art directors have numerous illustrated books of photographs and design through which they leaf in search of ideas about how to pose or dress a model, and borrow from them in designing the storyboards that they present to clients. They also use a grid system for illustration and copy layout. Photographers use different camera lenses, apertures, film, and so on to obtain different effects of light, mass, and perspective. Film directors use freeze frames, soft focus, background music, and other filmic conventions in their preparation of television commercials. In all these examples, individual temperament, or *habitus*, influences just which forms are adopted under which circumstances, but the finished work tends to adhere to established formal conventions.

This is not *necessarily* so, however. As we saw above, the introduction of new technology, together with its availability at affordable prices, can change these conventions, as well as the final form of creative products. With the arrival and common use of computers and digital photography, for example, it has become possible to make radical alterations to images. Faces are contorted, bodies twisted, limbs elongated. With a few clicks of a mouse stray wisps of hair can be removed from, or a beauty spot inserted on, a model's face. Airbrushing is the norm, rather than the exception. Digital technology provides art directors, photographers, and cameramen with new ways, and new conventions, to carry out their work (Moeran 2009). It also allows them to introduce new materials, such as the use of flat liquid-crystal display screens in the work of video artists. The development of industrially manufactured steel frames for guitars, together with amplifying equipment, led to a move away from large musical ensembles and to the formation of small bands, which itself instigated the emergence of the genre of rock music (Hutter 2008: 65–67, 69–70).

In a twist on this, musicians obliged to use a click-track found that they could become skilled technicians, but their playing lacked the complexity, spontaneity, and interaction that are the hallmark of professional competence and identity. Yet, it also gave them the opportunity to reconceive their aesthetic approach to the music they were required to play (O'Donnell). As well as *constraining*, therefore, materials and technologies *enable* – as we also see in accounts of how travel guidebook writers react to their editorial briefs (Alačovska), and a novelist rewrites her work in order to avoid being classified in a particular literary genre (Childress). This is the underlying power of *affordance*.

An artist normally works with paints on a canvas. But, as Michael Hutter (2008: 64) points out: 'Oil paints cause severe problems for painters: They react with untreated canvas, making it necessary to protect the canvas with a coating they tend to discolour over time, leaving a brownish tint; and they take weeks to dry, making it necessary to structure the workflow around the drying periods.' This in part explains modern American artists' embrace of acrylic paints, which use synthetic resins rather than oil as a binder, and enable colours to be applied directly to the canvas without leaving signs of a brushstroke. They also dry extremely fast and are cheap enough to be bought by the gallon. In this way, as with Impressionists' adoption of a synthetic cobalt blue (rather than continued use of the priceless ultramarine developed from lapis lazuli), a new painting style of aesthetic expression (Abstract Expressionism) came into being (Hutter 2008: 62–65).

Another material condition comes from the product itself. In the production of the folk art pottery mentioned above, for example, particular sizes of pots (large lidded jars or umbrella stands) can be fired only in particular parts of the kiln. Given the effects of temperature on glazes and the nature of the kiln being used, this means that large wares tend to be fired in certain colours (brown, transparent), not others (black, green). Similarly, in advertising, different products give rise to different styles of advertising. Alcohol and fashion items tend to be image driven, for example, while washing powders and other staples rely more on information in making their sales pitch. Besides the functions they perform, products are likely to attract or repel consumers because of a particular combination of audio, visual, tactile, olfactory, and/or gustatory properties with which they are imbued. Any one or more of these may be picked out as a way of advertising the product as a whole: for example, *At 60 miles an hour the loudest noise in the new Rolls-Royce comes from the electric clock* (Ogilvy 1983: 10). The product, therefore, particularly when it is a *brand*, conditions the direction in which creative expression will go – whether it will tend to simplicity and economy; adopt a quiet and persuasive or light-hearted style; develop an emotional or rational personality, and so on (Burnett 1971: 72–73).

## Temporal conditions

A second set of conditions surrounds the use of *time* in the creative industries. Time is important in three, rather diverse, ways. First, there is what Richard Caves (2000: 3) refers to as the 'time flies' property. *When* a creative product has to be ready for a particular event or the market has a backwards effect on its planning and execution. Deadlines have to be established and met. A book manuscript such as this must be delivered by a certain date for it to go through peer review, copyediting, first-proof printing, proofreading, revisions, second-proof printing, final revisions, indexing, and final printing processes in order for it to be distributed to retail outlets and placed on store shelves 4–6 months ahead of the start of a new academic year, thereby enabling course adoption where appropriate. Similarly, the fixing of a particular time and date for a fashion show or concert obliges participants to calculate backwards the various tasks that need to be completed – designing, sewing, fitting, and modifying a dress, for example, or musicians' rehearsals and accompanying sound and lighting arrangements – in order to be properly prepared to go on stage and perform in front of an audience. Such deadlines are more, or less, complex depending on the cultural product in question.

Temporal conditions concern not just the process of producing a cultural good but also the practices of evaluating it when finished. The *Michelin Guide Book* has to come out on a particular date (Christensen and Strandgaard Pedersen); a film's release date can help or hinder its chances of being nominated for an Oscar or other film award, while the sequence in which films are shown at a festival may well affect their chances of being awarded prizes. A film jury has to operate within very strict timeframes, but it is helped by the unstructured time that elapses between viewing a film and discussing it in a plenum session with other jury members. This enables individual members to lobby for or alter their initial perceptions and views through informal social interaction (Mathieu and Bertelsen).

Second, time can also be a conditioning factor depending on the medium or communicative channel used. For example, the fact that a fashion show conventionally lasts for an absolute maximum of twenty minutes affects how many items a designer can show, which in itself influences her choice of garments: formal and informal, office and sportswear, evening dress and casual skirt, bridal dress, and so on. Similarly, the convention that a film characteristically lasts longer than ninety minutes but less than two hours affects editing decisions and even story line (as we know from the alternate endings of *Cinema Paradiso* made available through the introduction of the DVD format). In advertising, a fifteen-second television commercial offers extremely limited opportunity for an advertiser to include very much more than its own name and the name of the product or service it is promoting, whereas a one-minute radio commercial enables a fast-talking narrator to give information about a product and even to repeat catchy sell-lines. The shorter the time available to broadcast advertising, the more likely it is that it will rely on 'mood' rather than 'information' as its mode of persuasion.

Finally, time is important in the sense that every cultural product is conceived, made, advertised, distributed, and received in an historical context of all similar products that have preceded it. Ideally, it should differ – if only marginally – from such previous outputs and, ideally, from comparable outputs simultaneously on the market (Hower 1939: 338). Creative professionals need to find the right balance between the brand and the 'non-brand,' between something that is recognizable but not quite recognizable. Thus, the young designers working on the HUGO BOSS Orange label were required to create something that was 'new' yet 'distinctly Orange.' Their collection had to be different from last year's Orange collection, as well as from competing offerings by H&M and other menswear collections. Similarly, all advertising campaigns should, ideally, differ from previous campaigns, both for the product being advertised and for competing products, in order to mark them off as 'recognizable, but unrecognizable.' Those that do so successfully are selected for prizes – such as the CINEVISION 'Watcher' campaign discussed by Timothy de Waal Malefyt, which received multiple awards at the Cannes Film Festival for its ability to capture the sense of the medium of outdoors while innovating within it.

Different gatekeepers may disagree, however, about the relative value of the 'recognizable' *vis-à-vis* the 'unrecognizable,' as when two competing restaurant-ranking systems (the *Michelin Guide* and the San Pellegrino World's 50 Best Restaurants list) seem to display opposing emphases on the merits of 'innovation' as a criterion of quality. Nevertheless, creative activity ideally 'takes apart the structure which was formerly created but restores it in a more complex form and gives to its components a new meaning, a new value, and a new structural role in the totality of the work' (Hauser 1982: 400). Here the field clearly affects not just the positions taken by individual creative individuals or organizations but the mode of communication that they adopt. Every fashion designer, every film director, every rock artist 'expresses himself in the language of his predecessors, his models, and his teachers' (Hauser 1982: 30). In other words, the constraints of time in the broader sense of historical continuity mean that creative expression is not 'created' so much as 'renewed.' In this sense, as Ana Alačovska shows in her discussion of travel guidebook writers, and Csaba and Ger of oriental carpets, evaluative practices are closely patterned on genre.

## Representational conditions

Representational conditions are fundamental to creative practices and products, even though creative people often express an inability to talk about their work (Moeran, Vangkilde), and even though what is *not* said is often as important as what *is* said. Indeed, creative work is often assumed to possess 'ineffable qualities' that are seen to characterize Art, Literature, Music, and so on – on the principle that, like pornography, you know it when you see, read, or hear it!

Although constraints in representation are primarily 'aesthetic,' they may also be derived from ethical and legal considerations, which may be formal and/or informal. In Japanese advertising, for example, advertisers are legally bound to include a *ping-pong* sound at the end of a TV commercial to signify to viewers that a medical product has been advertised. In many countries, cigarette advertisements must carry a health warning notice that extends to up to one third of the size of the ad itself. Incense manufacturers cannot now import agar wood and use it in their products because of a ban on its extraction. Perfumers have difficulty obtaining Mysore sandalwood because of Indian government restrictions on logging activities. Ursula Munch-Petersen and her colleagues at Royal Copenhagen Porcelain Factory had to find an alternative to glazes containing lead once it was recognized that this material could be deadly. All these legal restrictions oblige those working in the creative industries to find alternative solutions: using synthetic rather than natural oils in incenses and perfumes; creating glazes with materials other than lead.

Informal constraints also abound. In some countries (such as Japan) comparative advertising is considered to be in 'bad taste,' while in others (such as the USA) it is quite acceptable. In the fashion world, a recent development has been disapproval, or banning, of 'size zero' models from the catwalks because they are unrealistically thin. Proposals are also being put forward in one or two European countries' parliaments that the current practice of airbrushing models' blemishes so that they appear to be perfect be treated in the same way as cigarette advertising: with a warning to that effect. If passed, such proposals will become law and affect the representation of virtually all images in the media.

Different genres tend to encompass distinct representational constraints. Porcelain, faience, stoneware, and earthenware use different clay and glaze materials requiring or affording different skills that result in the end product being endowed with different aesthetic ideals. Similarly, different genres of music – classical, rock, and jazz – align different instruments together, as well as different ways of playing them. In book publishing, literary genres have separate conventions for paper size, title and cover layout, binding methods (cloth and/or paperback), and so on (Childress). Constraints on the appearance of consumer electronics can be quite different, depending on whether a device is designed visually to look good when not in use, or whether it is supposed to afford easy interaction with its user (Krause-Jensen). The merging of genres poses particular problems for the designer, who has to interpret which of two (or more) sets of representational constraints to adopt, and which to discard, when creating a product that is neither one genre nor another – witness the 'funky formal' approach to the Orange clothing line designed by the Talent Pool for HUGO BOSS (Vangkilde).

Aesthetic tastes form the main representational constraint in cultural production. No work that we think of as 'contemporary art,' no film that we see as an 'action film,' no music that we listen to for its 'rock' is ever marked by an aesthetic that is not an essential and accepted characteristic of contemporary art, action film, or rock music. Each carries its own set of aesthetic conventions – abstract daubs of paint on an unframed canvas, car chases, and the inevitable quartet of lead singer, drummer, rhythm and base guitarists in a rock band – that makes the creative product immediately recognizable. In this way, representational conditions sustain different genres. As Childress notes, a genre is 'a mutually constitutive and ritualized code of classifications' through which people strive to make sense of creative products at different stages in their production, distribution, and reception. Genres bring on 'disagreement, disorder, innovation, creativity, and strategy' at textual, contextual, and organizational levels. They thus constitute 'contested domains.'

Aesthetics is often inextricably tied in with material and technical conventions. A composer selects one key rather than another for a melody, and then one note or phrase rather than another because a particular aesthetics of music allows it and not the other (Becker 1982: 40–41). They also write for one instrument or group of instruments rather than another – because stringed, not brass, instruments are seen to be more 'suitable' for a romantic piece of music, for instance – and each of the musicians then makes choices about the phrasing or bowing of the final score (Becker 2006: 26). Such conventions allow us to call that score (classical, pop, jazz, rock, and so on) 'music' rather than mere 'noise.'

The borders of each of these genres can be pushed, but only so far. The five young designers charged with coming up with a line of clothes for the HUGO BOSS Orange label found themselves in a dilemma. What kinds of 'newness' could they safely introduce? At what point would a particular innovation, or combination of innovations, make their designs appear not to be 'distinctly Orange'? Somehow they had to find a compromise between 'too much' and 'too little,' and out of this dilemma funky-formal was born (Vangkilde). Similarly, Japanese advertising copywriters and art directors liked to talk of being just a 'half pace' – no more – ahead of society. If they were a full step ahead, or a half pace behind, nobody would pay attention to their work. Thus, in order to differentiate his client's product (a contact lens) from that of its competitors, an art director decided to colour the lens cut green rather than blue (the colour used in all competing ads) because he sensed the beginning of an environmental trend in Japan (Moeran 1996: 158–159).

Just how far borders can be pushed would seem to depend both on the nature of the product and on the social world of which it is a part. The looser the aesthetic constraints, the easier it is to innovate, and vice versa. In Japan, when the thirteenth-generation enamel overglaze artist Imaizumi Imaemon received a prestigious prize at a national exhibition, one of the judges summarized his committee's choice as follows:

Look. The Imaizumi family has been making bowls like this for centuries. Imaemon's father made one just like this, with its floral motif, and so did his grandfather. So did his great grandfather, and probably several other ancestors before him. But Imaemon has produced something different. He has painted the flowers pink rather than red, like everyone before him, and has painted them on a grey, rather than customary blue, background. That's why we gave him the Princess Chichibu's Prize. He was stretching tradition to the limit.[2]

This kind of comment reveals the power of judges, critics, and other professional reviewers in aesthetic (and other) evaluations. It is their

---

[2] Brian Moeran: interview with Yoshida Kōzō, Tokyo, June 1981.

decisions to award this or that prize that have a ripple effect, not just on the further reception of the creative products in question but on how similar new products will (or will not) be produced in the future, as art directors, chefs, film producers, musicians, and so on strive to be noticed, or in some cases (Malefyt, Christensen and Strandgaard Pedersen) contest decisions made. These evaluations may also have organizational repercussions. A favourable review of an earlier work in, for example, *The New York Times* can influence a publisher's decision to accept the same writer's latest manuscript and to promote it to 'lead title,' with all the content, formatting, and marketing adjustments that then need to be made (Childress).

## Spatial conditions

The organization of creative work is often characterized by spatial separation of one kind or another. A fashion designer and the seamstresses putting together his clothes do not work in the same room; nor do musicians and sound recorders, art directors, and account managers, and so on. It is often held that such physical separation enables creative processes, although there may well be other consequences. At Bang & Olufsen, design concepts were developed in a totally separate 'attic' known as *Idealand*, access to which was limited. Here was a space clearly marked out and separated physically from the rest of the organization. At the same time, the designers who worked there were seen to be 'elevated' and their aesthetic criteria to represent 'the apex of creative purity,' uncontaminated by 'petty market analysis or humdrum technical considerations' (Krause-Jensen).

We have already noted some effects of space on different forms of cultural production. Such effects can be material and technical. For example, the fact that large pots can be placed only at the top of a climbing kiln chamber if they are to avoid breakage means that they can be glazed only in some colours, not others. The move by film production companies from indoor to outdoor locations in the early twentieth century brought about the introduction of new filming techniques. But space can also lead to symbolic effects. In the studio shoot of an advertising campaign, different personnel are assigned to work in different areas of the studio and its annex, but there is a highly charged common symbolic space in which the two key actors, the art director and photographer, take up their positions and negotiate the work in hand. It is on this point, a photographic stand, that all converge between takes to offer advice or remain silent, and await further directions (Moeran 2009: 969–972).

Spatial constraints come to their fore in the institutions used to display or perform creative work. Theatres are of necessity much smaller than concert halls because a play of any kind requires that its audience hear actors' voices without the mediation of microphones, and can clearly see their facial and bodily gestures. This is not the case in a concert hall, where audibility, not visibility, is paramount. Similarly, rental costs contribute toward the comparatively small size of art galleries in downtown urban areas. As a result, they tend to exhibit the work of single artists when it comes to special one-man exhibitions. Museums of art, however, are able to display much more because of their size and, in the process, classify artworks into historical periods, styles and schools. Retail outlets – a jewellery store, for example, or department store gallery – use space to order goods on display: cheap objects are placed in the shop window and near the entrance in order to entice customers inside; once there, they are steadily drawn in to the most expensive items on display, often placed on plinths or behind glass to signify their value.

Perhaps the most notable example in this volume of the constraints imposed by spatial conditions is Shannon O'Donnell's discussion of rehearsals for Sir John Tavener's composition for four string quartets. The challenge was for string quartet musicians, accustomed to performing as a group of four in close physical proximity, to play coherently as four groups of four, seated apart. After all, in general, musicians' ability to work together depends on 'whether they are able, at a technical level, to hear one another in order to play in perfect time together and produce a balanced and integrated sound. Close spatial proximity becomes a crucial condition of this activity, insofar as it enables the musicians to hear, as well as see, corresponding visual cues.'

Here, physical separation hindered the creative process. After all, the use of sixteen rather than four musicians necessarily expanded the space between them. But then different venues added to the difficulty. In a museum of art, the quartets had to play on different levels of a spiral staircase; in a hall they were located seventy feet apart. As O'Donnell comments: 'At a certain distance and in certain configurations, the laws of physics make it impossible for the musicians to play in time and produce a balanced and integrated sound, as their hearing becomes distorted by delays related to the time it takes sound waves to travel.' As a result, they had to *see* one another in order to be able to take their cue from the leading violinist. Against everything that they felt and believed in as professional musicians, they found themselves obliged to adopt a pre-recorded cueing track delivered to the musicians through a wireless earpiece. This enabled each quartet located on each floor not only to hear the lead violinist's beat and time but to play more softly and to *hear* one another – something that had not been possible before.

Physical location can also be important symbolically, as opposed to technically, in the performance of creative outputs. Acting a part in *Hamlet* in the Shakespeare Theatre in Stratford-upon-Avon, for example, can be more inspiring, as well as more anxiety inducing, than playing the same part in a repertory theater in the north of England. Putting on a fashion show in the palace at Versailles can induce a thrill not experienced in a run-down warehouse in Seoul. Playing a Beethoven piano concerto in the concert hall of the Berlin Philharmoniker can be more uplifting than playing the same piece with a different orchestra in the Wigmore Hall, London. As we know well from our (televisual) participation in football matches and other sporting events, the atmosphere induced by an audience in a particular location often affects actual performance. Better a full house in a small venue than a half-empty concert hall or lecture theatre.

Spatial conditions often combine with other constraints to affect the appreciation of a cultural product. With oriental carpets, for example, certain combinations of spinning, knotting, or weaving techniques, sizes, stylistic elements, or other properties are known to be characteristic for a given region and era of production, and affect collectors' appreciation (Csaba and Ger). Probably the best known example of a spatial condition in this respect is that of *terroir* in the production of French wines.[3] By carefully 'limiting the number of appellations and the amount of winegrowing land that can be established in a given territory based on existing reputations' (Garcia-Parpet 2011: 125), the *Appellations d'origine controlée* 'turned terroir names into guaranteed income for reputable vineyards' and established, in contradistinction to

---

[3] In their chapter in this volume, Bo T. Christensen and Jesper Strandgaard Pedersen refer to the 'terroir' of New Nordic Cuisine, whose core values are associated with 'purity,' 'freshness,' and 'simplicity,' based on 'local, seasonal ingredients' ('Nordic terroir') and with a 'healthy, green, and environmentally friendly profile.'

the state-organized mass wine market, a limited field of cultural production, of the kind outlined by Pierre Bourdieu (1993).

Spatial conditions may thus affect the *form* of a cultural product.
Take this book, for example. The contract signed by the publisher and
editors stipulates that the manuscript should not exceed 120,000 words
in length. The underlying reason for this is primarily financial. 120,000
words translate more or less into 352 pages, while title pages, acknowl-
edgments, contributors' biographies, and indexes add a further 30 or so
more. Books such as this are bound in signatures, usually consisting of
16 or 32 pages, and it is the number of signatures that determines
the cost of printing. Publishers tend to think in terms both of print
runs and of x, y, or z number of signatures – as well, of course, as
page and typeface size – when deciding at what retail price a particular
book should be sold.[4]

The fact that the length of this book has been pre-established by the
publisher then affects the form it takes. For example, in our discussions
about how to edit the volume, we considered several different models,
each of which affected the length of each chapter and number of contributors. A chapter length of 10,000 words, for example, allowed for
twelve chapters, including this Introduction, while one of 5,000 words
would have doubled the number of contributions. But what form would
those contributions have then taken? Some chapters might have consisted of case studies, and others of theoretical analyses. In that case,
would some contributors not be allowed to analyse their own case
material? Should we then follow the standard format of edited volumes
and allow each contributor to write a longer piece in which they both
presented and analysed research data? How many cases did we wish to
include, anyway? Should we cover evaluative practices in *all* creative
industries (a near impossible task, given the word limit imposed by the
contract)? Or should we present an eclectic selection based on the rich-
ness of the research material and potential theoretical elaboration?
A different answer to each of these editorial moments would have
made the book somewhat different from the final result that you now
hold in your hands.

---

[4] The fact that this book is first published in hardback gives it, and its editors,
cultural capital as a 'serious work' (Childress), although it also encourages book
sales to libraries (which need durable volumes) and thus provides the publisher
with economic capital.

## Social conditions

One of the most important things characterizing a creative industry is that it provides 'a supply of interchangeable human parts' (Becker 1982: 78). This means that in the creative industries one can count on replacing people with others just as good. This in itself encourages a 'climate of collaboration'[5] and enables 'creative' work to be carried out in fairly routine ways, but the introduction of new personnel brings about new opportunities as well as constraints.

Social conditions of creativity may be broadly distinguished into three sub-sets: those stemming from the fact that most forms of cultural production consist of close contact and communication (Fukuda 1992: 147) among networks of cooperating personnel; those connected with the fact that much creative work is commissioned; and those that affect the content of the creative outputs themselves. Each of these highlights, to different degrees, the delicate balance between the unpredictability of individual *habitus* and the structured rules imposed by the field (Bourdieu 1993).

First, every creative industry has a pool of skilled personnel on which it can draw to carry out some specialized task. Some are in more demand than others because of the, generally technical, nature of their skills; there tends to be an over-supply of those whose roles are thought to contain some element of 'creativity' (Becker 1982: 77) and thus more than the market can bear (Towse 1996: 99). There are two basic organizational principles – one stable, the other discontinuous – underlying the work of the 'motley crew' (Caves 2000: 6–7) in cultural production. At one extreme, creative personnel are allocated particular tasks because they work for organizations – copywriters for an advertising agency, for example, or stylists for a fashion magazine publisher – and build networks, reputations, and careers through their organizational affiliation. Their work thus tends to follow established practice within the ad agency or magazine publishing house and to be subject to internal politics relating to hierarchy, promotion opportunities, gender, and so on (Becker 1982: 81–82).

---

[5] In creative industries generally, a lot of attention is paid to who can and cannot work or collaborate with whom. Persons with known animosities towards each other are not placed together in the same design or advertising campaign creative team, for example, while 'notorious assholes' are avoided when putting together film juries (Mathieu and Bertelsen).

At the other extreme, those forming a pool of support personnel are contracted for each task separately – a freelance copywriter for a single ad campaign, or a model and makeup artist for a fashion shoot. For the most part, it is established personal connections that enable one hair stylist or actress rather than another to get a particular job. Their professional specialization in a single task, however, can lead to an over-emphasis on the importance of their own contribution and to their paying little attention to, or even questioning (Moeran 2009: 973–975), other aspects of the creative work in which they are involved. It can also lead to their being 'type cast': this photographer is good for soft-focus images, that for food; this model for a magazine fashion story, that for a catalogue (and not vice versa) (Mears 2011).

Precisely because, first, creative work is guided in large part by personal connections, as well as by reputation established by previous assignments; because, second, the elements that go into a creative product cannot be determined; and because, third, there is great uncertainty surrounding the final result – what Caves (2000: 4) calls the *nobody knows* property – creative personnel have to build up relations of *trust* (Becker 1982: 87). In fact, trust can be a deciding factor in cultural production (Odagiri 1992: 109–110) and ideally exists at three different levels of organizational interaction.

In the first place, because creative partnerships – like those of copywriter and art director, or photographer and model – are hemmed in by constraints of one sort or another, those involved have to trust each other to be able to work together effectively. This is clear in the relationship between editor and author (Childress), as well as between members of four string quartets (O'Donnell). It has to be built between Ursula Munch-Petersen and those working in different departments of Royal Copenhagen (Moeran), and also among the five fashion designers placed together for the first time in HUGO BOSS's 'Talent Pool' (Vangkilde).

Second, creative workers have to trust those humdrum personnel outside the partnership to do what is necessary for them to get on with their job without interference. A composer has to trust that the musicians performing his piece know what they are doing and will do it according to his original conception. Designer, product manager, modellers, and glazing engineer have to trust that their company's managers know what they are doing, and vice versa. If trust fails to be built up satisfactorily by all parties concerned, or if existing relations of trust are for some reason broken down (because of, for example, a merger or acquisition and accompanying managerial incompatibility), then things go awry.

Third, the organization for which such people are working (whether provisionally or on a more permanent basis) often has to build up trust with other organizations involved – an advertising agency with its client, production company, studio, model agency, and so on; a fashion company or porcelain factory with subcontractors abroad. Similarly, an organization must itself be trustworthy. An oriental carpet or art collector, for example, must be able to trust that an auction house will not put up fake carpets or paintings for sale for him to be able to contemplate bidding. Trust, then, applies both to products and to those handling them.

All this is nicely summed up by Jakob Krause-Jensen in the context of Bang & Olufsen design. The company places trust in its freelance designer, who himself must trust and collaborate with concept developers for his ideas to be accomplished. The latter, for their part, must collaborate with engineers in 'the tube.' Establishing relations of mutual understanding and the trust that accompanies them *take time*. At Bang & Olufsen, it was built over decades between the staff of *Idealand* and the designer, David Lewis. These relations of trust between specific persons and groups also worked as social alliances and implicit cultural understandings that made it difficult for alternative visions and practices to be established.

Social constraints in creative work also arise from the fact that it is often commissioned. David Lewis, for example, is an independent designer who has been employed to design new products for Bang & Olufsen over more than five decades. Working to find a solution to each new problem put to him, he has time and time again come up with new product designs that have fashioned, and become synonymous with, the company's global reputation for design. In the art world, meanwhile, patrons over time have had an enormous influence on the selection of an artist's subject matter, materials used, size of work, and so on (Baxandall 1972). Collectors of contemporary art still commission work (witness Charles Saatchi's commissioning of Damien Hirst's infamous stuffed shark (Thompson 2008)); it is their likes and dislikes that determine what will, and what will not, come onto the market.

In the creative industries, such social constraints are often organizational. In advertising, for example, a client has a major role in the selection of campaign ideas put forward by an agency. It may also make certain demands with regard to selection of model, actress, or celebrity used in the campaign and the clothes she wears, and even interfere with details of the print ads to be run (Moeran 1996: 158–159), as well as tell a photographer how to do his work (Rosenblum 1978: 429). The client's or creative team's preference for one personality rather than another affects the style of an advertisement, since they will bring an already established image to the product being advertised and thus affect its representation (Moeran 1996: 156).

Organizational constraints also take place within a particular set of social relations. Since access to the independent designer David Lewis is extremely limited, those who *do* come into contact with him can leverage their authority within Bang & Olufsen's organization as a whole (Krause-Jensen). A travel writer has to consider the demands made by a guidebook publisher and somehow set the practicalities of the task in hand against its financial remuneration, so that she will be asked again to contribute to another guidebook project by the same publisher (Alačovska). A team of fashion designers finds itself considering not just the brand that it is required to develop but the creative director who will judge its efforts and the final result of its work, on the basis of his own immersion in the HUGO BOSS corporate culture and the Orange brand (Vangkilde). The finished product then becomes an adaptation to both stylistic and social/organizational constraints.

So, social constraints affect cultural products themselves in a number of ways. On the one hand, by commissioning work, patrons of one sort or another (businessmen, collectors, gallery owners, museum curators, and government departments) influence the form it takes; on the other, particular combinations of personnel can lead to particular, and predictable, styles of work. Indeed, the more people work together, the more likely they are to develop particular routines. Certain film directors (such as Pedro Almodóvar) work with a stable of actors on which they draw for each successive work and create a certain style; jazz instrumentalists team up to form groups that then develop a certain sound.

## Economic conditions

First, the general state of a country's economy almost certainly influences the extent to which a creative industry can or cannot be creative, since the bottom line tends to take on overriding importance in a recession. The so-called 'creative revolution' that took place in the British and US advertising industries (as well as in the fashion industry) during the 1960s was made possible by a strong economy; it was pushed aside by the recession following the oil shocks in the 1970s. Similarly, Japanese advertising flourished in the late 1970s and the 1980s, only to fade as the country slipped into a prolonged period of little or no growth. In times of prosperity, advertisers are prepared to give creative ideas a chance; in times of hardship, they focus on sales and are not prepared to take risks on 'creativity.'

Second, the budget put aside for film, rock concert, fashion show or advertising campaign has a huge effect on its form in terms of *what* can be done *where* by *whom*. The concert series, or 'spectacular', *This is it*, that Michael Jackson was rehearsing up to the time of his death, allowed for a multi-purpose stage with mobile ramp, ejection platforms, and numerous stage effects, including enormous robot machines and pyrotechnics, as well as a giant video screen with especially shot film, backing singers, musicians, dancers, and aerialist choreography. In contrast, a normal rock concert or festival allows for little more than the standard equipment (lighting and sound) that enables a series of rock groups to perform their music on stage in front of an audience.

Similarly, in advertising, a large appropriation affects the style and expression adopted in a campaign since it enables use of a mass medium such as television (with all its temporal constraints, noted earlier). At the same time, a large budget may well enable selection of a foreign (usually exotic), as opposed to domestic, location for filming; a small budget usually means that advertising creativity must be limited to print advertising and function within a studio frame.

A big budget also enables the contracting of (internationally) famous personnel to participate in films, concerts, advertising campaigns, and so on. A budget of $100 million buys more 'star power,' computerized pyrotechnics, and exotic locations than one of half that amount. This conversion of economic capital not only gives the finished product a certain cultural *cachet*, it usually influences its reception by the public.[6]

Economic constraints find their most obvious expression in price. An auctioneer relies on prices bid in previous auctions to estimate how much a particular item – in this case, an oriental carpet – will fetch at

---

[6] In advertising a large budget has a further economic effect in that it may well contribute to a campaign's reach and recall (McCracken 1989).

his own auction. Such estimates can be misleading, as happened when one oriental carpet fetched a price five times its estimate. In fact, the auctioneer had missed a sale at which the final price for a similar carpet had been well above his estimate, but which, fortunately, failed to reach the price at which his own carpet was finally knocked down (Csaba and Ger).

Prices are usually fixed according to the cost of materials and labour that go into a product's manufacture. By her own criteria, the ceramist Ursula Munch-Petersen reckoned that the retail prices for items in her *Ursula* range were too high. In particular, they failed to conform to her aesthetic philosophy that pots should be functional and therefore reasonably priced. But retail prices for *Ursula* tableware were affected by at least three different factors. One was the ceramist's perfectionism that required test pieces to be made and re-made time and time again. Another came about because the management of Royal Copenhagen decided to discontinue the production of the faience ware in Denmark and outsource it to a Japanese factory, where labour was by no means cheap. Finally, *Ursula* tableware retail prices were in part affected by the fact that Royal Copenhagen specializes in high-quality porcelain wares. Although faience wares could and should have been cheaper in terms of materials and labour, the company did not wish to detract from its high-quality image by selling some of its output at a lower price range than porcelain (Moeran). Here we have a not uncommon example of economic conditions being an outcome of material, organizational, and representational constraints.

## The name economy

The worlds of different creative industries such as those discussed in this book routinely create and make use of reputations: of individual actors, works, genres (often in the form of brands), and organizations. Like art worlds,

They single out from the mass of more or less similar work done by more or less interchangeable people a few works and a few makers of works of special worth. They reward that special worth with esteem and, frequently but not necessarily, in more material ways too. They use reputations, once made, to organize other activities, treating things and people with distinguished reputations differently from others. (Becker 1982: 352)

A theory of reputation for the creative industries follows to some extent that proposed by Howard Becker (1982: 352–353) for art worlds in that: (1) specially talented people (2) create products that are seen to be innovative, *different*, and thus exceptional in that (3) they exhibit a profound understanding of the genre (fashion, film, romance novel) in which they work, and/or (4) stimulate the sale of cultural goods that in some way better the lives of those who consume them. (5) The creative product's special qualities testify to its maker's (or makers') special talents, while the already known talents of the maker testify to the special qualities of the creative product.

Clearly, the theory of reputation in an art world is not quite the same as that for fashion, film, computer games, and other creative worlds. One major difference is that creative people are not necessarily seen as 'gifted' (the word used by Becker) in the worlds of advertising, music, and so on, although a system of awards may be designed to deny this by focusing attention on particular individuals (Malefyt). Rather, a creative person's recognized 'talent' usually stems from a mixture of personality, hard work, and experience, as well as from a certain 'literacy' *vis-à-vis* each field and its logics (Mears 2011: 156). Very often it should, in the judgement of peers, be more than merely 'cultural' and translate into commercial success.

Another difference is that not *all* those working in the creative industries build reputations that extend beyond their professional worlds. Some roles attract the attention of society in general: a few fashion designers, for example, or classical music conductors, as well as film directors, actors, and actresses. But others do not. It is rare, though not impossible, for advertising copywriters, orchestra musicians, or industrial designers to become household names. Rather, they tend to make their reputations among others working in the worlds of advertising, (classical) music, and design. The recent rise to fame of 'celebrity chefs,' such as Ferran Adrià in Spain or Jamie Oliver in the UK, attests to the fact that this need not necessarily be so and that roles are not fixed but fluid.

The fact that many of those working in the creative industries are employed – either permanently or on a freelance basis – by large corporations, and that the products that they make are marketed as brands closely associated with the names of those corporations, contributes to another difference in the two theories of reputation. In an art world, the theory of reputation focuses almost entirely on the individual artist. While an artist's reputation is built through an ability to exhibit, and ideally sell, work in a well-known gallery or museum of art, the mutual play-off between individual and institutional reputations tends to be played down in the public domain where the artist's name dominates media and other discourses. Inside the art world itself, of course, things are different. Participants know, and make use of, the hierarchies of prestige built around an art world's institutions (art schools, galleries, museums, and fairs). They follow closely which art gallery includes which particular artist in its stable, who among many collectors have (and have not) bought her work, and the resale value of that work established by auctions (Thompson 2008).

In many, but not all, creative industries, it is the centrally located organizations rather than individuals that become well known. Thus, as classical music *aficionados*, we may follow concerts given by a particular orchestra or string quartet (the Wiener Philharmoniker or Medici Quartet), and buy its latest CDs when they come on sale. We buy our, more or less, fashionable clothes at H&M, HUGO BOSS or Chanel, without knowing, or caring, who designed them. Companies wishing to commission an advertising campaign will go to Saatchi & Saatchi, BBDO, or a newer, more vibrant, 'creative shop.' Corporate, not individual, reputations are what count.

This is not always so, however. As classical music fans, we also like the music, and know the names, of individual composers and soloists. While many of us may know of film production companies such as MGM, Universal, or Miramax, thanks to repeated viewing of endless credits, we tend to pay more attention to individuals who direct and act in the films they distribute. We like, or dislike, Stephen Spielberg and Jane Campion, Viggo Mortensen and Jean Reno, Juliette Binoche and Meryl Streep. Similarly, we read books by Philip Pullman or J. K. Rowling and listen to pop music by Lady Gaga or The Beatles without ever being aware of the names of their publishers or record companies.

In spite of these differences among the various creative industries, we may state categorically that reputations *matter* to all concerned. They matter in particular because they define and sustain the different fields of fashion, film, publishing, art, architecture, and so on. This can be seen in the various systems of prizes and awards at work in each field. As Chris Mathieu and Marianne Bertelsen point out, one thing film festival jury members have in common, even though they work in different branches of the industry, is that each has an industry 'name.' This name may be old and well established, or new and interesting.

Most jury members have also recently been involved in a successful or prestigious film production – all factors which are used to boost the festival's reputation.[7] Here we have 'symbolic consecration' at work, of the kind also found in Bang & Olufsen's designs, which have not only won prestigious awards but are to be found in the permanent exhibition at MOMA, New York. Indeed, the company is ranked No. 5 in the list of the world's 'Coolbrands' (Krause-Jensen).

Names do not always sustain existing reputations; they may well contribute to industry innovations. Bo T. Christensen and Jesper Strandgaard Pedersen, for example, show how the Michelin star system and the San Pellegrino list of the 50 best restaurants in the world both define and enable the development of cuisine as a 'creative industry.' By ranking restaurants, each competes against the other to assert its name (a name based on 'stability' in the case of the *Michelin Guide*, and 'innovation' and 'authenticity' for San Pellegrino). Together, though, they create a spirit of competitiveness within the field and public interest on the part of consumers – something we have also witnessed in the rising (televised) awareness of the annual Nobel Prize awards, the Oscars, and seasonal fashion week catwalk shows over the past one or two decades. By establishing and sustaining a hierarchy of prestigious names, they bring in alignment the otherwise separate worlds of production and consumption.

So awards promote names. But, given the subjective and problematic nature of the theory of reputation outlined above (how should we define 'difference' or 'innovative'? What do we mean by 'profound' understanding?), award systems cannot openly display their practices. They may very well state certain criteria that are taken into account by adjudicators (as in the case of the *Michelin Guide*), but those who fail to meet those criteria are never told precisely how they failed to do so (Christensen and Strandgaard Pedersen). The language that film (and other) awards use, therefore, tends to be purposely ambivalent: 'best director,' 'best actress,' or 'best musical score' – leaving it to the jurors to decide among themselves what they mean by 'best' in each category (Mathieu and Bertelsen).

---

[7] At the same time, however, the informal pecking order within a jury, as well as the alliance and deference processes that take place therein, tends to be subject to branch-internal prestige and admiration rather than to popular notoriety or acclaim.

In addition to configuring a field of (artistic and thus restricted (Malefyt)) cultural production (Lampel and Meyer 2008; Moeran and Strandgaard Pedersen 2011), award systems serve a double function. One, as we have just noted, is to create and sustain a system of names. In this respect, their function is socio-cultural. They select either certain forms of cultural production that they regard as socially valuable, or the cultural producers thereof. Thus, in publishing, we find, among other awards, the Arthur C. Clarke Award for science fiction, the Golden Dagger Award for crime, the Astrid Lindgren Children's Prize, and the Booker Prize for 'best novel.' By selecting certain books or films, but not others, award systems build a *canon* of works in a particular field. They create symbolic capital (Malefyt).

But prizes also have an economic function, since they are one of several marketing mechanisms employed by creative industries to promote their products. They can bring relatively unknown film directors, artists, musicians, poets, and so on to public recognition, as well as enhance the reputation of those already established in their separate fields. They also turn the attention of the media to films, art, music, books, and so forth, thereby supporting their consumption more generally (Squires 2007: 92). They serve, in short, an 'economy of prestige' (English 2005).

Another facet of the economic function of award systems is their sponsorship. Take the Booker Prize, which 'aims to reward the best novel of the year written by a British or Commonwealth author.' Scholars have been quick to make a comparison between the sponsoring organization, Booker McConnell, its colonial business past, and the 'postcolonial' writers whose works are shortlisted or selected for the award (e.g. Huggan 1994). Clearly, as in advertising and sponsorship more generally, there has to be some sort of 'match' between the genre or brand and its sponsor. This is what enables and sustains an on-going exchange between, in Bourdieu's terms, cultural, symbolic, and economic capital.

Which brings us to the crux of the role of reputation in the creative industries. Our argument is that contemporary economies function according to a logic of *names*. Some of us drive a Toyota, smoke a Marlboro, or drink a Guinness. We might wear Nike shoes or an Yves Saint Laurent gown. In the office, we may well use Scotch tape and Post-its, at home a Hoover. Names are consistently confused in our everyday conversations. Sometimes we use people's names (a cardigan or sandwich), at other times companies' names (a Jaguar or Burberry), to talk about products. We also use abbreviations (a Coke, or a Mac), even metaphors (Golden Arches), and substitute a brand name for the thing itself (a Mackintosh or Walkman). Names are found in three distinct interlocking social spheres – of people (celebrities, personalities, stars, CEOs), products (brands), and organizations (corporations, government bodies, international organizations such as UNESCO). We make use of names to give 'personalities' to inanimate things and to forms of social organization – a form of 'animism' that Kasper Vangkilde discusses in the context of HUGO BOSS and its brands.

Names tend to take on particular importance in two ways in fields of cultural production. First, we find an active use and dissemination of names as part of the promotional strategies of different forms of popular culture. In the fashion industry, for example, the names of fashion designers and the houses they work for, of photographers and their assistants, of models, stylists, and hairdressers, as well as of fashion magazine personnel, are a crucial site for the functioning of the field as a whole. Each name strives to make its mark in a struggle for power and so legitimate fashion's 'categories of perception and appreciation' (Bourdieu 1993: 106).

Second, the primary means of linking organizations (corporations) to the products that they sell is through celebrities of one sort or another. So – and our example is again taken from the field of fashion – designers and fashion houses will take a lot of time and trouble preparing special clothes (which may not be worn) for actors and actresses attending the US film industry's annual Academy Awards (known popularly as the Oscars). Jewellers will also lend coveted necklaces and earrings to actresses for the evening, on the basis that they may be caught for a moment or two in the glare of network television coverage of the occasion.

In his contribution to this volume, Timothy de Waal Malefyt argues that the advertising creative awards ceremony is a naming system that both validates and celebrates creatives' ability to generate ideas that bridge multiple fields of cultural production. The celebrity status of advertising creatives, however, is not simply 'cultural,' for an agency that employs a famous copywriter or art director can leverage their name against other agencies in its competition for new clients. In this way, cultural capital is converted into economic capital, in a mutually reinforcing system of artistic and commercial categories. This may lead to the occasional anomaly, however. On the principle that even monkeys are known to fall out of trees, it is recognized that famous copywriters do not invariably write outstanding copy, nor art directors

produce great artwork. Yet the aura of their name tends to imbue each
new advertising idea (and associated advertising agency) with charisma,
or a certain *je ne sais quoi*, even though such ideas may in themselves
not be that outstanding or special – a point made clear by the fact
that some film festival jurors go on the reputation or previous work
of directors or production companies to make judgements about particular films (Mathieu and Bertelsen). Although initially marked by creativity, therefore, names can also mask a lack thereof.

As is evident from these examples, names involve a long-term accumulation of social and cultural capital that is then converted into economic
capital and back again. Names serve as 'cultural intermediaries'
(Bourdieu 1984: 354–365) operating in a particular commercial field
and are thus 'the crucial element in a mixed economy' that we might
well call a *name economy* (Skov 2000: 158; Moeran 2003). But they also
link different fields of popular culture – as when supermodel Naomi
Campbell makes forays into film, music videos, recording, publishing,
and the Fashion Café, as well as the by now customary crossover between
runway performances and fashion magazine spreads. At the same time,
Campbell is competing with other models such as Kate Moss and Nadja
Auermann, each of whom is trying to make her mark in different ways.[8]
It is the struggle among names that maintains a structured difference
synchronically and diachronically, within and between the fields in which
they operate. They create and sustain 'distinction' in and between different
creative industries and fields of cultural production.

## Concluding remarks

In this Introduction, we have argued that creativity is to be found in
neither product nor process as distinct entities, but rather in a concept of
product-as-process. This is because those employed in most forms of
cultural production – in particular in those associated with creative
industries such as fashion, film, music, publishing, and so on – need to

[8] Such competition is especially obvious in love relationships formed with other
celebrities. For example, over the years, Naomi Campbell has had her name linked
with that of singer Eric Clapton; Cindy Crawford with actor Richard Gere; Linda
Evangelista with actor Kyle MacLachlan; Tyra Banks with golfer Tiger Woods;
and Claudia Schiffer first with magician David Copperfield, then with art dealer
Tim Jeffries, who was formerly engaged to another 1980s' supermodel, Elle
Macpherson.

be aware of and take into account all other work in their field. A book publisher, for example, considers other works that he is publishing that year, as well as similar works put out by competing publishers, before committing himself to publishing a particular manuscript. He also needs to pay attention to what categories of books are selling well and adapt that manuscript accordingly, if at all possible. Similar editorial moments take place in deciding what fashion 'story' to print in a fashion magazine; what new pop singer, rapper, or boy band to promote; or how to auction an oriental carpet. Creative processes, and the improvisations that accompany them, are rooted in both synchronic and diachronic perceptions of cultural products.

Precisely because the present is informed by the past, and the future by the present, creative processes are never entirely free. For a start, there are the materials and associated technologies that can impinge on how something is conceived, designed, and made. Other limitations – like those of time and place – also come into play. Social relations also make their mark on creativity in terms of who works with whom, for whom, on what. And money has an obvious effect on how that 'what' turns out in the end. All the time, those working in different forms of cultural production put forward their aesthetic visions of a particular product and negotiate those ideals with others with whom they are thrown together in the creative process. Out of such constraints are improvisations and creativity born.

In this respect, creativity is *not* locked up in an 'iron cage' (Friedman 2001). Like Houdini, it can, against all odds, escape. When asked what creativity is, people – students, in particular – like to employ a similar metaphor. As Jakob Krause-Jensen notes, creativity is – like the HUGO BOSS creative director's claim for the HUGO brand (Vangkilde) – 'thinking out of the box.' This suggests that normal, everyday affairs are conducted in one box, while creative matters take place in another. Given that boxes have walls that prevent their inhabitants from seeing outside them, however, the notion of thinking 'out of the box' would seem to be misplaced, since what goes on in the 'creative box' cannot be seen by those inhabiting their 'everyday box' and thus goes unremarked. To recognize creativity, therefore, one needs to be sitting on the *edge of the box* because that enables one to look into it and, in Krause-Jensen's words, 'get a perspective on evaluative processes and the different criteria, dilemmas and institutional logics that inform creative choices.' By peering down on both sides, by seeing what is going on, one can compare products, processes, and products-as-processes. The exploration of creativity demands comparisons among cultural products that are, in Mathieu and Bertelsen's phrase, 'on the edge and not beyond the pale.'

Another way of putting this might be to say that creativity is more of a hop, skip, and a jump than a Great Leap Forward. While such a formulation is unlikely to lead to either cultural or intellectual revolution, it does allow us, at least, to explore realistically the ins and outs of innovation, design, and the arts.

And, as the 'clown prince' of Denmark, Victor Borge, used to say with great relish: that takes care of that.

## References

Baxandall, Michael. 1972. *Painting and Experience in Fifteenth Century Italy*. Oxford University Press.
Becker, Howard. 1982. *Art Worlds*. Berkeley and Los Angeles: University of California Press.
    2006. The work itself. In *Art from Start to Finish: Jazz, painting, writing, and other improvisations*, ed. Howard S. Becker, Robert R. Faulkner, and Barbara Kirshenblatt-Gimblett, pp. 21–30. Chicago and London: University of Chicago Press.
Boden, Margaret 1994. What is creativity? In *Dimensions of Creativity*, ed. Margaret A. Boden. Cambridge, MA: MIT Press.
Bourdieu, Pierre. 1984. *Distinction: A social critique of the judgement of taste*. Translated by Richard Nice. London: Routledge & Kegan Paul.
    1993. *The Field of Cultural Production*. Translated by Richard Nice. Cambridge: Polity.
Burnett, Leo. 1971. *Leo*. Chicago: Leo Burnett Company, Inc.
Caves, Richard. 2000. *Creative Industries: Contracts between art and commerce*. Cambridge, MA: Harvard University Press.
English, James. 2005. *The Economy of Prestige: Prizes, awards, and the circulation of cultural value*. Cambridge, MA: Harvard University Press.
Featherstone, Mike. 1991. *Consumer Culture and Postmodernism*. London: Sage.
Finke, Ronald A., Thomas B. Ward, and Steven M. Smith. 1992. *Creative Cognition: Theory, research, and applications*. Cambridge, MA: MIT Press.
Fiske, John. 1989. *Reading the Popular*. Boston: Unwin Hyman.
Friedman, Jonathan. 2001. The iron cage of creativity: an exploration. In *Locating Cultural Creativity*, ed. J. Liep, pp. 46–61. London: Pluto.

Fukuda Takayuki. 1992. Seiyaku wa kōkoku no haha desu (Constraints are the mother of advertising). In *Kōkoku no dai-nyūmon: kōkoku hihyō-hen (Great Introduction to Advertising: Advertising appraisal edition)*, ed. Y. Amano, pp. 143–153. Tokyo: Madora Shuppan.

Garcia-Parpet, Marie-France. 2011. Symbolic value and the establishment of prices: globalization of the wine market. In *The Worth of Goods: Valuation and pricing in the economy*, ed. J. Beckert and P. Aspers, pp. 131–154. Oxford University Press.

Gibson, James. 1977. The theory of affordances. In *Perceiving, Acting and Knowing*, ed. Robert Shaw, and John Bransford, pp. 67–82. Hillsdale, NJ: Lawrence Erlbaum.

Hauser, Arnold. 1982. *The Sociology of Art*. London: Routledge & Kegan Paul.

Hower, Ralph. 1939. *The History of an Advertising Agency: N. W. Ayer & Son at work*. Cambridge, MA: Harvard University Press.

Huggan, Graham. 1994. The Postcolonial Exotic: Rushdie's 'Booker of Bookers.' *Transition* 64: 22–29.

Hutter, Michael. 2008. Creating artistic from economic value: changing input prices and new art. In *Beyond Price: Value in culture, economics, and the arts*, ed. Michael Hutter and David Throsby, pp. 60–74. Cambridge University Press.

Ingold, Tim and Elizabeth Hallam. 2007. Creativity and cultural improvisation: an introduction. In Elizabeth Hallam and Tim Ingold, eds, *Creativity and Cultural Improvisation*. ASA Monographs 44.

Lampel, Joseph and Alan Meyer. 2008. Field-configuring events as structuring mechanisms: how conferences, ceremonies, and trade shows constitute new technologies, industries, and markets. *Journal of Management Studies* 45 (6): 1025–1035.

Liep, John. 2001. Introduction. In *Locating Cultural Creativity*, ed. John Liep, pp. 1–13. London: Pluto.

Löfgren, Orvar. 2001. Celebrating creativity: on the slanting of a concept. In *Locating Cultural Creativity*, ed. John Liep, pp. 71–80. London: Pluto.

McCracken, Grant. 1989. Who is the celebrity endorser? Cultural foundations of the endorsement process. *Journal of Consumer Research* 16: 310–321.

Mears, Ashley. 2011. Pricing looks: circuits of value in fashion modelling markets. In *The Worth of Goods: Valuation and pricing in the economy*, ed. Jens Beckert and Patrik Aspers, pp. 155–177. Oxford University Press.

Menger, Pierre-Michel. 2006. Profiles of the unfinished: Rodin's work and the varieties of incompleteness. In *Art from Start to Finish: Jazz, painting, writing, and other improvisations*, ed. Howard S. Becker, Robert R. Faulkner, and Barbara Kirshenblatt-Gimblett, pp. 31–68. Chicago and London: University of Chicago Press.

Moeran, Brian. 1984. Individual, group, and *seishin*: Japan's internal cultural debate. *Man* 19 (2): 252–266.

　　1996. *A Japanese Advertising Agency: An anthropology of media and markets*. London: Curzon.

　　1997. *Folk Art Potters of Japan*. London: Curzon.

　　2003. Celebrities and the name economy. In *Anthropological Perspectives on Economic Development and Integration*, Vol. 22: 299–321, ed. Norberk Dannhaeuser and Cynthia Werner. Amsterdam: Elsevier.

　　2009. The organization of creativity in Japanese advertising production. *Human Relations* 62 (7): 963–985.

Moeran, Brian and Jesper Strandgaard Pedersen (eds). 2011. *Negotiating Values in the Creative Industries: Fairs, festivals and competitive events*. Cambridge University Press.

Odagiri, A. 1992. Business o game ni suru (Making a game of business). In *Kōkoku no dai-nyūmon: kōkoku hihyō-hen (Great Introduction to Advertising: Advertising appraisal edition)*, pp. 109–118. ed. Y. Amano. Tokoyo: Madora Shuppan.

Ogilvy, David. 1983. *Ogilvy on Advertising*. London: Guild Publishing.

Rosenblum, Barbara. 1978. Style as social process. *American Sociological Review* 43: 422–438.

Skov, Lise. 2000. *Stories of World Fashion and the Hong Kong Fashion World*, Thesis submitted for the Degree of Doctor of Philosophy at the University of Hong Kong.

Squires, Clare. 2007. *Marketing Literature: The making of contemporary writing in Britain*. Basingstoke: Palgrave Macmillan.

Thompson, Don. 2008. *The $12 Million Stuffed Shark: The curious economics of contemporary art and auction houses*. London: Aurum.

Towse, Ruth. 1996. Market value and artists' earnings. In *The Value of Culture: On the relationship between economics and art*, ed. Arjo Klamer, pp. 96–107. Amsterdam University Press.

Williams, Raymond. 1976. *Keywords: A vocabulary of culture and society*. London: Fontana/Croom Helm.

Willis, Roy. 1990. *Common Culture: Symbolic work at play in the everyday cultures of the young*. London: Open University Press.

# 1 | *What's the matter with* Jarrettsville? *Genre classification as an unstable and opportunistic construct*

C. CLAYTON CHILDRESS

For Cornelia Nixon, *Jarrettsville* (2009) was first a family story. Nixon's story would be transformed into a work of historical fiction, or literary fiction, or maybe something skewed toward popular fiction that might garner readers to match Nixon's awards.[1] Or perhaps the story would ultimately be transformed into somewhat of a romance novel, or too much of a romance novel. For Charlie Winton, the CEO of *Jarrettsville's* publisher, Counterpoint Press, the manuscript that was created from Nixon's story was reminiscent of *Cold Mountain*: an investment in a second chance at catching lightning in a bottle. For Adam Krefman, *Jarrettsville's* editor, the manuscript was an intimate examination of a one-time secondary character's failings, his inability to do the right thing, and the actions and mistakes that young men like Krefman might uncomfortably occasionally relate to. For Krefman – at first, at least – the manuscript was also not just a manuscript. It was instead *the* manuscript written by *the* wife of a poet he admired and who had connections, like him, to the publishing house he yearned to work for again. These were not his primary motivations in advocating for *Jarrettsville* at Counterpoint Press. The manuscript was in his estimation a great manuscript, but it was also *the* manuscript written by *the* woman he had met casually at a reading several weeks before, which was not without importance in his evaluation. For Counterpoint's publicity staff, and for the regional field reps at Counterpoint's distributor, *Jarrettsville* was a work of literary historical fiction. It was 'literary' because both Nixon and Counterpoint were 'literary,' and it was historical fiction not only because the story was historical and a work of fiction but also because 'historical fiction' existed as a market category.

---

[1] Data for this paper were collected through participant-observational field research with the author and publisher of *Jarrettsville* from 2008 through 2010, in addition to observational research and audio data collected from twenty-one book groups across the United States which read the novel.

Importantly for Counterpoint, *Jarrettsville* was not just in the market category of historical fiction, it was *Civil War* historical fiction, a stable and dependable market category. That the entire story told in the manuscript took place after the Civil War, while acknowledged, was mostly incidental.

For reviewers, *Jarrettsville* was about the unanswered race problem in the United States, or the still lingering tensions of the Civil War, or an exquisite story about social conventions, emotional connections, and the human experience, or it was a failed effort rife with historical inaccuracies. For one reviewer the novel was reminiscent of Tolstoy and even worth reading for the impressive quality of the prose alone. For another reviewer, the writing was so bad it was 'timeless.' For a book group of women readers in Nashville, Tennessee, the novel was compared to what they jokingly referred to as the 'The Bible', *Gone with the Wind*. For a book group of men in Massachusetts the prose and story were too flowery, but reading the novel created an opportunity to discuss whether a woman can rape a man. For a book group of nurses in San Francisco *Jarrettsville* came to be about the history of one of the club's members who had grown up in Jarrettsville, Maryland. For a group of teachers in Santa Barbara *Jarrettsville* temporarily became about group members' own stories about racism in America. For the mothers of young twins it was about the relationships between men and women. For a group of lawyers and their friends in Santa Cruz it was about whether juries can break from a judge's guidelines and create their own convictions or acquittals for their own reasons. 'Is "justifiable homicide" something that a jury can use, doesn't that seem crazy?' a poet asked. 'It's rare, but juries can do whatever they want,' a lawyer replied. For a group of young women in Berkeley, *Jarrettsville* was not just about the two main characters' relationship, it was also about *their* relationships. For a group of men in San Francisco, the novel was a chance to learn more about a similar story in one of their members' family history, a family story he too had investigated and written.

If only briefly in all these instances *Jarrettsville* wasn't so much about *Jarrettsville* but about something someone was reminded of and chose to share. For readers in present-day Jarrettsville, Maryland, the story was not merely about long dead people whose graves merely happened to be down the road, the story was also about them. In the last 130 years had Jarrettsville changed, or was it still like *Jarrettsville*? Some things had remained the same. 'So, are we Northerners or Southerners?' The first question of the morning book club rang out and was met by a meditative pause. In a conference room in the new Jarrettsville branch of the Harford County Library, which sits across the street from rolling fields of sunflowers that are both idyllically pastoral and an investment in bird feed as a cash crop, the women launched into a discussion of where they live and what that means with reference to who they are. But for Cornelia Nixon, what would become *Jarrettsville* was first and foremost a family story. For a story ultimately to be a novel – for it to be written by an author, and to make it through a literary agency and into a publishing house and out the other end, and for it to be promoted by publicity staff and hand-sold in bookstores and evaluated by reviewers and connected with by readers – it must be multiple. For a novel to be a novel it must pass through the hands of many people, and for it to keep on passing through those hands and still be meaningful and worthy of passing on for each of them, it must be many things.

*Jarrettsville* was not *just* these things to all these people; it was *also* these things to all these people. It was a personal story, a work of fiction, a work of Civil War historical fiction, a saleable commodity, and a chance to reboot a career. It was an opportunity to re-activate embedded social ties within an industry around a new product, a text that had to be finished before a meeting, a leisure activity, a break from life that was 'perfect cross-country flight' length. It was a story that was really about a relationship between a mother and a daughter, a story that was, according to two women on opposite ends of the country who had never met and who were both dissuaded from this interpretation, really about the US occupation of Iraq. *Jarrettsville* was also moonlighting contract work for a copyeditor, another chance to flex a different muscle for the cover designer of travel books, and the day job of an editor in chief. The ultimate structure of the novel came through a publisher's rejection letter, the first sentence of the finished novel from an editor. The title came about through an act of friendship. The scene of Martha Jane Cairnes (the protagonist of the novel and an ancestor of Nixon) in her dress shooting a bottle off a fence, from a photo of Nixon's mother that she kept upon her writing desk. Nicholas McComas' arm, a beautiful arm, was the description of the arm of one of Nixon's students. The setting of a conversation in the trees between Martha and her friend, Tim – former family slave, and suspected father of her child – came from an old memory of the backyard of Nixon's husband's parents' house. Even Tim himself, his mother based on a woman from Nixon's childhood, emerged through a single sentence in a court transcript noting that there were rumors that Martha's child was not Nick's but came from a married man, or another man, possibly a freed slave. Martha's brother's beating of her fiancé, Nick, came from the historical record. There was no actual record of Richard Cairnes beating Nicholas McComas, but according to the Black Codes, a white man could legally whip another white man for having sexual relations with his property.

None of this is to say that the creative acts of writing and promoting and selling and reviewing and reading *Jarrettsville* were unconstrained. They were confined by what was possible. They were constrained by what could have happened in Jarrettsville at the time, by the historical record in cases where there was one, by Nixon's experiences, training, and method, by the feedback she received, the demands of the publishing house, the length and format of twenty-first century 'book length' fiction, by the conventions of authorship and careers, of intermediaries, organizations, markets, decision making practices, and readers of the place and time.

Yet one would err to reduce creative acts to a list of constraints, or amalgamations of them. Instead, even the activation of constraints as relevant to individual cultural works may itself be mediated and non-deterministically applied. Such may be the case with the application of a genre category to a creative work – frequently treated as a constraint on culturally creative activities – which may itself be a creative act. This chapter explores the creativity in negotiating and mediating the constraints of genres, particularly by those 'support personnel' (Becker 1982) who are tasked with fixing the meaning of cultural objects.

## Genre assignment and the negotiation of text and context

To lay bare the multiplicity of novels I focus – like some of the other contributors to this book – on the genre conventions through which *Jarrettsville* was made sense of and classified during the processes of creation, production, and reviewing. I leave genre to be loosely defined as a semi-stable, often amorphous but mutually constitutive and ritualized code of classifications through which people work to make sense of novels at different points in their life cycles. As the designations of genres are ontologically subjective, they exist as a form of contested terrain, both within creative industries in which their assignments serve as shorthand for action and in the collaborative meaning-making practices of readers. The assignment of genre categories to texts is one way in which creative acts can be temporarily tethered to serve immediate goals and purposes; they are cultural anchors that are used to make sense of novels. Yet the assignment of genre labels to cultural texts is much more than a unidirectional process of 'pinning down' meaning. The contested nature of both genre classifications and textual interpretation belies a reliance on mere *a priori* decision making when establishing what a work of fiction 'is.' Instead, the application of a genre to a creative work may require active engagement, creativity, and non-ritualized decision making. While intermediaries in creative industries may prefer fixed and clear genre assignments – they normalize both inter- and intra-organizational processes and allow for the targeting of market categories – what looks like a clear and ordered process of genre assignment after the fact is rife with disagreement, disorder, innovation, creativity, and strategy.

As such, the assignment of a genre category to a text can be conflicted, debated, and opportunistic. It can be mediated through the tripartite forces of need, possibility, and ingenuity in response to the particular and non-ritualized constraints between the former two. While one can lean on past experiences, training, and the embedded position of her role when making decisions such as the assignment and signaling of a genre category, as the economists say all cultural objects are 'experience goods'; new cultural works are by definition not exact replicas of old cultural works. The cultural object under consideration is not an exact replica of cultural objects that have been mediated in the past, and likewise, the organizational field through which the object is hoped to emerge from can have shifted from past experiences, and the consumer markets one might wish to target may have shifted too. In short, even the potentially constraining application of a genre category by support personnel may require creativity and ingenuity in negotiating between a new and unfinalized text, and a shifting sea of contexts. As a work of culture is transmuted into a piece of commerce, cultural workers must navigate between the interplay of text and context, and sometimes with competing agendas. When texts do not fit a preferred context, the text itself may change. And when the context of the text's fabrication as a piece of commerce is not deemed to fit, contexts must be mediated as well. The case of *Jarrettsville* highlights these processes in action.

As DiMaggio (1987) notes, the demarcation of genres is accomplished through an interplay of both cognitive and organizational

processes. In the broadest sense, genre can be considered as a cultural
and economic sorting mechanism, a way to take cultural objects and
categorize them relationally around similarities and dissimilarities. As
such the establishment of semi-stable genres is the end product of an
on-going taxonomy of cultural objects; a creation of categories that
are minimally dependent on some order of surface-level agreement
among interlocutors within industries. Yet the demarcation of genre
onto any object is also predicated on the establishment of both similarity *and* difference. To be 'of' a genre that is distinct from another genre,
cultural objects must first be of the same type, with 'type' being defined
by industries, market segments, outside evaluators, or communities of
users. For example, jazz music may be defined as a genre that differs
from rock music, but it is not defined as a genre that differs from
neoclassical painting – jazz music and neoclassical painting are unrelated genre forms, although they are both genres, and the same people
may enjoy both or neither of them. As the establishment of genre is
predicated on both a higher-order level of similarity and a same-level
order of difference, the precise demarcation points between related
genres are inherently fuzzy. From an ecological perspective, if one
were to map two music genres, pop and punk, the blending of these
genres ('pop-punk') exists at the borderlands of these two genres. Is
pop-punk part of the punk genre, part of the pop genre, or an overlapping sub-genre of both pop and punk? Sociologists have sought to
deal with this problem in several ways, yet have largely lacked access to
the on-the-ground negotiation of these borderland distinctions within
industries.

The academic study of genre operates along two competing axes.
As Lena and Peterson (2008) note, in the humanities the study of genres
is largely concerned with study of *texts*, whereas in sociology the study
of genre is largely oriented toward the study of *contexts*. In literary
criticism and related fields, the designation of genre is predicated on
typological distinctions that are internal to the textual object itself. Let
us consider the written genre of romance fiction as an example.
According to the Romance Writers of America (RWA) organization,
for a novel to fall within the genre of romance novel the text must
contain, first, a central love story, and second, an emotionally satisfying
and optimistic ending. That the love story is central is key to the textual
genre, as 'the main plot centers around two individuals falling in love
and struggling to make the relationship work,' although 'a writer can

include as many subplots as he/she wants as long as the love story is the main focus of the novel' (RWA 2011). Here we see that the genre takes a generic form: two people and only two people fall in love and experience hardships in that love. With regards to the second point the generic features of the genre are also clearly delineated: 'In a romance, the lovers who risk and struggle for each other and their relationship are rewarded with emotional justice and unconditional love' (RWA 2011). From a humanistic perspective, these two *internally* coded features of the text are defined as falling within the boundaries of the genre romance fiction. So is the case with a film set in the new frontier of the Old West about the conflicts between law and outlaw (a Western), or a thirty-minute prime-time show in which a bumbling husband is humorlessly exposed as less in charge than he thinks he is by his attractive and intelligent wife and children who are wise beyond their years (a situation comedy).

In contrast to the establishment of genres through content analysis of a text's internally coded features, sociologists forsake the decoding of the internal structure of texts and center their focus on the external building blocks of genre types: the *context* of textual creation. To return to the above examples, a sociologist might look at the romance fiction genre to examine the social, structural, and economic forces that have demarcated its rise, adoption, and relation to other forms. The question might be 'What impact has the prevalence of Harlequin had on romance fiction becoming a stable and defined market category?' or 'Does the Romance Writers of America organization compete with other romance writers organizations over a codified definition for the romance genre?' With regards to Westerns, what role did the US film industry's location in Los Angeles (a dry clime) play in relation to the filming of Westerns being an economically feasible venture (Hutter 2008)? For sociologists, the socio-structural context of genre formation and maintenance is key.

A second division in the study of genre can be found along another axis, this time between genre as it relates to cultural production and genre as it relates to cultural reception. As seen in Figure 1.1, the study of cultural production gives special attention to the issue of context and the creation of order through categories and conventions in genre distinctions, while the study of cultural reception more intimately deals with the interiority of texts and disorder in the reception of genres. Since the 1970s, the study of culture-producing industries in US sociology has worked within the production of culture approach (see Peterson and Anand 2004), with an emphasis on organizational forms and

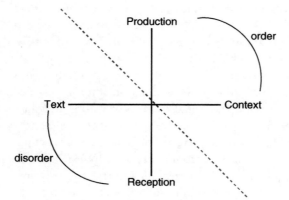

**Figure 1.1** Demarcations in the study of genre

institutional systems. In orienting toward contexts, production of culture scholars gave up on 'the problem of meaning' (Wuthnow 1989: 60–65) and instead investigated cultural objects relationally and through the structural creation and fabrication of their formations. Here, the establishment and maintenance of order finds prominence. In example of the order-inducing nature of genre, Becker (1982) highlights the collaborative power of conventions within art worlds; the establishment of rules and norms that allow creators and support personnel to work together without recreating the wheel anew for each cultural object. Given an established order of things, jazz musicians know the formulae for improvisation, and artists know that their works must be able to fit, or be made to fit, through doors and loading docks. With an established order of things, writers know that the raw material for a non-picture book cannot be 20,000 words, just as it cannot be 200,000 words.[2] In a collaborative work environment, as objects of culture

---

[2] These distinctions in length are partially a function of the demands of printing, the book market, and pricing structures. It would not be unreasonable to expect that the standard 'length' for books may have more variance with the rise of e-books (for example, Kindle Singles) and self-published authors, assuming of course, that there is a pool of self-published authors who are not simply failed industry-published authors. From this vantage point we may also reasonably expect a rise in the genres of self-published books which have been deemed unsalable by much of the publishing industry (for example, poetry and short story collections by new authors).

become objects of commerce, generic forms, and genres themselves, are used to maintain a system of order.

Such is the case in the world of book publishing, where literary agents and editors have areas of foci; they possess a passion, and compassion, for some genres and not others. 'Social circles' – networks of both business and taste – are the structural form through which book manuscripts pass (Coser *et al.* 1982). A literary agent who works in children's literature, for example, will not know what to do with a political biography, as his ties to publishing houses are with editors who work on children's literature. Harlequin will not buy a book about a plucky teenage detective, as Harlequin does not have the intermediary relationships, or knowledge of the market, for books about plucky teenage detectives to take a financial risk on a book of this type. On the production side of things, stable genre categories allow for specialization in industrial production, an institutional shorthand in decision making (Bielby and Bielby 1994), the targeting of specific markets (Hsu *et al.* 2009), and the co-optation of reviewers (Hirsch 1972). The system is not static, of course, as new genres can emerge due to best-selling titles (for example, 'paranormal teen romance' is a recently emergent genre as a result of the success of the *Twilight* series), or from outside the industry or from other markets (for instance, the rise of Japanese *manga* comics in the US). In the establishment of order, production-oriented studies have taken the internality of the text and 'thrown meaning overboard' as a form of 'disciplinary triage' (Griswold 1987). What is lost in these stories of context, then, is the text itself.

Whereas production-oriented studies concerned with genre are most centrally oriented toward context and the establishment of order, reception-oriented studies are more likely to examine the text, its ontological subjectivity, and surrounding disorder.[3] These works directly challenge the '"superstition" that genres have an ontological status' (Croce 1978: 449, quoted in Griswold 1987). For example, Denisoff and Levine (1971) find that teenagers skip past the 'protest' messages of the protest genre of music. For US indigenous populations, the Western

[3] Note that this is not the case with regard to the study of the social organization of different consumer groups, or the ways in which individuals may *use* culturally classificatory boundaries (see Bryson 1996; Bourdieu 1984). That said, in recent works the multiplicity of competing schemas of cultural classification does suggest an ontological subjectivity in these classifications, and a heavy order of disorder in their constructions (see Goldberg 2011).

film genre is about freedom and Native peoples' relationship and responsibility to the land; a good Western is marked by a hero who expresses bravery and toughness. For US whites, the genre is about their ancestral past (positively portrayed), and a good Western is marked by a hero who expresses integrity, honesty, and intelligence (Shively 1992). With regard to books, readers of romance novels find their own meaning within the genre's internal features and also use the genre as a temporary escape from omnipresent household obligations; both are social realities traditionally missed by academic readings (Radway 1984). Some readers even take genre forms and establish new genres with the 'pieces' of them, as is the case with reader-created fan-fiction (Jenkins 1992). In these works, genres aren't 'pinned down' into ordered types but instead are 'made up' of disordered textual meanings and the desires of readers.

While recent works have investigated how texts and disorder are fashioned into structural order in small-group reception practices (see Martin 2002; Childress and Friedkin 2012), the meaning of texts and negotiation of *dis*order in production processes may provide equally fertile ground. To borrow again from Griswold – a scholar who embraces both text and context as well as order and disorder – Baxandall's (1985) billiards metaphor may signal an integrative 'way out' of the production-reception dichotomy: 'an agent operating at time 2 bounces off a cultural object created at time 1, and the position of both is changed by the impact' (Griswold 1987). As a result of the strategic avoidance of the issue of meaning, and emphasis on categories, conventions, and genres as ordered and market-stabilizing processes, the interactive processes of text/context and order/disorder have been understudied in work on cultural production. The aim of this chapter is to provide a slight corrective by bringing both text and context back into conversation in industry process, to treat attempts to affix genre categories to creative works in the negotiation of text and context as potentially creative acts in themselves, and to bring the negotiation of meaning 'back in' to production-oriented studies of culture.

## From culture to commerce

Cornelia Nixon's first pass at what would become *Jarrettsville* was told entirely from Martha's perspective, and was appropriately titled *Martha's Version*. It was Nixon's third novel. Her first, *Now You See It*,

had received a glowing review from Michiko Kakutani, the influential
critic at *The New York Times*, although it had not sold well. This is not
to say that Kakutani's review did not help Nixon, as it appeared as a
blurb advocating for the quality of Nixon's writing on her next two
books as well. The cultural and social capital of Kakutani's approval
carried through Nixon's career, opening doors, and adding to the pile of
accomplishments that demarcate Nixon as a 'serious' writer in the
industry. Nixon's second novel, *Angels Go Naked*, was published by
Counterpoint Press, and it too received strong reviews but did not sell
well. It sold so poorly that Jack Shoemaker, Editorial Director at
Counterpoint, could not justify reprinting the novel in a paperback
edition, straining the relationship between Nixon and Counterpoint.
In the late twentieth century, after the 'hardback revolution' spawned
through the acquisition of hardback houses by paperback houses and
the growth of chain booksellers, paperbacks were a second chance at
life for books, and a second chance *Angels Go Naked* never received.
'I always felt bad about that,' Shoemaker would say a decade later,
'we're hoping the sales of *Jarrettsville* will be strong enough to warrant
the release of *Angels* in paperback.' While book publishing is a business
based on social relationships, the social relationships and the business
they are based on frequently do not align. The intersection of friendship
and business must be mediated, and when they become discordant,
efforts must be made to bring them back into harmony. Shoemaker
hoped that *Jarrettsville* could repair both the social and the business
damage done by *Angels*.

Cornelia Nixon wrote *Martha's Version* knowing that the story had
the potential to be popular with readers. She had first heard the story
from her mother while on an airplane at the age of sixteen, about how
one of her ancestors, Martha Jane Cairnes, had shot and killed her
fiancé, while pregnant with his child, in front of fifty witnesses during
a parade celebrating the fourth anniversary of the surrender at
Appomattox in a border town in Northern Maryland following the
Civil War. In a courtroom stacked with Southern sympathizers,
Martha, who was of Rebel family tied to John Wilkes Booth's militia,
was found innocent of killing her Union soldier fiancé on the ad-hoc
grounds of 'justifiable homicide.' Cornelia Nixon had the career that
any author would dream of, save for books that sold well. She had a
steady income from a professorship in English, glowing reviews in all of
the major within-industry and popular press publications, and she had

won numerous awards, including two Pushcart Prizes, for her short stories. But she had not attracted readers. Until this point she had been a career mid-list author, embraced in the rarefied world of fiction writers who had their work consistently accepted for publication, but not among the even more rarefied world of 'lead' authors. 'Mid-list' is a generic classification for authors whose books are deemed worthy of publication, but not worthy of full commercial promotion. As the market for book-length fiction tightened through the 1990s and 2000s, mid-list authors with poor sales records even found themselves at a disadvantage compared with first-time authors – for the latter, an editor could at least argue that there was no sales track record for a publishing house to base their expectations on.

But Nixon knew that the story of *Martha's Version* had the potential to be popular, and she wrote it with both this knowledge and the trajectory of her career in mind. She also used her training as a scholar – her first book was an academic treatise published by the University of California Press on the work of D. H. Lawrence – to inform the research process for her first foray into historical fiction. Yet *Martha's Version* was rejected by upwards of twenty publishers, the first major failing of Nixon's career, and the weak sales for her previous culturally celebrated novels surely played a role. In the rejection letters for *Martha's Version* – evaluations of the novel within the various genres it was interpreted to fit – was a series of often contradictory concerns. There was something wrong with *Martha's Version*, but what that exactly was couldn't quite be pinned down. Was the novel 'commercial' or 'literary'? Was it 'good' historical fiction or 'bad' historical fiction, or was it *too* historical even? At one of the most powerful publishing firms of literary fiction in the United States, the concern was precisely that 'it seemed to straddle the line between literary and commercial to [us].' At another literary house it 'seemed more plot-driven than character-driven,' easily decodable euphemisms for saying the work was too commercial and not literary enough.

Also troubling was the identification of the work as historical fiction. For one editor, Nixon was 'a lovely, lovely writer, and [in *Martha's Version*] she has captured this period and setting just perfectly, but without any of the self-consciousness I often find in historical novels,' despite other concerns. For another, 'Cornelia Nixon is obviously a gifted writer, but *Martha's Version* did not seem to soar above its category, the usual realm of historical fiction, through voice or sensibility.' Yet another editor found in the novel 'the usual problem I have with period fiction.' The quality of fiction was also questioned by an editor who wrote, 'while the story remains historically accurate, it might not be satisfying or fulfilling enough for a fiction reader.' Another editor, recognizing Civil War historical fiction as a saleable category, noted, 'I do worry that the language isn't quite powerful enough to make this novel competitive in the crowded market of Civil War literature.' Of course, working within a genre category with dependable sales also leads to more competition for those sales. Despite fully praising the novel, an editor explained in rejecting the manuscript that 'I think this would compete too much with one of our upcoming lead fiction titles ... (it's also a historical novel based on a real incident during the Civil War).' Yet falling within the more general category of fiction was also a problem for *Martha's Version*, as an editor opined, 'Still and all, it's a very well done novel and if I weren't so overscheduled with fiction right now, I might feel more comfortable pursuing. But the fact is I just have to be so careful right now.' And finally, for one publisher of literary fiction, the concern was that the novel may be confused for what is general anathema to a house with literary sensibilities, the dreaded and disregarded if widely selling genre of 'romance' fiction: 'It was the love story itself that bothered me. I know we're dealing with Martha's "version," but the writing seemed overwrought, over-romantic, unlike Nixon's style when she was relating the courtroom scenes.'

It was this last rejection letter, the one that noted that *Martha's Version* was 'over-romantic,' that mentioned 'And though it's not possible to get inside Nick's head, it was a letdown to be left with the feeling that he's not much more than your stereotypical cad.' Nixon took this disappointment and came to a conclusion about the problem with *Martha's Version*, the problem being that it was solely Martha's version of the story. Because *Martha's Version* was a work of fiction, the editor was wrong. It *was* possible to get inside Nick's head. The question of why Nick left his pregnant fiancée in Jarrettsville for the isolation of the Quaker countryside went unanswered in *Martha's Version* because Martha never knew the answer to this question. But there was an answer. Nixon had just failed to create it. She went back through her notes and rewrote the entire book at a torrid pace, with the first third of the story now told from Martha's perspective, the next third from Nick's, and the final third from the perspectives of other residents of the town. Nixon later noted that she didn't originally write from

Nick's perspective because at the time she couldn't understand him: 'Sometimes men do things, I don't know why.'

The challenge to figure out why Nick had done the things he'd done became a great accomplishment for her and he became the character she was ultimately most proud of writing: '*Martha's Version* not getting published is one of the best things that has ever happened to me, the book is so much better now.' *Martha's Version*, no longer Martha's version, became *Jarrettsville*, a title suggested by a member of her writing group ('why not just call it *Jarrettsville?*' Nixon recalled), and unlike *Martha's Version* the manuscript for *Jarrettsville* was a novel not only about the people but also about the place and its structural effects upon them. Counterpoint Press accepted the novel for publication in a two-sentence email to Nixon's agent: 'We have great enthusiasm for *Jarrettsville*. I'd like to discuss it further with you.' Acceptance letters, which unlike rejection letters do not require explanation if one wishes to maintain a relationship with the recipient, can be much shorter.

But Counterpoint Press was not without its own concerns. Counterpoint Press is a literary publisher. An editor at Counterpoint explained the types of books the Press publishes: 'I don't know, not highbrow, but well written fiction and nonfiction, not so much "genre" stuff . . . there has to be a literary quality to the writing, a book would have to be really special for us to do that.' The genre of 'literary fiction' is often defined through negation. Works labeled 'genre' fiction such as mysteries or thrillers or romance novels are not 'literary fiction.' When describing what defines literary fiction publishing employees often fall back on its ineffable qualities. As one employee noted: 'Would Justice Stewart's definition of pornography suffice for your purposes [of understanding what literary fiction is]? "You know it when you see it".' As a genre, literary fiction is colloquially defined as being *sui generis*, although this classification is surely more honorific than descriptive.

Yet, in other ways, the genre-spanning divide between 'popular' and 'literary' that could be attributed to *Jarrettsville* was quite right for Counterpoint as well. The firm's Publisher and CEO, Charlie Winton, had started his career in distribution and had a better sense than many publishers for both the demands on booksellers and their preferences; he had a trained eye toward the need of commercial appeal. In turn, the firm's Editorial Director, Jack Shoemaker, is an 'old school' publisher, an avuncular arbiter of taste, known for his work with celebrated poets such as Wendell Berry and Gary Snyder. As a publishing professional who regularly worked with Counterpoint said of the firm, 'Charlie really gets the industry and what sells well, while Jack is off buying Buddhist poetry and doesn't care what sales figures are as long as the books are great.' That these two men with their competing sensibilities work so well together not only makes Counterpoint somewhat unique, it also makes the publishing house the right home for a novel like *Jarrettsville*.

Also of note in the marriage between Counterpoint and *Jarrettsville* is that Counterpoint Press is an independent press. It operates on smaller margins than the conglomerate firms, relies on more stream-lined operations and smaller advances, and focuses on the money that can be made off of what would be thought of as mid-list or failing books at larger firms. According to an industry insider, signing manu-scripts by authors such as Nixon is 'kind of their strategy, taking great authors whose work has been neglected and trying to resurrect their careers.' As the conglomerates shied away from mid-list authors, a market niche opened in which smaller presses could compete for underselling writers deemed to be talented without being forced to compete over advances. Even the economic downturn and what was thought to be a flat-to-declining book market in 2008 and 2009 could be a good environment for a publisher like Counterpoint, because as Winton theorized, 'the advances at the majors have to come down, and that's good for us ... we can compete for authors, we might be able to attract some authors we couldn't get before.' Counterpoint Press is a literary publisher, but one with a particularly keen eye toward the overlap of popular appeal. As such, *Jarrettsville* was its type of book, and Nixon, with all of her accolades and limited sales, was its type of author.

Yet the balance between 'literary' and 'popular' which could be read into *Jarrettsville* had to be just right. The lists of publishing houses are a duality in that firms both create a publishing list and their identities are created by them. The identity of a firm is an amalgamation of the books it chooses to publish, and if the boundaries between high-status 'literary' fiction and low-status 'romance' fiction are impregnable, 'literary' work that could be confused for 'popular' work or vice versa is a Counterpoint book, whereas 'literary' work that could be confused for 'romance' work is not. As a result the possible incompatibility of a literary fiction novel which could be confused for a romance fiction

novel was a concern. Counterpoint agreed to publish *Jarrettsville* under
the condition that Nixon rearranged the structure of the book. The first
section of the manuscript, written from Martha's perspective, covers
the courting period between Martha and Nick, a love affair taking
place through letters and secret meetings in fields of flowers. Of course,
romance fiction is textually defined through a reliance on happy endings, and *Jarrettsville* has anything but a happy ending. The end of the
love affair is Martha murdering Nick, her trial, her regret, and her
bastard child who left Jarrettsville at first chance and didn't bother to
travel the thirty miles from Baltimore to collect Martha's possessions
upon her death. But the beginning of the book could indeed be confused
for a romance novel. As told by Adam Krefman, the editor at
Counterpoint who worked with Nixon on *Jarrettsville* and provided a
solution to this potential problem:

Everything was really strong about it but I had almost, the Martha section . . .
at one point I thought it was sort of like a sappy paperback Danielle
Steele kind of thing and I got really nervous that it was not publishable
[with Counterpoint], but I knew who Cornelia Nixon was and I just kind of
gave her the credit that this was going to be a good story . . . So then I got to the
next part, [Nick's section,] and it's really good and . . . the tension starts to
build and you really start to squirm. The big editorial question was how to
keep the reader interested past Martha's, past her very romantic section? So
the way that I suggested doing that was . . . I said 'let's bring in about four or
five of those peripheral characters [from the end of the novel] and move them
to the front and you get about 25 pages of tension just after the murder.' You
get this weird sense that something terribly wrong happened. You don't really
have the details, you don't know exactly what happened so you're drawn in
and then you get this love story but you kind of know that Martha has killed
him . . . You split [the end] apart and . . . it takes what was a sappy love section
and puts a really weird dark element to it hopefully . . . Then you're not
blindsided by a murder when you're reading a love story.

Nixon agreed to Krefman's suggestion. Both as a professor of creative
writing and through her experiences in a writing group, the benefits of
work-shopping stories were not lost on her. Given both Krefman's
creative suggestion and Nixon's creative ability to enact his suggestion
within the text, a novel that may have been initially confused for a
romance novel, and therefore not something that Counterpoint could
publish, became a 'Counterpoint book,' both in sensibility within
the text and in reality given the context of Counterpoint's position in

the industry. Yet questions of the boundaries between literary fiction, popular fiction, historical fiction, and romance fiction – and the potential to assign these genre categories to the text of *Jarrettsville* – persisted. How was an industry to make sense of a celebrated literary author who had written a book with popular appeal, a book that was still front-loaded with a burgeoning love affair in a field of flowers but is ultimately about racism, the unforgettable divisions of the Civil War, and a murder after the conclusion of the war that those divisions caused?

At the pre-sales distribution meeting at Publishers Group West, questions of how to make sense of *Jarrettsville*'s genre largely played out through discussions of its cover. In the intervening months, due to *Jarrettsville*'s overlapping literary quality and potential for public appeal as well as positive response to the novel from industry intermediaries from outside the firm, *Jarrettsville* had become Counterpoint's lead fiction title for the fall 2009 publishing season. It was Winton's background in distribution that allowed this to happen. Winton was against the practice of swiftly anointing lead titles within the firm, and instead fostered a belief in being circumspect, judging the early responses to new titles from the wider industry, and identifying lead titles as they emerged. The distinction of *Jarrettsville* as a lead title and not a mid-list title meant both the novel and its packaging and design would receive increased attention at the pre-sales distribution meeting.

The front cover of *Jarrettsville* is a silhouette of Martha Cairnes across the top and above the title, laid over a landscape of the region with a gun much like the one she used to murder Nicholas McComas. For the cover designer of the novel, this cover worked from a design perspective as it naturally led the eye in a backwards 'S' shape: from the butt of the gun to its tip, sweeping back down across the title, and back again across Nixon's name at the bottom. This was not the designer's personal favorite from the potential covers she had created, but she knew it would be selected by the firm. Her favorite cover was thought to be 'too historical' and not popular enough. A previous iteration of what would become the final cover was also changed so that the landscape would be more reflective of Jarrettsville, Maryland (see Figure 1.2).

With regards to what would ultimately become the cover, in a distribution meeting at Publishers Group West, Charlie Winton noted with a slight smirk, but not entirely un-seriously: 'Our thinking is that the gun might attract men, and the picture of Martha might bring in women.' As a newly minted lead fiction title, like the novel

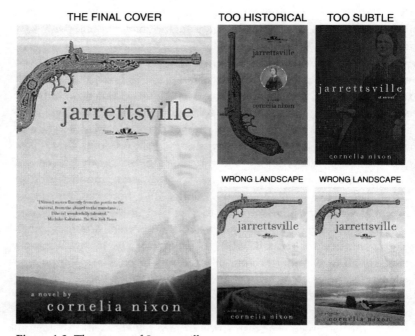

THE FINAL COVER        TOO HISTORICAL    TOO SUBTLE

WRONG LANDSCAPE    WRONG LANDSCAPE

**Figure 1.2** The covers of *Jarrettsville*

itself, *Jarrettsville*'s cover had to be multiple. A lily pad, with stylized ripples also drawing the eye in a backwards 'S' shape, had been placed below the title. What was it and why was it there? Was it too feminine to attract male readers? How could they signal that the book was Civil War fiction and not a Western, another genre of historical fiction. Might they replace the lily pad with two crossed flags, the Union Jack and the Rebel Flag, both defeminizing the cover and clarifying the story as taking place around the Civil War? This idea was dismissed as too literal, too on the nose, too trashy, and not literary enough for the balancing between popular and literary required for a book like *Jarrettsville*. The lily pad, also used to break up sections in the book, remained.

The next question pertained to putting a blurb for the book on the front cover. 'Is that acceptable [for serious literary works] these days?' People around the room offered examples of other literary books which had recently done so. The category of 'literary' is in itself unstable, the job of professionals to stay on-trend in its developments. As the lead fiction title, the book was expected to sell; it would be receiving increased promotion and publicity, and despite the popular maxim, people do judge books by their covers. Some estimates claim that covers can be responsible for up to 15 percent of sales. In an industry in which advertising directly to consumers is quite rare, treating front and back covers as advertising real estate is an important tool in the arsenal of publishers. If it was acceptable for works of literary fiction to engage in what was once the sole domain of market-oriented popular fiction (that is, the practice of putting blurbs on the front cover), then by all means a blurb should go on the front cover of *Jarrettsville*. Kakutani's blurb on the quality of Nixon's writing, from a review of her first book, was discussed but then rejected out of concern that Kakutani and the *Times* might take affront at having a review of Nixon for one book appear on the front cover of another, causing both *Jarrettsville* and the rest of Counterpoint's list to suffer in attracting future *Times* reviews. This was a major concern, as a positive review in the *Times* may not only signal a novel's 'seriousness' as a literary work, it might also generate sales; if one hopes for a literary work to become popular, garnering a positive *Times* review is the best place to start. A blurb from Ayelet Waldman, a friend of Nixon, wife of celebrated novelist Michael Chabon and a quite celebrated author in her own right, was selected: 'Haunting and powerful ... flawlessly capturing the authentic, earthy flavor of a blood-soaked land.' The blurb, while on the front cover, contained a conspicuous absence of the mention of a love story. Yet questions of the romantic qualities of the book had not entirely disappeared from discussions about the book's packaging. The 'flap copy,' the description of the book on its back cover, had been written by Krefman. On a blown-up printing of the front and back covers another editor at Counterpoint had circled Krefman's description of Martha and Nick as 'star-crossed lovers,' and written in pen along the side 'too romance-y?'.

Finally there was the question of the book's format. Although book sales had remained stable through the US economic downturn beginning in 2008, in 2009 the prevailing wisdom in the industry was that it was a 'down' time, and that the industry was in trouble. Although based on what was then a false premise, publishing employees were being laid off, the perception that money was more tight than usual was real, and people were justifiably skittish. The question was whether the book should be published first in hardback, or as a paperback original (PBO)? Much like a blurb on the front cover, had the PBO format grown acceptable in the literary marketplace? The argument for publishing first in hardback was that it signaled the importance of the novel, its seriousness as a timeless work. Given the tradition of this format for literary works, not doing so might also hurt the book in garnering reviews as well as in awards season. The trade-off, or the argument for publishing as a PBO, was that a PBO would increase the placement of the book in bookstores, as paperbacks with their lower prices and more convenient format are quicker sellers. They require fewer overheads and brick-and-mortar booksellers prefer them.[4]

Publishing in hardback was a pitch for cultural capital, a pitch to the literary quality of the work. Publishing in paperback was a pitch for economic capital, a pitch to the popular quality of the work. As a novel that straddled these lines, *Jarrettsville* was acquired by Counterpoint and made the lead fiction title for the Christmas season of 2009 because of its ability to be both of these things at once, and as such the answer to the hardback/paperback conundrum was far from obvious. Krefman strongly advocated for a hardback, even going so far as to surreptitiously switch the novel from a PBO to a hardback on the preliminary publishing schedule, which he managed. Yet Winton, coming across this clerical 'error' in a meeting, decided to publish the book as a PBO. Of concern was how Nixon would respond. As a literary author who had not sold well, her cultural capital was the capital she traded in. When Counterpoint refused to pay for an author photo by the industry's leading photographer for literary authors, Nixon paid for the photos. The photographer's name appears under the author photo, and an author photo from the right photographer signals to other literary authors and publishers the importance of the work. While a hardcover with a photo from the right photographer was important to Nixon, *Angel's Go Naked* was a hardcover that never had the chance to even become a paperback, and wanting a wide array of readers to actually read her work was of concern to Nixon as well.

Regional field representatives, the people who work with booksellers across the country on stocking decisions and who encourage them to

[4] Of note, by 2011–2012 the expansion of the e-book market had more affected the paperback market for fiction than the hardcover market, and the metrics used in deciding to publish as a PBO have changed. Given the shifting nature of the field, had *Jarrettsville* been published a few years earlier or a few years later it very well may have been published first as a hardcover book; the PBO strategy was very much a product of place and time.

give additional placement to titles that attention has adhered around, reported having strong success in getting placement for *Jarrettsville*. 'The decision to publish as a PBO made my job so much easier,' a field rep would later say. 'There are [book]stores that would have passed [on the hardcover] but took two or three copies just because it was in paperback.' Winton, relying on his background in distribution, had his sensibilities proven correct. Despite being a PBO, the novel would be reviewed in the major publications, and would twice be noted by the American Booksellers Association (ABA), first as a fall 2009 'Title to Watch For' and later as a summer 2010 title recommended to book groups. And despite not containing a single scene set during the Civil War, *Jarrettsville* would be consecrated as a serious and important work during awards season, winning the Michael Shaara Prize for Civil War fiction from the Civil War Institute in Gettysburg.

The wheels for these cultural consecration processes were placed in motion by Counterpoint's publicity staff, who also had to figure out their own genre distinctions for how to push the novel. They traded on both Counterpoint and Nixon's 'literary' capital. Counterpoint's publicity manager Abbye Simkowitz explained how to promote the book given Nixon's reputation:

Well, obviously she's a great literary voice, so all the top reviewers and top papers would definitely want to review her. So like the *New York Times Book Review*, *Harpers*, in *Bookforum*, the *New Yorker*. Those sorts of publications, as well as maybe some of the women's magazines that are a little bit less commercial, and maybe a little bit more highbrow like a *Country Living*, or an *O Magazine* or something like that, and maybe some NPR (National Public Radio).

Likewise, *Jarrettsville* fell into a different class of fiction because it told a true story that was from the author's family. This was a promotional 'hook' for *Jarrettsville* that differentiated it from other novels, a hook that could be attractive to media outlets such as NPR. As Simkowitz further explained, 'like [the public radio host] Diane Rehm or someone like [that] could also be an option. I'd say probably Diane Rehm, because Cornelia could talk about her family, she could really talk to her about the story and flesh it out some more.' Of course, also central to the pitch to media outlets was that *Jarrettsville* was the lead fiction title, not a mid-list book like Nixon's previous novels, and that Counterpoint was putting its weight as a publisher of quality books behind the novel. Simkowitz explained the order and contents of her pitch:

I would definitely tell them *Jarrettsville* is our lead novel for the fall season, because you want to establish what your priorities are for them. Especially if Counterpoint holds count with these reviewers, which it does, communicating to them what we consider some of our best books of the season is something that will go somewhere with them and something that they're interested in knowing. So I say, 'this is our lead novel of the season, the editors are just completely in love with it, they think it's brilliant. She has an amazing track record. She's gotten extremely well praised in the past and she's an incredible writer. And then I describe a little bit of the plot and maybe say that it's told in different perspectives, she has been influenced by Virginia Woolf' or something like that, some sort of a comp[arison].

Ultimately, *Jarrettsville* elicited praise in both of the major within-industry review publications, *Publishers Weekly* and *Kirkus Reviews*. Of particular note for Nixon was the strongly positive *Kirkus* review. She had never been positively reviewed in *Kirkus*, which has the reputation for being stingy with positive reviews (not least of which, many claim, because *Kirkus* reviews go unattributed). Although *Kirkus* noted the love story at the center of the novel, it focused on Nick's chapter, leading into a final evaluation:

His portions of the narrative painfully trace faltering will, self-doubt and moral decline. At Martha's murder trial, more than just one young woman stands accused. Thrilling and cathartic, this imaginative, well-crafted historical fiction meditates on morality and the complexity of motivation.

The ABA echoed this praise for the novel, calling the Jarrettsville of *Jarrettsville* a 'microcosm of America in the years following the Civil War.' According to the ABA, *Jarrettsville* was 'the story of neighbor fighting neighbor, old customs and quarrels dying hard, passion, friendship, and the complicated relationships between whites and blacks, all told exquisitely.' Both reviews treated the novel as literary fiction, and successful literary fiction at that. In contrast, *Publishers Weekly* honed in on the overlapping nature of the text, criticizing a lack of clear genre distinction, writing that 'the variety of voices and the disparate narrative elements – historical account, tragic romance, courtroom drama – renders unclear what kind of story the author is trying to tell.'

Writing in *The New York Times*, Adam Goodheart found even less to like in *Jarrettsville*, writing that it was poorly written, historically inaccurate, and tone deaf and offensive with regards to the voices of freed Blacks. In a discussion of forgeries in his review Goodheart also evoked Reese Witherspoon, the well-known film star of romantic comedies. Yet the implication that *Jarrettsville* might be a romance novel masquerading as a work of literary fiction was not much discussed, with defenders of the novel instead pointing out historical inaccuracies in Goodheart's review (an historian emailed *The Times*, Nixon, and the publisher), questioning his legitimacy as an evaluator of historical fiction given he is an historian and not a fiction writer, and what they took to be the 'mean spiritedness' of his review. Neither Goodheart's critiques of the novel nor Nixon's defenders' critiques of him were purely symbolic, as, given that his review appeared in *The New York Times*, it 'really punctured the buzz' that had built up for the novel, according to Counterpoint's CEO.

While Nixon could stomach most of Goodheart's critiques – 'poorly written' means 'not literary,' and the policing of those boundaries, as well as who may legitimately police them is up for debate – she was most disturbed by Goodheart's interpretation of her writing of freed Blacks as offensive, something some readers had felt as well. Nixon had struggled with the writing of freed Blacks as she did not have an historical record to depend on, and she elected to try – and maybe fail – to render them accurately instead of silencing them in her story (something Goodheart himself would later be critiqued for by *The New York Times* in a review of his own book on the Civil War). She pointed to Robert Goolrick's review in *The Washington Post*, as Goolrick thought *Jarrettsville's* treatment of race was the most valuable and centrally important accomplishment of the novel. Goolrick had also clearly staked claim to his interpretation of the novel as a work of literary fiction and not romance fiction in particular, while warning readers to discern the novel's placement in one category and not the other:

Just because the story is filled with hoop skirts, fainting ladies and dashing cavaliers on horseback, don't mistake it for one of those historical romances that feature hoop skirts, fainting ladies and dashing cavaliers on horseback. Nixon is too good for that.

While for readers of the *Times, Jarrettsville* was deemed to be too popular to be a serious literary work and it may have quite possibly been a romance novel masquerading as something 'literary' and less trivial, for readers of the *Post* the work was deemed to be literary, serious, and important – it might be confused for a romance novel, but this would be a mistake. In an effort to balance between 'literary' and 'popular,' the very nature of the text, its boundary-spanning potential with regards to genre and what would become its chameleon-like ability to be any number of things to readers, was at times a blessing and at times a curse. In the negotiation of text and context the potential misreading of *Jarrettsville* as a romance novel had not been scrubbed away entirely.

## Genre as an unstable and opportunistic construct

For Adam Goodheart *Jarrettsville* was a poorly written work of romance fiction that fumbled on the race question, while for Robert Goolrick *Jarrettsville* and Nixon were 'too good' for romance fiction, accurately captured the continuing salience of race, and were resultantly 'literary.' For Cornelia Nixon and Abbye Simkowitz, *Jarrettsville* was important because it was a true story from the author's family history, although this shared importance was felt for entirely unrelated reasons: for Nixon it was a personal connection, for Simkowitz a chance to garner publicity. For Adam Krefman the story was about Nick; for Nixon, it was first entirely about Martha and then about both of them. For Jack Shoemaker the novel was a chance to repair not only a business relationship but also a deeply embedded social relationship; the paperback for *Angels Go Naked* was finally released in the following Christmas season, in 2010. As a well-respected firm with an institutional identity as the publisher of 'quality' books, for Counterpoint Press *Jarrettsville* was important because it was its kind of book and Nixon was its kind of author, although even the text itself could be made to be more its 'type' of book, and the packaging and promotion had to be mediated to fit its goals. The boundary-spanning possibilities of the text between 'literary' and 'popular' had to be balanced, but those between 'literary' and 'romance' had to be erased. For the committee members of the Michael Shaara Prize it was decided that a novel about the Civil War did not have to be set during the Civil War; time and history can slightly shift when need be. Despite industry-oriented studies conceptualizing genre as a way to fix and 'pin down' cultural objects and as a way to stabilize a market order, we start where we began: for a novel to be a novel – for it to be written by an author, and to make it through a literary agency and into a publishing house and out the other end, and for it to be promoted by a publicity staff and hand-sold in bookstores and evaluated by reviewers and connected with by readers – it must be multiple. While authors and publishers and distributors and reviewers can temporarily pin down novels and orient them toward their needs and purposes, these purposes may differ for various people along the chain. While some level of agreement or order about the most basic characteristics of novels must ultimately be fixed, on the level of meaning, for a novel to be a novel it must pass through the hands of many people, and for it to keep on passing through those hands and still be meaningful and worthy of passing on for each of them, it must, if only temporarily, be any one of many different things. Despite after-the-fact appearances to the contrary, these shifts and adjustments when negotiating text and context are not purely rote or entirely inevitable. They, too, are creative acts engaged in by workers whose creative mediation of text and context all too frequently goes unmentioned in descriptions of their practices.

# References

Baxandall, Michael. 1985. *Patterns of Intention*. New Haven, CT: Yale University Press.

Becker, Howard S. 1982. *Art Worlds*. Berkeley and Los Angeles: University of California Press.

Bielby, William T. and Denise D. Bielby. 1994. All hits are flukes: Institutionalized decision making and the rhetoric of network prime-program development. *American Journal of Sociology* 99 (5): 1287–1313.

Bourdieu, Pierre. 1984. *Distinction*. Cambridge: Harvard University Press.

Bryson, Bethany. 1996. Anything but heavy metal: symbolic exclusion and musical dislikes. *American Sociological Review* 61 (5): 884–899.

Childress, Clayton C. and Noah E. Friedkin. 2012. Cultural production and consumption: the social construction of meaning in book clubs. *American Sociological Review* 77 (1): 45–68.

Coser, Lewis, Charles Kadushin and Walter W. Powell. 1982. *Books*. University of Chicago Press.

Denisoff, R. Serge and Mark H. Levine. 1971. The popular protest song: the case of 'Eve of Destruction.' *Public Opinion Quarterly* 35 (1): 117–122.

DiMaggio, Paul. 1987. Classification in art. *American Sociological Review* 52 (4): 440–455.

Goldberg, Amir. 2011. Mapping shared understandings using relational class analysis. *American Journal of Sociology* 116 (5): 1397–1436.

Griswold, Wendy. 1987. A methodological framework for the sociology of culture. *Sociological Methodology* 17: 1–35.

Hirsch, Paul M. 1972. Processing fads and fashions: an organization-set analysis of cultural industry systems. *American Journal of Sociology* 77 (4): 639–659.

Hsu, Greta, Michael T. Hannan and Özgecan Kocak. 2009. Multiple category memberships in markets: an integrative theory and two empirical tests. *American Sociological Review* 74 (1): 150–169.

Hutter, Michael. 2008. Creating artistic from economic value. In *Beyond Price: Value in Culture, Economics, and the Arts*, ed. Michael Hutter and David Throsby. Cambridge University Press.

Jenkins, Henry. 1992. *Textual Poachers*. New York: Routledge.

Lena, Jennifer C. and Richard A. Peterson. 2008. Classification as culture: types and trajectories of music genres. *American Sociological Review* 73 (5): 697–718.

Martin, John L. 2002. Power, authority, and the constraint of belief systems. *American Journal of Sociology* 107 (4): 861–904.

Peterson, Richard A. and N. Anand. 2004. The production of culture perspective. *Annual Review of Sociology* 30 (1): 311–334.

Radway, Janice. 1984. *Reading the Romance*. Chapel Hill, NC: University of North Carolina.

Romance Writers of America. 2011. Available online: www.rwa.org/cs/the_romance_genre.

Shively, JoEllen. 1992. Cowboys and Indians: perceptions of Western films among American indians and anglos. *American Sociological Review* 57 (6): 725–734.

Wuthnow, Robert. 1989. *Meaning and the Moral Order*. Berkeley, CA: University of California Press.

# 2 | *In search of a creative concept in HUGO BOSS*

KASPER T. VANGKILDE

In a meeting room inside HUGO BOSS, a group of five young talented fashion designers, the so-called Talent Pool, has just presented a fashion collection which is perceived to be neither funky nor formal but, precisely, funky-formal. All items in the collection have special features, an ergonomic cut, functional and eco-friendly fabrics, and are more widely aimed at both men and women. More than six months of intensive work with many long nights have passed, and the five talented designers can only sit back and wait. The Creative Director of the brand BOSS Orange looks carefully at the collection, touches the various features and fabrics, tries on the men's jackets and coats, and observes himself carefully in the mirror. Right from the beginning, he has emphasized that he does not want to see just another fashion collection. Rather, he wants the designers to come up with something truly creative and innovative. Now he breaks the silence: 'What you have done here is highly remarkable. It is really exciting. It is very close to what I had in mind, and you have done a remarkable job in interpreting and realizing my vision.' To be sure, the Creative Director is satisfied and impressed. The collection is 'classic but different,' as he says. In this sense, the Talent Pool designers have not created a spectacular collection, but this is, in fact, only positive. The hard part is not, as the Creative Director puts it, to design a shirt with three sleeves and thus create something exceptional. Rather, the key challenge is to make changes and still keep a balance. 'With all these elements,' he therefore concludes, 'I strongly believe that we have a very good opportunity to attract a new consumer to our brand.'

I am deeply indebted to everybody at HUGO BOSS and HUGO BOSS Ticino. In particular, I thank the then Director of Shirt and Neckwear for allowing me access to do my fieldwork, the Talent Pool supervisor for including me in the team, and, not least, the five Talent Pool designers for letting me participate in the Funky-Formal project and for sharing their knowledge and experiences with me.

In January 2007, the Creative Director of BOSS Orange initiated the Funky-Formal project. In HUGO BOSS Ticino situated in the south of Switzerland, a subsidiary within the HUGO BOSS Group, the idea of having a small group of talented designers employed for half a year to work on a specific project had been realized a couple of times before. This year, one Swiss, one Danish, and three German designers had been selected for the group, because they had created remarkable fashion collections as part of their diploma work in different European design schools, and were thus seen as talented, promising, and creative young designers. For the first time, the Talent Pool project involved the top creative management of the company personalized in the Creative Director of BOSS Orange, the more experimental and casual brand in the HUGO BOSS brand world. Known to 'offer leisurewear for men and women who enjoy dressing in style and sporting surprising looks,' as it says in the official brand profile, BOSS Orange had not hitherto offered formal wear as part of its collections. Offering 'versatile fashion ranges with a rich array of elegant "modern classics" in business-, leisure- and formalwear,' such clothing belonged instead under BOSS Black, one of the other HUGO BOSS brands. So if BOSS Orange were to create formal wear, it had to be done extremely carefully in order not to interfere with the identity of BOSS Black. According to the Creative Director, there was, however, a still untapped market potential in creating a concept of formal wear which would suit all those people who need to dress formally from time to time, but who nevertheless want to stand out and thus do not feel comfortable in formal wear, as we most commonly know it. Would it be possible, in other words, to create formal wear which would not be entirely formal but rather funky-formal? And what would such a collection look like? This was the challenge set before the Talent Pool designers.

Based on ethnographic fieldwork in HUGO BOSS, especially among the Talent Pool designers, this case study describes in detail how the Creative Director's initial idea of a funky-formal fashion collection gradually grew into the Talent Pool designers' more concrete creative concept for such a collection. In particular, we follow how the designers strive to get to know the HUGO BOSS *brands* and thus to adopt the particular perspective of BOSS Orange, how they seek to become truly *inspired*, entailing that they come to envisage BOSS Orange in a new way, how they struggle to transform all this into a compelling and valuable *concept*, which not only initiates a series of strategic exchanges but also leaves them hard put to make a clear-cut decision between a number of competing concepts, and, finally, how the Creative Director eventually makes the final *decision* and thus singles out the 'right' or 'best' funky-formal concept. Evidently, each of these processes involves a range of evaluative practices, or 'editorial moments' as outlined in the Introduction to this volume, which allow the designers to explore creativity and guide the creative processes onwards. In what follows, I zoom in on these, as I sketch the conditions and forces at play in the gradual movement from intangible idea to tangible collection. We begin with the significance of the brands – a theme that recurs in Timothy de Waal Malefyt's later chapter on an advertising campaign, but also that is present under the guise of 'genre' in several others (by, for example, Clayton Childress and Ana Alačovska).

## Getting to know the brands – or, adopting a brand perspective

As soon as the Creative Director of BOSS Orange had introduced the Funky-Formal project to the Talent Pool designers, the supervisor of the project initiated the next step. Over the next two weeks, the designers were to thoroughly explore the HUGO BOSS brand world with particular focus on the three most prevalent brands: BOSS Black, BOSS Orange, and HUGO. Based on various sources of information such as the official brand profiles and previous collections, the designers created three mood boards – a kind of poster design or collage composed of images, text, fabrics, and any other kind of object – which were to express the particular 'mood' or 'feel' of each of these brands. The mood boards were then presented to, and evaluated by, the Creative Director in an upcoming meeting. We shall, therefore, spend a few minutes in this meeting.

The first brand to be presented is HUGO. The designers ask the Creative Director to focus attention on the mood board for HUGO, while a short piece of rock/electro music by a band named Check is played on the computer. The mood board consists mainly of a number of pictures in predominantly dark colors, showing young people, urban environments, and various kinds of objects, for instance, a laptop, a record player, and some barbed wire. When the music stops, Lisa, one of the designers, says that HUGO can, in their eyes, be portrayed in three keywords: sexuality, youth, and rebel. She explains that these words indicate that HUGO is at once avant garde, retro, provocative, daring, urban, and rock 'n' roll. Following this portrayal, she continues by saying that the HUGO consumer can be imagined as a single guy who lives in a loft in Pigalle in Paris, spends his holidays in Saint-Tropez or Tokyo, works as an event manager for a record company, listens to electro and lounge music, drinks champagne with raspberry and mango, and prefers sushi for dinner.

The subsequent presentation of BOSS Black follows exactly the same structure. While we listen to the song 'Santa Maria (*del buen ayre*),' a jazz and swing track by the Gotan Project, we glance at the mood board for BOSS Black, which displays an elegant and classic atmosphere that is created by means of a number of different pictures: for instance, a man dressed in a dark blue suit, a shiny Audi, the *International Herald Tribune*, a glass of Martini, as well as some fairly exclusive pieces of furniture. Rebecca, another of the designers, explains that the essence of BOSS Black can be summed up in three keywords: intellect, grown-up, and professional. These terms denote the fact, she continues, that BOSS Black is, by its nature, sophisticated, exclusive, elegant, classic, and minimalistic. It follows that the BOSS Black consumer is, contrary to the HUGO consumer, a married person who works as an editorial journalist or banker, lives in Zürich, and goes on holiday to New York and St Moritz, reads *The New York Times* and *The Wall Street Journal*, prefers swing and jazz, and enjoys red wine and *haute cuisine*.

Lastly, we turn our attention to BOSS Orange, which is presented to the rock and funk sound of 'Can't Get Enough' by The Infadels. The mood board is composed of pictures displaying primarily young people in various contexts, often dancing, jumping, or being otherwise dynamic. Katja, yet another of the designers, explains again that the identity of BOSS Orange can be encapsulated in three words – that is, spirit, child, and feeling – as these capture the playful, open-minded, casual, adventurous, dynamic, as well as surprising, nature of this brand. The Orange consumer is, moreover, imagined as having a girl- or boyfriend, working as a graphic artist, illustrator, or communication manager, living in Prenzlauer Berg in Berlin, listening to funk and Britpop, drinking Desperados beer, and eating shawarma. For his/her holidays, he/she prefers to backpack in Eastern Europe either by train or bus, as this is a good way to get to know the local people. However, the Orange consumer often stays in exclusive hotels where different kinds of foods, along with wellness treatments and massages, can be enjoyed. In this way, he/she is truly a multifaceted character.

Now, it is time for the Creative Director to provide his feedback. He immediately zooms in on his own area of responsibility, as he stresses that BOSS Orange aims to attract a person who is very conscious of both his own background and the outside world. Contrary to the Talent Pool's portrayal, BOSS Orange is, therefore, neither childish nor immature but highly mindful and reflective about developments in the world. He is so, however, in a relaxed manner, although this should not be confused with being childish. Consequently, it is truly difficult to predict how BOSS Orange will develop in the future, because it has to reflect on the present or, as the Creative Director has it, on the concrete spirit of the time.

By comparison, BOSS Black, the Creative Director continues, is much more static as the message of this brand always remains the same in spite of constant minor changes in designs. HUGO, on the other hand, is more complex, because the brand is very avant garde in the sense that HUGO strives to 'think outside of the box' or 'cross boundaries.' This is not to say, however, that the brand is rebellious, as the designers argued, because BOSS Orange is, in fact, far more seditious due to its reflective attitude toward the world. Although both HUGO and Orange are thus individualistic, they are so in different ways, since Orange is clearly more reflective than HUGO. Orange is, of course, affected by its history, but it will not simply accept what once was; instead, it strives to find its own perspective and be distinctive, which is its very soul. For this reason, Orange is always unpredictable and, while the HUGO consumer might be called a fashion victim, the Orange consumer is, as the Creative Director puts it, 'not following, but reflecting.' As such, it makes perfect sense that he/she is backpacking one day and then check-ing into a five-star hotel the next. This, furthermore, indicates that the Orange person is not necessarily less rich than a Black or HUGO one but that he/she definitely does not enjoy flashing his/her affluence about.

During the meeting, I was truly overwhelmed with a number of impressions, not least that this evidently constituted a basic learning session in the sense that the exchange between the Talent Pool and the Creative Director served to further the former's understanding of the latter's ideas and thoughts about the HUGO BOSS brand world in general and BOSS Orange in particular. With the designers trying to describe the brands as accurately as possible and the Creative Director correcting the descriptions, their different structural positions within the HUGO BOSS organization were indeed manifest. As such, it was fairly clear, I think, that the designers had to get to know the brands in detail, so that their work would fit the particular identity of BOSS Orange. As the Creative Director explained in a presentation which he gave inside HUGO BOSS Ticino:

What is most important for me is to have a clear vision. When we are talking about Orange, this means always having a movie in mind, a long story or a book, which is divided chapter by chapter, and every chapter is one season. Then it is, one season after the other, a matter of finishing one chapter and opening another one, but in the end it is the same book, the same story, which is evolving every season.

So, it is relative to say what is right, and what is not right. When you have a movie or a book in your head, and you are, for instance, in front of a fantastic [prototype for a new] shirt, maybe it doesn't fit in your story, and then you simply don't do it. Because what is important is that everything fits together. It is no longer about a single item – a single shirt, a single t-shirt, a single piece of knitwear, or whatever – it is a combination of all the products together.

This spells it out quite clearly. Since the story or identity of BOSS Orange is so essential, it is obvious that the Talent Pool designers should thoroughly understand its specific features and attributes. The brand, in other words, thus functions as a kind of stabilizing framework (Mazzarella 2003b: 56) in the sense that different ideas are pursued or rejected on the basis of their compatibility with the brand identity. In this sense, the brand encompasses certain representational conditions (cf. the Introduction), not so unlike the way in which literary genres in book publishing also entail particular conventions, as Clayton Childress showed in the previous chapter.

By far my most overriding impression during the meeting was, however, a feeling of total confusion. I simply could make neither head nor tail of when the designers were talking about imagined human consumers and when non-human brands. Of course, I understood that human consumers could be imagined going on holiday, living in certain places, preferring specific types of food and drink, and so forth, but what really confused me was that the non-human brands were just as likely to possess equivalent characteristics and attributes. HUGO was described as sexy, young, provocative, and with a tendency to cross boundaries; BOSS Black as intellectual, grown-up, elegant, and sophisticated; and BOSS Orange as spiritual, open-minded, reflective, mindful, and relaxed, yet with an independent mind. Now, however, I realize that this confusion relates closely to what the brand theorist, David A. Aaker (1996: 141), describes as *brand personality*: that is, the set of human characteristics associated with a given brand. As Aaker argues, humans tend to 'interact with brands as if they were people, especially when the brands are attached to such meaningful products as clothes or cars' (ibid.: 142).

In anthropology, such tendencies to endow non-human entities, such as animals, spirits, or objects, with human dispositions, such as intellectual, emotional, and spiritual attributes, are traditionally known as *animism* (see, for example, Bird-David 1999). In previous discussions of such subjects as capitalist production (Sahlins 1976), advertising (Moeran 1996), and marketing (Lien 1997), however, emphasis has rather been placed on the related concept of *totemism*, which has been used to conceptualize the way in which differences between non-human entities (for instance, commodities or brands) relate or correspond to differences between human entities (for instance, particular groups of consumers). While totemism most commonly refers to relationships between natural species and social clans (see, for instance, Lévi-Strauss 1964), it is evident above that the same totemic logic may also be said to characterize the designers' way of thinking about consumers and brands, in that they see the former as forming different clans for whom the latter, as a kind of species, constitute totems. In the present context, however, we shall mainly focus attention on the fact that the designers' perception of the brands, with dispositions and attributes paralleling those of human persons, clearly represents a case of animism. Not unlike how Brian Moeran (1996: 162) argues that 'advertising often gives objects human characteristics and translates them into a social world,' it was not just the Orange consumer but, importantly, the *brand* BOSS Orange which was reflective and relaxed, yet with an independent mind. Of course, the designers distinguished between non-human brands and human persons, and they did not in any dogmatic way perceive phenomena and things with personhood all the time. Thus, animism is not, to quote Rane Willerslev (2007: 8), 'an explicitly articulated doctrinal system for perceiving the world' but 'something that emerges in particular contexts of close practical involvement.' Morten Axel Pedersen (2001: 416) argues further that animism depends on an unbounded potential for identification:

If people cannot perceive themselves as potentially being in the shoes of others, if people cannot imagine themselves as Others (whether human or nonhuman) and Others as themselves, then the very basis for animism is likely to break down because its ontological principle depends on an unbounded potential for identification.

In Willerslev's study of the Yukaghirs, a group of indigenous hunters in Siberia, animism emerges especially during activities of hunting, as the hunters tend to see their prey with person-like characteristics. What is more, the above-quoted ability to imagine oneself in someone else's position is precisely actualized in hunting activities, where the hunters, for instance when hunting elk or reindeer, seek to imitate the animals by moving, smelling, and sounding like them, or where, when setting up traps, they aim to think like the animals, for instance, a sable. In both these cases, the hunters strive to adopt the point of view of the animal in order to deceive it and ultimately bring it down (see Willerslev 2007, 2004).

It may perhaps seem that we have come a little far from the creation of fashion. My argument is, however, that this is only so at first sight. In fact, the animism of branding is equivalent to the animism of hunting. As Eduardo Viveiros de Castro argues, animism may be construed as a particular mode of knowing in that, for some people in the world, '[t]o know is to personify, to take on the point of view of that which must be known' (2004: 468). This obviously differs from the more objectivist ideal of knowledge according to which 'to know is to objec-tify – that is, to be able to distinguish what is inherent to the object from what belongs to the knowing subject' (ibid.). As a mode of knowing, then, animism grows from, rather than seeks to reduce, the knower's relatedness with the known: 'I know as I relate,' as Nurit Bird-David writes (1999: 78). Is this not precisely how we have seen the Talent Pool designers seeking to get to know the various brands, perceiving them with person-like dispositions and attributes?

What is more, much as in the case of hunting, these animistic tenden-cies entail designers becoming able to adopt the perspective of a given brand for the purpose of creating fashion collections from its point of view, so to speak. Just as hunters take on the perspective of an animal for the purpose of killing it, so do the designers assume the viewpoint of BOSS Orange in their endeavor to renew it. In this way – that is, by seeing things from the point of view of BOSS Orange – the designers uphold the particular brand identity, in that they are able to assess whether a given idea or design is compatible with it.

Crucially, however, the core ability of a hunter is not simply to adopt the perspective of an animal but rather to keep up a *double* perspective: that of the animal as well as that of himself as hunter. Only by being able simultaneously to adopt the point of view of the animal and uphold the intention of killing it may the hunter hope to bring down his prey. This goes for the designers as well – albeit for a different purpose. The challenge is not only to get to know the brands in detail and to adopt the perspective of BOSS Orange, but to ensure that the brand continually evolves. In this sense, the designers also have to uphold a double perspective: that of the *brand* and that of themselves as *designers*. In fact, it is in the latter respect, as we shall soon see, that the processes of inspiration take on their significance. The practice of going on inspiration trips can be construed as a way for the designers to counteract those instances where they seem to have become lost in the existing perspective of a brand. In those instances, it is common to hear them speak of a lack of inspiration and a need to experience or see (from) some other things and perspectives. In the designers' search for a creative concept or, in other words, in their endeavor to explore creativity, it is indeed crucial to get to know a given brand in detail and to adopt its particular perspective. But it is, at the same time, just as crucial to impose a certain distance on it. We now turn to this issue.

## Becoming inspired – or, envisaging BOSS Orange in a new way

In the second part of the meeting with the Creative Director, the designers went on to show a number of sketches and prototypes. All of these, they argued, were neither funky nor formal but, precisely, funky-formal. Although the Creative Director listened attentively to their explanations, he was not slow to tell them his overall opinion.

I have to be honest, there is nothing wrong with each sketch and prototype but it is, indeed, not what I am looking for. What you show here are fashion items, some of which may be nice enough for a season or two, but this is not your task. What you have to create is a distinctive and durable *concept*; that is, a concept which may form the basis for several collections and thus extend beyond just one or two seasons. Your task is to change Orange in five years.'

Clearly, this was not the response that the Talent Pool designers had hoped for, so the Creative Director hastened to elaborate:

You are one step too far ahead. You need to step back and create a durable concept within the overall funky-formal idea. Only when this concept is clear, should you begin to develop a range of exciting styles. This part is easy enough. It is the first part, to create the concept, which is the big challenge. And here, I have to be honest, you still need to work hard.

Not surprisingly, the Talent Pool designers were rather disappointed. As they now had no clear idea on how to proceed with the project, they soon decided that they needed to get away from the office in order to gain new inspiration. Early on a Wednesday morning in February, I thus joined them on a so-called inspiration trip to Milan. In what follows, I give a brief account of our tour in the fashionable Italian city.

Having arrived in Milan, our first activity is to visit the Galleria Carla Sozzani in which the Maison Martin Margiela Artisanal Collection is exhibited. Since its beginnings in 1989, the fashion company Maison Martin Margiela has accompanied its prêt-à-porter collections with more artistic and extraordinary pieces under the name Artisanal. A selection of the most important of these is on display in the galleria: for instance, a waistcoat for women constructed out of broken porcelain, a jacket made out of sandals, and a motorbike helmet transformed into a handbag. The Talent Pool designers are really excited; the exhibition is both fascinating and inspiring. When I ask why, Katja explains: 'It's just *so* cool when things are combined in a way that you don't expect – like, for instance, when sandals are turned into a jacket.'

Each of the designers carefully looks at all the exhibited creations. Rebecca tells me that she is not searching for anything in particular, as she is more focused on taking in the creations in their entirety. This, she explains, may give rise to some good ideas to reflect upon and perhaps incorporate into a concept or design of her own. Louise adds with a big smile that it is partly a matter of stealing other people's ideas with the purpose of making them one's own. She hastens to underline that she does not, of course, really mean to steal but rather to become inspired by observing and reflecting upon other people's ideas and creations in the light of the particular concept or style on which she herself is working.

The galleria is located at the famous address of 10 Corso Como, which is considered to be one of Milan's most fashionable spots. A bookstore as well as a store offering clothing, arts, and crafts can be found right next to the galleria, so it is obvious that we should visit these stores before continuing. There, the designers walk around more or less separately, looking carefully at all the different things. Not all of these are, of course, equally exciting, as some of them are almost ignored while others are seen as much more fascinating. The latter category includes not only bags, shoes, clothes, and other fashion accessories but, just as often, or perhaps even more so, things of a quite different nature. Katja, for instance, is very interested in a book, which she finds really cool. She shows me a few pages of the book, in which pictures of various CD covers from hard rock or heavy metal bands are surrounded by pictures of completely different things such as a teddy bear, a flower, a puppet, a sunset, or the like. She explains that she really likes this unusual and surprising combination, and Louise elaborates that it is always very exciting when you see something that you have not seen or thought of before.

After some time, we continue on to another museum, La Triennale di Milano, which is hosting the exhibition 'The New Italian Design.' This exhibition presents a wide range of designers in such areas as product design, graphics, food design, interior design, and much more, and, once again, the designers are extremely enthusiastic. As in the stores, it is not only things such as handbags, pieces of jewelry, and other accessories that attract the designers' attention. Rather, it is more often the other kinds of designs which they find truly fascinating. One creation, in particular, called *Un Seconda Vita* – A Second Life – inspires Rebecca. At first glance, the creation shows a broken bowl, but broken in a particular way so that each of the broken pieces has become a small plate. Rebecca tells me that she really likes this idea of something getting a second life, and she ponders over whether it could be applied to clothing as well. She says that she will indeed think more about this and, in much the same way, several of the other designs become sources of possible new ideas, because they are found to be surprising and quite exceptional.

After a few hours, we decide to turn our attention to Milan's famous shopping areas. Since our plan is flexible, we spend the next hours going from shop to shop, looking at all sorts of things, including furniture, antiques, interior design, books, art, magazines, expensive designer clothes, and more mainstream fashion. We visit all those stores which, for one reason or another, attract our attention: for instance because of a great amount of weird stuff in the window, an unusual interior

design, or something else. In these stores, the designers explore and
discuss a large number of different things, both the minor details and the
overall construction of what they examine. Some items of clothing are
even put on in order to see how they really look.

We leave Milan here on the more general note that the designers'
attention to things and people around them makes them appear very
much like a kind of 'urban hunter,' tirelessly in pursuit of things,
pictures, atmospheres, and other constituents that could provide food
for thought, so to speak. As they move from museum to museum, shop
to shop, street to street, the designers carefully observe and explore a
wide range of people and things, activating all their senses in the
process; that is, things are touched, materials smelled, people observed,
and so on. They go on for hours without leaving much time for breaks,
and with hardly any indication of losing their curiosity or focus on what
the next store, the next museum, the next street, or the next thing might
bring. This resonates quite well, I think, with what Catherine, another
educated designer in HUGO BOSS, replied when I asked her what she
finds to be significant in order to make a good fashion designer.
Although not part of the Talent Pool since she works as the style
coordinator of Product Development BOSS Black Shirts, Catherine's
explanations may nonetheless be pertinent in the present context. As she
explained:

I think that it is very important to always look at things in a new way and
never take things as they are. You have to be really open-minded, and I think
that you always have to, you know, look at everything that is happening
around you, take everything inside in a way.

In another context, the Creative Director of BOSS Orange explained
things somewhat similarly:

As a person, I am very curious. I see how people are dressed, what they are
doing, how they are, and what they want to communicate in the way that they
are dressing. So, I am always looking left and right, and sometimes it is too
much. I have to admit that it has happened more than once that people have
come up to me and said: 'Do you have a problem?' But the reason has always
been that I was just attracted by a pair of jeans, a pair of shoes, or whatever.

When the Talent Pool designers move through Milan, a similar kind
of acute attention to everything and everyone around them may be
said to be turned on to its utmost level of intensity, as they carefully

explore a broad range of people and things. As we have seen, a number of these things are perceived to be inspiring, because they are surprising, unusual, exceptional, wild, crazy; that is, somehow causing a stir and thus capturing the designers' attention. The things serve, in this way, as sources of inspiration in the sense that they contribute significantly to how the designers envisage a fashion collection. As Catherine added:

I could also take that lamp over there and say, 'Okay, this is my inspiration.' You can get something out of it. It is no problem. You can do a collection with this lamp as an inspiration. It just has to be your inspiration. I could see, for example, big white tops, and then really thin trousers. It is just an example, and that would run through. And then this round shape of it, you could try to have this as a topic going through as well. I would do big tops with thin trousers, and then I would find something else. I think that this round shape could be included as well.

This description could just as well, I think, be said to characterize the Talent Pool designers' engagement with the various things in Milan. Just as the lamp prompts Catherine to see big white tops, really thin trousers, and something with a round shape, so the things in Milan allow the designers to envisage a funky-formal fashion collection in a way that would hardly be feasible otherwise. In this sense, the inspiring things are certainly not passive objects but rather active agents in the sense of *affording* (cf. Gibson 1979) distinctive possibilities in the concrete engagement with them (on things and agency, see also Gell 1998; Ingold 2007; Latour 2005). As Martin Holbraad intriguingly suggests (2011: 18), things can, by way of their material characteristics, 'dictate particular forms for their conceptualization.' In other words, the things serve as a kind of talisman of thought, to paraphrase Pedersen (2007), in that they enable the designers to see or imagine BOSS Orange in a new way. Perhaps, we may even suggest that the things stare or talk back to the designers (cf. Elkins 1996; Holbraad 2011), making them envisage a funky-formal fashion collection in a particular way.

It should be added here that not just one but many things are found to be inspiring in Milan. This leaves us with a key question: how do the designers determine or evaluate what to do in the context of all the different things that they are inspired by? Faced with this question, it is more than typical to hear designers say things like, 'This is so difficult to talk about.'

What is more, they repeatedly refer to what they term the *zeitgeist*, or time spirit. Listen, for instance, to Rebecca, one of the Talent Pool designers:

I think that you have to know the time spirit. You have to have a feeling for the time, or era in which we're living. It is, eh, I don't know how to explain it. Just to have a special feeling regarding what is going on.

   [**KV**: Can you describe that feeling? Or can you describe how you think that you get ...?] No. I think that it is just a feeling. Some people are doing foresight research to tell what is going to happen, and I think that a good designer should have just a feeling, so that when he sees something he knows that maybe it could become important. Just a feeling about the time and what is going to happen. I cannot describe it exactly. It is just a feeling, I would say.

In his presentation inside HUGO BOSS Ticino, the Creative Director also argued:

It comes quite automatically for me. I don't have a crystal ball. I just have a feeling that tells me what is right, or what I think is right, and what is not right. [...] In a way, it is just to follow the wave because from my point of view a designer is a kind of shaman. It is a person who has a possibility of catching something which is not really visible; something which is in the air, which everybody can breathe, but which only some people have the possibility, or the faculty, of translating into reality, into real and concrete things.

According to Rebecca and the Creative Director – as well as several other agents in HUGO BOSS for that matter – it is largely their feeling for, or knowledge about, the time which makes them able to determine what to do. 'If you know a lot about what is happening in the world,' Catherine argued, 'you can also already imagine how things might be in one or two years' time.' In this sense, the Talent Pool designers' inspiration trip to Milan should not merely be interpreted as a matter of getting out of the office in order to see and experience new things and thus be able to envisage BOSS Orange in a new way. In addition, the trip served to enhance the designers' feeling for the time in the sense that being away from the office made them more in touch with trends and developments in the world. Crucially, the funky-formal concept ought not simply to reproduce BOSS Orange but to renew it, meaning that this sense or feeling for the time was indeed paramount.

   By thus engaging closely with the brands on the one hand, and going on inspiration trips on the other, the designers strived, in other words, to uphold *both* the perspective of BOSS Orange *and* the perspective of themselves as designers, acting in between identities, as it were. In this way, they struggled to enter a space betwixt and between, continuously balancing continuity and newness, in that the funky-formal concept needed to fit the BOSS Orange identity and, at the same time, be truly new. Creativity seems, in this sense, to be deeply rooted in a liminal space, betwixt and between relatively fixed or stable conditions, as Victor Turner (1967) so famously discussed the liminal period in *rites de passage*. Or, in other words, the concept should not be BOSS Orange and yet it should not *not* be BOSS Orange either. A representational factor, namely the brand, and a temporal factor, namely newness, had thus to be carefully balanced. The evaluative practices that took place concerned precisely, I think, this effort to enter a space betwixt and between continuity and newness; or, we may also say, betwixt and between being 'not brand' and also 'not *not* brand.'

## Generating a concept – or, engaging in strategic exchanges

When the Talent Pool designers returned from Milan, and later from Berlin (another inspiration trip), they felt better equipped to determine in which direction to take the funky-formal concept. However, the processes of moving from inspiration to an actual concept are not altogether straightforward and may also be somewhat difficult to grasp. In some cases, one inspiring thing may give rise to a concrete idea for a concept such as it happened: for instance, with the above-mentioned creation *Un Seconda Vita*. Based on this creation, Rebecca generated a concept which she termed Double Life, because it centered on what she saw as the dual demands of life. As Rebecca described the concept:

For me, Double Life means to achieve a balance between *who we are* and *how we act*. It is about the individual person and the society. Life has different demands: on the one hand we have to act according to rules, customs and structures; on the other hand we want to realize ourselves. So, because of the different demands we are playing different roles. Every day we try to combine the different roles/lives [...] The Double Life concept is about integrating individual features into the anonymity and uniformity of society. The formal wear, which is the standard uniform, is given a face.

In addition to these more abstract or general meanings, Rebecca suggested that Double Life might more concretely be realized by using double-face fabric, double layering, unusual cutting, etc. In this particular case, the relation between the inspiring thing and the concept was thus rather evident.

In most other cases, though, the processes were by no means as straightforward. As it was typical that not only one but several things were perceived to be inspiring, the Talent Pool designers often hastened, when they returned from one of their various inspiration trips, to create a number of mood boards composed of pictures of all the inspiring things they had seen. The purpose of these boards was not merely to take the designers back to the specific mood or feeling that they had had in Milan or Berlin, but also to give rise to more concrete concept ideas. In this respect, two distinct approaches in particular seemed prevalent: one largely deductive, the other largely inductive. Whereas Anne, Lisa, and Rebecca were focused on devising an abstract or theoretical concept before drawing any sketches, and so worked predominantly deductively, Katja and Louise were much keener on drawing a range of sketches in order to see where this might lead them. In this respect, they worked mainly in an inductive manner. Although the designers thus worked rather differently, they all tried hard to constantly keep the interplay between concept and sketches in focus. Not so unlike the combination of deductive and inductive reasoning in the development of advertising campaigns, balancing marketing data and concept ideas (Moeran 1996: 83–84), one of the key challenges facing the designers was to strike the right balance between abstraction and concreteness in the sense that a concept ought to issue concrete design guidelines *and*, at the same time, hold an overall story or message.

A couple of weeks later, the designers had, more or less individually, generated more than a few concepts. The task set them by the Creative Director was, however, not to be solved individually but collectively. This invites us to explore in more detail how the designers actually distinguished good concepts from bad. Or, in other words, what criteria did they use to evaluate the different concepts? As this evaluation mostly took place in a number of meetings, we shall now spend some time in these rather evident and explicit editorial moments.

It is Friday afternoon, and the Talent Pool designers, the supervisor, and myself are about to begin the meeting which has been planned all week. The designers are to present and discuss the various concepts, and Katja and Louise, who have been working rather closely together, are eager to begin. The first concept to be presented is called On Edge. Katja and Louise describe how raw, flossy edges and a used look have been a trademark of Orange in recent years, but On Edge 'suggests a more formal, sharper, and dressier way to continue the line of Orange.' By using specific cutting and finishing techniques such as laser cutting and glued edges, the idea is to maintain raw edges but now in a much cleaner and sharper way. This, they argue with enthusiasm, will express nothing short of a younger, more open, experimental, casual, and playful approach to formal wear and, they add, life more broadly.

The supervisor and the three other designers listen attentively but then the supervisor interrupts the presentation. 'I can clearly see what you mean, and your concept holds some interesting ideas. But I just wonder if much of it has not been done before.' Louise responds immediately: 'Perhaps some of our ideas have already been realized by others but always only as details, never as a general and consistent concept.' 'Precisely!' Katja exclaims. 'This is in fact what makes On Edge really new.' Neither the supervisor nor the other designers raise any objections, so we move on to the next concept.

This is Surface and Soul. Katja and Louise emphasize that because formal wear is generally very neutral, almost amounting to a sort of shield that allows the person inside to remain hidden, it is obviously at odds with 'the freedom and expressive personality connected with the Orange person.' However, now and then this person also has to dress in formal wear. For this reason, Surface and Soul is all about being able, as Katja and Louise put it, 'to present the world with a pleasingly formal attire, while remaining true to oneself.' By means of special buttons, creases and other such features, the concept thus centers on allowing the wearer to show additional details of pattern, decoration, and colors without compromising the formality, letting in this way a part of one's soul shine through the surface, so to speak – for instance, by unbuttoning a part of a sleeve so as to disclose another color or even some of the skin.

Now, the ball is in the court of the three other designers. It is the supervisor, though, who first comments that the concepts are, in her view, hardly workable as anything more than just themes for single collections. Katja and Louise object immediately that they truly think that both concepts can form the basis of several collections and that they can thus be reinterpreted and evolved continuously. Then Rebecca interrupts: 'Of the concepts, I would say that On Edge is my favorite. I find, however, that the concept ought to be understood more broadly, since it is far too limiting to reduce it to the edges only.' This prompts quite some discussion. While Katja implies that Rebecca has not really

grasped On Edge, Louise exclaims more directly that she does not at
all understand why Rebecca so unambiguously likes this concept more
than the other. Rebecca responds that they should not take her comment to mean that she does not like the other concept, but simply
that she likes On Edge the most. 'This is,' she says, 'just my personal
opinion.'

The meeting lasts for quite some time, as the designers discuss a
number of different concepts. In her well-known work on the meeting
as a distinct type of social gathering, Helen B. Schwartzman (1989)
points out that meetings constitute practical achievements in which
individuals 'transact, negotiate, strategize, and attempt to realize their
specific aims' (ibid.: 37). Meetings represent, in this way, constitutive
social forms in the sense that the processes of meetings contribute to the
construction of order, as well as disorder, in social systems. As such,
participants in meetings not only make sense of what they are doing and
saying but, just as importantly, also negotiate their own social positions
(ibid.: 312). One notable function of meetings is, therefore, *not* to come
to too clear-cut or definite conclusions in order to enable people to come
together again. This makes much sense in the present context, as the
meeting above ends without any decisions being made. None of the
concepts gains so much support from the designers that one stands out
as more valuable or better than the others. So the meeting does not lead
into more than a presentation and brief discussion. The supervisor
suggests that they should now try to rotate the concepts between
them, so that Rebecca works on some of Katja and Louise's concepts,
Louise on Anne's concepts, Katja on Lisa's and Rebecca's concepts, and
so on. This will likely show, the supervisor contends, which of the
concepts has most room for creativity, as well as revealing that some
of the concepts could appear stronger if combined.

We shall not go into detail over what happens in this other meeting, but
merely note that at various points, perhaps not so surprisingly, it gives rise
to fairly heated discussion. Again, much as it has been demonstrated in
various studies of advertising (Malefyt and Moeran 2003, Mazzarella
2003a, Moeran 1996), processes of negotiation and evaluation thus take
center stage. Rebecca states, for instance, that a concept called Combining
Free and Structured Forms does not, in her opinion, have much potential,
since it is far too narrow in focus and since its basic idea has been used
before. Katja and Louise, who have created this concept, evidently disagree, arguing that numerous different forms can be combined which

makes the concept truly durable. Louise, for her part, declares that a concept termed Knowledge of the Hidden is not exciting enough to form the basis of a complete collection, for which reason the concept should rather be seen as a set of details that may be added to another concept. Lisa then claims that a concept called Jeans Formal is nowhere near multifaceted enough, since it is far too simple to just 'stonewash suit fabrics,' as she phrases it. She admits, though, that the concept may work as part of a single collection within the framework of one of the other concepts, but it does not have what it takes to constitute the overall, durable concept. Needless to say, Louise, who generated this concept, disagrees. Quite the reverse, she believes that Jeans Formal contains exactly those qualities that make it an overall concept under which some of the other concepts might be included.

Now, to draw together some of these threads, it seems fairly evident that the designers are intensely involved in creating a certain degree of order out of the chaos that their various concepts appear to represent. Since each concept lays out a distinct design direction, it is momentous to make clear sense of, and evaluate in detail, all features of relevance, which, we may now sum up, revolve considerably around the following specifics. First, a concept must be perceived to be new in the sense of not having been used before. Second, a concept must fit well with the given brand, here the identity of BOSS Orange. Third, a concept must have a fixed content while simultaneously being flexible enough to allow for continuous reinterpretation, thus making it durable for more than merely a season or two. Fourth, a concept must strike the right balance between concreteness and abstraction, that is, between specific design guidelines and an overall story or message. Fifth, a concept must be realizable in terms of material as well as technological implementation. And sixth, it must be possible to present a concept in an exciting and somewhat positive way so as to make it appear truly compelling.

In a manner not so unlike the case of the multiple string quartets discussed by Shannon O'Donnell in the following chapter, these different criteria emerge and take on significance during the concept-making process. It is evident that the process is inherently social, and that each of the designers cares much about and takes great pride in their own concepts, thus epitomizing the so-called 'art for art's sake property' of creative industries (Caves 2000: 3–5, see also Moeran 2005: 173–175). The various presentations of concepts seem, therefore, largely to represent endeavors of persuasion, in that each of the designers struggles to convince all the others of the value of their particular concept. Hence, as Moeran stresses with regard to various forms of interaction in business more generally (2005: 2), the exchanges between the designers are to a great extent *strategic*, in the sense that they all seek to get something out of them. What appears to be at stake for each and every one of them is precisely their ability to turn inspiration into a compelling concept, which is, in a sense, also to say that their status as talented and promising young designers is the currency over which they are negotiating. Not so surprisingly, then, every one of them is really keen on making a distinctive mark on the concept generation and, preferably, to convince everybody of the value of their own concept, because this will feed back into their social position within both the group and the company overall. Schwartzman's point (1989) about meetings as constitutive social forms that function to construct both order and disorder seems clearly to make sense. In our exploration of creativity, the significance of such strategic exchanges, or what are discussed as social conditions in the Introduction to this volume, should not be underestimated.

## Making a decision – or, the creativity of uncertainty

One of the most striking features of the meetings above was, however, that they did *not* lead to any clear decisions. During the course of the negotiations, the designers critically scrutinized and evaluated the concepts, and although some concepts were, of course, dismissed or reworked, the designers reached virtually no clear-cut conclusions. Toward the end of one of the meetings, a manager of innovation and research projects was therefore asked to let us know his opinion, but even though he listened carefully to the concept descriptions and asked a few clarifying questions, he took no clear stand on the concepts. Somewhat spontaneously, the supervisor then suggested putting the concepts to a vote, in which those called Wildcard and Knowledge of the Hidden came to stand out as the concepts most well liked by the designers in general. But, rather tellingly, it soon turned out that the vote came to have no significance whatsoever. Not even once was it brought up or mentioned again.

Crucially, I think, this was due to fact that the decision of what would ultimately be the right or most valuable concept was up to the Creative Director. The challenge facing the designers revolved, then, not only around the demand to generate a concept but, even more crucially, around the fact that this concept should in principle not be the one in which they themselves believed the most but rather the one in which the Creative Director would believe the most. This fairly tricky position constitutes, however, not a unique case. In studies of advertising (see, for instance, Mazzarella 2003a; Moeran 1996), it is often demonstrated how advertising professionals find themselves in an intermediate position between the consumers, on the one hand, and the clients, on the other. Contrary to what one might suppose, advertising is, thus, not merely about targeting and persuading consumers by way of commodity images. As Moeran contends (1996: 96), 'it is as concerned with selling a would-be advertiser an image of *itself* as it is of selling consumers an image of that advertiser's *products*.'

Finding themselves between their own inspiration and ideas about consumers on the one hand, and the direction and views of the Creative Director on the other, the designers faced, by and large, the same challenge of having to address different audiences (see also Moeran 2005: 181–182). Over and over again, a discussion thus arose concerning the preferences of the Creative Director, and various strategies were initiated in an attempt to identify what he precisely tended to like and not like, and how he might, accordingly, be persuaded to believe in the value of the concepts. The designers carefully analyzed and discussed, for instance, a number of the collections of which he had recently been in charge, his specific criticism of their sketches and prototypes in previous meetings, what he had said and done more generally (including, to some degree, what the rumors said), as well as any other information that they were able to obtain. In an advertising agency, as Moeran describes (1996: 88–91), a significant task is likewise to identify the key people in a client's organization (that is, those who make decisions) and then to create the advertising proposal with primary reference to those people, taking into account every piece of information that one knows, or can possibly obtain, about their likes and dislikes. Also in this sense, then, it was indeed evident that the struggle to generate a concept was inherently social.

However, all these strategies notwithstanding, at the end of the day the designers had no way of knowing with absolute certainty what the Creative Director would prefer. As the latter had the final say, the designers were ultimately left in no position to avoid a level of uncertainty, not simply because of the inherent 'nobody knows property' of creative industries (Caves 2000: 2–3) but, just as importantly, because of their doubts about the concrete wishes and preferences of the Creative Director. This uncertainty explains, I think, a good deal about these evaluative practices, such as why the likes and dislikes of the Creative Director were so pertinent, why the making of clear-cut decisions was so hard (if not downright impossible), and why the designers eventually came to agree that the best strategy would not be to present just one concept to the Creative Director but rather to let him choose between a variety of concepts. For the Talent Pool designers, it seemed, uncertainty thus impeded anticipation to some extent. Or, as Marilyn Strathern notes: 'where the presumption is in favor of variability and keeping a range of possibilities open, *anticipation could be disabling*' (1992: 171, original emphasis). Contrary to what we tend to think, however, this uncertainty was not altogether problematic. In fact, it was productive, creative even. But before I elaborate on this, we should listen to the Creative Director as, in yet another meeting, he responds to the various concepts.

Now, the suspense is at its peak. The designers have no more to add and we all sit down at the table, anxiously awaiting the Creative Director's judgment. Apparently, he does not need much time to mull over the concepts, as he is immediately set to provide us with his feedback.

What you have to understand from the outset is that my comments do not concern what is good and what is bad but rather what fits best with what we are searching for in this context; that is, within the overall Funky-Formal idea. And in this regard, I believe that three of your concepts can, in combination, grow into something new and exciting.

A deep sigh of relief goes through the room. The Talent Pool designers have certainly not forgotten the previous meeting with the Creative Director, in which he practically dismissed everything that they had done. The relief is, therefore, unmissable. He then continues:

I have to add, though, there is nothing distinctly new in any of your concepts. But if you combine certain elements from three of these, you may potentially create something not yet seen; or something, which I, at least, have not seen before.

The Talent Pool designers are clearly content. They were not completely off track, after all. But now the suspense grows again. Which concepts? And which elements?

The Creative Director comments on only the three concepts that he finds of value, simply passing over the others in silence. The first of these is called Liquid Cut, or, more specifically, the aspect of organic or ergonomic lines. The Creative Director stresses that, although this is not a new concept in that such lines are used extensively in sports wear to create clothing that follows the movements of the body, it is surely innovative in connection with classic and more formal clothing, which tends to be rather stiff and uncomfortable. Therefore, he likes the fact that the concept respects the body and strives to make it more at ease by way of what could be termed ergonomic formal wear.

The second concept comes as a surprise to the Talent Pool designers or, at least to four of them: Energy. Katja, who really fought hard to have this concept included in the presentation, brightens up as the Creative Director explains that the idea of 'giving a sense of spa,' as it was described in the presentation, is truly exciting. He says:

In all big hotels nowadays, spa and wellness are paramount. This fits well with the aspect of organic lines, since these elements in combination will create formal clothing centered on wellness and stimulation of the senses. However, you need to work hard to come up with something new in this regard, as many things in this area have been done already.

The Talent Pool designers have still not said a word, being all ears.

Finally, and rather briefly, the Creative Director highlights Twisted, the concept that focuses on how a particular item of clothing may be used in different ways. He stresses that he likes how this concept allows people to use their clothing differently, which is always very surprising and thus of potential value.

At this point, the funky-formal concept became clear: a combination of something ergonomic, something energetic, and something to be twisted. The Talent Pool designers were clearly thrilled and relieved. Up to the meeting, they had been highly nervous and unsure about what the Creative Director might think of their different concepts. As already indicated, however, this uncertainty was not entirely problematic – from a certain perspective, it could be seen as productive or even creative. In her study of Shakespeare's dramas, Kirsten Hastrup (2004: 214) describes how the director of a theater play has to share his or her thoughts of the play with the players, but this sharing should by no means turn into an imposition; that is, into what has been termed 'directocracy' (a point also made apparent by Shannon O'Donnell's discussion of music ensembling in Chapter 3). While this might have worked in 1940, Hastrup remarks (ibid.: 215), today players are acknowledged as contributors to the play in the sense that they are not expected to copy the director but to do a whole series of actions on their own in line with the directions. In brief, '[b]reeding confidence is a way of making the players flourish' (ibid.: 211).

The point of this is that the director thus allows the unexpected to emerge; or, in other words, he opens up the prospect of those 'sudden leaps and moments of disorientation that may lead to unexpected discoveries in a territory that no map can mirror' (ibid.: 214). Crucially, this goes for the Creative Director as well. Instead of imposing his own ideas and preferences on the designers, thereby being guilty of directocracy, he leaves them in a state of uncertainty as to what precisely he wants (which, by the way, he might not even know himself). The uncertainty is, in this sense, simply an inevitable, or perhaps rather necessary, corollary of the creative process. It is not *in spite of* but *because of* the uncertainty that follows from the Creative Director not enforcing his thoughts and visions on the designers – other than providing, of course, the overall direction of funky-formal – that the designers are prompted to explore creativity, or the space betwixt and between, and thus to come up with a number of different concepts which may, in the end, lead to unexpected discoveries. If the designers simply knew the Creative Director's ideas and preferences with certainty, they would likely have begun to illustrate these, making 'sudden jumps out of the water' fairly improbable (ibid.: 221). To maintain a certain degree of uncertainty may thus be seen as a rather deliberate strategy.

## Conclusion

I end the case study here. A concept for a funky-formal fashion collection for the brand BOSS Orange had come into being. As a final note, though, it is crucial to stress that this is not to say that a funky-formal fashion collection could now simply be materialized. The creation of a fashion collection is not a matter of thinking up or constructing a creative design concept which may then be implemented more or less mechanically. Rather, it is a continuous process of growth or becoming by which a new fashion collection gradually grows forth (see also Ingold 2000, 2010). Crucially, this means that the process of materializing the funky-formal concept, that is, making it into a tangible collection, was also inherently creative in the sense that the engagement between the designers and the concrete materials with which they were working gave rise to further ideas, while involving them in a number of evaluations along the way (as Moeran describes in his analysis of faience tableware production in Chapter 4). To mention just a few of these, the concept had precisely to be turned into something tangible – meaning, for instance, that the concrete *materials* played a key role in shaping the collection; that the actual *human bodies* wearing the collection had to be considered; that the *production facilities* and *technological equipment* needed to be taken into account; that the concrete *presentation* of the collection in a photo shoot had to be kept in mind; and so on. Together with the various aspects discussed above, all these components contributed significantly to how the funky-formal fashion collection eventually came to look, making it – and creativity more broadly perhaps – something like *an entangled knot* of various threads and lines. Far from being an individual idiosyncrasy, creativity is essentially a dynamic potential of concrete relationships, emerging as and when the involved agents, human and non-human, make a difference to each other.

## References

Aaker, David A. 1996. *Building Strong Brands*. London: Simon & Schuster UK Ltd.

Bird-David, Nurit. 1999. 'Animism' revisited: personhood, environment, and relational epistemology [and comments and reply]. *Current Anthropology* 40 (Supplement): 67–91.

Caves, Richard. 2000. *Creative Industries. Contracts between art and commerce*. Cambridge, MA: Harvard University Press.

Elkins, James. 1996. *The Object Stares Back. On the nature of seeing*. San Diego, New York and London: Harcourt, Inc.

Gell, Alfred. 1998. *Art and Agency. An anthropological theory*. Oxford: Clarendon Press.

Gibson, James J. 1979. *The Ecological Approach to Visual Perception*. Boston, MA: Houghton Mifflin.

Hastrup, Kirsten. 2004. *Action. Anthropology in the company of Shakespeare*. Copenhagen: Museum Tusculanum Press.

Holbraad, Martin. 2011. Can the thing speak? *Working Papers Series* #7: Open Anthropology Cooperative Press.

Ingold, Tim. 2010. The textility of making. *Cambridge Journal of Economics* 34 (1): 91–102.

2007. Materials against materiality. *Archaeological Dialogues* 14 (1): 1–16.

2000. On weaving a basket. In *The Perception of the Environment. Essays in livelihood, dwelling and skill*, pp. 339–348. London and New York: Routledge.

Latour, Bruno. 2005. *Reassembling the Social. An introduction to Actor-Network-Theory*. Oxford University Press.

Lévi-Strauss, Claude. 1964. *Totemism*. London: Merlin Press.

Lien, Marianne E. 1997. *Marketing and Modernity*. Oxford and New York: Berg.

Malefyt, Timothy deWaal and Brian Moeran, eds. 2003. *Advertising Cultures*. Oxford and New York: Berg.

Mazzarella, William. 2003a. *Shoveling Smoke. Advertising and globalization in contemporary India*. Durham and London: Duke University Press.

2003b. 'Very Bombay': contending with the global in an Indian advertising agency. *Cultural Anthropology* 18 (1): 33–71.

Moeran, Brian. 2005. *The Business of Ethnography. Strategic exchanges, people and organizations*. Oxford and New York: Berg.

1996. *A Japanese Advertising Agency. An anthropology of media and markets*. London: Curzon.

Pedersen, Morten Axel. 2007. Talismans of Thought. Shamanist ontologies and extended cognition in Northern Mongolia. In *Thinking Through Things. Theorising artefacts ethnographically*, ed. Amiria Henare, Martin Holbraad, and Sari Wastell, pp. 141–166. London and New York: Routledge.

2001. Totemism, animism and North Asian indigenous ontologies. *Journal of the Royal Anthropological Institute* 7 (3): 411–427.

Sahlins, Marshall. 1976. *Culture and Practical Reason*. Chicago and London: University of Chicago Press.

Schwartzman, Helen B. 1989. *The Meeting. Gatherings in organizations and communities*. New York and London: Plenum Press.

Strathern, Marilyn. 1992. Reproducing anthropology. In *Reproducing the Future. Essays on anthropology, kinship and the new reproductive technologies*, pp. 163–182. Manchester University Press.

Turner, Victor. 1967. Betwixt and between: the liminal period in *rites de passage*. In *The Forest of Symbols. Aspects of Ndembu ritual*, pp. 93–111. Ithaca, NY: Cornell University Press.

Viveiros de Castro, Eduardo. 2004. Exchanging perspectives. The transformation of objects into subjects in Amerindian ontologies. *Common Knowledge* 10 (3): 463–484.

Willerslev, Rane. 2007. *Soul Hunters. Hunting, animism, and personhood among the Siberian Yukaghirs*. Berkeley, Los Angeles and London: University of California Press.

   2004. Not animal, Not *not*-animal: hunting, imitation and empathetic knowledge among the Siberian Yukaghirs. *Journal of the Royal Anthropological Institute* 10 (3): 629–652.

# 3 | Reconceiving constraint as possibility in a music ensemble

SHANNON O'DONNELL

I join fellow authors of this book, and sociologists such as Faulkner (1971), Becker (1982), and Becker, Faulker, and Kirshenblatt-Gimblett (2006), in the study of the arts as work. In particular, I build on the study of 'artful making,' in which Austin and Devin (2003, 2010, 2012) investigate the conditions and ways in which fine and performing artists carry out and manage their work, and propose these conditions and ways as a lens for understanding new shapes of business innovation and creativity emerging in the creative economy. While I might, with Becker *et al.* (2006), investigate artful making by looking at 'the ordinary problems of workers trying to get a job done' (ibid.: 18), in this chapter I offer instead an example of *extra*ordinary work: work that did not proceed under usual conditions, but rather under conditions that were stretched, primarily physically, to the point of making the work task nearly impossible. By exploring this unusual case, we increase our understanding of how collaborative creativity operates when the dial on constraints is turned up and the degree of difficulty increases, and usual collaborative methods and performance criteria are put to the test. Examining this process shows us what constraints these artists determined to be a critical threat to their work, how they experienced that threat, and how they opened themselves up to new possibilities for moving forward with the work while sustaining key performance criteria. This in turn helps us imagine other conditions and ways in which groups might perform collaborative creativity and achieve their usual standards of excellence.

An unprecedented musical experiment presented me with the opportunity to study the work of performing artists in extraordinary conditions. In 2009, multiple string quartets (many considered world class) organized in New York City and in and around London, England to perform a new composition by renowned British composer Sir John Tavener. The composition challenged four quartets at a time to perform as an integrated ensemble while sitting apart, in various configurations, and at spatial distances of up to 70 feet. The musicians appeared to experience this difficulty primarily as a practical problem that threatened their ability to perform together in precisely synchronized time, and to demonstrate professional competence doing so. However, as they explored ways to address the problem that included the option to incorporate a coordinating technology into the process, pragmatics gave way to passion, revealing that the musicians' professional identities, in terms of their standards and aspirations, were also at stake. These standards and aspirations were to realize the composer's vision to the best of their ability, to achieve a high level of mastery in their performance, and to experience a quality of ensemble and play in their work together making music. When either constraints or proposed responses to them threatened these objectives, the perceived crises prompted explicit evaluation of alternative solutions. At times these discussions were left unresolved, and the group remained open to future discovery; they chose to live with uncertainty rather than resort to certain compromise. At other times, members of the group were able to reconceive constraints as unanticipated opportunities that made it once again possible to realize their objectives. In most instances, performance objectives did not 'break' under the duress of increased constraint, but rather the way in which the musicians conceived of and went about their work altered.

## Standards and aspirations

Realizing the composer's vision presented a near impossible challenge to start. In the introduction to his composition, titled *Towards Silence: A meditation on the four states of Atma*, Tavener calls for four string quartets to play together, seated in a cross formation, in a resonant building, 'sounding unseen from high galleries' when possible. He allows that the position of the quartets will vary with location, but asks that the music be meditated on by the audience as opposed to heard and viewed as concert music. Project leader and first violinist of the first quartet, Paul Robertson, described the challenge inherent in Tavener's directions:

He's written a score that is completely coordinated and orientated as an integrated ensemble, but then invited us, or actually demanded, apparently, that we sit apart. There's actually an essential contradiction there.

As far as the project participants knew, this composition introduced a form that had never been attempted, with new constraints that created a new kind of problem: how can string quartet musicians, accustomed to performing as a group of four in close physical proximity, achieve a quality of ensemble as four groups of four, seated apart? Addressing this problem would take the work of string quartet playing to the edge of a new frontier – as informants admitted, potentially beyond what would be possible for the quartets to achieve. Cellist of the first quartet, Anthony (Tony) Lewis, underscored the uncertainty: 'I'm not sure [Tavener] was quite sure himself [it would work].'

To increase our understanding of the difficulty they had to address to pull this off, we can consider the way in which spatial proximity impacts the work of musicians. First, their ability to work together depends directly on whether, at a technical level, they are able to hear one another in order to play in perfect time and produce a balanced and integrated sound. Close spatial proximity becomes a crucial condition of this activity, insofar as it enables the musicians to hear, as well as see corresponding visual cues. Enlarging the size of the work group from four to sixteen members, as Tavener did, naturally increases the distance between each member and the farthest member from them, at which point it becomes difficult for each member to hear every other member. Stretching the groups' configuration by placing them, for instance, on the landings of a six-level staircase or at opposite ends of a 70-foot-long ballroom, as the diverse event producers did in response to Tavener's directions in the score, increases the distance further, making it more difficult to hear, and now difficult as well to see, every other member. At a certain distance and in certain configurations, the laws of physics make it impossible for the musicians to play in time and produce a balanced and integrated sound, as their hearing becomes distorted by delays related to the time it takes sound waves to travel, further confounded by architectural barriers and echolation. In these conditions, the musicians' ability to demonstrate mastery of their craft is challenged.

While the ability to hear one another in order to synchronize and balance the sound they make is critical to their work, these musicians do not consider coordination an end in itself, but a foundational capability to enact while aspiring to achieve a special quality in their performance: ensemble. String quartet musicians often describe ensemble as a perfectly synchronized and aesthetically balanced yet dynamic conversation between four distinctly articulated voices (Blum 1986; Moritz 2005). This special quality to which they aspire emerges from a highly attuned conversational process that involves group members in the activity of listening deeply to and responding to one another's musical choices in the moment. To do this requires a high level of practice and preparation. World-class quartets spend years together mastering the capability of performing as a unified group, in the case of the Guarneri String Quartet, for example, developing over time a 'complex system of leads' to sustain precision and unity with seeming effortlessness (Blum 1986: 10). Each new composition itself, and its specific technical demands, needs to be learned and mastered to the degree that the musicians can perform the fundamentals reliably and focus attention on improvising in relation to the emerging choices they are all making. When they achieve this quality of dialog, the informants say, they are 'making music' and report an experience of 'play.' Given that the emergence of ensemble and play rely on the musicians' ability to sustain precise coordination without it dominating their attention, this exercise in spatial distribution put more at stake than the musicians' ability to achieve technical proficiency. The musicians' artistry was also at stake.

I've suggested that the musicians involved in this project 'reconceive' constraints as opportunities, and we will look at examples of this in my description of their work. The practice of reconceiving is particular to collaborations that exhibit the quality of ensemble (Austin and Devin 2003). Makers reconceive when they combine the contributions of colleagues with their own ideas to create wholly new ideas that are greater than the sum of contributions and beyond what any one member of the group could have anticipated (Austin and Devin 2003). Reconceiving happens spontaneously in groups that routinely engage in work as a dynamic conversation in which no one person or logic dominates, but all members of the group participate as equals (Austin and Hjorth 2012). It presents an alternative to other forms of collaborative work in which diverse or conflicting ideas give rise to negotiation or compromise, in which ideas are modified to accommodate one another, or competition out of which one logic emerges victor, either on merit or on social grounds such as member clout or rank. Reconceiving, meanwhile, thrives on a multiplicity of voices, encourages the instability that keeps multiple possibilities alive until the group converges on one, and sees conflict as opportunity to imagine new alternatives.

## *The* Towards Silence *project*

I will now offer a description of the project as it unfolded, and the ways in which I observed the quartet musicians respond to the difficulties and opportunities inherent in their work together. In this telling, I emphasize moments in which conflict or concern in rehearsal was met either with a preference to leave the difficulty unresolved at that moment, or with new proposals that reconceived the current dilemma in a way that framed future possibility. In the last section of this chapter, I reflect on what caused the musicians to feel that their standards and aspirations were at times threatened, and how these moments of uncertainty were reframed as possibility.

The musicians involved in the *Towards Silence* project were members of seven string quartets. The Medici String Quartet, one of Britain's finest music ensembles, was joined in the US by a set of three well-established American string quartets with group tenure ranging from three to thirteen years, and in the UK by a set of three promising British ensembles either recently formed or newly formed for the project. While these seven quartets enjoyed varying tenure as groups, all musicians were considered top performers in their generation. With Medici first violin Paul Robertson as project leader, they addressed the project in phases, as follows. In February 2009 the UK team of quartets assembled for two days of 'pre-rehearsals' of the piece, with the main objective of understanding better how to make practical preparations for and rehearse this new work in anticipation of summer performances. In April the US team gathered at the Rubin Museum of Art for five days of rehearsal culminating in one sold-out, live premiere performance. At this stage, the use of a simple coordinating technology called a 'click-track,' a pre-recorded cuing track delivered via wireless earpiece to one member (typically the first violinist) of each quartet, was instigated. In June and July the UK team, implementing the click-track from the start, reassembled for four more days of rehearsals, followed by four evening performances (each preceded by 1–3-hour afternoon rehearsals in which new spatial configurations were tried) in four different locations in and around London. Producers at each of the five performance venues, which ranged in type from the Rubin Museum's six-level spiral staircase to the expansive Winchester Cathedral, differently interpreted Tavener's directions for configuring the event. The musicians also expressed their own preferences for how to configure each event in order to best realize Tavener's vision, at times in conflict with the producers' plans. We'll look next in more detail at each of these phases as they unfolded.

## Pre-rehearsals, February 2009

Pre-rehearsals take place in the barn-cum-studio at The Old Farmhouse, Paul's home, in West Sussex. To begin, the musicians arrange themselves in a half-circle, which over the course of the first day gradually morphs into a full circle, the quartets ordered by number clockwise Q1-Q2-Q3-Q4. In a later interview, Paul claims that the only way he knows for the group of four quartets to rehearse *Towards Silence* is to begin in this way, sitting together in one large circle, despite Tavener's direction that the four groups sit apart. He explains why: 'Until we actually know the score well enough to be able to play it with *complete* confidence sitting in a circle, there is no way we can attenuate the connections or the lines of sight – because it's not just visual, that's the trouble, you actually have to hear it.' Sitting in a circle affords the musicians the best opportunity of hearing one another at this stage.

Paul, who has recently suffered a near fatal aortic dissection and doesn't feel well enough to play at the beginning of the day, spends the first few hours acting as a kind of conductor for the larger group from a seated position: he cues them when and where to start and offers feedback to individual musicians. While external direction simplifies coordination efforts, Paul is ultimately resistant to functioning as a leader in this way. He describes it as antithetical to the work:

The nature of the piece, the way it's composed ... is such that it would be grotesque if there were only one person leading. And it would just be wrong. The music demands the initiative from [many] – and ... it's not just first fiddles. There needs to be and should be and has to be leadership from every individual at different times.

Even while Paul conducts, he differentiates his gestures from the strong, codified leads of a conductor to informal waves of the hand meant to suggest leads. The second violin of Q3 leans over to his first violin, remarking to her that the current leadership they are receiving won't be a normal condition of the work: 'We're going to need to have something to latch on to; it's easy now with Paul to guide us.' Conducting serves as a temporary support, so that practice can proceed, but it isn't proposed as a long-term solution. The musicians will need to find another way to sustain coordination.

After 3pm, Paul, still weak from his illness, goes into his house to rest. In his absence, the group attempts to work without a conductor, not without first wondering how they will be able to play in time. They consider, then discount, the option of using a metronome to replace Paul. The two remaining present members of the Medici Quartet, second violinist Cathy Thompson and cellist Tony, attempt to lead, but the group resists. Others test the water, offering input, and voicing opinions and suggestions on how to proceed. At 4.30pm, Paul rejoins the group but not as a conductor: he picks up his violin to play. The unspoken proposal Paul makes with this action could be understood as follows: we will now try to organize ourselves without a dominant leader. Realizing this, the eyes that were once on him search out clues from other members of the group as well. The group sorts out which quartets at which moments need to give the others clear leads, as dictated by the needs of the score. These leads, as the musicians in Q4 tell me later, begin to present an order amidst the chaos of sixteen voices, provided the musicians attend to them. Still, many express difficulty hearing what they need to hear in order to play in time with the other quartets, even while seated in a close circle in one room. What will it be like when they are stretched further apart, at Winchester Cathedral for instance, they wonder.

On the second day, Paul brings a metronome to rehearsal and clips it to his music stand. He tells the group that, ideally, they would have set up rehearsal so that one quartet was in each of the two lofts in the barn, and two on the ground floor, to simulate the performance configuration, but he determines they are not ready for that yet. They still need the physical proximity of a circle to learn the piece and each other. A discussion of timing and how they will take cues when they can't see each other in the performance space emerges and is left unresolved when Paul cuts it off, saying they can't know what they will need until they are in the space on the day of each performance, and they will need to adapt on the fly. The metronome for now provides the support necessary for them to at least practice the music. But as a learning tool, meant only for rehearsals, it presents a temporary guide, leaving the quartets to wonder what they will ulti-mately 'latch on to' – a lingering question Paul does not attempt to resolve at this point.

Reflecting on those two days of rehearsal, in interviews after the fact, several of the musicians report that, as a composition, *Towards Silence* is not that much harder to play than a 'regular' quartet piece; it involves the same kind of work. Often the quartets play as units, almost as if each quartet is one voice in a larger quartet. The challenge is being able to hear each other. The first violin of Q4 tells me that what happened in rehearsals was 'what you kind of expect if you put four lots of people who don't know each other's groups into the same room and ask them to interact together. Which is slightly chaotic, slightly disorganized, but fundamentally not ineffective.' Most agree that they achieved their primary objectives for these rehearsals: to get to know the other players, to get a concept of what the piece is, to find and feel the 'pulse' of the piece collectively, and to at least begin to determine what kind of leadership or other support will be needed to pull this off.

While they express little concern over the fact as pre-rehearsals wrap up, the musicians remain uncertain as to whether or not they will be able to achieve Tavener's vision. In conversation with Paul in his home on the evening of the second day, he expresses general satisfaction with the progress they have made, assessing that they had 'got past the most uncomfortable, incoherent stage' typical, in his experience, to the development of a new work. When I ask Paul how he expects to translate the group's work, which in rehearsals so far has been configured in a circle, to the yet untried configurations of the performance venues, he shares his uncertainty over whether they will be able to achieve the spatial distribution Tavener calls for:

At the moment, I don't see any way that we can attenuate this shape. I think the most we might be able to achieve if we had a big enough space, a suitable space, is to sit in a cross form, with the four quartets facing inwards to each other . . . Sort of four clusters, like four nubs. But that's not what [Tavener]'s asked for. I'm going to take a lot of convincing that anything beyond that is possible.

Paul explains that this uncertainty makes the US premiere particularly tricky, because they have already committed to performing across four levels of a spiral staircase, and he still doesn't know if that will be possible. But Ivo-Jan van der Werff, Medici's viola player who is now based in the US, had traveled to the Rubin Museum earlier that month and agreed to the producer's proposed configuration. 'I hope Ivo wasn't over-eager to please, but he said to [the producer] we can do it. So they've sold tickets now on the basis that we can do it in that shape,' says Paul. Then he informs me of the back-up plan: 'It may be that the only way that we can perform it in that space, in that shape, is for everyone to have headphones, and we play it with a click-track. Which is like, effectively like we'd be playing to a metronome, but only *we* would be hearing the metronome.' Though he groans as he says it, Paul confesses he believes 99 percent of the audience won't know the difference: 'Most people have no idea that there's an aesthetic or difference in sensibility between listening and playing to something that's clicking. But to me, it's like a negation of everything I believe in.'

Nonetheless, Paul ends on an upbeat, putting his trust in the composer and suggesting that it may work in a way that he can't anticipate until they try it. This is the usual way of beginning to rehearse any new work, he explains: 'Things that were simply impossible when first learning a piece become easy when you know it.' The only way to get through impossible to easy, in his experience, is to be 'in it,' to play the music as a group and learn the signals, the shape, and the needs of that particular composition. Until they do that, he considers it unproductive to doubt Tavener's ability to create a composition that can be effectively performed. Their task is to believe it can be done and find the best way to do it.

## Rehearsals and a world premiere, April 2009

Paul, much to his disappointment, isn't well enough to travel to New York in April to participate in the world premiere. The Medici Quartet enlist a friend of Cathy's, Fenella Barton, to play second violin to Cathy's first. I'm at the Rubin Museum when the provisionally constituted Medici Quartet arrives Sunday evening, ahead of the younger American-based quartets who are coming Monday. After a period of enthusiastic introductions, producer Tim McHenry takes us all on a quick tour of the 'Spiral,' the centerpiece of the museum's architecture and the site of Thursday's performance. The staircase (see Figure 3.1) scales six floors, pausing at each in a sunburst-shaped landing to release travelers into the open exhibition rooms, and resolves under a massive skylight.

Tim informs Medici that the aim of performing across different levels of the Spiral is to exploit the sound funnel the staircase creates, and to experiment with transmitting vertical sound through the audience, who

**Figure 3.1** The Gallery Tower. (Photo: Peter Aaron / Esto)

will be seated on each floor, facing the exhibitions, in the kind of meditative exercise for which Tavener asks. The Tibetan Singing Bowl, which is also in the score, will be played by a musician seated on the very top floor. Despite contrary suggestions offered by Tony, Tim insists that the four quartets be spread out over four floors, this experiment being a primary motivation for the commission. Ivo takes the lead in suggesting the layout: Medici (Q1) will be positioned on the fifth-floor landing, Q2 on the fourth, Q3 on the third, and Q4 on the second.

Tim then invites the Medici musicians into the museum café for tea and a chat, during which they troubleshoot problems they might have in achieving an integrated performance across four floors. Slight time delay due to the distance sound must travel from Q1 to Q4 is considered (disrupting aural communication), as well as the difficulty they will have in seeing more than one or two other quartets at any given time (restricting visual communication). Several possible solutions are proposed for solving the problem, and all discarded as insufficiently precise, save one: Paul has recorded a click-track of the entire score with which to cue the first violinists via the use of wireless earpieces. However, Cathy reminds the others that, according to the score, two quartets always play in relationship to one another, which might in itself provide enough aid for coordination. Perhaps, and ideally they agree, they will be able to solve the divide without any kind of artificial support. Maybe 'ears will simply have to listen harder,' Tim suggests.

Medici begins rehearsal in the museum theatre, seated in usual proximity; the maximum distance between two members is 8.5 feet. But their curiosity over how this will work in the performance configuration gets the better of them, and the musicians soon carry their instruments out into the Spiral. Tony and Fenella perch on the fifth-floor landing where Medici will sit in performance. Cathy takes the role of Q2 on the fourth-floor landing opposite the Spiral from Medici, while Ivo travels down to the third floor, the site for Q3, from which vantage he can see Cathy, but not Tony and Fenella as he is directly underneath them. 'Can Tony see down?' Ivo asks. They seem concerned only to prove that they can see and hear one another to some degree, and they determine trade-offs: for instance, only the first violin needs a view of the opposite quartet, not the second violin.

The four experiment with playing parts, each representing a quartet in the full score. Cathy exaggerates the musical beats physically while she plays, to try one method of communicating across space, and is teased for it. Ivo and Cathy figure out how to coordinate communication with Q4 for a crucial passage in which Q1 and Q4 play together; Cathy decides she can stand up from time to time at her position on the fifth floor, for when she stands at the landing rail, she discovers, she can see Ivo, who is now acting as first violin of Q4 on the second floor, and give him visual cues. While they aren't yet sure what they will or will not be able to hear across such a distance once all sixteen musicians are playing (it is 36.2 diagonal feet from the fifth-floor landing to the second-floor landing, rail to rail), they seem encouraged by the possibilities they're inventing. Ivo states: 'I'm feeling more positive now.' They report to Tim their belief that the four-floor split is possible and their resolve that they won't need the click-track after all. 'It won't be music' with a metronome 'banging away' in their ears, Cathy asserts.

However, the click-track comes up again the next morning, as the Medici Quartet discuss ways to enable communication between groups. They begin with the organic approaches: each first violin will need to act as a conductor and gesture cues to the other quartets; Q2 will be able to see Medici's bow changes even if they can't hear them; Q2 can beat out a rhythm to cue Q1 and Q3; Q3 will have to coordinate with Q2 and Q4; the whole activity will be like a relay race, passing the baton. However, as they talk through these options they acknowledge that it becomes hard to be still, as the music requires, when communication objectives oblige them to be hyperactive with their bows. Tony brings up the use of the click-track solution again, *just for a section of the music*. But his colleagues remain convinced that the click-track will isolate each quartet from the other and make it more difficult to hear. This is seen as detrimental to their art. Listening, says Fenella, is the way musicians make music with one another. Cathy argues that they have to 'give it a go' without the click-track, but also agrees to remain open to giving the click-track a try.

The American-based string quartets arrive Monday evening, and the collective work begins. Unlike their British counterparts, who were lacking a few musicians, these quartets rehearse with the benefit of full attendance. They are energetic and on task, bubbling with intra- and inter-quartet conversation. They sound better prepared than their pred-ecessors, an observation Cathy supports later with her own assessment. They begin their work as the UK team had in February, seated in the configuration that allows the closest proximity and maximum lines of sight – a circle – at the base of the Spiral. They jump right into the tasks of sorting out leads, synchronization, and interpretation collectively. Questions are typically directed at discerning whom a particular musi-cian or quartet should be listening to at a moment in the score, in order to play in time together. Q2 and Q4 alone play a passage together to sync up; the chance to hear them play that passage turns out to be helpful to Q3. Some of their interpretive negotiation relates to volume adjustment, so they can hear each other, and sorting out difference in textures, so they aren't all playing at the same level. Other discussion focuses on finding a mutual understanding of Tavener's written direc-tions, and marking the breaths to take together between sections. In the midst of this work, Cathy acknowledges appreciatively that the group is working well together by collectively leading: 'I feel a sense of leading and not leading, all of us.' No metronome, click-track, or conductor has been proposed.

The American quartets soon begin to reiterate, with some variation, the concerns about spatial constraints that Medici had exercised prior to their arrival: will they be able to hear one another once they are seated in the Spiral? Since they are used to seeing one another while they work, what will happen when they can't? The second violin of Q4 reports experimenting in this configuration with not looking at Q2 during a passage. Deprived of visual leads, she discovers she is no longer able to stay in time with them and is alarmed. Despite these concerns, the quartets continue to use their time together in a circle to explore textures, taking away vibrato in one passage, playing another as if 'petrified.' They enjoy good feelings, good attention, and productive work.

Later that evening, the quartets migrate upwards to the staircase landings in the Spiral. Here they try all kinds of acrobatics in the effort to coordinate their playing without artificial aid. For instance, Q3 is seated on the third floor directly underneath Q1 on the fifth, and, as Medici had discovered in their earlier experiments, the two quartets cannot see one another, but both can see Q2 on the fourth-floor landing opposite. So the first violin of Q2 takes on the role of communicating between Q1 and Q3 by exaggerating his bowing, and even conducting at moments with broad gestures. Q3 then relays beats and downbeats to Q4 on the second floor, who can see no one but Q3 and hear little, their eyes and ears craning upwards. In order to relay, Q3 delegates tasks among themselves: the cellist will express the pulse physically, with an animated bounce, while the first violinist will embody the downbeat, in a more subtle but perceptible way.

These efforts continue the following day, short Q3, as the quartets work in the Spiral. The click-track has been proposed as an option this morning, but the musicians consider it to be 'Plan B.' Q4, in the absence of Q3, splits its members across the second-and third-floor landings to facilitate communication with Q2 on the fourth floor. While this serves to make coordination easier for them to start with, Q4 struggles with the perceived sound delay and inability to hear what the first two quartets are doing above. The delay makes it difficult for them to diagnose problems, such as who is out of time, and adjust. Their cellist lets loose a sudden cry: 'We're in jail down here!' Lina, their second violin, climbs the stairs to Q2's landing and pleads with the others to at least try the click-track.

Her plea meets with vigorous debate, as the musicians gather on the fourth-floor landing, instruments in hand. Q2's first violin J argues against the click-track. His concern is that the click-track, being a fixed, pre-recorded track, cannot accommodate and adjust for the natural reverberation of sound through this space, as the musicians can. If not born of listening to the space and one another, J argues, it won't be 'music' they perform. Lina counters: 'If it's not together, it can't be musical anyhow.' She suggests the best approach is to use the click to play precisely in time together, so that they can focus on developing the layers of sound the audience will perceive.

Finally, they agree to at least try the click-track, and technicians visit each floor delivering the earpiece to each first violin. The use of the click-track brings a host of changes to the nature of rehearsal. First, every time the musicians stop mid-score, they have to wait for the technicians to re-cue the click-track before starting again at an agreed-upon place. Second, they now work on playing in time with the click-track rather than with one another, and to do this the musicians in each quartet focus on their 'leader,' the first violin, to communicate the cues he or she is receiving through the earpiece, a new task for that leader. Almost all physicalized and visual communication between quartets has ceased. Gestures subside. Cue relay is a thing of the past. Folding chairs spring open, and musicians sit, circling into their own groups, where once they stood at the edges of the landings peering up and down across the divide.

Once they've tried the click-track, some revisions of opinion occur. Lina, its strongest advocate, admits that it's hard to 'play music' with a click in your ear, and expresses discomfort with the 'military' feel it causes. The musicians feel constrained by the click in terms of the range of character they can explore within its rigid structure. J remains dissatisfied with this solution. He argues that the click-track takes away the essential struggle of four quartets coming together across distance, and the dynamics of this struggle experienced in both the qualities of the process and the music made. He considers this struggle essential to realizing Tavener's vision and for creating that special quality of ensemble. He claims the music sounds different as a result of the change.

However, the advantages are also weighed, in terms of both technical proficiency and aesthetics. The musicians discover they can play softly now, as the score is written, rather than play loudly to be heard and in ways that distort the musical aesthetic. Given that they are now playing more softly with less overt physicality, and given that they are now playing more precisely in time together via the click-track, they can actually *hear* one another better – a promising condition. The result, heard by those musicians who leave their seats and wander the staircase to listen as the others play, is more 'musical.' It sounds better. Ivo gives the group a new way to think about the click-track, suggesting that, as he hears it, 'Tavener's music is an absolute inner pulse with stillness around it,' and the click actually supports the aesthetics of the piece by being that absolute pulse.

Tony builds on this possibility, making a proposal to the group: 'As we get familiar with [the click] we can expand it.' By which he means, as they master the click, they can begin to play less rigidly *with* it, and more *in relation to* it, creatively, as they would work normally with a metronome in rehearsals. Eventually, they will be able to reduce the amount of effort and attention required to play in time via the click-track. It will help them sustain coordination, but will cease to dominate, and a more dialogic relationality can emerge. Lina suggests that while 'temporality is taken away' from them, they can find other ways to create changes in character.

After these discussions and playing through the full piece with the click-track, the group opinion coalesces around the decision to use it. Ivo declares the music better with the click. The music now wafts through the sound funnel. 'It sounds more clear,' says Cathy. A more 'ethereal' effect can be pursued, as Tavener intended. The click also alleviates difficulty: musicians no longer have to strain to hear or be heard. Q4 is delighted with the overall effect. Q2 concedes, telling me in a later interview that they do so because they believe the decision ultimately rests with the Medici Quartet, since this is 'their project.'

Reflecting Friday morning, after the Thursday evening premiere, Fenella tells me that, in her opinion, they became more playful once they added the click-track. Being able to hear one another gave them freedom to listen, and tightness of coordination afforded play. She declares that 'the whole thing came together' in performance, and that she was persuaded for the first time that the composition works in different levels and can work in different configurations. Tony reports on audience feedback: 'Everybody says it's beautiful to listen to.' Several others involved in the performance offer their own evaluation by writing letters to Paul, which he posts to his blog. McHenry calls the performance 'phenomenal,' declaring that the conception of the levels worked. Q4's violist says that despite the challenging configuration, 'you could feel a genuine connection between all of the groups.' Reviewer Matthew Gurewitsch reports: 'Though divided into four movements and punctuated by chant-like calls from the singing bowl, the composition unfolded in one shining arc . . . Those who attend are in for a singular experience' (Gurewitsch 2009). An audience member describes that experience as follows: 'In the performance the distinction between sound and space sometimes seemed to dissolve, so perfectly did the music and the museum complement one another.' Paul receives, to my knowledge, one critique of the performance that he does not post to the blog because he 'doesn't want John worried.' While mostly favorable, the writer exposes the use of the click-track (which was meant to be imperceptible to the audience) and claims the piece should have been composed for the Spiral configuration more precisely.

## Performing in multiple venues, June–July 2009

Scheduled before the world premiere of *Towards Silence* in the US was perceived and blogged a success, the UK premiere at Winchester Cathedral in July arises next on the agenda. Here, the musicians are promised the ultimate test of this exercise: to perform together at the extreme distance afforded by one of the most expansive cathedrals in Europe, completely out of sight and, likely, hearing of the others. Leading up to this performance, the UK quartets have two concerts in London, one for The Study Society at The Colet House, and one for Westminster Synagogue, which, being private concerts (even if sold out to audiences of 200), Paul considers to be rehearsals for the premiere. Following Winchester, a final performance will occur at St Mary's Church as the opening to the Petworth Festival.

To achieve performance of *Towards Silence* in four radically different spaces, and based on the perceived success of the US exercise, the UK quartets begin rehearsals with the click-track. No time is spent considering alternatives, though Cathy mourns the loss of the connections built by working first without the click: 'It's like rushing straight for a Cesarean section instead of trying natural birth first!' However, Ivo and Tony have returned from the US true believers in the click and proselytize to the others. Ivo tells the violist of Q2 that with the click 'you have the rhythm, so it gives you more freedom. It feels horrible, but it's amazing.' The musicians have spent the morning hours of the first day of rehearsals focused on the opening act of these concerts, Vivaldi's *Four Seasons*, with a plan to play through the second act, *Towards Silence*, only once that afternoon. Tony explains: 'I'm not worried about *Towards Silence*. We have the click-track.' The US experiment appears to have solved the problem for this group.

Reconvening in Paul's barn, the four UK quartets organize them-selves into a configuration that disrupts, as much as possible, their sight lines, so that they may begin to practice playing with limited visual communication. They work first with the click-track played over the barn's sound system, for all to hear. By the second day of rehearsals, they use the wireless earpieces. As they rehearse, Tony reports on interpretive decisions made by the quartets in the US. Ivo steps out of his seat to listen, and offers input. When Cathy says that the music doesn't sound as clear as in New York, Ivo supports her assessment, ascribing the change to the room they are in. Physically, they are 'on top of one another' in this space. More distance between quartets is needed to hear the music properly. Ivo coaches the group to adjust dynamics to the space, feedback he will offer differently to suit each of the spaces they travel to. In the barn, dynamics need to be 'on the lower edge.'

The last hours of rehearsal focus primarily on 'playing right with the click,' including sorting out the leadership needed from each first violin responsible for communicating cues to colleagues. While the musicians make some preliminary choices regarding dynamics, these choices stay open to revision, as they anticipate that they will need to adjust balance to each performance space. Four days of rehearsals in the barn end in good spirits on the evening of July 3. The musicians plan to meet at The Colet House the next day, early enough in advance of their evening performance to rehearse *The Four Seasons*, and then work *Towards Silence* in the performance hall one hour prior to opening the doors to the audience.

## Private concerts

The Colet House performance goes more or less smoothly, with the occasional technical glitch and musician error (a faulty earpiece, a dead battery, getting out of time with the click) from which the quartets quickly recover by checking in with whichever musician is seated closest or within sight. They perform in the configuration planned in advance by Tony and Artistic Director Jude James, who have called for the four raised platforms on which the quartets sit to be situated in each corner of the 70-foot-long rectangular hall. The hall is filled to the brim on this hot evening, and 200 people meditate in unison (they train in meditation at The Study Society) to the 35-minute piece. Jude is so affected by the performance that she attends every following event. When I ask her about her experience at the final concert, she tells me she 'can't get enough of it' and that as a personal spiritual experience, it is 'transforming' her.

The Westminster Synagogue performance is also experienced as a success, although (or because) nothing proceeds as planned. Tony and Events Coordinator Renee Salamon agreed in advance that all four quartets would be seated together on the ground floor, with the sound wafting up an open staircase to the audience seated on the first floor above. However, when the musicians gather at 5pm to try this out, they discover that the space at the bottom of the staircase is too cramped; they are seated on top of one another, as they had been in the barn. There is a 'too close' problem as well as 'too far.' The musicians rebel against the configuration, claiming the music will sound muddled and won't be audible enough to the audience on the first floor. After some debate whether to play upstairs and/or downstairs, they decide on a more radical option: to play in and around the staircase itself. While there are still difficulties with this configuration – Q2's violist becomes alarmed when she realizes she won't be able to depend on Q4 for two visual cues; Renee is alarmed by the change and requires problem solving related to fire codes – the quartets proceed with this arrangement, minutes before the audience's arrival. As they finish rehearsing, Paul, Ivo, and Tony agree it sounds 'ravishing' on the stairs. Paul praises it by comparison: 'Didn't get that sound in Colet!'

## Winchester Cathedral premiere

The Winchester Cathedral event introduces an altogether different and unanticipated difficulty: since 8am (it is 2pm now) two crews – a recording crew from the BBC and a television crew hired privately with generous funding from an unnamed patron – have been setting up extensive video camera, audio recording, lighting and electrical equipment around what they have defined as a central 'onstage' space. Doing so, they indisputably dictate precisely where the performers are to sit, within a rather tight space in front of the choir. Malcolm Creese, who is not a quartet musician but the bass player for the Vivaldi *Seasons* and the producer of the next performance at the Petworth Festival, expresses his horror at this layout to quartet musicians as they arrive. All were led to believe that the whole point of playing at Winchester was to reach a climax in the distributed design, to push the boundaries of this unique endeavor to its very spatial limits. Malcolm is organizing an uprising.

Malcolm and the mobilized quartet musicians exercise their arguments, along the following lines:

Didn't we all begin this peculiar project with the vision of Winchester as the pièce de résistance of distributed quartet playing? Didn't Paul from day one take pains to describe, in detail, his vision for how *Towards Silence* will be impossibly performed in the four extremities of the cross-shaped Cathedral? Wasn't a performance at Winchester in fact sought after precisely because the Cathedral boasts the longest nave and overall length of any Gothic cathedral in all of Europe?! What was the point of all that hassle with technology? We struggled to integrate the damn click-track so that we could become capable of playing in any space, and especially this one! Winchester is finally the space in which we can achieve Tavener's vision – no stairs to contend with, no wide-open and well-lit hall. But if we proceed with this publicity-induced absurdity, we'll all be seated together, practically on top of one another! Tavener says 'this is not music that should be heard as concert music [as in under hot lights, on a stage!], but rather meditated on.' We'll all be mercilessly exposed to the audience under television lights, which is nothing at all like being enshrouded in the secret corners of darkness about a Cathedral. We will be watched instead of listened to.

And Tavener himself is coming, today no less, and might die any moment! Shouldn't we be giving him the performance he asked for? It's disaster!

When Tony arrives, we learn that this layout was in fact pre-arranged by Tony and Paul, in negotiation with the BBC and television crew. When the opportunity for filming came up (that is, funding), the trade-off was made: to sacrifice the aesthetic experiment in favor of media benefits. Unfortunately, no one had bothered to tell the rest of the musicians about the change in plan, and priority. When Paul arrives with his familial entourage, he confirms this decision and layout. He refuses to listen to any dispute on the matter, and settles himself in his first violinist's chair to survey the crew work in progress, displaying his physical weariness as a barrier to any further disputation. Malcolm retreats.

By dinner break, Q4's disappointment in the Winchester configuration seems to have flourished into full-blown disillusionment with the project. Now that they are seated 'practically in a circle' at Winchester, the click 'feels pointless.' Back stage, Q4's violist, who is usually the most animated of the group, slumps in his chair. He calls his work today 'a job,' by which he means to differentiate it from projects that involve 'passion and love.' He adds: 'I feel like this is still just a professional product at the moment.'

By Q2's post-performance assessment, the Winchester experience suffered in comparison with the Synagogue, which was for them more pleasurable and more integrated. 'We were almost audience members ourselves [at the Synagogue],' second violinist Natalie says. 'I loved the fact that it was so informal, that it seemed really friendly.' Whereas at Winchester, seated 'higher up on an altar,' they lacked the interaction with the audience, and Q2's cellist felt for the first time as if they were separate groups rather than one whole ensemble working together. 'Tonight, to be honest,' continues Natalie, 'we could have been sitting in a string orchestra situation playing individual parts. Whereas [at the Synagogue], it was the effect of having four groups, that kind of surround-sound ... and I thought that was what Tavener was wanting with it.' This quartet expressed their perception that, given the set performance configuration at Winchester, they were not allowed to realize Tavener's vision, neither in terms of their use of the space nor by becoming an integrated ensemble.

Ivo, however, expresses a different experience. He describes the sound at the Synagogue as being 'too loud almost' so that 'you couldn't tell the detail quite so clearly.' He enjoys the effect of being in a large space, which he says allows him to hear better what's going on, and thinks the audience at Winchester had a more complete experience of the whole piece. At least one reviewer, Andrew Clements, criticizes the layout as failing to honor Tavener's directions, and blames the cameras for taking 'the edge from any sense of spirituality' (Clements 2009). Tavener himself is thankful, but remarkably silent.

## Constraint and possibility

As the quartet musicians involved in the *Towards Silence* project addressed the problem of performing as an integrated ensemble while seated apart and in varying configurations, much effort was dedicated to solving the immediate problem of playing together precisely in time. While they temporarily relied on external methods for coordination such as a conductor, a metronome, and the click-track, the musicians repeatedly considered these methods as learning tools inappropriate for performance, artificial, and ultimately antithetical to their professional standards and aspirations. They preferred to address the problem of coordination in ways that made it possible for them to pursue their objectives to achieve the composer's vision, demonstrate a high level of competence, and achieve a quality of ensemble and play in their collaboration together. In other words, the musicians determined that some were better ways to respond to new constraints than others, 'better' being based not on efficiency or ease but on the quality of collaboration that response called forth.

The click-track in particular was characterized by many of the quartet musicians as a serious threat to their work. When Paul introduced the possibility of the click-track in February, he differentiated between the activities of 'listening' and 'playing to something that's clicking,' calling the latter 'a negation of everything' in which he believed as a musician. Playing accurately to a click-track is the work of a skilled technician, while making spontaneous revisions of opinion to an emerging performance that is born of listening and responding to one's colleagues with intimate awareness is the work of a master quartet player. This capability is achieved at great cost over years invested in rehearsal together. Quartet musicians stake their careers on their ability to regularly demonstrate a high level of competence in performance, and that competence, for a string quartet player, goes beyond technical achievement, to the ability to express complexity, spontaneity, and the special quality of relationship between members that becomes evident in their music. The regulated pulse of technology threatened these pursuits, turning the musicians' debate over its use into a debate about whether they were artists or technicians.

When string musicians shortcut their usual process, as they might with a click-track, their professional identity is at stake. Paul chose to pursue a career as a quartet musician because he was 'in love' with the intimacy of relationship that could be created in a group of four, and determined it to be 'the highest aspiration for a string player' (Austin and O'Donnell 2007: 4). During a particular moment of crisis in the Medici Quartet's long career, several members turned to studio work to supplement their income, and Paul referred to the new efficiency they displayed in rehearsals as an 'inward cancer of the musical soul' (Austin and O'Donnell 2007: 10). In Paul's experience, the impact of efficiency on rehearsal was that 'all the love went out of it.' Faulkner (1971: 56) describes a merciless dichotomy, instilled in string musicians by the socializing force of early training, between committing every action in service of the work and selling out for financial gain. This dichotomy emerged in evaluation of the Winchester premiere, when media benefits overruled artistic experimentation and the potential to realize Tavener's vision. Here we learn what happens when the musicians' fears are realized: Q4's violist described that event as the moment in which *Towards Silence* lost the 'love and passion' of an ensemble project, and became for him 'just a professional product.' His colleague Natalie felt that being seated together on stage at Winchester in close physical proximity was the same as being in a string orchestra. They had lost their sense of identity as quartet musicians, conversing across four groups as Tavener had intended, and found themselves unable to realize their objectives.

In the US, the Medici Quartet discussed and rejected the click-track in theory, believing that it would isolate each quartet from the others and decrease their capacity for listening to each other and for producing an integrated performance as an ensemble. Doing so, it threatened to separate the pursuit of coordination from the pursuit of ensemble. While playing precisely in time together is a necessary condition for playfulness, the two activities are integrated. In order to increase the likelihood that they emerge together, coordination cannot be addressed separate from 'making music.' The activity of giving leads is an example of how coordination and play are integrated in action: the leads musicians give each other, whether pre-determined or spontaneous, function both to coordinate the group – they create an order out of chaos, as Q4 in the UK described – and to sustain a balanced and collective engagement in the dialog. The US quartets preferred to pursue coordination organically, as the struggle of four voices coming together across distance resulted in, as Cathy reported later, a higher quality of listening and that special quality of ensemble.

In order to accept the click-track, the musicians not only needed to reach a dead-end in their other efforts, they needed to *reconceive* its role and their approach to using it, so that it no longer threatened their identity or objectives. The first breakthrough came when the US quartets tried the click-track and discovered that it enabled them to hear each other, so that they might listen. Contrary to expectations, it brought them out of the isolation they were experiencing ('We're in jail down here!') by giving them a means by which to hear each other. Binding them to an absolute structure, the click-track conversely freed the musicians to listen to each other and to play. Its role changed from one of domination and the suppression of artistic aim to one of enabler of ensemble. As part of this breakthrough, the musicians reconceived the click-track as part of the aesthetic of the music, and therefore a constraint that played an important role in helping them to realize Tavener's composition, which they interpreted as an absolute inner pulse immersed in stillness, exhibiting an ethereal quality.

In the UK, the click-track also played a role in helping them to realize Tavener's vision of distribution, in multiple spaces. Faced with the difficulty of achieving precise coordination in varying configurations, the quartets managed to do so with increasing efficiency. Starting rehearsals in June by learning to play with the click-track helped them spend their limited rehearsal time in each performance venue – in some cases as little as 30 minutes – on discovering the unique configuration in which they could produce the most pleasing listening experience, while improvising supporting visual cues to ensure they stayed together or could recover in the event of a technical glitch or human error. Had they been able to exercise this new flexibility in Winchester as well, it might have been determined a success: that incident was not an example of failure to reconceive the click-track but an example of failure to honor the shared objectives of the group.

Conceiving of a new role for the click-track, as a support for demonstrating competence as a string musician, for realizing Tavener's vision, and for achieving ensemble, was not enough in itself for achieving their objectives. The way in which the musicians conceived of and engaged in their work with it over time mattered. They worked with the click-track much as they might do with a metronome in rehearsal, not as a solution to the difficulty of coordinating their work but as a tool to temporarily attend to in order to master coordination, with the aim eventually to use it to sustain coordination while directing their attention to activities involving dialog and play. By the third performance in the UK, Ivo observed that the musicians were working with the click in 'a more relaxed fashion.' He said the click had become subliminal, like a heartbeat, making it possible to 'withdraw your awareness of it' and achieve the dual attention necessary to prioritize other collaborative efforts. Tony's observation of the UK groups' development over time illustrates how the musicians used the click-track to support collective leadership:

[The first violins are] physically leading beats, and making sure everyone's together in their own quartet. And you can see also there's leads going on within each quartet. So [the quartets] actually are playing within themselves as well. So it's not just a click-track, but they are actually playing together and trying to lead each other, which is good.

Over time, members of the group appeared to be taking 'more responsibility and leading more,' suggesting that a dialogic relationality was emerging as the group found ways to work creatively in response to the click-track.

As they encountered new constraints and suffered the threats inherent in some of these, the musicians took care not to compromise their objectives in favor of resolving difficulty early. Even when they could see no viable way forward, or know with certainty whether they could deliver promised performances, they chose to live a bit longer with uncertainty and remain open to emergent possibilities. Taking the approach Paul described as 'believe it can be done and find a best way,' they kept working, and doing so created an open space for something unforeseen to enter. By allowing the problem to exist rather than resolving it in a way that compromised their standards, aspirations, and thereby identity, they were able to discover unanticipated ways of meeting those objectives in stretched conditions. This learning introduced alternative ways of integrating coordinating technology into the work of ensembles, in ways that kept alive multiple possibilities and enabled them to create effective performances in very different kinds of spaces.

In this chapter I have described how these string quartets used the practice of reconceiving to sustain their professional standards and aspirations, while performing under intensified constraints in such a way that standards and constraints were able to productively co-exist. While the musicians could have directed their efforts in this project at simply achieving a high degree of coordination – a noteworthy feat in itself given the unusual conditions of the project – they didn't compromise. Rather, they defined the problem as one of ensemble and addressed it together as a group. As a result, constraints were reconceived as an aesthetic feature of the work process and outcome. The click-track that was antithetical to everything became the foundation of a new aesthetic logic and practice. The musicians used their new capabilities to exploit (when allowed) spatial distance and distribution in ways that optimized the performance of Tavener's composition and the audience's experience of it.

As this chapter resolves, I invite a re-opening. While this discussion emphasizes moments in which I understood constraint to be reconceived as possibility, there are other ways to focus the story, and more detail behind these descriptions. No doubt the reader has perceived possibilities beyond those I can address in this chapter, and may be already at work on new conceptions.


## References

Austin, Rob and Lee Devin. 2003. *Artful Making: What managers need to know about how artists work*. Upper Saddle River, NJ: Financial Times Prentice Hall.

2010. Not just a pretty face: economic drivers behind the arts-in-business movement. *Journal of Business Strategy* 31 (4): 59–69.

2012. *The Soul of Design: Harnessing the power of plot to create extraordinary products*. California: Stanford University Press.

Austin, Robert D. and Daniel Hjorth. 2012. The unlikely conversation: How the economic 'lives with' the aesthetic in creative companies. Working Paper.

Austin, Robert D. and Shannon O'Donnell. 2007. Paul Robertson and the Medici String Quartet. *HBS No. 607–083*. Boston: Harvard Business School Publishing.

Becker, Howard S. 1982. *Art Worlds*. Berkeley and Los Angeles: University of California Press.

Becker, Howard S., Robert R. Faulkner and Barbara Kirshenblatt-Gimblett. 2006. *Art from Start to Finish: Jazz, painting, writing, and other improvisations*. University of Chicago Press.

Blum, David. 1986. *The Art of Quartet Playing: The Guarneri Quartet in conversation with David Blum*. New York: Cornell University Press.

Clements, Andrew. 2009. Towards Silence: Winchester Cathedral. *The Guardian*. July 9, 2009. www.guardian.co.uk/music/2009/jul/09/towards-silence-review.

Faulkner, Robert R. 1971. *Hollywood Studio Musicians: Their work and careers in the recording industry*. Chicago: Aldine, Atherton, Inc.

Gurewitsch, Matthew. 2009. Unsung: Sir John Tavener's 'Towards Silence' received its world premiere. April 24, 2009. www.beyondcriticism.com/2009/04/sir-john-tavener-towards-silence.

Moritz, Reiner E. 2005. *4 Better, 4 Worse: The anatomy of a string quartet* (documentary film). United Kingdom: Opus Arte.

# 4 | *The* Ursula *faience dinnerware series by Royal Copenhagen*

BRIAN MOERAN

In 1993, Royal Copenhagen broke with its porcelain tradition and launched a new faience dinnerware series, which it called *Ursula* after the potter who designed it, Ursula Munch-Petersen (b. 1937). The fourth generation of potters living and working on the island of Bornholm in the Baltic Sea, east of Denmark and south of Skåne in Sweden, Ursula Munch-Petersen worked as 'artist in residence' at the Royal Copenhagen Factory in Frederiksberg (a borough of Copenhagen city) from the late 1980s into the early 1990s. It was then that she designed the *Ursula* series, and, together with a number of colleagues at the factory, nursed it into production.

This chapter explores the creative process by describing various evaluative practices, or 'editorial moments,' that took place during the conception, design, manufacture, distribution, and sale of the *Ursula* series. In the process, it reveals actors' perceptions of Ursula Munch-Petersen as a potter and craftswoman, as well as of Royal Copenhagen as a company.

## A tale of two factories

Ursula Munch-Petersen's training in ceramics was broad and closely linked to mass-production practices. After childhood exposure to her

The material presented here is based on two visits to the Royal Copenhagen factory in Glostrup, Copenhagen, as well as on interviews with the potter herself; with Finn Næss Schmidt, product development manager at Royal Copenhagen during the time that *Ursula* was developed and put into production; with Peter Poulsen, chemical engineer who worked on the glazes used in the series; and with Ole Jensen, a designer who was also an 'artist in residence' at Royal Copenhagen with Ursula Munch-Petersen. I would like to thank all those concerned for their time, enthusiasm, patience, and mutual respect.

It was a custom to use working people's names for designs made at Aluminia, one of Royal Copenhagen's factories. A green glazed ware was called *Sigurt*, for example, and another, blue glazed, product line was called *Sonja*.

mother's pottery, Ursula worked for a couple of years in a well-known Danish pottery turning out 'functional art' wares (*brugskunst*) before starting at the School of Arts and Crafts in Copenhagen, in 1956. After graduation in 1960, she spent a year working in her grandfather's terra-cotta factory on Bornholm before finding employment in an experimental workshop located in the Bing & Grøndahl ceramics factory (where her aunt Gertrude had worked from 1949 to 1959). This gave her an opportunity to show her work in a number of exhibitions both in Denmark and abroad. From 1970 to 1975, Ursula worked at home on a series of salt-glazed wares for home use. During this period, she was employed at the School for Arts and Crafts (*Skolen for brugskunst*), where she held a position until 1990. In 1982, she published a book titled *Clay Forming* (*Lerforming*).

Her work has been strongly influenced by folk craft utensils, as well as by her long-standing interest in botany, whose methods of taxonomy influenced the form typologies that she eventually developed for the *Ursula* faience dinnerware. The latter was put into production by Royal Copenhagen in 1993, with considerable initial success, winning the Design Plus Prize that year in Germany. Ursula Munch-Petersen has, since then, tried to combine precise, functional internal forms with 'accidental' and natural external forms and decoration.

In 1985, after spending the best part of a decade working at the Bing & Grøndahl, pottery factory in Copenhagen, Ursula Munch-Petersen was invited to make a dinnerware series by Erik Magnussen, a fellow student during her years at the School of Arts and Crafts, who was then artistic consultant to the company.

This was when the *Ursula* idea all started, although the year before I'd made a 'serving set' (*serveringsdele*) for a show at the Industrial Arts Museum (*Kunstindustrimuseet*) in Copenhagen. The well-known cookbook writer, Camilla Plum, used it in the museum café to serve food on one weekend. I decided to develop this idea and design a simple set of serving dishes: a large oval dish, three or four smaller dishes, and a raised cake plate of the kind Camilla Plum had used.

While she was perfecting her designs for the *Ursula* series, however, Bing & Grøndahl was taken over by the Royal Porcelain Factory (*Den Kongelige Porcelensfabrik*), and in 1987 the new company of Royal Copenhagen was formed. After a period of uncertainty, Ursula suggested that Royal Copenhagen produce a simple series of pots that she had in mind for serving food – a large oval dish, four other smaller dishes, and a cake plate. The new management, however, was unable to come to a decision: at times it said yes, at other times, no. In 1988, just as she was beginning to despair, Ursula was awarded a three-year bursary by the Danish Arts Council (*Statsfonden*). This obliged Royal Copenhagen to provide her with a workshop, and with what she called a 'symbolic salary' as she gave up teaching and devoted herself full-time to designing the *Ursula* series.

Things did not go at all smoothly, however, in large part because of the new company's management style. Finn Næss, product development manager at the time, explained things in detail:

One of my jobs was to oversee all the young artists who were taken on by the Royal Porcelain Factory at that time. So when Ursula Munch-Petersen arrived, she naturally came under my care. I had to deal with all sorts of so-called 'artists' and a lot of them were extremely egocentric and self-confident. But not Ursula. Ursula immediately came across as different. She was really humble, right from the start. She was someone who wanted to *learn*. I liked that. We all did.

When she came to the factory, Ursula brought with her a limited range of utensils that she'd made in her studio at home. But they were still pretty primitive so far as their development as products was concerned. The forms weren't properly finished, and the glazes weren't at all even, or anything like that. All in all, you could say that they were very much based on a concept of something that was *hand* made. So we had a lot of work to do to develop that concept into something that could be sold as a Royal Copenhagen product.

A major problem, however, was how best to reconcile different corporate cultures. Finn Næss continued:

Compared with the Royal Porcelain Factory, Bing & Grøndahl always treated its artists extremely well and the company developed a milieu that enabled both close contact with management and fine artistic work. The trouble was that a lot of this artistic work didn't *sell* very well. And because there was a lot of it coming off the production line, Bing & Grøndahl found itself with a large stone hanging round its neck, dragging it down. That's why it was taken over by the Royal Porcelain Factory and the two of them merged into Royal Copenhagen.

Unlike Bing & Grøndahl, the Royal Porcelain Factory didn't place all its artists together in one big workshop. Rather they distributed them around according to their particular speciality. So a sculptor would be placed in the modelling room, and a painter in the painting room. And so on and so forth. This meant that, after Bing & Grøndahl was taken over, it was difficult to separate their artists physically because they were used to being all together.

There was also a totally different chemistry between artists and management. At the Royal Porcelain Factory, senior management didn't come and see what their artists were up to every day or two or three times a week, in the way they used to do at Bing & Grøndahl. Instead, they told their artists to display all their work in one room once every three months and the new Royal Copenhagen leadership would turn up in their fine suits and ties, look around at what was on display, and say things like, 'that's OK,' 'that's no good,' and so on and so forth. This was the way they selected work for further development or rejected it for the dustbin.

During this process, the artists weren't allowed to be present. So it was my job to find out what was right or wrong about each of the products and let the artists concerned know. But they never got a chance to hear anything directly from senior managers. Nor were they able to question their decisions or explain to the leadership why they were doing things the ways they were.

Of course, two or three of Bing & Grøndahl's former managers were there, too, because they'd also become part of Royal Copenhagen after the merger. So there were two totally different worlds at work in the same room. On the one hand, there were the old Royal Porcelain Factory lot, in their fine suits and colourful ties. And, on the other, there were these really down-to-earth production-oriented people from Bing & Grøndahl. And, of course, they had totally different opinions about what was 'good' and what was 'bad', about what was worth developing further and what wasn't.

And Ursula's work was something they *really* disagreed on. The Royal Porcelain Factory managers thought her work was 'a little primitive' and asked what the point was in having her kind of work included in the Royal Copenhagen production line. The Bing & Grøndahl people, with whom Ursula had developed very strong connections during her time there, thought it really exciting and imaginative.

As you can imagine, this was a dilemma for both sides. What were they going to say to Ursula who, let's face it, had a big vision? The Royal Porcelain Factory managers just didn't like this kind of work, while the Bing & Grøndahl managers obviously did. In the end, the Royal Porcelain Factory lot *pretended* to like what Ursula Munch-Petersen was doing. Privately, though, they said her work would never sell. It was all a matter of internal management politics. The two groups had to keep face.

## Clay and glazes

Corporate structure, management, and production practices all had an effect upon the final outcome of the *Ursula* dinnerware range. But there were also a number of technical aspects that came into play, particularly with regard to form and decoration (glazing).

There was sound reasoning behind Ursula Munch-Petersen's decision to work with faience clay, rather than with porcelain. As she put it:

I personally like faience, what people call the 'poor man's porcelain' (*fattig-mands porcelain*), but most artists or craftsmen at that time preferred the real thing: porcelain. In fact, even though the production of faience is said to be 'cheap,' it's just as expensive as, perhaps a bit more so than, porcelain. This was when people were producing stuff that was the last of the Bauhaus effect. Everything had to be B&O kind of design – very clean, very minimalist. The designer Greta Meier's dinnerware is probably typical of the period. Minimalist colours like grey and brown were used for *every*thing in the 40s and 50s . . .

Anyway, so far as I was concerned, faience was what was interesting because you could get such fantastic colours with it. Royal Copenhagen had bought up a faience factory called Aluminia quite a long time previously. As a result they had a treasure archive of glazes that nobody ever used. It was these that I wanted to try out on my *Ursula* line.

Faience ware is fired twice. First, pots are fired to a comparatively high temperature of 1160° or so. Then they are spray glazed and re-fired to a lower temperature of about 1065°. The two firings prevent the pots from being porous. Both the clay and the transparent glaze materials – feldspar and quartz – are natural and purchased from Cornwall in England. Synthetic pigments are weighed, mixed, and added for the different coloured glazes. Peter Poulsen added:

We don't have any problems with new batches of materials nowadays, although we did in the past. Everything's advanced a lot technically speaking, so materials are almost 100 per cent consistent from one batch to the next, and we don't need to make adaptations to our recipes. Still, we tend to draw on old and new batches of mixed ingredients at the same time, just to make sure.'

Although not trained in chemistry, like Peter, Ursula, like all potters, used to make glaze tests in her kiln at home and wrote down all her recipes and results meticulously to ensure repeat results. However, working with faience at Royal Copenhagen proved to be a challenge – first, because faience is very different from earthenware or stoneware, which Ursula was used to, and second, because of the different kilns and firing methods used.

I soon learned that firing glazes at home and firing them at the factory were rather different things. In my own kiln, I could make adaptations as I went along, by increasing the temperature, adding more air to the fire, and so on. But Royal Copenhagen used a tunnel kiln. Pots went in one end and came out the other. There was nothing you could do in-between.

The man she worked with closely on developing glazes for the *Ursula* series was Peter Poulsen:

Ursula's samples had been glazed at home and were for earthenware basically. Not for faience. This meant that they had to be adapted, and that we had to find glazes that would fit the faience clay body used by Royal Copenhagen. That was my job, and Ursula and I worked quite closely together, making adaptations to test results as we went along. We'd agree that one glaze was a bit too transparent, for example, and needed more yellow in it. Things like that.

Although they clearly got on very well, they soon found themselves in difficulty. Ursula explained:

There were two problems. Firstly, we couldn't use a lot of the old glazes because of new working environment improvements that came in during the 1950s and 60s. A number of restrictions were introduced on materials like cadmium and chrome, for example, that poisoned the atmosphere in the workshops. This meant that a lot of old glaze tests that were really nice just couldn't be used any more.

So we had to develop new glazes or adaptations of old ones. At first, I wanted ten different glazes: yellow, blue, reddish brown, light green, green, dark green, grey, lavender blue, black, translucent white, and transparent. I planned to use as many as I could, within reason, on each form, so that a medium-sized dish, for example, would be made in all ten colors.

This led to a second problem. In pottery factories in Germany, for example, a minimum number of forms are manufactured in a large number of different colors. Royal Copenhagen, on the other hand, was exactly the opposite. It produced a large number of forms in just one or two colors. I wanted them to change to the German style, because it made financial sense, and the pots would look better. I mean, you can change production colors from one day to the next, but not forms. They take ages to get right. But Royal Copenhagen refused. They're still working in the same way today. Multiple forms and few colors.

Exactly why the company refused to cooperate or what the problems were remains unclear. Peter Poulsen later commented:

I think Ursula was too ambitious in one respect. She wanted to have every single one of the pots in the *Ursula* dinnerware range in *all* of the colors that we developed. Her ideas were all right in principle, but they were too difficult to carry out in actual production.

After starting out with ten different glazes, therefore, potter and chemist found themselves having to drop grey, black, and transparent. Ursula continued:

But then, the dark green became a problem because of the tiny amount of lead in the recipe, and we had to drop it. I wanted black instead, but the Royal Copenhagen marketing people wanted nothing of it and eventually we settled on the grey. They also wanted much more yellow than I did. I myself would have preferred to have had much more white than there currently is.

During our talks, potter and chemist disagreed about the effect of lead in a glaze. According to Ursula:

Lead doesn't actually do any harm for the most part, even though people make a lot of fuss about it. You see, the fact that a glaze is vitrified prevents harmful substances from coming to the surface of a pot – except if you put some sour liquid in it and leave it there for a considerable length of time.

Peter Poulsen was less sanguine:

The dark green glaze that we started with had to go, unfortunately, because it contained copper, and copper can seep through a clay body and make it porous. And that won't do with dinnerware that you have to eat off and wash up all the time. I don't care what Ursula herself says. This is the fact. You can't have lead in a dinnerware glaze. So that was the end of the dark green glaze, even though it was really beautiful. Still, we did keep it on the handles of the *Ursula* cups, because nobody's going to lick them or anything like that. But we couldn't put it on the dishes, or bowls, or jugs, or any of her other dinnerware pots.

Lead wasn't the only problem the two of them faced during their many glaze tests. One dark green glaze that they succeeded in developing (without lead as an ingredient) was rejected because it affected another part of the production process. As we stood in her kitchen admiring a large dark green jug, Ursula explained:

That glaze isn't so bad either. It's a thinner version of the other . . . The trouble is Royal Copenhagen said it made their *sorting* too difficult. You see, the glaze varies in thickness and colour as it melts down the jug's outer form, and in places it's a bit speckled. Royal Copenhagen has always been *very* particular about sorting firsts from seconds. Look!

She picked up a very large blue-rimmed white oval dish and showed it to me.

**Fig 4.1** *Ursula* ware pitchers. (Photo: Brian Moeran)

This is a second because it's got flaws on it here. [She pointed to a red crayon mark on the surface of the pot near the rim, and then to another in the centre.] And here. Not those red marks. They wash off. They're there just to indicate where the flaw is. On the rim, it's this tiny spot here. See? In the middle, I don't actually know where it is. And frankly, as a potter, I don't think it matters at all. Anyway, a slight imperfection can add to a pot.

Still, you can see that, if they're going to be so picky about tiny little spots like these, the sorters at Royal Copenhagen would *never* be able to work out what was right and what was wrong in a glaze that's *designed* to vary in colour on different parts of a pot. So that was the end of that glaze experiment!

There were endless small problems like this all the time I was working with Royal Copenhagen. Take my jugs, for example [Ursula stood up and went to the far end of the table at which we were sitting to demonstrate]. Ideally, you should lightly wipe the rim of each jug after it's been glazed. Like this. She brushed the lip of a jug with a rectangular sponge. That way, the glaze won't become too thick at the tip of the spout so the jug will pour better. But Royal Copenhagen refused to do this. I don't know why. It's a little thing perhaps, but it could have made the design just that little bit better and more practical.

## Design and form

Initially, Ursula Munch-Petersen designed the *Ursula* series in the same way that she designs a lot of her work, starting with two-dimensional sketches which she then converts into three-dimensional forms at home. After making a number of different shapes and sizes, she selected those that she thought were best and took them along to the factory to get samples made, glazed, and fired.

I prefer *not* to keep details exactly the same when I design things. So, while the handle here [she pointed to a middle-sized jug] is straight, on the large jug I have indented it slightly. It's the same with these plates. Royal Copenhagen said they should be oval like the dishes, but I said no. So we kept them round.

Sometimes there's no system in making a design, so you just cannot draw what you're thinking of. Like this bowl here. [She showed me a faceted white bowl that was lying on its side just in front of me.] I did this in an afternoon, working with plaster of Paris, cutting off each side as I went along, until I ended up with this nine-sided bowl. There are a lot of things like this that you can do, but just can't talk about coherently.

Ole Jensen, the designer who worked in the room next door to Ursula in the old Royal Copenhagen factory in Porcelainshaven, had this to say about her design process:

Ursula used to make a lot of clay models. A lot of them went into the waste bin, but some went on to the next stage when they were made in plaster, and from these a few moved on to the model makers and were cast in moulds. It's really hard work because a lot of things need to be changed all the time. Remember, she wasn't working in a digital age then. There was no digital equipment at the factory, so everything was based on manpower in those days. It was really, really close to being ... old fashioned. For sure, it's a good way to learn.

Finn Næss explained what happened then:

Once we got the go-ahead to develop Ursula's ideas, I took her off to the Modelling Room and introduced her to the people there, in the same way that I did for other artists whose work we decided to develop. Ursula was very energetic and demanding – in the good sense of the word. She was very particular, for example, about the exact angle at which a handle should be fixed to the body of a cup, or how *precisely* a spout should be formed at its tip. This contrasted with the rather primitive look of the work that she'd made at home in her studio and then brought in to the factory.

Ursula had more to say about teapots and spouts:

I've made at least ten different teapot designs over the years. Some of them have had squarer handles; others lids over the top, rather than fitting inside; some spouts that are tapered, other that are cut off, and so on. [She lifted the lid of one of the two teapots standing on the table between us.] It's difficult to get a really good fit when the lid is placed over the top of the teapot, and that's why I prefer this other style where the lid fits into the top. Ideally, too, a spout should be tapered like this teapot here, because that allows the tea to pour much better without dripping. This means I can make the spout itself a slightly different shape and angle to the body of the teapot. But, precisely because the tip of the spout is tapered like this, it is fragile and can get chipped easily. Hence this cut off style, which Royal Copenhagen wanted.

Another example of a problem with form concerned the spherical lids that were designed to act as both jug lids and small bowls in themselves.

I designed these to be both lids and bowls in their own right. This is how I like to work – making multifunctional wares. There weren't any problems with these bowls as lids for as long as Royal Copenhagen made everything here in Denmark. But some years ago, they started to have some of the pots made abroad. This jug, for example, was made in Portugal, I think, before later being made by Nikko, a well-known porcelain factory in Japan. But the lid

Fig 4.2 *Ursula* ware oval bowls and plates/lids. (Photo: Brian Moeran)

continued to be made in Denmark. But because there was more shrinkage in the Danish clay, the lids ended up being too small for the jugs, so they'd be too loose and sometimes fall into the jug itself. It was such an elementary mistake to make. But they made it!

Both Finn Næss and Peter Poulsen agreed with Ursula about this, although their perspective was somewhat different. Finn explained:

There were a couple of things that happened that should never have happened with the *Ursula* series. One concerned production, the other stock.

The first problem stemmed from the fact that Royal Copenhagen management began to get more conscious of production costs and started outsourcing. They decided to have the *whole* of the *Ursula* production done in Japan by Nikko. This meant we had to start production all over again, right from scratch. In other words, we found the original models, made copies of them, and sent the copies out to Japan, together with test moulds. Nikko then had to use these moulds with *their* clay, make adaptations, and send them back to us for inspection and approval. Ursula and I would examine them closely, make comments about how we wanted forms improved – pinching a lip here, softening a line there. I'd write everything down long hand in Danish and then give it to a secretary who'd translate it into English. Then we'd send the English instructions back to Nikko, who then made more tests, which they sent back to us for further examination. And so on. It was a lot of extra work, but, to their credit, Nikko did a really excellent job and their quality has always been really good.

The second problem concerned stock. There was a time when a lot of stock was kept over in a warehouse in Malmö in Sweden . . . and orders were being taken here before being sent over there. This caused everyone a headache because the *Ursula* series consisted of *so* many different items. I mean, you had all the dishes, jugs, cups, and so on in the first place – a couple of dozen or more different forms. And then you had each of them glazed in all sorts of colors – dark blue, light blue, russet brown, and grey for the big bowls, for instance, and all seven colors for the little ones. That made for an awful lot of stock items, because each one had to be labeled differently – 1189 571 for a small bowl with a dark blue glaze; 1189 575 for a middle sized bowl; and 1189 576 for a large bowl, both with the same glaze. Keep the same pot but change the glaze and you had a different stock label – 1188 576 for yellow, for example, or 1187 576 for dark green. You can see how easily pots could get mixed up. And they did. Either we got our customers' orders wrong, or we just couldn't deliver the right orders in time. As a result we lost a lot of customers – big ones, too. In this respect, you could say Ursula's concept was too complex.

Peter Poulsen continued:

You see, one tends to simplify things once production gets started. With the *Ursula* series, for example, we started with a transparent white glaze on the underside of each dish, within the foot rim, and glazed the rest of the dish in green, yellow, grey, or whatever colored glaze. But once we started production, it became simpler to glaze the whole of each pot in the same color, top and bottom. This is the sort of thing that goes on with every production line. It's normal procedure to change things as you go along during the first one or two years. But *stock* was something we should've thought about and worked out beforehand. Whether that was Marketing's or Ursula's fault isn't clear in my mind. But one thing I *do* know. If she'd been told about the potential problem, she would have *listened* to advice.

What, then, was the role of the Marketing Department in development of the *Ursula* series? Did the marketing people talk to Ursula about consumer tastes or advise her to change her designs at all? At this she laughed sadly:

Designers weren't *allowed* to participate in meetings with marketing people. I know it sounds crazy, but that's how it was. I don't know why. Maybe it had something to do with the fact that we designers are immersed in design history and are influenced by one aesthetic movement or another, while the young girls in fashionable clothes and high heels who were in marketing knew absolutely nothing about Bauhaus and design schools like that. It struck me that marketing people were more concerned with copyright than with design.

So I wasn't ever involved in a discussion of forms with marketing people. At the very beginning, they insisted on my making round serving dishes because they said that the oval ones wouldn't sell. In fact, they were quite wrong. It was the oval dishes that sold, not the round ones, which were then discontinued! They also wanted me to develop the series beyond just serving dishes. That's why cups were added, for example.

Ole Jensen concurred:

The Marketing Department in Royal Copenhagen was much more focussed on luxury products than on selling everyday common pieces. It was more trained to tell stories about luxury life in contrast to daily life. This is one of the reasons, I think, that the *Ursula* series hasn't worked commercially.

It was, therefore, the product development rather than the Marketing Department that gave advice on designs, forms, and glazes, as Ursula explained:

Finn Næss acted as intermediary and was really helpful during my time at Royal Copenhagen. He was involved in all kinds of meetings and told me what to do, saying things like: 'Now you should write a letter to the Director of the company,' or 'You'll just have to accept this glaze, or the whole things ends right here.' It was Finn who told me that my idea of having a kitchen series of ten bowls nestling inside one another had to be modified to five, so I agreed, even though I really wanted ten.

The factory's mould-makers had a favourite word they used all the time when talking about making forms. What was it now? Ah yes! *Compensate.* You had to *compensate* for this or that when making forms. It's sad, isn't it? Words like this are part of a lost language, now that production's been shifted abroad and pots are no longer made in Denmark. Anyway, they would talk about how to *compensate* for what happened to the clay during drying and firing and so on. You know, the clay would sag a bit, so they had to *compensate* by making the forms more vertical. Things like that. And I had to go along with these adaptations, although I think that perhaps in some cases I shouldn't have.

## Corporate practice

One of the sticking points through the entire development of the *Ursula* series was the fact that Royal Copenhagen's management did not seem to want it to go into production. Ursula enjoyed telling the story of what happened:

At the end of three years, the company said it wasn't interested in my designs. I wasn't prepared, though, to take no for an answer. I countered that I had to show something for the Arts Council bursary I'd held while at the factory designing the *Ursula* series, and told them I wanted to hold an exhibition of my work. Very reluctantly, the company agreed to let me show fifty pieces of each design for a month in its city centre store. That was at the end of May 1991.

The show turned out to be a great success and everything sold out very quickly. Then the fun started. A well-known journalist, Henrik Steen Møller, wrote a fantastic review of my exhibition in the newspaper *Politiken*. A few weeks later, he wrote a scathing critique of a Royal Copenhagen product in the same newspaper. This led to an exchange between the CEO of Royal Copenhagen and the Editor-in-Chief of *Politiken* when the two men were sitting together on some board or other. The former complained about the newspaper publishing a critical article like that about a Royal Copenhagen product, so the latter asked to visit the factory to see things for himself. And, since he liked Steen Møller, the Editor-in-Chief took him along when he went.

As they were going around, looking at all the work there, Henrik kept asking: 'Why don't you produce Ursula Munch-Petersen's work? Is it too difficult? Are there technical problems, or what?

And the Royal Copenhagen people couldn't answer these questions, so the CEO eventually said: 'Of course, it will come.' And once he'd said that, Royal Copenhagen *had* to do something about the design – especially after Steen Møller wrote about it in *Politiken*. They couldn't back out of things after that. Still, it took them some time to find the models and glaze tests we'd made while I'd been there, because they'd all been put away somewhere hard to find. As a result, things didn't get going for another two years or so.

Finn Næss had this to add:

In a way, Ursula has always been her own marketing machine. She's been good at networking with people who matter – Erik Magnusson, for example, who was artistic consultant at Bing & Grøndahl; Camilla Plum, the well-known cook; and, of course, Ebbe Simonsen, boss of Bing & Grøndahl, who was Jewish and had his own connections with fellow Jews like the Editor-in-Chief of the *Politiken* newspaper and – I think I'm right in saying, though I may be wrong – Henrik Steen Møller, the journalist.

But connections or not, things didn't proceed smoothly.

Ursula could see that the board of directors wasn't really interested in her work, but it didn't take account of her personality – of the fact that she was really engaged and believed in what she was doing. She'd move around the factory at will, pursuing her objectives with the Modelling Room, Glazing Room and so on, and everyone liked working with her. And as a result, *everyone* wanted to see the *Ursula* dinnerware project succeed.

What was missing in all this was that management didn't have any confidence in Ursula Munch-Petersen's decisions, even though all the factory floor workers did. As a result, everyone working with Ursula owed their loyalty to *her*, rather than to the company that employed them. We all wanted her to succeed.

Ursula herself clearly appreciated this, in spite of her reservations about the factory's management style.

There were a lot of really good people working on the factory floor and I really learned a lot from them. They were all very different from one another, too, because in those days each 'room' (*stue*) had a very different cultural environment from the others. So the Modelling Room (*modelstue*) was totally different from the Decorating Room (*malerstue*), which was again different from the Glazing Room (*glasurstue*).

But the factory as a whole had a special culture of its own. You always learned to look behind you and hold the door open for people carrying heavy loads of pots, for example. At the same time, some of the workers had almost been born in the factory so, as you can imagine, there were always plenty of intrigues going on. But I made really close friends with some of them.

What emerged during the course of discussions was that Royal Copenhagen's management had trouble envisioning how the *Ursula* series should be positioned *vis-à-vis* the company's other products. Ole Jensen expressed this most clearly:

Royal Copenhagen met with enormous success with its *Mega* floral design in the 1990s. This changed the company's international ambition and shifted its focus from artistic wares to its traditional designs. The *Mega* design was *extremely* important because it enabled the factory to survive and thrive. Perhaps it could have survived on the *Ursula* series and on my own designs, I don't know, but neither of these was *typical* of Royal Copenhagen ware – unlike the *Mega* design, which had a close link to the factory's classical tradition.

If a company like Royal Copenhagen is to compete internationally, either it needs to be big and rich, or it has to focus on new pieces. Royal Copenhagen chose to focus on its tradition, and this is one of the reasons the *Ursula* series hasn't been a big commercial success. The Marketing people didn't feel comfortable with this kind of work.

This observation led to Ole elaborating on Ursula's overall approach to pottery design *vis-à-vis* Royal Copenhagen's:

When you buy Royal Copenhagen, you're buying luxury. Within this concept, the *Ursula* series is a kind of *simple* luxury, but in fact it represents much more a kind of ... *un*luxury. It's a sort of schism, a paradox. When Ursula makes an unluxury product in the context of a luxury brand, then something's wrong.

He expanded on this observation in the following manner:

If you spend a lot of time in a porcelain factory, you begin to get interested beyond unique pieces in doing daily kitchen ware or dinnerware for common use ... You get interested, too, not in mass production as such, but in production and in the reproduction of artistic qualities. So, from that point of view, Bing & Grøndahl offered a really good chance to a young ceramicist like Ursula.

At the same time, you find all sorts of different skills and different specialists in a factory, so you need to harmonise with them in order to be able to do your work ... I think the *Ursula* series represents the very *best* of a craftsman's qualities, the best of Ursula Munch-Petersen herself, and the best of the art industry itself – I mean, of the engineers, painters, formers, and so on ... For this reason, I think it's a pity they've stopped making it this year.

The quality of the *Ursula* design, the details, the sensitivity, the glazes and shapes are first class. Still, sometimes when you're working with factories and so on, even if you've done a good piece, you're never sure if it'll be a commercial success or not. This is because a lot of parameters have to be met beforehand. Artists often have no control over this part of ... the game.

So perhaps Ursula collaborated with the wrong company. Perhaps she could have had more success elsewhere. I don't know. How can I put it? As an artist, she had some eggs to lay, but perhaps she laid her eggs in the wrong nest. Sometimes, as an artist, you just can't control things. I think this is what happened with Ursula.

Nevertheless, and in spite of discontinuing the *Ursula* series in 2011, Royal Copenhagen has occasionally taken advantage of its acclaim to boost its image. Peter Poulsen said proudly:

We *worship* Ursula Munch-Petersen. And we worship the *Ursula* series. A year ago, to commemorate fifty years of something or other, the company used *Ursula* as a logo or icon to tell the world what it made. *Ursula* has become its flagship design. But they never said it was Ursula Munch-Petersen who designed it. Instead, they just took the credit themselves. That was *scandalous*. I wrote and complained to management.

Ole Jensen added:

From the very, very beginning I'm sure Royal Copenhagen thought Ursula was going to be one of the big ceramicists in Denmark, and for sure, one of its cleverest and most important. But, at the same time, the company thought she was in opposition to what they liked and what they wanted to make and do. And it's true. She has been a little bit in opposition to the brand.

In a way, Ursula is looking for opposition. In her line of thinking, to be an artist is not simply a matter of making the right form, or of being a craftsman. It's a way of searching for the opposition role – in a positive sense. As a designer, you have to be in opposition, and a company like Royal Copenhagen needs designers whose way of thinking is in contrast to everything that's accepted, both in the market and within the company itself.

Sometimes, being in opposition means you can change something in the factory's mindset. But, in the case of Ursula, although she's produced important artistic work that is respected, what she did *not* manage to change was the mindset inside the company – the management's mindset, that is. I'm sure

Ursula spent a lot of time discussing things. She's a rebel in the best sense of the word and you need to be a rebel when you collaborate with the business part of design. I don't mean that you need to enter into a big discussion all the time about the ideal way of doing things. You can be a rebel without being one in *everything* you do. In the beginning, Ursula was in opposition to how to do business, but – as I said – this creates a kind of schism: you're against being a part of the business because you're a part of it. I think Ursula could have learned a *little* bit about how to be more dynamic in the situation in which she found herself.

## An aesthetics of production

Unlike many potters or other craftsmen, Ursula Munch-Petersen is known for being articulate about her work and about what makes a pot 'good' or 'bad.' Ole Jensen commented on her ability to see the potential in a design very early on in its process. She has a good 'eye' and uses her thoughts to formulate and explain why something is interesting, or not. He continued:

She is also one of the few ceramicists with the intellectual power to write down her thoughts. She's written and talked a lot about handmade craftwork. You could call her, perhaps, a little too intellectual. But she's much better than a lot of artists, craftsmen, ceramicists, textile weavers and so on who aren't any good at talking. Their power is based only on the expression found in their work. Ursula likes to discuss her work in an intellectual way and she's always been very, very articulate.

I've learned a lot from Ursula – in terms of technical ways of doing things, of course, but mainly through her ideas about why one should make a new product. Ursula finds it difficult to make something new just because the market is looking for it. It's not that she's a romantic or anything like that; rather that it's important for her to find the right reason for making a new piece. For Ursula, it's extremely important to be critical – not in a negative, but in a positive way – to enable her to communicate human, rather than just commercial, values. Of course, working in a company can be very stressful, because it consists of many different parts, and you have to take part in the game. But the whole thing about *Ursula* was not to make a new collection as such, but to produce something that consisted of human and functional values.

Such comments express an aesthetics of production, as seen by a designer. But Ole Jensen's ideas were shared by others working at the Royal Copenhagen factory. Peter Poulsen, for example, who is a chemical engineer by training, gave a succinct summary of his attitude to work:

In our kind of work, we have to know what's 'good' and what's 'bad.' And that isn't something you can talk about or explain. It's not up for discussion at all. That's the way it is. Ursula knows what's good, and I like to think I do, too. To be able to make this distinction between 'good' and 'bad,' you have, first of all, to know your *materials*. You have your transparent glazes and your matt glazes. You have to know which materials dissolve, and with what effects, and which don't. Things like that.

And then you have to *communicate*. You have to enter into dialogue with other people, learn to speak the same language as they do, in order to be able to make the necessary adjustments to the thing you're working on. Ursula was really good at this sort of dialogue.

Thirdly, you have to *work*. It's as simple as that. For me, I have my basic glazes that I then have to develop to create this effect or that. And that is simply a matter of work. Nothing else.

And the driving force behind materials, communication and work is the *idea*. Without an idea, you've got nothing at all.

At the same time, though, you've got to understand other people's work. Otherwise you can't communicate. That's why the Royal Porcelain Factory used to give us a training in *every*thing. I mean, I first trained as a painter. That means I can paint *Flora Danica* – not well enough for production line purposes, maybe, but well enough to understand decorators when they talk to me about a problem they face.

I also learned how to make moulds and press clay, and how to fire, of course. I had to, in order to be able to communicate and understand different people's problems. In the old Royal Porcelain Factory, all of us were trained as generalists before we became specialists. That's all gone now, of course.

The fact that the *Ursula* series has now been discontinued was cause for reflection by those to whom I talked. Both Ole and Peter, in their different ways, felt that the *Ursula* series represented a craft tradition that was now lost. First, let us hear Ole:

There are still a lot of buyers – you may prefer to call them consumers – who can tell the difference between high and low quality. But when you no longer have the opportunity to make something in absolutely the best quality, then the public's ability to distinguish between good and bad quality disappears, in a way. This isn't to say that Royal Copenhagen now produces bad quality products. It's just that it's not possible any more for designers to be close to other craftsmen, like the model makers, painters, and so on. The *Ursula* service really represents the kind of quality you get in your hands when a designer works closely with the craftsmen and people who produce it. In a way, this is what the art industry has lost during the past 25 years, but it was probably unavoidable.

It's a pity *Ursula* isn't in production any longer. I wonder why it's not possible to make money out of making and selling her dinnerware, although I'm sure it will be a very important part of Danish design and ceramic history for a lot of years in the future, because of its sensitivity and uniqueness . . . But one of the reasons why production has had to be stopped is because it's too expensive. For a commercial success, you need a good balance between production costs and retail pricing. The *Ursula* series has been a little bit *too* expensive in its production because of its high quality.

This has always been the craftsman's dilemma, right through history. It was a dilemma for William Morris, a dilemma for the Bauhaus. What happens is that work based on an idealistic tradition of producing the best and highest quality pieces for everyday users ends up consisting of luxury items. Their prices are always a little too high.

Peter Poulsen talked about this sense of history and loss from his viewpoint within the company:

If there's one thing stops me from walking out of this job, it's history. I mean, I've *inherited* other people's hard work. The transparent glaze that we still use was first made by the founder of the Royal Porcelain Factory more than two centuries ago. It's basically still the same recipe. Of course, over the years, we've added to it, and we're still doing so, but I don't want all that accumulated knowledge to disappear just because I retire and there's nobody left at the factory who knows what I know and who can continue my work.

So that's what keeps me going. That and the fact that the people I work with here are fantastic. They're so committed, you know. Committed to the work they do and to what they produce. In spite of everything.

And it seems to me that it's all going to be lost. In the same way that we've almost lost the skill of how to decorate porcelain. In the old days, the Royal Porcelain Factory in Frederiksberg used to employ two *thousand* people. Now, we've got just *fifty* women working in the Decorating Room here in Glostrup, *eighty* of us overall.

I learned the basics of chemical engineering from my teacher at Technical University, of course, but since then everything I've learned has been through *experience*. You learn through your *fingertips* in my job. [Peter rubbed two of his fingers on his thumb.] This isn't knowledge that you can see or read about, even though some people believe all you have to do is make a video of something for other people to be able to do what's wanted. But learning with your fingertips isn't knowledge you can see or pass on just like that. A lot of people just don't understand that.

## Theorising craftsmanship

This case, like several others in this book, is about craftsmanship: about conceiving, making, modelling, glazing, and firing clay, in such a way that the finished product – an oval platter, lidded jug, or cake plate – is appealing in itself, while contributing to a class of other products, in this case tableware manufactured by Royal Copenhagen.

Craftsmanship of all kinds is founded on highly developed skills: here, a potter's or modeller's bodily understanding of the plasticity of clay and the accompanying possibilities and limitations of form afforded by it; and a chemical engineer's hands-on experience with certain ingredients – quartz, feldspar, and a variety of pigments – that, mixed in the right proportions, produce attractive colours appropriate to the forms. Their relentless pursuit of excellence (of the kind discussed, too, by Shannon O'Donnell) allowed Ursula Munch-Petersen, Peter Poulsen, and their co-workers to take pride in their work, while anchoring them in tangible reality (Sennett 2008: 21). The case reveals the interaction between head and hand, as those concerned sought, through many trials and occasional errors, to 'grasp' at solutions to the problems they faced. As Peter Poulsen succinctly summarised a lifetime of working with glazes (coincidentally echoing the thoughts of Richard Sennett [2008: 238]): 'You learn through your *fingertips* in my job.' Touch is the arbiter of both form and colour when working with clay.

Clay, like food, is both good to eat (*bonne à manger*) and good to think (*bonne à penser*). In one formulation, 'earth must no longer be what men eat but must instead be cooked, like food, in order to enable men to cook what they eat' (Lévi-Strauss 1988: 176). A shapeless mass is first prepared, then given form, before being dried, decorated, and cooked in a kiln. No wonder, then, that there are parallels in the myths explaining the origin of cooking fire and those explaining that of clay (Lévi-Strauss 1988: 50).

The pots that emerge are used primarily for food and drink. That is the purpose of *Ursula* dinnerware: to be *usable, practical, multipurpose,* and *sturdy*. But in addition to this functional discourse, people talk about Ursula Munch-Petersen's (and other) pots in a different way. Cups, jugs, and dishes form a *family* (Munch-Petersen 1991), which has 'grown up' over many years of hard work (Nielsen 2004: 145). Individual pieces 'mingle on the table in appetising *harmony*' with their '*rich* forms and *generous* sizes' (Royal Copenhagen pamphlet). Words such as *care, fresh, friendliness, gentleness, joy, mild, natural,* and *warmth* are used to express the potter's, as well as users', relations to the *Ursula* range (Figueroa 2011). Here we find ourselves immersed in a discourse of functional beauty, which, in the tradition of nineteenth- and early twentieth-century craft movements in both England and Japan (Moeran 1997), imbues inanimate objects with human character- istics, and sets the artificial apart from the natural. Thus is the meta- morphosis of clay transformed into the anthropomorphosis of material culture (Sennett 2008: 120–141).

Clay is good to reflect upon in another way. The fact that Ursula Munch-Petersen decided to use a medium that she hadn't experienced before, faience, forced her to think of a different way to conceptualise her tableware. Yes, it should be functional. Teapot spouts had to pour properly; their handles should enable a balanced grip. But it should also be multifunctional where possible. Oval plates could serve as lids to similarly shaped bowls; different sized bowls could nestle inside one another to save space when not in use. In the potter's words: 'the shapes of our utensils are like pictures of our actions.'

But faience is not porcelain, like the other products made at Royal Copenhagen; and it is not stoneware, of the kind that Ursula has been accustomed to working with. Faience might make use of decorative motifs, but it is remarkable first and foremost for the clear colours with which the clay can be glazed. Glazes, then, are good to think. Not only did Ursula envisage a tableware series glazed in more than a dozen colours, she realised the economic advantages of such an approach. It was clay forms that required the most labour; the more forms, the more labour was required to press or mould them; and the more labour required, the more expensive was production. By designing fewer forms, fired in multiple colours, Ursula Munch-Petersen provided the opportunity for a radical innovation in Royal Copenhagen's production line. She fulfilled the craftsman's role of being, as the designer Ole Jensen said, 'in opposition – in a positive sense.' Her thinking had that 'sharp social edge' required of thinking like a craftsman (Sennett 2008: 44).

That such a radical line of thought about clay did not materialise (or, in Ole Jensen's words, 'change the mindset inside the company') reflects another aspect of craftsmanship. There is a difference between how something *should* be done and then getting that something to work in the way that it should (Sennett 2008: 45). Both Peter Poulsen and Ursula Munch-Petersen concentrated on what they perceived as 'objective' standards: on the function, form, and colour of the pot itself. But their discipline and commitment were thwarted by the corporate structure in which they found themselves. Their desire to do a thing well for its own sake came up against other standards, other evaluations of their work (Sennett 2008: 9). They faced the truism that 'every new experience, every new impulse to communicate meets with obstacles in the process of expression, and at least a part of its originality, its immediacy, and its liveliness is sacrificed to these obstacles' (Hauser 1982: 21). It may be the *idea* that is the driving force behind an understanding of materials, the ability to communicate, and sheer hard work, as Peter Poulsen so succinctly said, but the evidence suggests that Royal Copenhagen's managers wanted to whittle the 'big idea' into something as little as politically possible, without throwing it out altogether.

Or does it? At this point in time, it is hard to tell fact from fiction, and memory is often a false ally when it comes to relating the past. But what if Ursula had been given free rein – full artistic license – to do what she wanted? Would she have been successful in realising her vision? I am inclined to think not. Perhaps, then, every creative vision needs an 'enemy.' It is the enemy (in this case, management – the worker's classic opponent) who spurs the craftsman on to realise something greater than he or she at first imagined possible. Could it be that Royal Copenhagen's managers *purposely* adopted a negative attitude in order to ensure the necessary quality?

That Ursula Munch-Petersen had a vision is not in doubt; nor was her ability to work hard and learn about materials. Was it, then, an inability to communicate that let her down? Not exactly. She was well connected with people outside the factory, and communicated well with enough people who 'mattered' to be her own 'marketing machine.' Moreover, time and time again, people commented on how well she interacted with those working in the modelling and glazing rooms at the factory, on how much people were prepared to do for her, and to work for her rather than the factory as such, because they wanted her to succeed. The only apparent failure to communicate on her part, therefore, lay in her dealings with the factory's management.

As Richard Sennett (2008: 54) has noted, the craftsman's workshop is 'a productive space in which people deal face-to-face with issues of authority.' It can glue people together through shared practices and procedures stemming from highly specialised skills, as Ursula herself remarks about Royal Copenhagen's 'factory culture.' But it also reveals who commands and who obeys. Informally, the potter's obvious skills and willingness to learn from others created a charisma that encouraged those on the shop floor to see her as some sort of leader. Formally, however, as artist in residence, she was – like the Bang & Olufsen designer David Lewis, discussed in Chapter 5 – more or less outside the corporate structure of Royal Copenhagen. Unlike Lewis, however, she had no direct access to managerial staff and thus no opportunity to communicate her ideas in person.

Being an 'outsider,' and perhaps something of a 'rebel,' may have blinkered Ursula Munch-Petersen from realising fully that what was relayed as a difference in managerial outlooks (Royal Copenhagen versus Bing & Grøndahl) was in fact a difference in genres, and that the problem she faced was not social but in a sense material. Generally speaking, every newly created work owes more to previous work of that genre than to the inventiveness and originality of its creator (Hauser 1982: 31). While working for Royal Copenhagen, therefore, Ursula needed to subject her idea about multi-coloured faience tableware to the company's 'rules of grammar' (that is, the Royal Copenhagen brand) and its stylistic principles (hand-painted flowers in cobalt on a porcelain body) if she was to achieve fully her purpose (Hauser 1982: 433).

The fact that she opted for faience and disregarded hand-painted motifs in cobalt in some way, surely, singled out the potter as a maverick in the eyes of Royal Copenhagen's management. Although trained in conventional ways, Ursula Munch-Petersen worked unconventionally. How, then, was she to solve the riddle of Kant's pigeon, whose flight is made possible by the very atmospheric pressure that seems to hinder it? By developing two lines of social relations to circumvent, as best she could, management resistance. First, she cooperated closely with factory floor workers; second, she activated external networks with the power to voice public criticism. She was not able to get rid of the constraints that went with her, in many ways advantageous, position in Royal Copenhagen (Becker 1982: 236) because, however rebellious, she could achieve production of the *Ursula* tableware series only by remaining a part of the company. So, she was also a professional who changed some decorative conventions, introduced varieties of multifunctional forms, and had to accept, more or less, everything else thrown at her.

In this respect, as Howard Becker (1982: 244) points out, it is sometimes hard to 'draw a firm line between the innovating integrated professional and the maverick.' But, in the end, her designs did take off and 'fly,' though not with quite the success, perhaps, of your everyday pigeon.

Because the actual connection between inner impulse and objectification is unclear and in some ways puzzling, those to whom I talked resorted to stories as a way of talking about – at times, perhaps, idealising and dramatising – the genesis and development of the *Ursula* dinnerware series. These stories were not quite as bold as Beethoven's attribution of his *Eroica* symphony to the fate of Napoleon, or as surprising as Schubert's hearing the theme for his String Quartet in D Minor in the workings of a rusty coffee mill, but the linking, for instance, of an early version of *Ursula* to the decision by the well-known cook, Camilla Plum, to use it over a weekend when serving food in the Museum of Industrial Arts in Copenhagen provided as important an anchoring device as the biblical tale of Adam and Eve in the Garden of Eden – not that either 'explanation,' of course, explains the genesis of anything.

In a sense, as almost all the chapters in this volume show, 'everything is a story, a narrative, a sequence of events with characters communicating an emotional content. We only accept as true what can be narrated' (Zafón 2009: 139). People tell stories for two reasons: first, to transform private into public meanings (and sometimes vice versa); and second, to provide a sense of agency in the face of disempowering events (Jackson 2002: 14–15). Both strategies involve evaluation.

Stories change our experiences of events. In talking to me about things that happened more than twenty years ago, my informants began to reflect and go over the ground of their lives, retracing their steps to rework reality and render it comprehensible, both to myself, an outsider, and to themselves as participants. Finn Næss, Ole Jensen, Peter Poulsen, and Ursula Munch-Petersen all remarked at some point about how long ago the events that they were relating had taken place, about how much they had forgotten, but also about how much came back to them once they stopped to think about the people and the sequence of activities in which they were all involved. None of this would have happened without the intervention of the anthropologist (who, in other circumstances, might have been a journalist, a detective, or consultant of some kind).

The term *anthropology* derives its origin from 'the words of human beings.' An anthropologist lives off the tales he is told by those he meets and, in turn, writes stories based on the stories he hears. In this respect, the anthropologist begins to draw near to the potter. He shapes his stories from a jumbled mass of data, just as a potter at the wheel shapes his vessels from a lump of wet clay. Each leaves his handprints on the material being worked (Benjamin 1968: 92). Thus does each try to 'grasp' and 'give shape' to reality.

## References

Becker, Howard. 1982. *Art Worlds*. Berkeley and Los Angeles: University of California Press.

Benjamin, Walter. 1968. *Illusions. Edited and with an introduction by Hannah Arendt*. New York: Schoken.

Figueroa, William. 2011. Ursula Munch-Petersen. Online at: www.williamfigueroa.com/ArtAndDesignCollections/UrsulaMunchPetersen/ursula.html. Accessed May 18, 2011.

Hauser, Arnold. 1982. *The Sociology of Art*. London: Routledge & Kegan Paul.

Jackson, Michael. 2002. *The Politics of Storytelling: Violence, transgression and intersubjectivity*. Copenhagen: Museum Tusculanum Press.

Lévi-Strauss, Claude. 1988. *The Jealous Potter*. Translated by Bénédicte Chorier. University of Chicago Press.

Moeran, Brian. 1997. *Folk Art Potters of Japan*. London: Curzon.

Munch-Petersen, Ursula. 1991. En prøveproduktion i fajance 1991 [A test production in Faience]. In *Hverdagsstel Munch-Petersen Fajance fra Royal Copenhagen* [Service for Everyday Use Munch-Petersen Faience from Royal Copenhagen]. Royal Copenhagen A/S.

Nielsen, Teresa. 2004. *Ursula Munch-Petersen*. Copenhagen: Rhodos.

Sennett, Richard. 2008. *The Craftsman*. London: Allen Lane.

Zafón, Carlos Ruiz. 2009. *The Angel's Game*. Translated by Lucia Graves. London: Weidenfeld & Nicholson.

# 5 | *Looking into the box: design and innovation at Bang & Olufsen*

JAKOB KRAUSE-JENSEN

Bang & Olufsen – or B&O as every adult Dane knows the company – is a producer of audio-visual home electronics familiar to most upper- and middle-class consumers around the world. Along with Lego, Royal Copenhagen, and Carlsberg, the company is one of the crown jewels of the Danish manufacturing industry. Originally influenced by Bauhaus functionalism, and the softer Scandinavian versions thereof expressed in Danish furniture classics from the 1950s and 1960s, for about half a century the company has built its reputation around its user-friendly, minimalist designs focused on shapes, textures, and materials. Over the past decades, however, televisions have become two-dimensional and consumer electronics have been *digitalized*, calling for new ways to think about design and innovation practices.

One of the deepest theoretical problems of the social sciences is to find explanations that give satisfying accounts of both change and continuity. This theme underlies many discussions of structure versus agency, system versus individual, and consensus versus conflict. In Bang & Olufsen the permanent pressure to innovate means – as we saw in the case of the Talent Pool's attempts to come to grips with the HUGO BOSS brands – that a balance between continuity and change is a predominant practical problem and a continuous concern: to invent something 'new' and accommodate to rapid technological developments without jeopardizing the company's celebrated 'name' and design tradition is an ever-present challenge in the creative and evaluative practices in the design processes of Bang & Olufsen. In this chapter we shall see how B&O has solved this problem in a seemingly paradoxical way, securing the company's design consistency by *excluding* the designer from the organization. Exemplified by the development of a particular product, *Beosound 5*, which tried to break with existing design traditions, I will show how the development of this product challenged long-established evaluative practices of the company and raised questions about the criteria of 'good design.'

146

In the present context it is useful to maintain a distinction between 'creativity' and 'innovation.' Over the last decades these two concepts – and particularly the notion of innovation – have become keywords in the Raymond Williams (1976: 14) sense: 'particular formations of meaning – ways not only of discussing but at another level of seeing many of our central experiences.' The point of such keywords is that they don't have fixed denotations, but that their significance (in both meanings of that word) changes historically as the keywords become central binding concepts within specific discourses, by being connected with other meanings and embedded in certain forms of thought. For instance, according to a short dictionary definition, 'innovation' simply means 'a new idea, a way of doing something, etc. that has been introduced or discovered.'[1] In this very broad sense, the word is synonymous with 'creativity' and, indeed, the two concepts are often used interchangeably, as we have seen in the Introduction to this book. The term 'innovation,' however, carries connotations that distinguish it from the broader notion of creativity and tie it to a context of production and market that makes it useful as a central mobilizing concept in contemporary policies and discourses of globalization. Organization theorist Peter Senge (1999: 15), for example, makes the point that the Wright brothers were undoubtedly original and creative when they invented the airplane in 1903, but that this invention became an 'innovation' only when Boeing commercialized the idea after World War I. When in the following I analyze the design and evaluative activities in Bang & Olufsen, I am referring to creative processes as 'innovation' in this restricted sense, which clearly ties the creative processes to the material (for example, technological development) and economic conditions also mentioned in the Introduction to this book.

Innovation is commonly described as 'out-of-the-box thinking.' It is seen as a matter of drumming together creative brains with green thinking hats (de Bono 1999) to come up with great ideas and unexpected solutions. In this chapter, I want to approach innovation from a different angle by taking a closer look 'into the box' to get a perspective on evaluative processes and the different criteria, dilemmas, and institutional logics that inform the creative choices in Bang & Olufsen. If, in other words, we want to explore creativity and get a deeper understanding of

---

[1] *Oxford Advanced Learner's Dictionary*, http://oald8.oxfordlearnersdictionaries. com/, accessed on October 30, 2011.

processes of innovation, we are well advised to keep in mind Schumpeter's seminal definition of innovation as 'creative destruction'. Creative processes are not only inhibited and constrained by external factors, they are lodged in an institutional and political environment with personal rivalries and different views on aesthetics competing for recognition. I want to show, first, how Bang & Olufsen has solved the problem of stability and change in a particular, if not paradoxical, way by cutting the designer off from corporate power hierarchies and influences. My suggestion here is that anthropological theories of power and the sacred can help us shed light on this apparent paradox and understand the lasting influence and position of the freelance designer. Second, by focusing on the development of a specific product, I want to show how practices of innovation are embedded in complex social, political, and cultural contexts that are often papered over in descriptions of creative processes in current discourse on innovation.

## The role of the designer

Organizations are socio-topes established to achieve specific ends. In a business organization such as Bang & Olufsen the ultimate purpose of the creative process is to generate a profit. Thus, to be successful, new designs must turn out to be 'innovative' – in other words, they must appeal to a group of consumers and must come at a relatively affordable price. The creative process that goes into the manufacturing of products thus involves a number of criteria, which are not purely aesthetic but which also include the functionality of the product, and the time and cost of its production. Bang & Olufsen, however, has created its particular niche on the AV market by giving unprecedented priority to the aesthetic criteria of the *designer* in its product development.

Conventionally in the AV industry, the designer's job was seen to be *post facto*, and had to do with a bit of styling and ergonomics (Du Gay *et al.* 1997: 63). This is not the case in Bang & Olufsen, which, since the early 1960s, has protected the artistic freedom and aesthetic priorities of the designer. As journalist Jay Green (2007) puts it in his *Business Week* portrait of the company: 'At B&O, the designers dominate. Far from being team activities, design and engineering are separate functions. Designers do their creative thing and then tell the engineers to execute.' This bet on design costs money and time. Thus, Bang & Olufsen releases only a few new products every year, but it is often able to keep those models on the market for decades, a fact that distinguishes the company from the rest of the industry. A case in point is the loudspeakers *Beolab 8000* designed by David Lewis in 1992: twenty years after their release they are still produced and being sold for a price of 20,000 Danish kroner (US$ 3,800) a pair.

It might seem odd that a company that puts such emphasis on design does not have a single full-time designer on its payroll. Bang & Olufsen uses a handful of freelance designers. Among them one stands out, however. For the past forty years David Lewis has been responsible for the majority of Bang & Olufsen's portfolio. He has been knighted by the Queen of England for his design work, and three of his Bang & Olufsen creations are now included in the permanent collection of the Museum of Modern Art in New York.

Since 1972 and until recently (see below) a small organizational skunkworks unit, *Idealand*, has mediated the external designer's contact with Bang & Olufsen. *Idealand* is the liaison between the contract designers and the engineers in Product Development. Physically *Idealand* used to be situated in the attic of the old factory building, now home to the Product Development division. Access was restricted. A sign on the door warned: *No access for unauthorized personnel – use of mild force authorized.* Inside *Idealand* product prototypes were covered in black velvet. Whereas employees were free to access all parts of Product Development around the clock, *Idealand* was locked after 4pm. It was populated by a handful of 'concept developers.' In addition, a few technicians and engineers from Product Development were handpicked for shorter periods to solve particular tasks. As is often the case, the 'creative personnel' who worked in *Idealand* were seen to be '"rebels" against corporate order and general non-conformists' (Moeran 2006: 85), although their difference from corporate decorum was far from the flamboyant style usually associated with creative staff (ibid.: 87). An observer from marketing thus described the personnel of *Idealand* as 'creative geniuses, engineers who don't give a damn about their outward appearance (*med hængerøv i fløjlsbukserne*), who have their fling up there in the attic. Some weirdos on whose unconventional thinking the company depends' (Krause-Jensen 2010: 107).

## The TOP model

The design process at Bang & Olufsen typically starts with the external designer's idea materialized in a cardboard or plywood mock-up. After that Bang & Olufsen design processes ideally follow the so-called TOP model (*Tempo Og Produktivitet*, or Time and Productivity) (see Figure 5.1), which is a chronological description of the product development process and its various stages from the initial idea to the actual product.

In the TOP model the initial stages in the creative process are depicted as a cloud. This process takes place in *Idealand*. As anthropologists Peter Lilleheden and Anders Høgsbro Holm pointed out in their study of the design process (Holm and Lilleheden 2009), the metaphors 'cloud' and 'tube,' which symbolize different departments and different stages in the creative process, also point to dissimilar approaches to the creative process in product development as they connote different substantial states – that is, water as vapor and water as liquid. Vapor is 'light' and is not affected by gravitational forces to the same extent as liquid. Liquid that runs in a tube can be controlled and directed, whereas the molecular movements in the cloud are turbulent and unpredictable. In Bang & Olufsen, a concept ('the cloud') is not just the initial fluffy idea in the designer's head, it is a comprehensive plan or program of a product idea, including all aspects: aesthetic, functional, social, and economic. For instance, a concept should also take into account and work systematically with user scenarios. It can thus be seen as a mapping of the entire innovation process that takes place before the actual product development starts. 'Condensation' (*inddampningen*) is the emic description of the stage in the development of new products where engineers from Product Development work with the external designer and concept developers in *Idealand*. The latter here are thus brokers between the aesthetics and sensibilities of the designer on the one hand, and the technical know-how of the engineers on the other.

In 'the tube,' management of a particular project is in the hands of a project manager (*produktlederen*), who has financial responsibility for the development process 'downstream,' as it is known locally. In Product Development, calculations are made about the expenses and expected revenues of the particular product. So, economic and technical considerations are both criteria of Product Development, or 'the tube.'

Since *Idealand* was founded in the early 1970s, it has been believed that the designer should not communicate extensively with the engineers, because such contact is thought to compromise the originality and artistic potential (*idéhøjden*) of the designers. As an engineer from

TOP

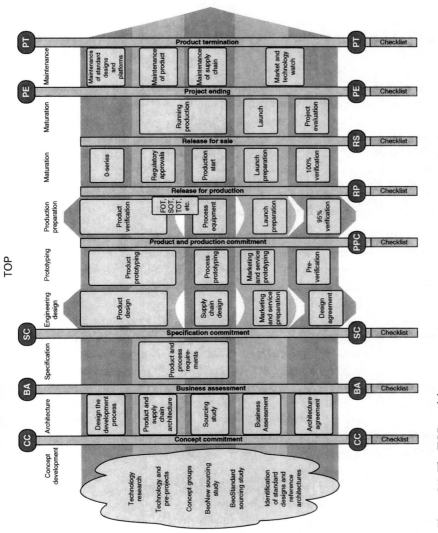

Figure 5.1 The TOP model

Product Development recounted: 'When David Lewis arrives with his cardboard model of a speaker that looks like a pencil, when he comes with an upright CD player displaying six CDs, the technicians scream: this is damn impossible! But this is what distinguishes us. We depend on that contradiction' (Mads, project manager).

Considering the fact that Bang & Olufsen has made design its pivotal selling point, it seems reckless to keep the designer on a freelance contract. Yet it is a curious fact that David Lewis' association with the company spans half a century. This kind of long-term bond with the company might still be found among a few local workers, but it is unparalleled among employees placed high in the organizational hierarchy. But how is it possible to make sense of the paradoxical fact that the 'Design God', as David Lewis is sometimes referred to by the locals (Krause-Jensen 2010: 109), is an organizational outsider?

## Design is the great *taboo* in Bang & Olufsen

One serendipitous moment occurred when, two weeks into field-work, an HR manager asked me to write a note, memo-size, on 'taboo in the organization' for senior management: 'don't spend a lot of time on it,' he told me. Obviously it was some sort of 'test' of the anthropologist intruder, but as Crapanzano (2010: 65) has observed, 'a test is a way one's informants learn something about you.' Yet, aside from being a test, it also reflected management's ideals that the organization should be transparent. Seen in this light 'taboo' was a bad thing. Like the sacred cows in non-Hindu discourse, taboos were irrational and counter-productive and should be gotten rid of as quickly as possible. By retaining a richer analytical meaning of 'taboo,' however, I think it is possible to get a clearer understanding of the evaluative process and its outcomes if we realize that design is *taboo* at Bang & Olufsen.

I ended up spending most of the week on the task, handed in the memo – and never heard anything about it from senior management. The assignment, however, provided me with a clue about how to explore the idea of design as 'taboo' more systematically. *Taboo* is connected to the sacred. In his theory of *The Elementary Forms of the Religious Life* (1976: 37), Emile Durkheim famously argued that religious and social life is ultimately based on the ability to classify. He argued that the origin of all classification, and thus the foundation of all social life or *conscience collective*, is the ability to distinguish between profane and sacred. And he pointed out that 'sacred' means 'set apart.' Thus, a characteristic of the sacred is that it is precisely *not* transparent and open. On the contrary, the sacred is characterized by secrecy, or, as the anthropologist Mary Douglas puts it, 'the sacred needs to be continually hedged in with prohibitions' (Douglas 1986: 3). *Idealand* can be seen as such a space clearly marked out and separated from the rest of the organization, and the designers even more so: elevated and in some sense above the attic of *Idealand,* their aesthetic criteria were seen to represent the apex of creative purity, which should not be contaminated by petty market analysis or humdrum technical considerations. David Lewis, who has been with the company for more than fifty years, is not an employee of Bang & Olufsen but is attached to the company on a freelance basis. He has his own workshop in Copenhagen, and every Thursday night he drives the 350km to Struer to participate in Friday meetings in *Idealand.* He is 'protected' from the rest of the organization, or, as one engineer put it: 'I and many others think that Eigil [the person who headed *Idealand*] overprotects David. The circle around David is very small. Access up toward him is limited as far as possible. And the few that communicate with David … they increase their external authority in that way' (Krause-Jensen 2010: 111).

On the surface of it, this lasting influence of an outsider appears counter-intuitive: after all, an important aspect of externalizing functions – of outsourcing and of employing consultants and workers on temporary contracts – is to make the organization more 'flexible' – in other words, to make it easier to hire and fire people. And such employment strategies seem to work against deeper commitments as they are normally a way to avoid long-term social dependence (see Sennett 1998). But by drawing on notions of the sacred and conceptualizations of power associated with it, we can perhaps begin to understand the deeper meaning behind this surface contradiction.

The French anthropologist Louis Dumont makes a useful distinction between secular authority (*power*) and spiritual authority (*status*): 'Status and power, and consequently spiritual authority and temporal authority, are absolutely distinguished [. . .] In India there has never been spiritual power, i.e. a supreme spiritual authority, which was at the same time a temporal power. The supremacy of the spiritual was never expressed politically' (Dumont 1980: 72). One of the most important differences between the two forms of authority is that the hierarchy of status is less open to change than the hierarchy of political dominance (ibid.: 198). The CEO has considerable executive power, limited only by the board of directors. The designers, on the contrary, have no executive power. They are outsiders; they can fire nobody. But, as is apparent, the Chief Designer has tremendous status. In the course of my fieldwork nobody ever blamed him for the ill fortune of the company. Despite a turbulent and dramatic corporate history, his name stands unblemished.

Clearly the external designers have their champions and opponents in the political system within Bang & Olufsen. The point is, however, that they are not themselves directly involved in the politics of the organization. David Lewis' authority in matters of design is absolute and his autonomy is protected, but he dominates nobody. He has tremendous influence in that he embodies the 'design consistency' or the 'good idea' on which the existence of Bang & Olufsen depends, but he has no formal or executive power within the organization – he can fire nobody. Supported by the distinction made by Dumont, however, it can be argued that it is precisely the limit to his power that helps protect his prestige: David Lewis competes with other external designers (notably Anders Hermansen, as we shall see below). Senior management, which has the power in the organization, has no say or influence when it comes to the aesthetics and functionalities of particular prototypes, but it is the group of senior managers which decides which of the suggested designs they will put their money on. All designs have to be approved by this group, and when a prototype is finished it has to be judged financially viable by senior management before it is sent further down 'the tube.' In this respect, Bang & Olufsen's management does not differ that much from the management of Royal Copenhagen, discussed in the previous chapter, although the latter *does* have a say in the aesthetics and functionalities of particular prototypes.

Bang & Olufsen has staked its reputation on its design and appealed to 'distinction' and the good taste of its customers, rather than chasing after rapidly changing technology fads. The rationale is that design has a relative permanence that transcends fashions and fleeting customer preferences. As we have seen, the longevity of the products and the durability of its designs find their counterpart in the lifespan of the designer: David Lewis has been working with Bang & Olufsen for more than fifty years, the last twenty-five years as Chief Designer. So, in a world of technological change, financial ups and downs, and organizational turbulence, the designer has been a point of unusual *stability*. In organizational terms, rather than being a paradox, the permanence, consistency, and 'transcendence' of design are emphasized and secured by placing the designer outside the circuits of organizational power.

This argument is an inversion of Pierre Clastres' theory of Indian chieftainship. In his book *Society against the State* (1977), Clastres claims that the Indian chieftainship represents an intermediary evolutionary state in which the group ('society'), defined by relations of generalized reciprocity, tries to protect itself from the disruptive influence of institutionalized political power (the 'state'). This is done by symbolically recognizing the chief by offering him presents and gifts, while at the same time isolating him from society by denying him the possibility to return those gifts. Thus, in an argument inspired by psychoanalysis, Clastres asserts that the group recognizes 'power,' but only as the negation of culture and society. By allowing it a marginal symbolic space, power is kept at bay. Contrary to Indian chiefdoms, in a business organization such as Bang & Olufsen, institutionalized power is an obvious and ever-present reality, but also a highly volatile and unstable one, because organizational power structures reflect changes in a notoriously unpredictable market. In the case of Bang & Olufsen, 'transcendence' or continuity resides not with 'the group' but with the external chief (!) designer. Compared with the lifelong influence of David Lewis, the power of the managing director depends on the nervous flickering of the cardiograms on the stock exchange, and his lifespan is, therefore, considerably shorter. On January 9, 2008, Bang & Olufsen's stock fell almost 30 percent in one day. A day later, CEO Torben Ballegaard Sørensen was dismissed 'with immediate effect.' In the period between 2000 and 2011 covered by this chapter, the company has been headed by four CEOs, and all of them have been fired as a result of the company's poor financial performance. So, at Bang & Olufsen, the problem of change and continuity is solved by making a distinction between status and power reflected in institutional arrangements and embodied and represented symbolically in the distinction between the *designer* and the *managing director*. If the CEO is the 'change agent' *par excellence*, enmeshed in corporate power struggles and who must prove himself to turbulent stock markets, the external designer is the guardian of stability and 'transcendent' aesthetic values.

## Change is underway: the case of *Beosound 5*

The institutionalization of the creative encounters at Bang & Olufsen has been remarkably stable and consistent. For more than thirty years, *Idealand* has occupied a mediating role between Product Development and the external designers, and in the same period David Lewis has been a dominant figure. However, a recent product development process reveals that technological development has forced Bang & Olufsen to rethink its institutionalized practices. The following case is based on a three-hour interview with Birger and Adam,[2] two employees (not designers), who work with concept development and thus the processes close to 'the cloud.' At the time of the interview (March 2011), Bang & Olufsen had just appointed a new managing director, Tue Mantoni, and the company was reorganizing, so the interview took place in a vacated room amid a few products, moving boxes, desks, and scattered chairs. The focus of the 'case story' in this chapter is a particular case of product development: *Beosound 5*, an audio player launched in 2008 (see Figure 5.2).

'Control *Beosound 5* with the sturdy and welcoming aluminium navigation cylinder for direct and easy interaction with your songs and albums, which are shown flawlessly on the beautiful screen. No greasy fingerprints, no flimsy plastic. The compact shape is unmistakably Bang & Olufsen: Bold and beautiful lines, the best materials, and a deep sense of function over flash.'[3]

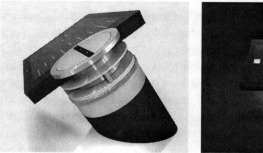

**Figure 5.2** *Beosound 5*: 'Touch the music that touches you'

---

[2] Birger and Adam are pseudonyms.
[3] www.bang-olufsen.com/beosound5, accessed on April 12, 2011.

Such is the official presentation of *Beosound 5*. I guess Adam and Birger chose to tell me about the product, not because it was particularly successful, nor because it was 'representative' in the meaning of 'typical' or 'average,' but rather because it illustrated a break with the established practices described above, and thereby clearly exposed institutional structures, norms, and differences.

When I asked who designed the product, Adam and Birger said:

Birger:  It was actually a process that had many fathers – depending on the sales numbers ... [*laughter*].

Adam:  The concept had many fathers, but its quality was really improved by an intern, Wilhelm Horst. Don't forget to mention him in your description. He worked in *Idealab* and developed a prototype with a wheel and all, a prototype that worked well enough to show to the CEO and the designer. David Lewis also saw it, but Anders Hermansen was the one who eventually took up the challenge ... And then the concept was developed until, design-wise, it was rather strong. And then it went back and forth, and we decided which 'handles' we needed. Those 'handles' were then sent to our specification department, whose task was to make it into an audio-player. And they didn't like it. They said: 'Well, it needs two additional controls. You need an "up-and-down" control! We can't make it without an up-and-down control.' This meant that from the very start they had this negative attitude. Instead of loving that 'otherness' (*anderledeshed*), they hated it. And instead of helping find a great solution, they said: 'Well, it is not our fault. If we were designers we would have put more controls on.'

I argued above that the designer occupied an unusual extra-organizational position: a role which was at once marginal and permanent. As indicated by the quote, however, the design process at Bang & Olufsen is also fiercely competitive. Apparently, the personal rivalry between two competing external designers had at one point been so intense that 'systems were designed with guards posted to make sure that they did not meet each other in the corridor' (Adam).

## Two designers

As mentioned earlier, the most influential designer at Bang & Olufsen over the past few decades has been David Lewis. But he is contracted and in principle competes with other designers, notably Anders Hermansen, who has been involved with Bang & Olufsen for more than twenty years. At one point there had been two *Idealands: Idealand 1* working with David Lewis, and *Idealand 2* working with Anders Hermansen.

At the time *Beosound 5* was developed there was another division between *Idealab* and *Idealand*. At some point Bang & Olufsen managers concluded that design in the B&O market space had to encompass more than physical function and form. As televisions became two-dimensional screens to hang on the wall, and as the industry went digital, it became clear that the old furniture-way of thinking about design was insufficient. Pleasant sounding motors and brushed aluminium surfaces were no longer enough. 'Design' had to encompass virtual space and take into account software- and network-based interaction with other products and services, and this required skills, ideas, and forms of evaluative practices different from the usual institutionalized ways. So *Idealab* was formed as another skunkworks unit meant to complement *Idealand* by developing digital concepts that could be handed over to designers to create new products geared to meet the demands posed by development in computer technologies. *Idealab* experimented with 'supplementary innovation' as a way of injecting new ideas into products from outside the institutionalized process described above.

Set up to collaborate, in practice *Idealand* and *Idealab* often competed, because their focus implied different criteria and views of the design process. According to the people in *Idealab*, the designer should work more closely with the end users, focus on software and the UI (or user interface), instead of the form and the exterior of the product, which had been the classical priorities of Bang & Olufsen (and *Idealand*). As Jesper Holm, who was then a concept developer at *Idealab*, expressed it: '[David] has never been interested in what happens on the screen itself. He has seen it as his principal task to create a television that looks good in the living room when it is turned off. A television is turned off most of the time, and it should be beautiful to look at' (quoted in Holm and Lilleheden 2009: 110).

As Bang & Olufsen works with other freelance designers, important editorial moments (Becker 1982) are often organized as blind reviews. For instance, when televisions turned digital and flat, Bang & Olufsen staged a competition between half a dozen designers from all over the world to come up with a new flat-screen TV concept. These designers were anonymous, but eventually senior management chose David Lewis' design. According to Birger, this cultural continuity had obvious explanations:

Anders Hermansen has worked with Bang & Olufsen for almost twenty years ... He just hasn't won many of the competitions. And it is a fair question why David Lewis ends up winning all the time. ... [The] people who ultimately decide what we bring to the market are people who are employed and have earned their position because they are good businessmen or good at running a factory. They haven't been employed because they are good trend spotters. They work at Bang & Olufsen and ... when they need to make a decision with the CEO about what products to develop, they look at three different televisions from three different designers and say: 'That one! That is bloody Bang & Olufsen!' And who designed it? Well, David Lewis, because he knows how to make 'a Bang & Olufsen television.'

*Beosound 5* was an unusual product because it was not a David Lewis design and because, for the first time, the company had placed confidence in a concept from *Idealab* rather than from *Idealand*. In this respect, *Beosound 5* represents a break with traditions and the cultural continuity described above. It was a concept from *Idealab*, and the rivalry and differences between *Idealand* and *Idealab* continued, even after the formal distinction between the two was abolished and the departments fused in a new comprehensive *Idea Factory* in 2007. According to Birger and Adam, the fate of the product was also affected by political resistance throughout the Bang & Olufsen Product Development organization, where David Lewis and his supporters in *Idealand* were dominant and exerted their influence, both explicitly and implicitly.

Birger:  Well, some things happened. It was a confrontation beween *Idealand* and *Idealab* at the time. *Idealand* was not author of it. Svend talked about it [*Beosound 5*] condescendingly for a long time. Svend was then head of *Idealand* and he eventually [in the course of the process] became head of the *Idea Factory*. So Svend, who was responsible for taking it further [in the development process] didn't love it. [I admit] there are things about the concept which are not perfect, but I don't think enough effort was put into trying to correct these things. ... *Beosound 5* is a 'user-interface concept.' It is really the wheel ...

Adam:   That's for sure! What went wrong was that when Hermansen returned with a piece of brilliant design, we handed it over to people who were used to developing David Lewis' products, and said: now you should do what you usually do, only with a design that is radically different. They should have given it back to the people at *Idealab*.

## Two CEOs

Adam and Birger's story points to the fact that the ultimate fate of the product is not in the hands of the designer. Rather, the concept is shaped in the tube, and must be carried through by committed employees there as well. They go on to explain how research and development (R&D) policies and evaluations and the criteria that govern them are also – and ultimately – determined by CEO priorities. *Beosound 5* was developed under Torben Ballegaard, but the final product was launched in 2008 under Kalle Hvidt Nielsen after the financial crisis had hit Bang & Olufsen, and Torben Ballegaard had been fired. Ballegaard and Hvidt are described as having different approaches to the R&D process.

Ballegaard was 'extremely involved in the cloud' and took part (or interfered?) in the work of *Idealand* and *Idealab*:

Adam:   To Torben Ballegaard, *Idealand* and *Idealab* were the heart of the company. According to him, this was where the essential creativity was. This was where new value was created. Afterwards, when some engineers had to sit down and – well, [according to him] that could be outsourced. The *tube* should be outsourced, because then you could just scale it up and down according to need. As long as you had these creative people who could come up with the right and bright ideas, anybody could do the rest.

Birger:   In the time of Torben Ballegaard there was a mass of wonderful ideas. A lot of ideas and suggestions about what could be produced – and no products came out of it, because 'the tube' was

completely clogged. Sales were f\*\*\*\*\*\* great (*skidegodt*). But our
pipeline was empty . . .

Hvidt, who replaced Ballegaard as CEO, came from Brüel & Kjær, a
company which produces instruments to measure sound and vibration.
Hvidt's claim to fame was to have turned its fortunes by initiating
the development of a new unifying PC-software platform for Brüel &
Kjær products. The hope was that he would do something similar at
Bang & Olufsen. According to Adam and Birger, he was 'an engineer.'
If Ballegaard was enveloped in the 'cloud,' Hvidt was focused on the tube.
Adam explained the strategic emphasis of Kalle:

Now this company needs to be able to make good electronics for a product. It
was his focus, and one of the things I remember making us slightly uneasy was
when he said: 'Well, in the design department they must be able to figure out
how to make things to fit with our electronics.'

Birger:   It was a complete reversal. We make some electronics, and they need
          to make some boxes around it.

We would probably expect concept developers like Adam and
Birger, who look at the R&D process from a cloud perspective, to
regret such gravitation toward the tube. But even if they expressed
some concern about the radical shift of emphasis, they both
acknowledged the drawbacks of the previous strategy that gave
exclusive priority to the cloud and imagined that everything else
could be *outsourced*.

## 'Low-hanging fruits' and 'white elephants'

Adam:    *Beosound 5* was born in the heyday of this outsourcing idea, which
         means that focus was actually to hit on the ideas, and the priority and
         work went into showing that idea [and not the subsequent product
         development]. And then, when it was actually there on the table, [. . .]
         then the next step was: 'Let's outsource it and get it produced.' How
         difficult could that be?

Birger:  It's called 'low-hanging fruits.' I've learned that 'low-hanging
         fruits' are apples that hang so low that you only need to
         [*he clicks his tongue*]. That's bloody easy. We only need to feed
         it into the outsourcing machine then. . . . Now I know. There's
         no such thing as a 'low-hanging fruit'. . . . Well, in the process

of this *Beosound 5* [we held a workshop, where] we talked about 'low-hanging fruits' [i.e. elements from previous products that could be reused in the new product], and we looked in our portfolio, and we found something called Beo-media, which was this black box, which just went underneath, behind or below the television, and then it could provide some sound. Maybe we could produce a smart little UI to go with it? Or a neat little 'handle' and do something ... But it was not very iconic. ... It was fruits from the wrong tree. Oh, I hate that word!

Short cuts turn out to be detours. Strategies that look efficient and easy on paper happen to be counter-productive. Similarly, the TOP model, with its milestones and commitments meant to make the process rational and efficient, was also a deep source of regret in the development of *Beosound 5*. The evaluations and decisions made at particular stages were irreversible and introduced a rigidity that ultimately detracted from what Birger and Adam described as a near-perfect initial idea: 'At the conceptual level it [*Beosound 5*] is really good, and the industrial design is great. It is one of the best iconic audio players you will find out there' (Birger). The initial idea, however, met with resistance and the rigidities of the development process. This problem was particularly clear on the UI or software side of the design process.

Adam:    Bang & Olufsen is much better at making iterations on mechanical design, and these processes are missing in software.
Birger:   We run some stage-gate processes ... some milestone programs.
Jakob:   Concept commitment?
Birger:   Exactly. At that point we commit ourselves to making a particular concept. But on the software side it is still up in the air, when we reach 'cc' [=concept commitment]. It doesn't hang together in the same way as hardware. But the die is cast and at the 'cc' some things have been sealed, which shouldn't have been closed down quite so fast, because you haven't done enough iterations. We might have made a decision to have only three rubber controls one week before 'cc,' but the software side has not had the opportunity or time to work with a concept with three controls.

Redefining design to take into account digitalization was not a straightforward matter. Software was difficult, not only because the organization had not yet developed adequate iterations around it, but also because of the nature of software itself. Even if it was recognized as necessary that design concepts needed to take user interface (i.e. software) seriously, it was also clear that a bet on software platforms was a risky venture because software changes quickly, and therefore platforms and projects are in danger of becoming obsolete even before they are launched. Furthermore grand platform projects could easily turn into white elephants, as Adam explained:

[They] become white elephants that cannot die. Part of a company's asset is its investment. If you invest 100 million Danish kroner in making a software platform, then it is worth 100 million on the balance sheet. Which means that when we borrow money, we put that up as security for our loan. [If we choose to] throw that platform away, we have admitted that it's not worth anything – and then we are 100 million short and become insolvent ... That is a good reason for the immortality of the white elephants.

*Beosound 5* was not chosen because it was 'average' or represented a typical Bang & Olufsen creative encounter. Quite the opposite. *Beosound 5* stood out because it wasn't a smooth creative process (if ever there was one?) and because it didn't follow the institutionally recognized and celebrated tension between the designer (that is, David Lewis) and engineers. Instead, it described a moment when new ideas and criteria clashed with old practices and institutional forms. In other words, this particular case was significant because it was not about 'innovation' but about the attempted *innovation* of innovation. In the process, old ideas about design and the role of the designer were challenged. It is clear from the case that the creative process is not a smooth process but one full of contingencies and constraints. As we can see, constraints also provide participants in the process with opportunities to explain failure. As Brian Moeran (2006: 99) points out in his book on creative process: 'Creativity exists only because of the constraints present in any creative industry. Such conditions are necessary because they provide those working in the creative industries with reasons or excuses for things not going as planned.'

## Bang & Olufsen and the name economy

So far I have focused on the on-going evaluative processes and editorial moments that take place when a concept is formed and eventually becomes a product. But as Brian Moeran points out in the Introduction to this volume, equally important are post-production evaluations that seek to compare and rank cultural producers and goods. It is clear from the contributions to this book that such post-production symbolic classifications play a large part in the creative industries. This is certainly true for Bang & Olufsen. In the past four decades the company has earned a multitude of national and international design prizes, such as the *if-design award*, the *red dot award*, and other prestigious prizes. On top of these acknowledgements, the ultimate post-production recognition mentioned in every Bang & Olufsen chronicle (see Bang 2005: 477; Poulsen 1997: 136) is to have had several of the company's products canonised as *objets d'art* and included in the permanent exhibition at the Museum of Modern Art in New York. Furthermore, in 1978, MOMA hosted a special exhibition covering the company's entire product portfolio (Jensen and Olesen 2003: 51).

These systems of awards and recognition work as a symbolic exchange in their own right, relatively independent of market success or failure. As we shall see later on in Timothy de Waal Malefyt's discussion of an advertising campaign's awards, the fact that Bang & Olufsen has time and again been recognized for its designs helps to establish its reputation, commands respect and attention, and contributes to other more commercial brand rankings. For instance, in 2010 Bang & Olufsen was positioned No. 5 in the Centre for Brand Analysis' ranking of the world's top 'Coolbrands,' a list compiled by consumers and a panel of lifestyle magazine editors and brand consultants.[4] So these symbolic consecrations, which are known in many fields of cultural production and are discussed in this book in terms of advertising, film, and *haute cuisine*, are also relevant in the increasing segments of industrial production focused on 'design.' In such corporate contexts, Bourdieu's (1997) crucial point that symbolic capital can be converted to economic capital is relevant, as such post-product evaluative moments influence market performance

---

[4] www.rankingthebrands.com/The-Brand-Rankings.aspx?rankingID=64&nav=category, accessed on August 4, 2011.

and serve to 'add value' and justify the relatively high price of Bang & Olufsen's products.

In the branding or 'name' economy, the value of the name is pure attribution. It is expectation of a particular experience, a certain quality, or aesthetic signature. Even if the protection of a brand, as the etymon suggests, demands a piece of concrete graphic design to be attached to the products, brands are abstract objects. They have no extension in time and space (Klein 1999: 21). A well-established brand creates a loyalty and emotional attachment between itself and the consumer, 'ostensibly [allowing] consumers to identify with brands on an intimate level' (Malefyt 2009: 202). As the nature of this relationship is emotional, the designer is important as a key person seen to be able to infuse products with emotional appeal.

Even if Bang & Olufsen's products have been incorporated into art museums, they are not works of art. Even if the designer enjoys unparalleled autonomy, and even if many Bang & Olufsen employees and some aficionados in fact see David Lewis as gifted, he is a designer and not an artist, and he works under specific constraints. He is commissioned to solve a task, and to come up with an idea for a specific concept to be developed into a product to be sold on the market. The industrial designer can thus be viewed as a 'cultural intermediary' (Bourdieu 1984: 16; Du Gay *et al.* 1997: 62) because he joins the world of products and engineers with the world of the markets and consumers by infusing technology and products with emotional significance. Even if the designer has built a reputation, and even if, like David Lewis, he is well known and widely esteemed throughout the organization, the products are primarily associated not with him but with the two names of the company's founders: Bang & Olufsen.

## Cultural creativity and corporate constrictions

As mentioned in the Introduction to this volume, 'in the creative industries there is a continuous – often unresolved – tension between creativity, which we may define as the ability to push boundaries, and constraints, which uphold them.' Products must be new, yet bear a clear family resemblance to the existing portfolio. The cultural tradition, social environment, and institutional setting define what can be counted as creative. This is true in general, but it is obvious and concrete in the context of industrial product innovation in general, and of Bang & Olufsen in particular, where specific constraints frame the creative process and where 'ideas' and concepts not only have to be aesthetically appealing but also have to take into account technological developments and have to be judged at least potentially profitable to be realized. This is clearly brought forth in the case of HUGO BOSS, where designers are given the double binding mandate to make something that is 'surprising' and distinctly 'new' yet resonate with the brand, and to add to the ambiguity, this novel creation should be funky-formal (Kasper Vangkilde in Chapter 2). As Moeran observes in this case, 'renewal' is probably a more appropriate term than creativity.

Likewise, design and innovation at Bang & Olufsen take place in the context of a well-established brand. The market asks for 'newness' but, like other well-established brands, companies such as Royal Copenhagen and Bang & Olufsen live off a venerated tradition, and their brand name is associated with a particular aesthetic signature, which brings unstated yet very real criteria into the evaluative process. As mentioned above, ideas have to have a certain unspecified 'potential' (*idéhøjde*) to meet the recognized standards of the brand. Senior managers, who take the final decisions, talk about their criteria of judgement in imprecise and non-technical terms – like the necessity for the prototypes to have a 'Bang & Olufsen DNA.' Similarly, when judging designers' prototypes, they appeal to what is commonly known as the *eight-second rule* – 'a new concept has to make your jaw drop within eight seconds' (Holm and Lilleheden 2009: 125–126). Obviously this rule privileges traditional aesthetic criteria of design, as the evaluation of a product's software, UI, and other functionalities clearly requires more time. The rule also privileges 'intuition' in the evaluative process, and resonates with a particular image of the designer as an 'artist' who uses his (*sic!*) genius or intuition to access the sensibilities of the customer (and managing directors). As one managing director once expressed it: 'We wish to cooperate with designers, who can create unique products that stay on the market for ten or twenty years and don't become outdated. We think this is an intuition, a gut feeling the designer has [. . .] It is something artistic' (Verner Kristiansen, manager, quoted in Holm and Lilleheden 2009: 63). This view of the designer-as-artist is confirmed elsewhere in accounts of the company's approach to creativity. Design historian Christian Holmsted Olesen writes about Bang & Olufsen's approach to the designer: 'A completely satisfying experience of value cannot be generated on the basis of qualitative or quantitative market analysis, and this gives the designer a specific role as artist in the company' (Jensen and Olesen 2003: 69).

In an exploration of cultural creativity, anthropologist John Liep points out that during the Enlightenment the concept of creativity was bisected: 'Creativity became the mark of the engineers and scientists. At the same time artists became separated from the dependency on and support of feudal and ecclesiastical patrons . . . Creativity thus took two forms, represented as the contrast between the material and the spiritual' (Liep 2001: 3). The latter is tied to the romantic notion of artistic inspiration and intuitive insight; the former connects with systematic and analytical work. We might recognize a similar distinction in the division between different views on design at Bang & Olufsen. At one end of the spectrum we have the spiritual, artistic vision of the designer-genius, represented by the separation and sacralization of the designer; at the other, we see new ideas necessitated by digitalization, which seem to require a more systematic and collaborative effort between designers, engineers, and users.

Anthropologist Jonathan Friedman talks about 'the iron cage of creativity.' 'Creativity is only recognized in terms of its constraints. It is the latter that determine the nature of its intelligibility. The constraints are products of an organization of shared experience, of shared implicit attributions of meaning to the world' (Friedman 2001: 48). It is important, however, to recognize that this is not only a question of ideas being out of sync with 'interpretive schemes' or 'mental models,' as the romantic vision of creativity might lead us to believe (see Hill and Levenhagen 1995: 1057 and 1061). It is not a matter of an 'out-of-the-box-thinking' freelance designer vision being up against a recalcitrant 'collective' or system. As this chapter demonstrates, we should acknowledge that different 'new ideas' are connected to institutional interests and enter into power struggles within this system.

## Editorial moments

Creative processes are punctuated by 'editorial moments' (Becker 1982: 198). As pointed out in the Introduction, these moments describe the actual choices people make at different stages during the production of a creative work. Such editorial moments make it clear that creative processes are social and cooperative ventures (Becker 1982: 201). Consequently, as Becker (1982: 87) points out, creative personnel have to establish relations of *trust*. This is as true of ensembling in a chamber music performance (see Chapter 3) as it is in the development of a Bang & Olufsen sound system. The company places trust in the designer, and for his ideas to be accomplished he must trust and collaborate with concept developers, who for their part must collaborate with engineers in the tube. An additional point that becomes evident from the Bang & Olufsen case is that it *takes time* to establish such relations of mutual understanding. Thus, at Bang & Olufsen, trust was built over the years between the staff of *Idealand* and David Lewis. But, as the material reveals, these relations of trust between specific persons and groups also worked as social alliances and implicit cultural understandings that made it difficult for alternative visions and practices to be established.

At Bang & Olufsen, it is the senior management group which has the ultimate editorial power. It has to accept particular designs and choose which of the concepts put forward by the different designers will be continued in the tube. As testified by the predictable outcome of the competition to develop a new flat-screen concept, this affects corporate priorities and strategies, and builds a certain cultural inertia into the process. Birger and Adam lamented that such important editorial moments were put in the hands of people with a financial, technical, or administrative background – people who were neither trend-spotters nor designers. Considering the socio-economic segment of the typical Bang & Olufsen customer, however, it might not be such a bad idea to let senior management decide as it would be difficult to find a 'focus group' that fits the target consumer more adequately in terms of socio-economic position.

At one level it is true that creative processes depend on trust and editorial moments on mutual understanding. But, as this chapter shows, such events can sometimes be 'social dramas' in Victor Turner's sense (1974: 34–35), i.e. moments when the stakes are down and social differences are articulated with rare clarity. As such they are inherently conflict-ridden and marked out as 'hot' events – i.e. points in time when a lot is at stake and choices are made that affect organizational priorities and can have deep personal consequences. These are occasions when 'winners' are announced – and losers implied. One such event is the decisive editorial moment, when a group of managing directors has to decide which of the designers' proposed concepts they will support. So, editorial moments in the context of a large corporation make it clear that processes of creativity or innovation are not only social activities in the sense of requiring a collective or common effort. When people in organizations attempt to accomplish things by *acting* among each other – *inter-est* – each actor has particular *inter-ests* expressed in the negotiation and struggle to obtain concrete and symbolic resources (Bourdieu 1977).

The three cases of industrial design analyzed in this volume – HUGO BOSS, Royal Copenhagen, and Bang & Olufsen – represent three different product temporalities. At one end, HUGO BOSS operates in a market of fashion clothes that changes by the season. At the other end, the traditional luxury tableware of Royal Copenhagen is craftwork considered as a paradigmatic heirloom and thus passed on from one generation to the next. Bang & Olufsen falls somewhere in between these extremes. It stakes its reputation on minimalist, user-friendly design, implying a view of its TV sets as pieces of furniture. This has been a strategy of longevity and a way to avoid having to cater to incessant changes in technology. But the demands and constraints imposed by the digital world clash with some of the fundamental premises of Bang & Olufsen. David Harvey has alerted us to the fact that, in the age of global flexible capitalism, technology and consumer preferences change at an ever-increasing pace, and product lifespans are continuously diminished. The average product lifetimes in the age of Fordism was 5–7 years, but in some areas such as the textile industry it has been cut to half (Harvey 1990: 156). This tendency, which Harvey described twenty years ago, is even more pronounced in today's area of digital technology and software. In this light, Bang & Olufsen's bet on the longevity of its products is a swim against the tide. But perhaps the only way to find that much-hyped 'blue ocean' is to swim in that direction.

Innovation is commonly described as out-of-the-box thinking. The implied view of the designer and the design process keeps design – and questions about its evaluation – beyond the gaze of sociologists. However, as this chapter has revealed, to get beyond the anodyne language of *win–win* and out-of-the-box thinking, when studying such phenomena we are well advised to keep in mind the full implications of Schumpeter's definition of innovation as 'creative destruction' and to explore the social and cultural dialectics implied in this oxymoron by realizing that creative processes are social encounters full of incompatible criteria, compromise, and contradictions.

170                                                    *Jakob Krause-Jensen*

## References

Bang, Jens 2005. *Bang & Olufsen: fra gnist til icon*. Struer, Denmark: Bang & Olufsen.

Becker, Howard. 1982. *Art Worlds*. Berkeley and Los Angeles: University of California Press.

Bourdieu, Pierre. 1977. *Outline of a Theory of Practice*. Cambridge, NY: Cambridge University Press.

   1997. The forms of capital. In *Education: Culture, economy, and society*, ed. A. H. Halsey, pp. 46–58. Oxford University Press.

   1984. *Distinction: A social critique of the judgment of taste*. Cambridge, MA: Harvard University Press.

Clastres, Pierre. 1977. *Society against the State*. Oxford: Mole Editions.

Crapanzano, Vincent. 2010. At the heart of the discipline. Critical reflections on fieldwork. In *Emotions in the Field: The psychology and anthropology of fieldwork experience*, ed. James Davies and Dimitrina Spencer. Stanford University Press.

de Bono, Edward 1999. *Six Thinking Hats*. London: Penguin.

Douglas, Mary. 1986. *How Institutions Think*. New York: Syracuse University Press.

Du Gay, Paul, Stuart Hall, Linda Janes, Hugh Mackay and Keith Negus. 1997. *Doing Cultural Studies: The story of the Sony Walkman*. London: Thousand Oaks.

Dumont, Louis. 1980. *Homo Hierarchicus: The caste system and its implications*. University of Chicago Press.

Durkheim, Emile. 1976. *The Elementary Forms of the Religious Life*. London: George Allen & Unwin.

Friedman, J. 2001. The iron cage of creativity. An exploration. In *Locating Cultural Creativity*, ed. John Liep, pp. 46–61. London: Pluto.

Green, Jay. 2007. Where designers rule. *Businessweek*. November 5.

Harvey, David. 1990. *The Condition of Postmodernity: An enquiry into the origins of cultural change*. Cambridge, MA: Basil Blackwell Ltd.

Hill, Robert C. and Michael Levenhagen. 1995. Metaphors and mental models: sensemaking and sensegiving in innovative and entrepreneurial activities. *Journal of Management* 21 (6): 1057–1074.

Holm, Anders H. and Peter Lilleheden. 2009. At skabe nyt – på den gamle måde. En empirisk undersøgelse af sociale processers betyding for innovation på Bang & Olufsen. *Institut for Pædagogisk Antropologi*, Aarhus, Denmarks Paedagogiske Universitetsskole. Unpublished Master's thesis.

Jensen, Jacob and Christian H. Olesen. 2003. Designeren og mesterværket. Jacob Jensen og Beomaster 1900. *Bang & Olufsen 1960–1990. Fra Dansk Kvalitetsmærke til Internationalt ikon*. Højbjerg: Hovedland.

Klein, Naomi. 1999. *No Logo*. New York: Picador.

Krause-Jensen, Jakob. 2010. *Flexible Firm. The design of culture at Bang & Olufsen*. Oxford, NY: Berghahn Books.

Liep, John. 2001. *Locating Cultural Creativity*. London: Pluto Press.

Malefyt, Timothy de W. 2009. Understanding the rise of consumer ethnography: branding technomethodologies in the new economy. *American Anthropologist* 111 (2): 201–210.

Moeran, Brian. 2006. *Ethnography at Work*. New York: Berg.

Poulsen, Per Thygesen 1997. *Break point. Anders Knutsen og Bang & Olufsen*. Viby: Centrum.

Senge, Peter M. 1999. *Den femte disciplin*. Århus: Klim.

Sennett, Richard. 1998. *The Corrosion of Character: The personal consequences of work in the New Capitalism*. New York: Norton.

Turner, Victor. 1974. *Dramas, Fields, and Metaphors: Symbolic action in human society*. Ithaca, NY, London: Cornell University Press.

Williams, Raymond. 1976. *Keywords: A vocabulary of culture and society*. London: Fontana/Croom Helm.

# 6 Creativity in the brief: travel guidebook writers and good work

ANA ALAČOVSKA

This chapter shows how travel guidebook writers, who are committed to doing as good a job as possible within the constraints imposed upon them by their publishers, go about their work in practice. Because travel guidebook writers care profoundly about the products they create, they constantly employ craft standards or inner criteria of excellence by which they judge good or bad performance. The practical doing of guidebooks is an everyday achievement based on a concatenation of daily evaluations of work. In what follows, I continue Moeran's earlier discussion of craftsmanship, by analysing how a craft ethos underpins guidebook writers' evaluations of good work in the process of *doing* their job, and not just made sense of after the fact. This is all the more important as travel guidebooks have long been considered a lowly genre – 'fit for moral ejaculation' (Barthes 1993: 75), a sanctuary for 'second-rate literary talents' (Fussell 1980: 212), 'unashamed dilettantes,' and 'opportunistic journalists' (Holland and Huggan 2000: 12–13).

What producers evaluate as 'good' is assessed not in a vacuum but with a view to a range of conflicting demands. On the one hand, they are contractually bound to obey institutional requirements and audience preferences, which are embodied in the editorial brief. On the other hand, cultural producers are self-avowedly accountable to the ethical and aesthetic principles (norms, conventions) of the genre they produce, separately from managers, administrators, and markets. This is because the cultural product is doubly articulated: it is both a commodity and an artistic object. It follows from this that the practical making of cultural products is an ambiguous and ambivalent, habitual yet often reflexive, reconciliation of the tension between commerce and culture.

The editorial brief and the genre interlock and co-construct each other. Genre theory has long argued that genres in fact function as 'institutions within institutions' – autonomous and independent 'models for writing' (Todorov 1990: 18) that in turn are backed up by the material and commercial institutions of cultural industries (Altman 1999: 91). A genre is an independent regime which defines what it is appropriate to do in a particular situation and professional genre community. It is not always written or explicit, but it lays down tacitly obligatory and practically obliging rules of text-making that are recurrent, shared, and sustained in a locally and historically specific 'community of genre' (Devitt 2004: 37). Only afterwards is it incorporated in the relations of capital and pragmatically institutionalised in the editorial brief.

The editorial brief is a template for action, as well as a regulatory and legally binding document, developed in-house by editors and aligned with corporate financial charts. The writer delivers in accordance with the brief, which functions as a disciplining tool that allows a publisher to audit, measure, and reckon his or her performance. Writers get chastised for failing to meet the brief's demands: in particular, with regard to addressing audience needs, heeding the bottom line, and executing work on time. The brief is thus conceived of as a controlling mechanism that casts a scrutinising, undercover eye on freelance writers who, in principle, do not work in spatial or temporal proximity to their managers (Hirsch 1978).

As it is inherent in genres to stabilise the voluntary and thus self-governing 'contract' between producers and audiences (Genette 1997), managerial strategies generally counter the uncertainties of cultural markets by linking pre-established consumer trends with pre-sold products (Bielby and Bielby 2003). As a result, the genre was eagerly used to render the 'unruly' creation 'rationalised' and 'bureaucratised' by steering producers toward repetition and predictable outcomes via genre-related norms, models, and formulae.

It can be said, then, that the travel guidebook genre is sanctioned in the editorial brief, which in turn enforces a standardized plan (Adorno 1975: 12) or format (Ryan 1991: 160) in the guise of structured conventions and company-advocated rules of text-making that have been presented to writers as a set of stringent regulations, detailed stylistic guidelines, extensive product manuals, and meticulous instructions. The brief thus underpins authorial intentions and ensuing aesthetic and ethical choices (Griswold 1987: 7). Fulfillment of its requirements leads to writers becoming entrepreneurial, creative individuals (Christopherson 2004), who try to boost their income by expediency and efficiency of execution. This increases their chances of repeated commissions (especially if they court editors), reduces their working hours (by mixing research and writing with family and vacation time), and leverages the experience and content gained from guidebook work (by selling adjacent stories to magazines and newspapers).

The guidebook genre itself represents a less obtrusive set of rules than those of the brief, but rules all the same, which are embedded in corporate culture, inscribed in the unwritten conventions of professional perform-ance, and underlain also in the tacit agreement pertaining between pro-ducers and consumers. The genre seamlessly blends independent codes of making with commercial imperatives: 'formatting transforms the usual rules of a form into *necessity* in the workplace' (Ryan 1991: 172, original emphasis). Guidebook writers thus have to follow the editorial brief, but also work within autonomous rules of the genre with its independent trajectories and sovereign conventions of form.

The brief and the genre play off each other in a practical manner while underpinning the craft ethos to work. The coupling of the brief and the genre affords resources and schemes of text-making that are deeply contradictory and conflicting. Together, they represent constraints in addition to affordances, or those properties of objects that help structure, organise, and order action (DeNora 2003; Born 2005). In other words, it is how they are used that matters, not what they mean and how they are to be critically reinterpreted. In order to illustrate this point, I will now describe how Daisy, an experienced travel guidebook writer, judges her work while doing it, as I follow her engaging with, mobilising, and employing both brief and genre. At the time of my ethnographic work she was commissioned by a renowned global travel (guidebook) publisher to write anew a guide to the capital city of Elbonia.[1]

## Spreadsheet culture: 'Stick to your brief'

[The company] loves spreadsheets. I spend most of my time figuring out how they work, why some cells are bigger than others, and so on. I must follow the pattern they give me: how many words I'm supposed to use for a hotel review, or particular neighbourhood. . . . They use an incredible number of abbrevia-tions. It took me forever to learn them. For example they say POI for Point of

[1] The Republic of Elbonia is a fictional country in the popular comic strip *Dilbert* authored by Scott Adams. On several 'gossiping' occasions I have witnessed travel guidebook writers referring to Elbonia when intent on avoiding mentioning a specific destination and thus invoking the names of the authors who are experts on it. Emulating this practice, I use *Elbonia* in order to protect the privacy of my informants.

Interest, referring to the process of updating info – like hotel names, addresses, telephone numbers, things like that.

I need to follow the brief. It represents a sort of outline of the work I'm supposed to do. I'm really grateful they did it because it says everything here and all I need to do is follow it. I always keep that to hand and close to my heart when writing. Just to make things in accordance to what they ask and expect. Actually, the more constraints I have, the better job I do. That may sound strange, but it's true. I take pride in delivering in accordance to the brief. I thrive on positive feedback from the editors. It is about pleasing the editor. If they like what I do, they'll commission me again, especially now that [the company] doesn't give you the faintest hint that they'll contact you again with a gig.

The brief undergirds writers' calculative and consequential agency. Writers anticipate their future (in terms of employability and income) by projecting whether they have the capacity to finish the job on time, within budget, on target, and above all according to the expectations and regulations set out by the editors. They express that paradoxical feeling of being both overwhelmed and inspired by a publisher's directions and rules – not least by the company's internal jargon (for freelancers are, of course, external) – in their agitation to deal with spreadsheets. At its core, travel guidebook writing is filling in a grid of cells that organises content creation just like an arithmetic operation. The spreadsheet enables an efficient and expedient deployment of massive amounts of content. By enforcing impersonal censorship, it automatically calibrates the number of words written, leaving no space for excess. What doesn't fit in the spreadsheet doesn't belong in the guidebook. The spreadsheet affords an overview, chart, and totality of the process of making that produces a homogeneous, uniform, and coherent voice which, in turn, is overridden by the publishing brand, rather than by the author's name. To this end, the spreadsheet erases the idiosyncrasies of the individual writer and acts as an agent of homogenisation (Law 2002: 27), as it moves purposively from the sphere of statistical and economic calculability to that of creativity. What, then, of those unclassifiable, residual, and aesthetic choices that writers make? How do they cope with the arithmetic restrictions of the spreadsheet?

The travel writer needs to find solutions to the constraints contained in the spreadsheet, including space, word limit, and overall outlook. In order to meet such contingencies, writers not only keep the brief 'at hand' (as a tool) but also 'close to heart' (as a goal). It is interiorisation of the brief that first and foremost has a bearing on a writer's self-evaluated ability to do good work. Daisy devoted herself to the implementation of the brief requirements for two reasons: first, to profile her credibility and please her editors, in order to build up credit for possible future employment (Faulkner 1983), and second, to take personal pride and enjoyment in a successful, timely, and efficient realisation of the brief.

The brief dictates in minute detail a writer's assignment: what is to be included in, or omitted from, a guide, as well as the tone of the review to be adopted, the pitch of voice, the angle, all informed by meticulous audience and market research. Words need to be carefully chosen and always measured against the overall word limit, which needs to be rigorously adhered to in order to avoid inflating editing and printing costs. As one brief stresses: 'Please stick to the word counts assiduously.'

I haven't had the chance to write more than forty-five words on any given subject in about five years. That's why, maybe, I began to write a blog. What I'm not allowed to say in the guidebook, I put on my blog. So when editors censor me, fine! I have my blog! Whatever drops out of the guidebook – you know, word limits, practicalities, suitability – is not wasted, it goes out there. The Internet is unlimited. I cannot write about that quirky wig shop, almost a wig museum, down a dark ally in a guidebook. The editor would immediately say: 'that's a bit off. . . . A wig isn't a memento of your trip to Norway, is it?' It doesn't make any business sense, at least not to editors.

The brief, then, determines what it is appropriate to say and write in a particular situation. Although the writer has to fall in line with the institutionally determined logic of appropriateness, she can also translate it into a margin of freedom elsewhere, and not just in terms of her future employability. What she can also do is set up a private publishing space, free from imposed limitations, which escapes close scrutiny. In this way, new media technologies upset the established publishing value chain by eliding editors and publishers (Thompson 2010).

Some writers felt that spreadsheet-induced censorship was especially disturbing because the brief explicitly demanded personality and subjectivity: 'write with colour and flair'; 'the author should include an angle'; 'find some interesting twist to the coverage – we must cover the Statue of Liberty, for example, but can we lift the coverage beyond the ordinary?' Daisy interiorised the brief to the extent that she unwittingly, yet approvingly, reiterated editorial demands as part of her own style and benchmarks. She hoped to present content which the editors would find compelling and appealing, but also which she herself was going to be proud of; in other words, content that would be not just functional, accurate, factual, and objective, but also 'atmospheric', including 'prose with an angle.' Daisy developed her own standards of excellence – aligned with genre-specific discourses – that could not be reduced to editorial requirements or bureaucratic specifications. Her sense of having achieved quality was often perceived as inventiveness within the conventions of the genre – usually through a critical and reflexive engagement with the genre regime. This was especially evident when she questioned the truthfulness or factuality of the genre, and when she reprimanded other writers for failing to uphold its 'referential' regime:

AA:      When do you feel happy with what you write?
Daisy:   When I've caught the spirit of the place. Captured the atmosphere. It is important to get the angle on the place.
AA:      How does one capture an 'atmosphere'? How do you know how wide the angle should be, so to speak?
Daisy:   [*hesitating*]. Let's say that you need to review a sleepy seaside village. You've been there, as once happened to me, and said: 'The place is full of veteran fishermen. Beware, they all tried to hit on me.' This succinct explanation reveals the atmosphere of the place. It may not tell the truth about the place itself, but it reveals the truthfulness of the author's experience of the place. Or if you describe a small town, woefully conservative for generations now, from the perspective of its central square sculpture, which is all nakedness – basically a couple on the verge of having sex – then you can spice things up. You aren't boring, or tempted by clichés. You're factual, but at the same time you've got that twist.
        This is a strange sort of genre. It inflicts the need to use clichés, even on the most eloquent of writers. It's a daily combat against clichés. It is so funny. Great writers otherwise, write texts full of worn-out phrases. That resembles more a third-grade essay than serious guidebook prose. 'You can wear a bikini all year round, although the majority of people are Muslim' or 'you'll encounter smiling faces despite being so deprived.' That's abominable.

Writers reflect upon the interrelationship between the brief and the genre, even though it is fussy, vague, and undifferentiated. That interrelationship underpins choices of appropriateness, with a view not only to the brief but also to generic trajectories. In Daisy's account, the boundaries separating the brief and the genre are blurry and indeterminate: 'the brief is rigid,' maybe, but also 'the genre is demanding' and 'sort of strange.' Choices are made at the intersection between the two. The genre is judged as 'demanding' and the brief as 'stifling.' Clichés and 'flowery language' are not appropriate for a 'factual' genre, and certainly inappropriate for the thrifty economy of words as regulated by the spreadsheet. Writers can be critical or appreciative of what they have achieved on the basis of their assessment of the outcome of their work.

Together with short deadlines and skimpy budgets, fighting off clichés that corrupt the genre and defy editors' expectations is a constant source of anxiety and burn-out. Equally, however, it can form the basis for enjoyment and pleasure in one's work when successfully navigated:

Travel guidebook writing is a very demanding style of writing because the genre itself is really demanding. First of all, you have very tight and precise word lengths; you have to learn how to express ideas very succinctly, leaving aside a lot of flowery language or descriptive excess. I found it exacerbating to always need to come up with a fresh perspective, or fresh turn of phrase. It's almost robotically searching for freshness. Look now, for example, about how best to describe the restaurants and bars we visited today, and those of tomorrow and the day after tomorrow. I go: tasty goat sandwich, yummy olive spread, delicious lentil soup. Then I try mouth-watering, lip-smacking. But then what? This is gruelling. ... But once you've got the word in place you say: that's that. That works well. Eventually everything falls into place. Just like in a mosaic.

Daisy simply 'knew' when the words were appropriate and when they 'felt a bit off.' She would just convince me that something 'didn't work well' because she 'knew' it 'wouldn't click.' 'The search for the fresh turn of the phrase' was 'gruelling' and time-consuming because she was determined to get the job done well, and not just to get by. She was not content with regurgitating the same old adjectives or clichés – that would be taking the easy way out. Being aware of a range of alternative linguistic devices at her disposal, Daisy defined what she believes (while endorsing both editors' and customers' expectations) 'doesn't work,' what doesn't pair together, what doesn't describe well, what doesn't capture truthfulness appropriately. At the same time, a source of apprehension – the incessant search for the 'right' word – is also a source of pride. The development of skills turns into a joy of learning and refining, a never-ending pursuit of excellence. At this level, Daisy's daily choices become aesthetic choices, which are relational because they are always evaluated in context and *vis-à-vis* other possible alternatives. Daisy evaluates again and again the qualities of words, the potential of a specific turn of phrase, the *blasé* character of epithets. By constant trial and error, she painstakingly puts together 'the mosaic' of the guide. She obsesses over words until they feel right and in place – in other words appropriate to both the brief and the genre.

Most importantly, it is the long-term, pretty consistent, self-avowed commitment to writing 'good guidebooks' that prevents the temptation to do 'bad guidebooks.' This decision buttresses a writer's perseverance through periods of disillusionment, tight deadlines, and poor pay. Daisy, for example, was resolutely committed to doing good work. Even if lacking an obvious formal theory or doctrine, this writer devised her own standards of judging good work on the basis of her experience with, and professional understanding of, the genre regime, as well as of lessons learned from previous editorial work.

I'm feeling the burn-out even in this first week of research. My head is filled with addresses and URLs and random mental notes. I have yet to commit anything to paper because I've been biking the whole day. I feel the time pressure. Being late in [the company] creates a black spot – a stain. You can be a bad writer, but being late means that you aren't going to be hired any time soon. Hence, people might do a crappy job to avoid being late and to catch up. I want to write good guidebooks, so that will make me stay away from bad guidebooks.

The melding of the brief and the genre contributes to individual reflexivities that are part of wider professional or collective reflexivities. At the interface of the brief and the genre, practitioners critically and self-reflexively re-evaluate their writing practices. This is a mode of professional engagement, with the two institutions, the publishing company and the genre, made manifest mainly through irony and resistance. One such instance of resistance was clear when Daisy tried to negotiate the appropriateness of a review she had been unconditionally requested to 'execute.' The editorial brief made a review of Elbonia's War Museum compulsory. The writer, though, was convinced that this was an overrated and boring experience, which needed to be played down in importance, not highlighted. The editor, however, had other ideas, as the following extract from the brief reveals:

Elbonia's War Museum – [*comment from the author written in green*]: Honestly I find it a little bit of a ho-hum experience, as the crowds are too off-putting. Am I cruel for saying that? It is heartless not to make this a highlight.

[*Comment from the editor marked in red*]: From a marketability/sales point of view, this should be a highlight. It is one of the top draws for visitors (about a million visitors per year, hence the crowds) ... emphasize that the crowds can taint the experience, and give tips on what time of day to visit/best time to avoid crowds. But you must write about it.

The blurb of the guide to Elbonia makes the museum a highlight and a main selling point in spite of the author's objections.

When I later met Daisy and asked how she felt about 'having' to write in spite of her personal beliefs, she explained: 'The traveller needs to figure out himself that it is an overrated experience, though. That's the catch. I've seen so much disappointment but also victory on their faces when standing in front of it.'

While Daisy dared to interpret the brief requirements in a matrix alien to the brief's consequential logic, her interpretation turned into a conflict of interpretations. Ultimately, it was resolved by an instrumental and yet appropriate evocation of 'the audience': 'the audience' that is measured, charted, and market researched (as represented in the brief) and the audience that is made of flesh and blood, *bona fide*, here and now (as is intended, imagined, and encountered 'out there' by the author).

## Aesthetic choices

Travel guidebook writing involves a practical mastery of discernment and quick immersion in new places and cultures (a practice commonly referred to as 'parachuting'). The practical mastery comes from a bodily awareness of a place and this kind of sensuous perception is clearly made visible when the writer seamlessly and effortlessly navigates her way through a place evaluating tourist establishments. This is well demonstrated in the following two episodes drawn from fieldwork:

We have been walking in light drizzle for almost an hour now. It's pouring with rain and we're soaked from head to foot. Daisy considers stopping off at some random place. As we pass by a bar, she hesitates for a moment. Soggy and tired, I hope we are finally going in. But she is adamant: 'No. This bar is totally uninspiring. No, I won't lower my criteria. This isn't a good bar. Let's go a bit further. Our bar is somewhere here. I was here two years ago but I can't remember exactly every street. Anyway it's a maze around here.'

I somehow manage to ask what's wrong with the bar we've just passed and, for that matter, with another half a dozen along the way. 'It has neither a fancy aura, nor a cosy feeling. It's just ordinary,' Daisy replies.

After almost an hour of roaming without any (at least to me) fathomable purpose, I ask: 'Daisy, do you know where we're going? Do you have something special in mind?'

'Not really!' she replies. 'I've developed an inner compass of the place. I can feel the place. I've got the place at my feet. I've developed a mental sifting process. I sift through the data and rely on my taste and judgement. I don't care any more if I'm not capable of seeing everything. I just want to be sure I do the best job possible.'

I still have difficulty understanding and ask her to clarify what really she means by 'the best job.' 'I want to merge seamlessly into the background, listen to the city sounds, and sort of touch the place. I have a nose for quirky places. A good writer must be able to follow her nose and discover the place instinctively. When I feel I've got the place in my feet, it's time to stop. That is that. I just want to wave my flag and say, "Hey, I was here!"'

Suddenly, she exclaimed: 'Wow! Wow! That bar! Let's go in!'

I possessed neither the 'nose' nor 'the feet,' let alone the 'inner compass,' onto which Daisy was so successfully, and sometimes even stubbornly, clinging. From years of practice, she had painstakingly worked out and reworked an inner evaluative mechanism, her 'wow' criterion. Devoid of that embodied knowledge (superbly captured in the bodily metaphors she uses), I was at pains to make sense of the ostensibly haphazard itinerary and even worse, to assess instantly what was a 'fancy' or 'cozy' feeling in what seemed like an indistinguishable string of bars.

Here the difficulty writers have in explaining their actions and describing their practices is self-evident. The reference to bodily senses and sensibilities remedies the inadequacy of language to formally capture embodied knowledge. Daisy's 'taste' and 'judgment' were shaped by an intangible ability to feel the place in 'the feet,' to develop 'a nose,' 'to touch' the place, to follow 'the inner compass,' and 'merge' into the place by 'listening' to its sounds. Her post-rationalised account of what it is she was doing becomes 'intelligible' only when she openly makes clear her authorial intentions: 'I want to show that I have been there' and 'I want it to be a good read.' In this way, the making of guidebooks goes beyond a spreadsheet culture, with its formal editorial mechanisms and control devices. The challenge to write efficiently within editorial formulae, as a purely cognitive, rational, or consequential task, blends with the calling to most appropriately (intimately and bodily) understand a place, and conversely most appropriately to convey the meaning of that place to readers.

It is in 'being there' that bodily sense-perception comes into being (Geertz 1988). Bodily or situated choices are sensuous, and *ipso facto* aesthetic in essence, thereby surpassing narrow functionality as an expressive ways of knowing (Polanyi 1998). The basis for the evaluation and expression of sensory qualities is nested in the craft ethos to work: writers care about what they produce in practice, and act as (often ruthless) critics of their own performance. Even in the case of travel guidebooks that serve the practical purpose of guidance and are written with a view to affecting readers' actions, instruction can be, and indeed is, expressive: a result of aesthetic choices and evaluation when the execution of good work is at stake. It is the goal of achieving expressiveness that melds technical craft with the imagination, as Sennett (2008) so convincingly demonstrates when discussing the production of the equally mundane and lowly genre of cooking recipes.

As the writers clearly value the sense of 'being there', their authorial intention is to create 'expressive instructions' (Sennett 2008: 179) which are functional, but not boring; which are both factual and inspiring; and which make navigation in space and time seamless and safe. It is about *showing* a place from an insider's perspective, and not merely *talking about* it. The regime of the genre pre-supposes that a writer will visit a place before writing it up. In alignment with this, the editorial brief recommends as a minimum a four-week stay. 'Being there' is the prerequisite for obtaining intimate knowledge of the place, and thus making a good guidebook, both contractually and generically. It underpins a writer's sensual perceptions, bodily awareness, and discernment in making situated choices. As a result, travel writers take pride in writing in a sense of their presence in order to show that they have indeed been there. This is Daisy's paramount goal since a sense of presence is both an index of good work and a function of intimate knowledge. To capture the mood of being there exonerates the very act of writing from distrust, qualms, or misgivings on the part of both editors (who do not oversee the writing directly, but expect and pay for a truthful 'as is' account) and readers (who expect and pay for a first-hand, accurate, and factual description pursuant to an actual trip). Both editors and readers take good work for granted (Faulkner 1983). Hence, crafting a sense of presence is an immanent insurance against bad work, but also a well-gauged investment in building trust relations with both editors and readers.

Daisy has developed a range of strategies to exhibit 'being there.' One is a focus on detail; another involves wearing 'readers' moccasins'; and a third is premised on the senses, especially smell and touch. Smell is powerfully evocative and atmospheric, and thus adds to the 'angle of writing' and the capturing of ambience, while touch implies a direct connection to and physical contact with a place, and so reconfigures the truthfulness of 'I was there' poetics. Daisy would often stop, sniff, and touch. Once, I even caught her thinking aloud:

Artificial flowers and a cheap distasteful room-refresher. Does that make a four-starred hotel?

When urged to post-rationalise her strategies for conveying a sense of presence, Daisy resorts to instrumental rationality. Yet, the writer is not a totally calculative subject. Her work involves sensibilities, senses, ways of perceiving and evaluating that are not subject solely to organisational constraints or spreadsheets (editors as controllers), but emerge out of a deep engagement with the genre, the place, and the readers. When trying to describe how and why she strategically employs her senses, she explains how difficult it is to describe things 'freshly' and anew when they look 'exactly the same.' The use of senses helps differentiate guidebook reviews by supplying an 'angle.' It is also a tool against boredom that helps steer clear of an ugly (dull, bad) write-up.

Daisy:   When you have visited the umpteenth hotel, a giant generic room haunts your spirit. They all look exactly the same. The room is [*she changes her voice to ironic*] nice, beautiful, clean, moderately clean, spacious, relatively spacious. It has a chair, a desk, a bed, double, single. So what?! That doesn't work. You cannot write that ugly stuff. The editors don't want that, and the readers for sure hate raw reality. I need to show that I've been there. I've seen for myself, and also for them. I've sampled a place, I've touched it, rubbed my fingers against the furniture, smelled the flowers in the vase. You cannot know about the smell of the lobby or the texture of the sofa unless you've actually been there. I think the editors like that, and it makes an interesting read. It's a concrete sign of having been there and having seen and smelled and touched more than a chair, a desk, and a bed. You can see the hotel rooms on the Internet and then how they're described, call the staff from home to check the opening hours, but the smell or tactile sensations, these give a lingering sense of presence.

AA:    But is this enough? Is there anything else you can do to show your presence?

Daisy: When I think better, I like to exaggerate a detail. To take something totally mundane or unimportant – a feature, a facet – and play with it. It may be the strange smell of hay and horses, or the colorful door plaques with a hidden history, or that exotic talkative parrot in the lobby. Or I write: 'regulars are locals, and a big fat cat.' I want the guidebook to be accurate, but also to make a good read.

The utilisation of senses and the exaggeration of detail to achieve expressive representation of actuality are stylistic and aesthetic actions *per se*. However, practical mastery is required to instantaneously and spontaneously bring them out in practice. To strive to leave an indelible impression of being there, to try to present the familiar 'generic hotel room' so as to make it appear 'interesting' and maybe even surprising to the readers, to aim to expunge the obvious and 'the raw reality,' is not only to blindly and uncritically follow the requirements of the brief to lift the review 'above the ordinary.' It is, in fact, a deep engagement and instinctive play with the stylistic devices, tools, and instruments, conscious or not, at a writer's disposal to enable expressive instructions.

A good travel writer should not succumb to the pernicious tendency to 'automatization' by reiterating formulaic patterns. Instead, like the HUGO BOSS designers struggling with the Orange brand, she should resort to stylistic tools to de-familiarise the familiar: the 'raw' and 'dull' actuality of myriad bars, cafes, hotels, and so on. In this she engages in what Russian formalists called 'a device of making strange' or 'technique of defamiliarization' (Shklovsky 1965: 21). Their craft ethos drives travel writers to counteract the constraints of routine and sameness by showing rather than telling – but showing with an 'angle,' either through the senses or by hyperbole of certain details. And this is not only a subjective decision. It is a submission to compelling, craft-sanctioned, good work. 'Show, don't tell' is the principle dictum passed on to students of creative writing. Showing is 'a good way,' telling 'simply bad' (Booth 1983: 28).

However, a travel writer carefully gauges how far she can go in making things strange. Often an inarticulate dose of 'just enough' prevents the guidebook from lapsing into fiction or poetry, or trespassing on the territory of some other field and thus encroaching on some other rules of the game (a challenge faced by Cornelia Nixon when rewriting *Jarrettsville*). The careful juggling of 'just enough' aesthetic choices so as to preserve the specificity of the genre while fighting off automatism is most obvious when travel writers research and write 'unique' items – such as boxes, highlights, and snapshots, which are supposed to be 'brief and snappy,' 'quirky and interesting,' or 'inspirational and fun' ways of writing. Being as unspecific as they are, these requirements give leeway for creativity and allow a writer to show that behind the book there is indeed a 'real' writer.

The freedom accorded in the boxed texts poses other kinds of constraints and responsibilities, however. Here a writer's subjectivity, sincerity, and judgment must shine through. She must make herself out to be an expert who is entitled to make judgments and recommendations about other cultures, and not least to make jokes about others. Even though accompanied by a sense of unease, such opportunities allow writers to take pride in discussing places and cultures with wit and eccentricity. Personal stories, opinions, mental pictures, intimate experiences, and anecdotes give symbolic meaning to the physical travel.

You cannot really tell what is bad and blatantly ugly. You need to know how to couch an argument, and not offend anybody. For example, I hate Elbonian liquorice lollies, and Elbonian people adore them. So I write about all the shapes, colours, and wrappings they come in. And write a warning!

These unique items with their relatively unstructured guidelines often call for re-examination of the writer's craft, as when Daisy decided to devote one of her snapshots to marijuana smoking and felt uneasy about it:

I'm certainly not the one most suitable to judge weed or a joint. How can I write about it when I've only tried it once, and almost died! So I need to write in a manner that, say, stops younger people from getting too enthusiastic about smoking, and doesn't put off those who are a bit older.

This quotation points to the fact that writers must address the tastes and preferences of their audience, to write 'just enough' quirky, fun, and snappy stuff to neither offend nor bore their audiences.

I need to cater to an audience that is youngish, cultured, and smart; that lives in a big metropolis, is probably childless, and can afford to spend a day or two, or a long weekend, somewhere nearby, and not be particularly bothered with the prices.

Consumer demand is paramount. Market research has been employed extensively and consistently in the design of the brief, involving a large-scale quantitative study in terms of market size and segmentation. Audience research assists publishers in rationalising the production process and minimising costs by offering simplified, reified, and sche-matised representations of the audience. The results of such research define what is appropriate to the guidebook and how it should be covered:

Research shows that the city-break market is aged 25–40 years, professional and educated, . . . the average length of stay is between two and five days. . . . Our market is intelligent, interested, discerning, relaxed, experience-led, and hungry for a memorable time. . . . they realize that immersing oneself in a city isn't a matter of ticking off eight sites in one day (though they may wish to do this) but might be about sitting people-watching in a local café all morning or spending an afternoon browsing the market.

Although the audience is an object of calculation, administered, sche-matised, and integrated from above by the culture industry (Adorno 1975), the match between writers' intentions and the intended audience is never completely straightforward or functional, let alone cynical or malicious. Daisy takes pride in identifying with her readers, acting on their behalf, and not just in uncritically following the brief. It is about assuming the reader's point of view. She rejoices in meeting travellers, potential readers, on the road and objects to their being thought of as numbers, typifications, or impersonal markets. Craftsmen imagine their audiences (Sennett 2008). As Born (2000: 415), in her study of the BBC, also says, 'producers engage imaginatively with the audience' and do not just follow the results of institutional market research. Yet, for travel writers who meet their readers on the road, audiences are not just anticipated, but tangible and real: it is they who frown at a meal in a restaurant or ask for directions.

Good work is when you put yourself in your readers' moccasins, and try to imagine what they would like to do and say. When one is passionate about the job, nothing is impossible.

Readers want advice about where to spend their hard-earned dollars. I cannot slack off. We travel writers are responsible for their good time.

Every time I need to work in scorching heat or torrential rain, I remind myself that my reader may one day be right on this corner baked, or drowned, and lost. I need to get this job done, and done well.

Daisy engages with her imagined audience almost magically through the simulacrum of the moccasins. She sympathises with the audience through her own vulnerability. She retraces her steps emotionally in the process of making so as to provide 'good' guidance. Moreover, she operates on the assumption of a shared genre identity – 'we travel writers' – that takes the genre which instructs 'good' ways of travelling seriously on its own terms.

## Conclusion

Travel writers constantly judge their own performance so as to arrive at a personally satisfactory assessment of 'good work.' When building a more authentic relationship with their work, in the face of strict adherence to company-advocated rules and the need to make a living, cultural producers trade autonomy for a habitual, yet self-reflexive craft attitude to work. The skillful cultural producer set standards of excellence for herself while engaging with the independent genre regimes or models for writing, by which she judges work. No matter how lowly, normative, or prescriptive the genre is (as was the case with travel guidebooks), it is thought to provide the craft modes of achieving aesthetically and ethically sound work.

One of the most durable residues of Romanticism is probably the conviction that art is a pursuit of self-expression beyond economies and pecuniary benefits. The great works of art are produced in violation of, not in compliance with, market principles. Bourdieu even argued that commercial producers were 'mediocre and failed writers and artists' (1996: 347). For Adorno (1996), the producers (and recipients) of popular culture suffered from 'pseudo-individualism' as they needed to conform to prefabricated patterns and formulae. In contrast, Gans (1974) was an early sociological voice to propound the notion that aesthetic criteria applied to popular genres, and not solely to 'high culture.' Thus, aesthetic criteria need not be only about beauty and taste but also about craft values, intellectual and emotional benchmarks. Producers are neither failed nor pseudo-individuals just because they work with, and inhabit, low or popular genres.

The sociological approach to creative work, most superbly exemplified by Faulkner (1983) and Fine (1992), has shown empirically that the incursion of markets into creative work at a micro level (day-to-day practices of low-status cultural production such as studio-music making or cooking, respectively) entails turning art into craft worlds. Within craft worlds, the emphasis shifts from expressiveness and autonomy to issues of virtuosity, acting in accord with one's top expertise; judgments oriented toward editors and readers; skills, discipline, and above all a long-term commitment to skillful and good performance; and a honed sense of style, quality, and sensuality commensurate with available resources (Becker 1982: 288–293).

Recent scholarship on creative work from within media and communication studies has revived the interest in commercial media work. Mainly through interviews, these scholars contend that producers in media industries take pride in their work, and derive pleasure and satisfaction when making good cultural products (Hesmondhalgh and Baker 2011; Kennedy 2010). In spite of the culture industries' impending commodification of culture, craft values are still vigorous and vital (Banks 2007).

Following in these footsteps, I have shown, through a detailed ethnographical account, how cultural producers negotiate in practice the tension between aesthetic choices and more calculative rewards. Instead of focusing on what is commercial or formulaic in travel guidebook production, I asked what is aesthetic, sensory, and expressive, on the grounds that all 'good work' involves making aesthetic choices.

At the level of technical and practical mastery, the production of how-to, instructional accounts such as travel guidebooks becomes the production of expressive instructions. Well conversant with the history and principles of the genre, travel writers make choices that escape managerial control and editorial impositions. Thus, craft standards are embodied in a producer's ability to balance conflicting demands or constraints: the market and its commercial imperatives, on the one hand, and the aesthetic and ethical, autonomous requirements of the genre, on the other.

Acting at their best, travel writers become severe yet productive critics of their own performance. 'The expert judgment' provides a sense of righteousness and purpose. And here again, the commitment to doing the job well is relational: finding its *raison d'être* in an imaginative engagement with audiences, rather than in market research and ratings.

# References

Adorno, Theodor W. 1975. Culture industry reconsidered. *New German Critique* 6: 12–19.

    1996/1945. The social critique of music. *Kenyon Review,* June 1: 229–236.

Altman, Rick. 1999. *Film/Genre.* London: British Film Institute.

Banks, Mark. 2007. *The Politics of Cultural Work.* Basingstoke: Palgrave.

Barthes, Roland. 1993. *Mythologies.* London: Vintage.

Becker, Howard. 1982. *Art Worlds.* Berkeley: University of California Press.

Bielby, William T. and Denise D. Bielby. 2003. Controlling primetime: organizational concentration and network television programming strategies. *Journal of Broadcasting and Electronic Media* 47 (4): 573–596.

Booth, Wayne C. 1983. *The Rhetoric of Fiction.* University of Chicago Press.

Born, Georgina. 2000. Inside television: television studies and the sociology of culture. *Screen* 41 (4): 404–424.

    2005. On musical mediation: ontology, technology and creativity. *Twentieth Century Music* 2 (1): 7–36.

Bourdieu, Pierre. 1996. *The Rules of Art.* Palo Alto, CA: Stanford University Press.

Christopherson, Susan. 2004. The divergent worlds of new media: how policy shapes work in the creative economy. *Review of Policy Research* 12 (4): 543–558.

Devitt, Amy J. 2004. *Writing Genres.* Carbondale, IL: Southern Illinois University Press.

DeNora, Tia. 2003. *After Adorno. Rethinking music sociology.* Cambridge University Press.

Faulkner, Robert. 1983. *Music on Demand. Composers and careers in the Hollywood film industry.* New Brunswick: Transaction Publishers.

Fine, Gary A. 1992. The culture of production: aesthetic choices and constraints in culinary work. *American Journal of Sociology* 97 (5): 1268–1294.

Fussell, Paul. 1980. *Abroad: British literary travelling between the wars.* Oxford University Press.

Gans, Herbert. 1974. *Popular Culture and High Culture: An analysis and evaluation of taste.* New York: Basic Books.

Geertz, Cliford. 1988. *Works and Lives: The anthropologist as author*. Stanford University Press.

Genette, Gerard. 1997. *Paratexts: The thresholds of interpretation*. Cambridge University Press.

Griswold, Wendy. 1987. A methodological framework for the sociology of culture. *Sociological Methodology* 17: 1–35.

Hesmondhalgh, David and Sara Baker. 2011. *Creative Labour: Media work in three cultural industries*. London: Routledge.

Hirsch, Paul M. 1978. Processing fads and fashions: an organization-set analysis of cultural industry systems. *American Journal of Sociology* 77 (4): 639–659.

Holland, Patrick and Graham Huggan. 2000. *Tourists with Typewriters: Critical reflections on contemporary travel writing*. Ann Arbor, MI: University of Michigan Press.

Kennedy, Helen. 2010. Net work: the professionalization of web design. *Media, Culture and Society* 32 (2): 187–203.

Law, John. 2002. Economics as interference. In *Cultural Economy*, ed. Paul du Gay, and Michael Pryke. London: Sage.

Polanyi, Michael. 1998. *Personal Knowledge: Towards a post-critical philosophy*. London: Routledge.

Ryan, Bill. 1991. *Making Capital from Culture: The corporate form of capitalist cultural production*. Berlin: Walter de Gruyter.

Sennett, Richard. 2008. *The Craftsman*. London: Allen Lane.

Shklovsky, Victor. 1965. Art as technique. In *Russian Formalist Criticism: Four essays*, ed. Lee T. Lemon and Marion J. Reiss. Lincoln, NE: University of Nebraska Press.

Thompson, John B. 2010. *Merchants of Culture: The publishing business in the twentieth-first century*. Cambridge: Polity Press.

Todorov, Tzvetan. 1990. *Genres in Discourse*. Cambridge University Press.

# 7 Celebrity status, names, and ideas in the advertising award system

## TIMOTHY DE WAAL MALEFYT

An unusual event occurred in the advertising world in 2008. A digital shop, which had assisted a highly celebrated advertising campaign, complained publicly that the advertising agency which won the award and the awards festival granting the award had failed to give it proper credit for its contribution. The criticism launched by the digital shop was followed by a counter response from the creative director of the winning agency, denying the digital shop any original involvement for the winning idea. This then ignited a debate in the advertising industry over the nature of evaluation in advertising awards. The publicized conflict offers a rare glimpse into the unspoken relationships between advertising agencies and the various contingents that contribute to an advertising campaign. At issue is not only the question of who takes credit for successful advertising campaigns but also from where creative ideas are generated, how they propagate, who contributes what, and to what ends. It also questions the advertising awards system that evaluates ads and grants recognition in the first place.

This chapter explores the struggle over defining a creative narrative claiming idea rights to an award-winning advertising campaign. It traces the trajectory of ideas at each juncture of a campaign: from various ensembles of people and stages of idea development, to how creative ideas were finally evaluated and awarded. The narrative concludes with a description of the contestation over idea rights in which a digital vendor called for a revision of the system. In the end, the awards ceremony remained unchanged. Nevertheless, the conflict exposed a truth in the evaluation of advertising: creative ideas are the valued currency of advertising agencies, and notions of their origination and ownership are not equally shared. Notably, a system that resists change is found in the creative awards ceremony, which is structured to valorize and elevate advertising creatives singularly as legitimate sources of ideas against others who might make counter claims.

To be sure, an elite advertising awards ceremony, such as Cannes, in the South of France, provides a major artistic diversion for advertising creatives apart from their everyday commercial world of advertising. But more significantly, it represents a glamorized site not only for honoring creative talent but also for resolving conflicted categories of advertising work that reveal the other mundane and unpleasant side of advertising. The awards ceremony offers an effective counter system for distinguishing, elevating, and sustaining creative power within the industry. It positions advertising as elevated art apart from advertising as commercial business.

The ensuing discussion will show that for advertising creatives the commercial world of advertising bears an everyday reality that is often considered drudgery and highly competitive. The business end of advertising requires advertising creatives to regularly develop campaigns that are generally dull, selling ordinary products in support of their clients' trade. Creatives labor hard and fast to sell to consumers mundane stuff from fast-food chains to headache remedies. Another commercial reality of advertising requires that advertising agencies frequently compete against other agencies to gain a client's business. An advertising agency as a collective whole labors long hours and often successive weekends to win accounts against other agencies in pitches. In the build-up to a pitch, much of a copywriter and art director's creative effort is dismissed or passed over for other work deemed more appropriate. While the everyday commercial world of advertising requires churning out ads that sell products to consumers and competing against other agencies for new clients, the world of the award ceremonies presents another reality.

Contrary to everyday work in an agency, the award ceremonies represent a special world of elite connections and artistic merit. Agency creatives band together and cooperate to award each other's work. Awards are given at ceremonies for creative ideas that both serve commercial purposes (sell products) and recognize novel approaches to campaigns. The awards thus validate a creative's skill in linking both the mundane consumer/client world and the celebrated world of artistry in distinctive ways. Moreover, this ability to cross domains results not only in winning awards but also in gaining a name. Awards reveal a special system for developing an all-important name in advertising. Because advertising creatives gain a name through winning awards, they also develop an aura to their work, which further imbues their ideas and their advertising agency with charisma and status, and thus provides standout value within a competitive industry. Hence, the advertising award system proves to be a critical evaluator and differentiator of ideas for creative talent, and offers a vital mechanism for generating and advancing celebrity name status in the advertising world.

## Beginning the narrative

Advertising is a highly collaborative enterprise. Any given advertising campaign enlists assistance from a multitude of specialists, both internal and external to the agency. Advertising agencies are organized into a number of divisions that function with distinctive roles and responsibilities that work independently as well as collaboratively. The office of the president is the figurehead; the financial office maintains costs efficiencies; the media-buying office deals with newspaper, TV, Internet, outdoor placement; account services attempts to secure new client brand accounts and maintain current ones; account planning undertakes consumer research for a brand; the creative department dreams up advertisements for clients' brands (Malefyt and Morais 2010; Moeran 1996: 3, 4; Morais 2007).

These departments within an agency are also assisted by various independent vendors which offer support services. These include model agencies, film, photographic, and recording studios, fashion and hairstylists, as well as research vendors such as ethnographic, and focus group or survey researchers. Increasingly, with the rise of digital commerce, digital experts such as website developers, graphic artists, and web advertisers are also enlisted for campaign development and execution. As Becker notes, any work of art involves implicit and explicit contributions from relations among multiple constituents along the way: 'All the arts we know, like all human activities we know, involve the cooperation of others' (Becker 1982: 7). Indeed, the various arrangements of the relations within and external to the agency create the products that the general public sees as advertising (Moeran 1996: 27). Nevertheless, as we shall soon learn, the multiple levels of interaction are also often fraught with potential difficulty (Malefyt and Morais 2012; Moeran 1996: 21). This was the case for the final awards of a campaign made public by an irate digital vendor, where the build-up to the campaign reveals many contributing factors that begin much earlier.

The CINEVISION 'Watcher' project began in May of 2006, when BIG SHOP, a large, traditional, New York-based advertising agency, was given an assignment to explore consumers' attitudes towards the cable network station from a branded perspective.[1] According to the history of CINEVISION the quality of its programing changed people's perceptions of cable viewing and raised the standard of expectations in television. The problem was that other cable TV channels were copying its model of distinct programing. CINEVISION needed to differentiate itself with a new advertising campaign. The research challenge was to discover what CINEVISION as a brand meant to consumers, how it could differentiate itself, and what message would best represent this to audiences. The account team of BIG SHOP sought a novel approach to understand the ways that consumers related to the cable channel and enlisted ethnographic research to find out.

Two anthropologists (Malefyt and a colleague), accompanied by two agency account planners and two videographers, were divided into teams and sent out to homes in the greater New York City area to observe, interview, and film twelve avid TV watchers loyal to CINEVISION. Viewers were screened for age, education, TV viewership, and opinion of CINEVISION. Importantly, the selected viewers were instructed *not* to watch or discuss any CINEVISION programing or content with friends, colleagues, work associates, or family members for two weeks prior to the scheduled interviews. Viewers were also instructed to keep a journal of their thoughts and feelings in place of watching CINEVISION. This methodology of 'deprivation,' requiring avid viewers to *not* 'tune in' to CINEVISION, proved to be critical for uncovering insights among the consumers interviewed.

During in-home interviews, consumers discussed their deep and extended relationship with TV viewing. Most described themselves as unabashed TV watchers who spoke of TV as a source of bonding with their family and friends. They expected 'more' from TV, and CINEVISION delivered what they described as 'authentic, intelligent, and risky programming.' They detailed the artistic merits of CINEVISION programs as possessing 'smart writing, good acting, rich character development, complex plots,' the reason for their loyalty

---

[1] The names BIG SHOP, CINEVISION, BIG DIGITAL, and 'Watcher' used in this chapter are all pseudonyms.

to it. They said its quality programs were the first of their kind to 'get you involved, draw you into the debate.'

This discussion led the anthropologists to observe the highly social nature of CINEVISION viewers and their deep involvement with programing. The anthropologists further noted that viewers spoke of watching TV as if they 'participated' in the episodes. Viewers said that watching CINEVISION episodes on weekends frequently involved inviting friends over to one's home as a social event. The 'ritual' marked off special time for viewers, requiring certain foods for the night, favorite seats taken, and cell phones turned off. Especially on Sunday night, CINEVISION original programing began a social 'ritual' that initiated their whole week.

Nevertheless, it was through the forced 'deprivation' of *not* watching CINEVISION that the anthropologists discovered a deeper social meaning of the brand to its viewers. When program content was removed from their lives, viewers claimed they could no longer properly engage in conversations with their friends, family, and colleagues. Not being able to watch CINEVISION had a profound effect on them socially. Viewers said during normal activities at work or out with friends they felt 'out of the loop' or 'disconnected from others.' The power of the brand lay in fostering discussions and debates about related issues in everyday life. Watching the cable network played a critical role in mediating personal relations and allowing viewers to share opinions with others, which linked to concepts of self-identity. The deprivation technique proved to be highly innovative in uncovering and exploring consumer insights for the brand.

## The agency meeting and idea transformations

Back at the agency, a briefing was set up by the account team to discuss the ideas garnered in research for creative implications. The ethnographic research findings were discussed for how they might stimulate new thoughts and offer new directions for the brand. According to the planners, there were plenty of ideas gathered in research that were presented in a deck and also developed into an ethnographic film from the interviews. The account planners led a discussion based on the anthropologists' research, detailing the consumers' unique relation to CINEVISION compared with 'regular' TV. The planners sought to harness the social role that CINEVISION plays in people's lives and so developed a Creative Brief to instruct the creative team on key consumer insights.

The Creative Brief, a one-page document that leads creative direction like a blueprint and is written by the account planners and approved by account executives, sought an inspiring way to motivate the agency creative team. The Brief instructed the creative team to persuade enthusiasts who demand a variety of high-level entertainment to relish the enriching CINEVISION experience. It also encouraged it to inspire CINEVISION fans with bold and intelligent stories. Responding to the socializing behavior that the interviewed fans displayed, the Brief stated that CINEVISION wasn't merely a cable network. Rather, it was an 'essential cultural force' that motivated people to socialize and tell stories to others.

The advertising creatives responded with enthusiasm to the research findings that CINEVISION viewers 'needed' to socialize with others. The agency creatives were then instructed to develop a multimedia campaign based on the idea of storytelling. The charge proclaimed by the chief creative director was to make 'CINEVISION the greatest storyteller in the world.' The campaign idea was to extend beyond TV advertisements in a series of connected interactive media that was 'risky, authentic, and provocative,' to use the fans' own words, and in a big way that was unprecedented. The production team, briefed with the assignment, partnered with a hired vendor, BIG DIGITAL, known for digital creativity, to carry out the execution in a multimedia campaign. What is not known is how exactly the 'storyteller' idea evolved into such a groundbreaking execution.

A new CINEVISION campaign launched in the summer of 2007 with an on-the-ground 'guerilla' marketing approach. Street teams were sent out and targeted heavily trafficked pedestrian areas of New York City. They handed out special invitations to passersby for a summer's evening event. The invitations directed people to the Lower East Side of Manhattan where, using two high-definition projectors that BIG DIGITAL had designed for the event, a film was projected on to the outside wall of a building, with an illusion that the wall itself had been removed. Audiences had a virtual cut-away view into the fictitious homes of eight different apartments. Attending viewers on the street could hold up their invitations and see clues to the different stories being projected on the wall. The stories in each apartment were dramas about life, death, birth, and redemption, each of them linked to the dramas taking place in other apartments. The promotion for the story also aired on TV and in movie theaters. The teaser campaign in movie theaters and on TV read: 'See what people do, when they think no one is watching.' The promotion drove viewers to a website. The website showcased the same film that was projected onto the wall for the event. Audiences online could zoom in and follow the stories of each apartment and discern what was going on. Viewers were also invited to go to CINEVISION on-demand to see a created film, 'The Watcher.' The film allowed audiences to see through the eyes of the Watcher (much like the Hitchcock film, 'Rear Window,' with Jimmy Stewart and Grace Kelly). The website also encouraged people to connect to a blog, where the story became more involved.

New York media raved about the advertised campaign. BIG SHOP and CINEVISION garnered much public attention for it. *New York Magazine*, for instance, lauded the project as 'brilliant and high-brow' in its approval ratings.[2] CINEVISION fans shared their positive opinions about the campaign on online blogs and forums. More than 1 million viewers sought out the website within the first three weeks of its launch. Moreover, over half of CINEVISION loyalists also watched the stories. The campaign line read: 'There are stories. Then there are CINEVISION stories. It's not TV. It's CINEVISION.' The campaign was hailed a great success.

## Conflict over creative 'ownership'

In 2008, BIG SHOP won top honors at the awards festival in Cannes, which represents the pinnacle of achievement in the advertising awards. The 2007 CINEVISION 'Watcher' campaign was deemed by the Cannes jury most innovative for its broad use of a single branded campaign idea that crossed over multiple consumer mediums: from outdoors, to online digital, to film and TV broadcast. It earned two Grand Prix trophies in the outdoors and promotion categories, plus another five Gold, one Silver, and one Bronze medals in media, cyber, design, promotion, and film. The credit for most original campaign idea went solely to the creative team of BIG SHOP, and in particular to its chief creative officer.

---

[2] *New York Magazine*'s 'approval matrix', July 16, 2007.

What the judges at Cannes emphasized in their evaluation of the CINEVISION campaign was its originality and ability to disseminate an idea. They said that the campaign both 'captured the medium of outdoors' and integrated with other mediums across the consumer marketplace. 'Often you find work that is just replicated from other mediums and converted to outdoors,' said the Cannes jury president, the regional executive creative director of Asia Pacific for a major advertising agency in Mumbai, India,[3] 'but this campaign idea captured the sense of the medium and innovated within the medium.'

Another juror representative, the chief creative officer from a Los Angeles advertising agency, announced that the CINEVISION campaign had brought about a 'change of mind' among the jury. He announced that the campaign was evaluated for its 'paradigm shift.' 'We saw a lot of great advertising, but this was a signal for something entirely different. It was part of a bigger picture and it was the initiator . . . a catalyst,' that succeeded across categories. He continued, stating that the 'average consumer looks at a billboard for three seconds, this thing captivates you for four minutes . . . It's redefining categories.'[4]

The week after BIG SHOP was highly awarded at Cannes, the digital shop hired by the agency, BIG DIGITAL, which had originated the work for the campaign, publicly contested the award by claiming that it deserved more creative recognition than it had received. The CEO of the digital group argued that a single award given by the jurors to the agency did not reflect the reality of advertising. He explained that advertising awards, like those given at Cannes, permitted only a single winner for each award and contended that 'marketing campaigns are more complex today, engaging consumers in more ways and places. Advertising agencies are not the lone source of creativity that they were in pre-Internet days.'

The chief creative officer of BIG SHOP then countered this claim, stating that his agency 'was the source of the idea' and so deserved all the credit it had received. 'Ideas are timeless,' he continued. 'Ideas are what inspire people. Ideas are the root of execution. [We] thought of the idea, shot the idea, then brought in BIG DIGITAL to do what they do. They did a great job. What's the issue?'

[3] *Advertising Age*, June 17, 2008.    [4] *Ibid.*

For his part, the CEO of the digital group challenged this counter-argument by claiming: 'This isn't about digital agencies getting credit, and it's not just about BIG SHOP and BIG DIGITAL. It's a larger problem and it's about shifting the tenor of the industry overall. We are in a brave new world, a networked world, and you will never find a single agency that can handle all the various works of executions. Anything that runs against innovation and collaboration succeeding should ultimately be choked out.'[5]

The publicized fractional fighting between agencies stirred up a lively discussion among advertising and media representatives. At issue was the question of who should receive credit for an advertising success. The parleying responses revealed much about the nature of idea generation and working relationships in the advertising industry. Discussions deliberated over who was, and who was not, acknowledged for idea generation in a successful campaign. Opinions were divided. Some wrote that BIG DIGITAL should have received more recognition, while others wrote that they did receive attention and that it was their job as hired venders to work for the advertising agency. The author of the *Advertising Age* article, Rupal Parekh, wrote that a new model of relations was emerging in the ways that agencies acted more like 'hubs that marshal other resources, from digital experts to production companies, on behalf of their clients.' Others disputed this model, claiming that relations were still hierarchical and that a vender's role was to 'serve' the advertising creatives.

Curiously, what those involved in the discussions did not dispute, and therefore complacently accepted, was an assumption about where creative ideas originate. Whether vendors, such as digital shops, received more or less credit for their *executional work* was disputable, the credit from where the idea *originated* was not. Discussants assumed that creative ideas are generated by advertising agencies. This is telling since all of the commentators were mostly senior members of other advertising agencies, and agreed that the initiation of ideas and flow of creativity begins with agency creative executives and continues into the production and execution of campaigns. What was not considered or debated was how creative ideas often emerge from small adjustments, trial and error, and finally larger breakthroughs, which lead to a new way of thinking (Sawyer 2007). To be sure, in advertising, production

[5] Quoted in *Advertising Age*, June 25, 2008.

adjustments are continuously and collaboratively made at various junctures, and therefore often go unnoticed. The discussants' complacent agreement only reinforced the notion that creative ideas are legitimized and authenticated solely by creatives in advertising.

Notably, multiple versus singular authorship is treated differently in other creative industries. For example, in the film industry (see Chapter 8) the making of a movie requires extensive collaboration, which results in the awkward long list of credits fraught with tradition and symbolic capital. In the writing industry (see Chapter 1), the sole credit goes to the writer, despite the myriad negotiations and discussions that occur throughout the process. In the advertising industry, advertising creatives are esteemed for their role as 'idea generators' who then hand off concepts for others to execute. They are 'the arbiter of ideas' in spite of the multiple others who assist in bringing campaigns to fruition.

We can now explore the ways in which the awards system in advertising, and the judges – themselves creatives in advertising agencies – foster evaluative practices to sustain a network of elite relations apart from outside vendors, commercial interests, and internal agency departments. The awards system accomplishes this by holding awards *for* the separation of ideas, and acknowledging creative work *apart* from campaign executions, advertising production, and consumer research – even though these elements necessarily contribute to the overall advertising campaign. Importantly, the system of assembly and cooperation among advertising creatives contrasts with the everyday commercial reality of advertising. The awards ceremony offers a special site where creatives gather to acknowledge and validate each other's artistry, which contrasts with the competitive rivalry among agencies outside in the marketplace and the everyday labor of making mundane ads for consumers.

## Awarding honor: collaboration against competitiveness and ordinariness

In the commercial world of advertising, agencies compete against each other for client business. As scholars have shown (Miller 1997; Moeran 1996; Schudson 1984), fierce competition among agencies often leads to outright animosity, as they are 'constantly looking for ways to poach clients from each other' (Miller 1997: 160). Economic capital and cultural capital are gained through securing clients from winning campaign ideas and this represents the business end of advertising. Given that lucrative client accounts are hard to come by, and client loyalty to agencies has declined over the years, the competition for, and shifting around of, 'blue chip' accounts can appear like a 'game of musical chairs' (Moeran 1996: 45). Gaining client accounts is further complicated today by many new shops and digital companies also competing for attention. The influx of new technologies, media platforms, and novel ways of marketing to consumers adds challenges to the practice of pitching business and securing clients (Creative X 2011).

Another commercial reality of advertising is that much of the creative work in making ads is quite mundane. The so-called creative flair, writes Moeran, generally tends to be a 'humdrum affair' (1996: 134). This is because filling out all the required demands of a client's marketing and advertising campaign leaves little room for novelty and experimentation. In fact, the need or requirement for something 'fresh and different are all too rare – perhaps ten percent of total output at the most' states Moeran (citing Mayle 1990: 58). Moreover, much of what is labored over and dramatized in advertising campaigns is quite trivial. A great deal of advertising treats ordinary and mundane products of everyday life (pharmaceutical drugs, cosmetics, soaps, cleaners, soft drinks, toilet paper, liquors, and beers). In dealing with the everyday, advertising 'attempts to make the insignificant seem significant,' writes Kottman (2010: 31), and so creatives must regularly 'deal with the trivial' and accentuate brand differences among ordinary commodities to stand out as exceptional in the minds of consumers.

The advertising award system, however, operates against these currents of ordinariness and competitive rivalry. It is a venue that celebrates ideas and their originators for artistic value, apart from economic capital. A creative's artistic, and hence symbolic, currency is sorted out and elevated by the unique structure of the award ceremonies. Since award ceremonies, such as Cannes, are a regularized activity, occur in a designated place, for a discrete period of time, with certain objectives and evaluations carried out, they offer a frame of analysis for understanding specific roles, relations, and divisions in the agency world (Goffman 1979; Malefyt and Morais 2012; Moeran 2005: 43–57). Frames in a business context are not only useful for understanding agency creative life but also for interpreting and understanding various sets of relationships, both in and out of the agency (Moeran 2005: 63–79). The judging structure at Cannes and other advertising awards ceremonies is composed of a collection of senior-level advertising creatives, themselves from rival agencies. Even though agencies compete for clients economically outside in the consumer marketplace, advertising creatives collaborate artistically within the awards ceremonies to evaluate each other's work. They cooperate as a jury to award honors for the 'best' ideas to certain creatives. In this way, advertising creatives develop autonomy in formulating their own set of rules of form and style, from which they evaluate their ideas among themselves (Bourdieu 1993: 112–115). As such, judges in award ceremonies form an elite system of collective artists that operates in a field of 'restricted production' within and counter to the larger arena of commercial economic production. This field of restricted production creates a specialized frame, where creatives assemble as judges to make sense of their own community and their actions taken therein (Moeran 2005: 14). In this frame of interaction, their work assumes 'artistic value' and is evaluated as such, which contrasts the outside world's economic objective of selling goods in mass markets for commercial purposes. The frame of the elite system in the awards ceremony is thus developed relationally and in opposition to the proliferation of mass advertisements for a generalized public.

This frame owes its position within the structure to the opposition between a field of restricted production that produces artistic ideas, and the field of large-scale works for the general consumption of goods. This oppositional relation makes sense when we compare ideas valued for artistic merit and those valued for selling goods to consumers.

In the advertising and marketing world, advertising creatives are known for their idiosyncrasies and oddities that stand them apart. Since the beginning of the so-called 'creative revolution' in the 1960s, advertising creatives in European and US agencies have been distinguished and valorized for their quirky social behavior, long hair, and idiosyncratic actions (Moeran 2005). The creative artist is esteemed for being highly individualistic and unique. He (or she) is one who sanctifies an idea for a product that he 'discovered,' which would remain otherwise a 'mere natural resource' (Bourdieu 1993: 76). Consumers, in contrast, represent a 'natural resource' and broad material base from which artistic ideas are developed, and which constitute the raw material or data that are ultimately transformed into unique campaign images.

Consumers as a commercial category and the object of daily creative work are unexceptional and standardized, compared with the highly idiosyncratic nature of advertising creatives. The difference between the idealized character of the advertising creative and the ordinary consumer is that no one cares what the consumer does as an individual, only what she does collectively. Uniformity is desired from a targeting standpoint since, in typical marketing studies, consumers are recruited for common characteristics among cohorts of other 'like' users. Brand targeting and forecasting – against which ads are created, produced, and distributed – require a baseline on which to build marketing plans, since consumers reflect what is essential to the brand target (Malefyt 2003). Deviation from an average not only threatens the integrity of a marketing plan but also confounds a 'natural resource' from which creatives transform 'raw material' into a 'cooked' execution (Moeran 1996: 126–132 citing Levi-Strauss 1966).

Nevertheless, consumers are vital to advertising creatives in several ways: as a resource from which to draw initial campaign insights, and as a final destination toward which campaigns are launched and distributed. Creatives acquire ideas from reports of consumers' relations to brands so they, in turn, can transform cultural capital (the meaning of brands to consumers) into symbolic capital (advertising ideas for consumers), and then back into economic capital (consumers' purchase and use of brands). Consumers complete a relationship with advertisers and their clients in the dialogic exchange of ideas and business (McCabe and Malefyt 2010). From another perspective, consumers represent the cultural and economic capital that consumes the symbolic capital which creatives produce, transforming products into brand images in advertising campaigns. In the same way that consumers are intrinsic to the structure of commercial capital, their relationship to creatives as symbolic capital is oppositional. Consumers aid advertising creatives as a source material, but creatives are charged with molding that material into something artistic and unique. Furthermore, since consumers represent a 'natural resource' from which ideas are transformed, others associated with consumers, such as market researchers, data collectors, and consumer anthropologists, stand in opposition to creatives. In an elite economy of restricted production, market researchers and anthropologists are typically not elite.

The awards system, like Cannes, represents a frame for evaluating the symbolic merits of an artist's ideas, apart from other influences, yet within the larger frame of commercial economic interests. This is evident in the lead judge's criteria for the winning BIG SHOP's campaign when he stated that 'Watcher' won because it both 'captured the medium and innovated within the medium.' In other words, the campaign represented the artist's innovation for an idea within a medium and also played to the commercial interests of that medium. The awards system thus recognizes and evaluates artists who stand apart as innovative and original, and who also operate within the commercial necessities of creating popular campaigns. This recognition leads to winning awards for creative work, and eventually to winning a name.

## The name economy

According to Levi-Strauss (1966), names are strategically used by 'natives' to classify, distinguish, and elevate cultural phenomena. Brian Moeran (1996, 2003) develops this notion further to show that celebrity names are powerful symbols which circulate in the public domain and operate across three distinct but interconnected social realms: individual names, products (brands), and corporations. Names are used in these realms as promotional strategies to advance celebrity fame, elevate brand recognition, and increase corporate association, and to link different fields of cultural production (fashion, sports, film, and so on) through advertised endorsements with other brands (Moeran 2003: 300). As such, names are powerful symbolic strategies that both elevate and distinguish, while they connect across to disseminate cultural material.

The 'name economy' (Moeran 2003) represents a potent transfer system for increasing symbolic and commercial capital. Celebrities such as sports figures, movie stars, and fashion models develop names that garner much attention. Corporate sponsors seek to use these names for product endorsements. Because names have auras they also imbue objects and brands with charisma and status. An important feature of using a name is its ability to cross, connect, or transfer *across* domains – such as cultural, economic, and symbolic categories of society. Sean Connery's rugged yet refined film character when associated with a 12-year-old scotch allows the scotch to be recognized in multiple settings. Celebrity names are thus 'cultural mediators' effectively transferring symbolic capital and associations across fields of cultural production (Moeran 2003: 308).

Likewise, the advertising creative awards ceremony relies on the name economy to develop its ideas of creativity and charisma for a creative person. The advertising awards ceremony is a naming system that validates and celebrates a creative's ability to cross and connect advertising domains: mundane with sublime, commercial with artistic, functional with inspirational. By winning awards in these ceremonies the advertising creative gains a name, which generates attention. Advertising agencies then leverage this name against other agencies back in the commercial world to gain more clients. Because creative names gain auras with success they also imbue their ideas and associated advertising agencies with charisma and status, and thus provide celebrity value within the industry.

It is the quality to both elevate and distinguish while connecting across cultural material that is an important characteristic of the awards system for generating celebrity names. Advertising creatives become distinguished names by winning awards for generating ideas *that also connect* across multiple fields of cultural production. They gain celebrity status as a name and increase their worth to an agency by winning awards for creative ideas that connect artistic with commercial categories.

This is evident in one of the judges' comments for BIG SHOP's award when he stated that the creative work was 'an initiator' and 'catalyst' that 'crosses boundaries or barriers ... the beginning of joining of hands of different mediums together' (Parish 2008). The 'Watcher' campaign was awarded for an idea that crossed commercial media categories of outdoor displays, digital, print, and TV. In other words, the winning creative name at BIG SHOP effectively transferred symbolic capital across other fields of cultural and economic production. Advertising campaigns are thus awarded to a creative name for his or her ability to cross consumer mediums and link various executions through a singular idea.

At the center of a celebrated name lies the notion of a charismatic artist. Bourdieu reminds us that the 'charismatic ideology' is the ultimate basis of belief in the value of a work of art (1993: 76). Walter Benjamin (1969) concurs that an original work of art has a unique 'aura' that cannot be copied, and through distance of time and space gains authentic value. Names are like brands that are unique and differentiated. According to Callon *et al.* (2002), a specialized good, like a brand, is meaningful through a relational dynamic that has particular intrinsic value. It becomes *singularized* beyond its generalized or functional value. Thus, the basis of the artist's role in advertising is to gain charismatic *and* singular identity through distance and distinction, like a brand. The ideology of branding a name directs attention to a creative author while suppressing the question of what or who else authorizes the author (Bourdieu 1993: 76–77). So, even when an advertising campaign is aided by multiple sources of innovative research, collaborative meetings, and exchanges with digital teams, these 'others' become peripheral to the centrality of the unique charismatic artist. Ideas from artists are evaluated and awarded for their singularity, separateness, and disjuncture from others – for their 'paradigm shifting' originality, as we heard from one judge. Creativity here is judged in temporal acts, differentiated and individualized, apart from a generalized world of others. This is what Ingold and Hallam (2007: 5–7) describe as the novelty of exceptional acts imagined of charismatic individuals who achieve something extraordinary against a mass of conformity and standardization. In other words, the creative is evaluated paradoxically as an artistic individual *against* a world of mass consumption, as he also works *within* and across a field of commercial and popular interests.

Back in the commercial world of the agency, the creative name is valued for his promotional significance, which is leveraged in competitive pitches and presentations for gaining clients against other agencies. Presentations are part of the political economy of values (Moeran 1996: 93, 94); they are performances where all the activity of a given participant on a given occasion serves to influence in any way the other participants (Goffman 1959: 15). The essence of a presentation is *direct interaction* meant to influence others (Moeran 1996: 86). Creative names are thus valued for their charisma and charm in presenting ideas in agency pitches, where business is won (or lost) through client interaction. The creative idea as well as the creative himself is on stage. As one creative director is quoted as saying: 'The spotlight is on you. You have the chance to convince someone that something you have created is worth the world seeing' (in Malefyt and Morais 2012). In other words, ideas are evaluated not as abstract thoughts but as personified embodiments of the creative individual. Copywriters do not merely present advertising ideas, they present *themselves* (Kover 1995: 604). The presence of the creative and the performance of the idea become one. This notion is affirmed by the commentator who mentioned that 'bigger agencies often *own the relationships* and are able to *sell through a BIG IDEA* that a small interactive shop would never be able to convince a client to do' (Parekh 2008). Creatives guard ideas personally because in a literal and figurative sense, creatives *are* their ideas.

Since a name links with a particular creative individual, it has to be singular and distinct to be authentic. As such, creative ideas are always presented *directly and personally* by the lead creative themselves, and not channeled through others, such as department heads or even the advertising agency CEO or president. The creative's work therefore cannot be associated with others, shared by committee, or attributed to anything else. This means not only that the creative is and has to be sole originator of an idea but also, in the act of presenting that idea to others (in meetings, pitches, and so forth), that none other can replace, present, or fill in for the creative himself. Since advertising agencies and advertising creatives do not produce material objects – commodity 'things' as their clients do for consumers – but rather ideas, the ideas take on objectified meaning as a valued currency. The creative *is* a name and the name needs winning ideas and celebrity recognition to validate, sustain, and distinguish it. Thus the awards ceremonies give great power, personality, and further status by naming the creative individual. This makes the singular production and individual owner-ship of ideas all the more critical in a competitive environment.

Names are thus used in advertising award ceremonies as promo-tional strategies to distinguish and elevate campaign ideas *and* to advertise a sole individual as originator of a winning idea. Celebrated names thrive on narratives in media and agency pitches that glorify their artistry, individualism, and originality. In fact, we may note that awards are given after the fact, since a name must prove a degree of commercial success and gain media attention which 'looks back' at a narrative of his uniqueness and artistry. Even if scholarship indicates that creativity is rarely the result of isolated individual acts, but rather of collaborative efforts and achieved over time (Hallam and Ingold 2007; Moeran and Strandgaard Pedersen 2011; Sawyer 2007), the awards system evaluates creative ideas as distinctive and detached, attributed to the 'aura,' fame, and charismatic singularity of a name. As such, the advertising awards ceremony both separates and distin-guishes from others the putative efforts of advertising creatives, as it elevates to celebrity status those creative names from whom campaign ideas ostensibly originate.

## Conclusion

Ironically, in a fast-paced consumer marketplace that promotes inno-vation and forward thinking, the evaluative framework for the crea-tive awards ceremonies indicates that the advertising industry maintains conservative practices. What becomes evident in this 'tournament of values' (Appadurai 1986; Moeran and Strandgaard Pedersen 2011) is not merely a contestation over claiming rights of one creative against other departments, hired vendors, and support relations. The conflict indicates an adherence to old ways of practicing advertising while resisting the encroachment of new ways: a 'survival' from another time.

The evaluation of creative ideas in the advertising awards system thus reinforces practices of modernity and tradition at the same time. Modernity, on the one hand, is produced in the way advertising creatives are awarded for utilizing new mediums (the Internet) or for reinventing old mediums (outdoor) to transmit novel ideas in campaigns. Awards are given for 'integrated campaigns' that link an advertising idea with newer technologies, and execute a campaign idea across multiple points of engagement in the consumer marketplace. Tradition, on the other hand, is reproduced in the way judges of award ceremonies recognize creativity as a singular idea of a creative person. They further promote 'innovation narratives' to which they attach a name, by 'reading creativity backwards in terms of its results, instead of forwards, in terms of the movements that gave rise to them' (Ingold and Hallam 2007: 2–3). A hierarchical structure and elite community are thus maintained among advertising creatives in advertising agencies, which both preserve artistic identity and link idea generation to an agency's unique competency in the marketplace against other agencies. The award system celebrates creative names to elevate individual talent in advertising agencies and to promote the agency through symbolic capital, which then bolsters cultural capital for its clients. While advertising campaigns are developed and executed by various departments and vendors as an economic product, creative ideas that generate celebrity status and symbolic value for an artist are guarded as a benefit of the name economy.

## References

Appadurai, Arjun. 1986. *The Social Life of Things: Commodities in cultural perspective*. Cambridge University Press.

Becker, Howard. 1982. *Art Worlds*. Berkeley and Los Angeles: University of California Press.

Benjamin, Walter. 1969. The work of art in the age of mechanical reproduction. In *Illuminations*, ed. Hannah Arendt. New York: Schocken.

Bourdieu, Pierre. 1993. *The Field of Cultural Production.* New York: Columbia University Press.

Callon, Michel, Cecile Meadel, and Vololona Rabeharosoa. 2002. The economy of qualities. *Economy and Society* 31 (2): 194–217.

Creative X. 2011. The industry doesn't need a Bogusky. In *Advertising Age.* Online at: http://adage.com/print/148251, January 17.

Goffman, Erving. 1959. *The Presentation of Self in Everyday Life.* New York: Anchor Books.

1979. *Gender Advertisements,* p.10. Cambridge, MA: Harvard University Press.

Hallam, Elizabeth and Tim Ingold, eds. 2007. *Creativity and Cultural Improvisation.* Oxford: Berg.

Ingold, Tim and Elizabeth Hallam. 2007. Creativity and cultural improvisation: an introduction. In *Creativity and Cultural Improvisation,* ed. Elizabeth Hallam and Tim Ingold. Oxford: Berg.

Kottman, E. John. 2010. Truth and the image of advertising. In *Advertising: Critical readings,* Vol. 4, ed. B. Moeran, pp. 29–32. Oxford: Berg.

Kover, Arthur J. 1995. Copywriters' implicit theories of communication: An exploration. *Journal of Consumer Research* 21 (4): 596–611.

Levi-Strauss, Claude. 1966. *The Savage Mind.* University of Chicago Press.

Malefyt, Timothy de Waal 2003. Models, metaphors and client relations. In *Advertising Cultures,* ed. Timothy de waal Malefyt and Brian Moeran, pp. 139–163. Oxford: Berg.

Malefyt, Timothy de Waal and Robert J. Morais. 2010. Creativity, brands, and the ritual process: confrontation and resolution in advertising agencies. *Culture and Organization* 16 (4): 333–347.

2012. *Advertising and Anthropology: Ethnographic practices and cultural perspectives.* Oxford: Berg.

Mayle, Peter. 1990. *Up the Agency: The snakes and ladders of the advertising business.* London: Pan books.

McCabe, Maryann and Timothy de Waal Malefyt. 2010. Brands, interactivity, and contested fields: exploring production and consumption in Cadillac and Infiniti automobile advertising campaigns. *Human Organization* 69 (3): 252–262.

Miller, Daniel. 1997. *Capitalism: An ethnographic approach.* Oxford: Berg.

Moeran, Brian. 1996. *A Japanese Advertising Agency.* Honolulu: University of Hawaii Press.

2003. Celebrities and the name economy. In *Anthropological Perspectives on Economic Development and Integration,* Vol. 22: 299–321, ed. Norberz Dannhaeuser and Cynthia Werner. Amsterdam: Elsevier.

2005. *The Business of Ethnography: Strategic exchanges, people and organizations.* Oxford: Berg.

Moeran, Brian and Jesper Strandgaard Pedersen, eds. 2011. *Negotiating Values in the Creative Industries: Fairs, festivals and competitive events,* Cambridge University Press.

Morais, Robert J. 2007. Conflict and confluence in advertising meetings. *Human Organization* 66 (2): 150–159.

*New York Magazine.* 2007. The approval matrix. July 16. Online at: http:// nymag.com/arts/all/approvalmatrix/34444/.

Parekh, Rupal. 2008. HBO 'Voyeur' collaborator calls Cannes prizes unfair. *Advertising Age,* June 25. Online at: http://adage.com/article/special-report-cannes-2008/hbo-voyeur-collaborator-calls-cannes-prizes-unfair/127988/.

Parish, Nick. 2008. BBDO, New York, wins outdoor Grand Prix for 'Voyeur'. *Advertising Age,* June 17.

Sawyer, R. Keith. 2007. *Group Genius: The creative power of collaboration.* New York: Basic Books.

Schudson, Michael. 1984. *Advertising, the Uneasy Persuasion.* New York: Basic Books.

# 8 Evaluation in film festival prize juries

CHRIS MATHIEU AND MARIANNE BERTELSEN

This chapter focuses on juries which award prizes at film festivals. A prize jury usually awards a preordained set of prizes to films from a preselected slate according to criteria that are usually up to the jury itself to formally or informally establish and administer. The consequences of film festival prize jury allocations can affect many different groups and individuals. The most obvious beneficiaries are those who are associated with the films and roles that win prizes, although what the tangible benefits of winning them are is still a matter of debate and depends on both the prize and the festival concerned. The film festivals themselves and their leadership are also impacted by the jury and its decisions, since these may build or erode legitimacy and publicity for a particular festival.

Despite the relatively widespread interest in film festivals (de Valck 2007; Iordinova and Rhyne 2009; Mezias *et al.* 2011) and prizes and awards in the film industry (Dodds and Holbrook 1988; English 2005; Lincoln and Allen 2012), surprisingly little scholarly research has been carried out on *how* decisions about which films and individual efforts to be rewarded are arrived at (one exception is de Valck and Soetman 2010). This is paradoxical, given that festival prizes are a crucial aspect of film festivals, and a central motive for film companies' participation in festivals, to the point that they may withhold release of films or speed up production in order to have a film shown in competition at significant premier festivals.[1]

Factors that might explain this have to do with the high visibility of juries and its members on the one hand (that is, jury composition is usually highly publicized by the festival, and the jury is frequently seen

---

[1] 'Premier' festival in this sense denotes festivals where the films in competition must be premiered at the festival, and not be in general release prior to it. There are also festivals that show and have films in competition that are already in general release.

and visually depicted at the festival site and in media reports) and on the other the closed-door and secretive nature of the jury's work. Visibility gives the impression of familiarity with, comprehension of, and confidence in the jury. The closed nature of jury work makes it difficult for researchers to access its actual processes first hand and heightens the sense of mystique, suspense, and surprise about what may emerge, leading to (publicity-generating) speculation where nobody outside the jury itself really knows what is going on, and even jury members may still be very much in the dark about a result right up to the final decision. A parallel can here be drawn to the nature of restaurant ranking systems discussed by Christensen and Strandgaard Pedersen in Chapter 9. In our case, film festivals can be perceived as arenas where the standards for what is 'good' and what is 'bad' film are explored, negotiated, and developed. In this, festival juries have a leading role, but only the results (usually with just a short justification) and not the process are made public. This opens up for both expert and popular speculation about the process, and heightens its publicity.

In this chapter, we look into the black box of prize-jury work. Via our informants we first examine context-setting issues – what role juries play at festivals and how the selection of jury members takes place (compositional issues) – before moving on to issues relating directly to the evaluation process – how directions (or lack thereof) given to juries impact their evaluations and work; how individual evaluations of films and artistic contributions are made; and how the collective process of evaluation and awarding takes place.

Since direct access to actual jury processes is virtually impossible, as they are invariably closed-doors processes, this chapter relies on accounts of such processes by twelve Danish filmworkers who, all told, had sat on roughly seventy film festival prize juries, ranging from 'A' to minor festivals, and including documentary, fiction, short, and genre film juries. Most of the twelve have sat on juries in at least one well-recognized festival such as Cannes, Berlin, Venice, Toronto, Sundance, Busan, San Sebastian, Karlovy Vary, Amsterdam, or Copenhagen (the last two being renowned documentary festivals). Thus, what is reported on here is not a single process. Nor is it even restricted to a single film festival's jury processes (as in de Valck and Soetman 2010, who focus on one festival), but covers multiple jury processes over time. As rendered here, film festival prize-jury work is a historic and multi-sited episodic 'phenomenon' that is internally heterogeneous, with both convergent and divergent aspects. Like most phenomena, there are both objective facts (such as who sat in the juries, which films were awarded which prizes, which films competed, and so on) and myriad subjective interpretations.

In the following analysis of film festival prize juries, multiple opinions are expressed – some of them contradictory. This can have to do with different experiences at different festivals, as well as differing opinions about degrees or levels of phenomena experienced, and their desirability. To give a more substantive 'feel' for how many of the described processes play out, composite vignettes based on the accounts given in the interviews are presented. These vignettes are directly based on quotes and descriptive information from one or more of our informants. None of the substantive content is fabricated, but in some cases similar observations are synthesized from different interviewees. The vignettes allow us to *consolidate* information that was given at various stages of an interview with a single informant, as well as illustrate points that traverse the experiences of different informants.

The jury process starts with what in social psychology would be called basic 'group formation,' entailing learning both the formal and informal expectations on and of the group and its members. This process is usually planned for and facilitated by the convenors of the festival in terms of explicit information to the jury, as well as social opportunities for group members to get to know one another. Prior knowledge about the other members, the festival, and jury work plays a significant part in this initial phase (as illustrated in the vignette below), a phase where basic viewpoints and informal status orders are explored or developed.

## Juries: composition and deliberation

*The group sitting at the table looks like a Benetton commercial for film making: each person – to the extent possible – different in what continent they originate from, their occupation in filmmaking, their gender, and age. One could almost picture the people in charge of recruiting the jury: 'Well, if we pick her, we can check off Asian, woman, and producer. And if we pick him, we can check off writer, director, American, and male.' One thing they have in common is that they are 'a name' in the industry – an old, well-established name, or a new, interesting name; usually they have also recently been involved in a successful or prestigious production – all of which is relevant for boost-ing the festival's image as being up to date in the industry.*

The jury president welcomes them and lays out the ground rules for the meeting of the day. His experience tells him that people will comply with the 'raise your hand to speak' rule and keep a constructive diplo-matic focus on the positive qualities of the films for the first hour or so. As the group gets more familiar, formality will dissipate and eventually also even politeness. This, in his opinion, isn't necessarily a bad thing, as an honest and open discussion is what is aimed at. The night before, most of the group had gathered for an unofficial welcoming dinner, and based on this people were already quite comfortable in each other's presence. The group was already beginning to discover or confirm which genres people were leaning toward, who the loud people were, who one might connect with, and so on. A very good start for a healthy discussion, he thought. 'As you know, we will have two shorter meet-ings following the first and second third of the films, where we will deliberate and agree upon a shortlist of three to four films, which will go on to be discussed at the third and final deliberation.'

Everyone around the table nods in agreement. It's almost impossible to keep the entire line-up of films in one's head, let alone evaluate, discuss, and compare them against each other cumulatively, as several days can pass since seeing the first, and only a few hours since seeing the most recent. 'Let's try to keep the initial meetings at three to four hours and the final deliberation at four to five hours. The goal of course is to reach a shared agreement, but there is no point in wasting anyone's time by discussing pointless candidates.'

The group nods again. They have all heard stories about juries sitting up all night, trying to agree on a winner; having members walk out in protest or mere frustration; ending up taking a vote and agreeing on a winner that was no one's favorite.

The central characteristic and reason for convening juries is to be able to gain a *reasoned* assessment and verdict from a group selected on some form of representational criteria on a specific given topic or matter. Two things are thus of central importance – the composition of the jury, and the process whereby it reaches its judgment. With regard to composition, juries tend to be of two types: expert juries and lay/peer juries. Lay/peer juries are convened to gain an assessment of what conforms to the norms of the given social group from which peers are drawn. Expert juries are convened to make assessments that require knowledge, insight, or experience that exceeds common or lay understandings, but that also recognize that purely technical assessments (which could be made by a single trained individual) are not possible, and thus several individuals with similar, complementary, or divergent expert backgrounds are convened.

Most research on jury processes focuses on one or sometimes both of these issues (Neilson and Winter 2008)[2] – the impact of composition in terms of 'peerness' and representation on jury outcomes and processes (York and Cornwell 2006), and the 'quality of deliberation' understood in terms of the opportunity to make arguments and have the content of arguments rather than other individual or social factors impact the outcome of the jury process. Gastil *et al.* (2007) operationalize the concept of deliberation in terms of sufficient time and respectful attention accorded to both the opinions of all jurors and the facts of the case and instructions given to the jury. Deliberation can thus be summarized in terms of collective and collaborative attention paid to discerning the rules of the context one is in and how one should operate, establishing the facts of the matters at hand, and respectfully listening to and considering the perspectives and opinions of all jury members in an effort to come to a collective decision. Habermas' (1990; 2008) famous 'ideal speech situation' is a prototypical normative model of how deliberation should take place (see also Bohman 1996; Bohman and Rehg 1997; Dryzek 2002; and Gutmann and Thompson 1996 for theories of political deliberation). A common expectation in jury work is that a *reasoned* assessment will occur via deliberation. Whether deliberation actually occurs in (criminal trial) juries has been the object of empirical investigation, and Gastil *et al.* (2007) find in a study based on selfreported data (by jury members) that by and large juries do deliberate in an advanced and sophisticated manner.

With regard to the composition issue, film juries, like academic peerreview grant-awarding bodies (Lamont 2009), are an interesting mix, being at one and the same time both 'peer' and expert, as the peers of filmmakers are generally experienced experts in a variety of realms of

---

[2] When focus is on both, it can either be on them individually, or on how composition impacts process, usually in terms of how group homogeneity or heterogeneity impacts the deliberation process. A third field of focus in jury research looks at the impact of procedural rules and mechanisms (see Tindale, *et al.* 2002).

filmmaking. On the issue of composition, relative consensus among our informants can be seen on several topics.

The first is the basic observation that juries are convened for only one occasion (that is, for only one particular film festival, and they do not return together in subsequent years) and for a specific purpose – usually confined to one section, classification, or competition.[3] In other words, the films that a jury evaluates are distinctly demarcated, and a jury is rarely asked to award prizes in two or more competitions at the festival. This means that juries are 'one-off' arrangements, with a very well-defined field of competitors to select from in one competition. Juries do, however, usually award multiple prizes within the competitions they judge. The categories for the various prizes follow occupational and often gender lines, such as best screenplay, best director, best music, best cinematography, best male and female lead, and supporting actors, as well as what is usually the most prestigious prize, best film.

Second, juries are composed on a principle of breadth or diversity. This means, as mentioned above, that the organizers of film festivals seek to ensure a wide degree of representational breadth on juries. The most common categories for breadth are occupational (that is, securing representation of a broad group of occupations, from film distributors to directors, editors to actors, film critics to composers), sex (males and females), age, and ethnicity/national origin. Composition of some juries may take into consideration genre specializations, and 'commercial' versus 'art' traditions or reputations. Most informants reported that compositional criteria were used in their own selection (such as, 'I was the female editor on that jury') and that festival conveners usually succeed in attaining diversity in juries. A number of reasons were given for seeking to attain diversity. The first is the simple matter of having as many perspectives on film and film-related performance as possible in order to obtain as well-rounded an assessment of the field as possible. This means occupational as well as 'cultural' perspectives that might evolve in distinct national, regional, or genre environments. As the overarching criterion for awarding prizes – 'best' – is a very vague term, perspective diversity is one way of ensuring that a variety of interpretations about what 'best' is comes into play. Another often

---

[3] At a given film festival there may be several competitions in various categories or sections within which films compete against each other but not [generally] across sections, categories, or competitions.

stated reason for seeking diversity is 'power-based.' Diversity is sought to 'balkanize' the jury, so that no single perspective, occupation, or socio-demographic group can dominate the process, at least from the outset. These are the 'work process' reasons for diversity. As mentioned in several interviews there are public expectations and public relations reasons for diversity as well – 'it has to look good' to the press, public, and industry.

It was also stated that conveners of juries have a stake in making sure the juries function well, and that the jurors have a positive experience which then reflects well on the festival as a whole and creates long-term goodwill. This leads to considerations (if possible) about who can and cannot work or collaborate with whom, and persons with known animosities toward each other are not placed in the same jury, as well as not selecting what one informant termed 'notorious assholes' for juries (though apparently some 'less notorious' ones get through sometimes).

If the festival leadership has strong preferences or desires with regard to rewarding a particular film in competition, or a type or genre, a jury may be composed to increase the odds of an outcome in accord with the festival leadership's desires. One respondent mentioned being consulted once by the leadership of a festival about the likelihood of someone known to our interviewee supporting a particular type of film, and then noticed that when the reply was that the person would probably not be disposed toward such a film, the person in question was not selected for the jury that year. So apparently jury composition can, in some cases at least, be done strategically, though this far from secures a given outcome. This example may also be interpreted to indicate that it is at this stage that festival leaderships seek to exert influence, as more proximate intervention in the awarding process is more apparent, illegitimate, and dangerous in terms of causing affront and backlash.

Juries almost invariably have an appointed chairperson. What this role entails formally and informally varies from festival to festival, incumbent to incumbent, and jury to jury, and examples of both authoritarian and 'facilitative' chairpersons were reported. This is one of the few, if only, formal differentiations or divisions of labor reported in juries. Informal divisions of labor and expertise arise surreptitiously, often along the lines of occupational expertise, experience, reputation, or accomplishment. On this point it should be remembered that in most aspects of film production, there are role hierarchies that are well engrained in work processes, practices, and culture. This means that an appointed leader or chairperson is not an alien concept, but who the chairperson is may run counter to established occupational hierarchies or hierarchies of the national film industries that the incumbent comes from. At the same time, juries are usually expected to operate on participatory, deliberative, and possibly even consensual principles. There is thus a sub-theme of a tension between 'leadership and democracy' present in most jury settings, based on the presence of a chairperson with a sometimes ambiguous role. However, the jury is expected to deliver decisions about the prizes it is charged to distribute on time, and it is the responsibility of the jury's chairperson to ensure that these decisions are made.

Another structural issue has to do with the number of jurors on the jury. Juries usually comprise at least three members (the lowest odd number above one) and rarely come up to double digits in order to facilitate face-to-face interaction and dialog. Another more practical reason for limited numbers is that jury work is often voluntary and requires, as one respondent stated, 'ripping a whole week or more out of my work schedule'. This can make it difficult to enlist a high number of jurors, especially to less glamorous festivals. Juries also tend to comprise an odd number of members, so that in the cases where consensus cannot be reached, a decisive vote should be able to be taken.

Finally, it was noted by many that prizes are given and juries selected and convened to attract publicity and media attention. Therefore, some 'headline names' and photogenic individuals are included in juries if possible for these reasons. As one of our interviewees noted with regard to a Cannes jury, 'all the men on the jury are celebrities, and all the women are really stylish.' While 'celebrity' status may carry over into the jury and jury work, branch-internal prestige and admiration were generally reported to structure the informal pecking order and deference and alliance processes in juries – more so than popular notoriety or acclaim. There is a general norm that jury work is a form of 'community service' and thus jury members do not get paid directly for participating in the jury work but rather enjoy the level of luxury and prestige that the festival can afford. Nevertheless, a couple of interviewees noted that some very prestigious celebrity jury members, as opposed to the rest of the group, are paid for their time at the festival, including their work with the jury.

With regard to deliberative processes, most respondents stated that there were no substantive or qualitative rules given by the festival organizers to inform the jury's work, other than that they meet the deadline for when the group's decisions should be completed. It was reported that some organizers go to great lengths to support coherent deliberative processes, by such things as providing transcriptions of jury proceedings so that what was said earlier can be recalled in an indisputable manner, or by having someone present during the deliberations who can give clarifications on technical details or formal rules. However, most respondents stated that it was up to the jury to decide for itself on *both procedural and substantive* issues. With regard to procedural issues one respondent stated that there were 'no rules' – it was up to the jury itself to decide how it wanted to operate, how it was to proceed, aside from which prizes can and must be awarded, and by when they needed to reach their decisions. Juries normally can decide about the levels of consensus aimed at, when and how often to meet, whether to promote plenum discussions and suppress discrete discussions among jury members, or not. With regard to substantive issues, it was again stated that defining, identifying, and rewarding what was 'best' was entirely up to the jury and its members. However, as discussed below, many hierarchies and substantive conceptions of what should be rewarded and what constitutes good and great, the foundational elements for making the comparative judgment 'best' (and worthy of mention), exist both collectively and discretely among jury members.

## The jury work process

*Dana is tired; it's been a long day and it's not over yet. The film they are watching is okay, but the stuffy air and dark theater are slowly lulling her usual sharp focus to sleep. The film critic in the group, an older gentleman to her left, is snoring gently. She looks embarrassedly toward the row in front of her, where the team behind the film is seated, hoping they haven't noticed the critic dozing off. They regularly take quick glances over their shoulders in the hope of getting just a hint of the jury's verdict, any small signs of disappointment, amusement, enthusiasm, indifference. She thinks she sees them starting to whisper, demoralized, amongst themselves . . . or maybe it's in her head. She gently nudges the critic with her elbow, waking him up with a groan. The row in front of her quietens down again.*

*She focuses back to the screen after doing her bit to uphold the honor of the jury by keeping the critic awake. This has brought her out of the flow of the film. 'Focus now!' she thinks. She looks over at one of her co-jury members and notices, first with a snitch of embarrassment, that one of them has tears in her eyes. She feels awake again, feeling that she has missed something, and tries to get back in the desired state of surrendered focus, trying to give way to the film and let it touch her. She tries to let go of the official jury role and become just a viewer, leaning back in the big soft theater chair and focusing with dedication on the strong closing scene on the big screen.*

*Leaving the theater she glances at the other jury members, noticing hidden sniffs and wet handkerchiefs being stuffed into pockets. She makes eye contact with a few, and exchanges a mutually agreeing and pleased smile.*

*Later, back at the deliberating table, the attention turns to that film. Everyone agrees that it was special, except the one member who had seen it alone at his hotel room the night before, due to conflicting obligations at the festival that afternoon. He had not felt that the film had anything new to offer, and struggled not to fall asleep toward the end. Dana begins to wonder what she had felt, what she should have felt, and what she would have felt if not affected by her surroundings during the screening.*

## Viewing the films

Juries are usually charged with viewing a rather long slate of films and by rule do so together as a group; a sequential process, usually stretching over several days, sometimes more than a week for larger festivals. In general, the films are viewed publically with the other jury members, and often also with a broader festival audience, which may also include the film makers, cast, and crew of the film. Sometimes a single film is seen per day, sometimes multiple films are viewed, especially for documentary, shorts, or other film forms briefer than full-length features. It is generally the festival program that governs which films are seen when, and in what sequence. It was remarked, however, that it is possible for jury members to see films on DVD or special showings under extenuating circumstances, although this is a solution of last resort reserved for emergency situations or to accommodate the needs of especially prestigious jury members whom the festival has an extra interest in catering to. This means that sometimes films can be seen in different sequences and settings, sometimes even at a jury member's home. As a rule, however, the jury acts as a unit and the films are seen collectively, publicly, and in the same sequence.

Our informants had several perspectives on the viewing process. One group of comments focused around the composition of the group or slate of films in competition. Jury members are not involved in the selection process. This is usually done by a committee or individual in or appointed by the festival management, and frequently these individuals or committees work over a number of years, in contrast to the 'one-off' nature of the juries. Some respondents noted that it is possible to see the orientations, or likes and dislikes, of these programmers in which films they have chosen for the festival and competition, and what they omit. As with jury composition, the composition of the field of competing films is also reported to be based on a principle of diversity – to put on display and in competition an array of different types of films, and films of 'varying quality.'

This latter comment is quite interesting, as some respondents argue that the field of films in a competition is composed in order to produce contrasts rather than an even or level group of films. Some argue that this is intentional: including mediocre as well as great films makes some films stand out in relief to others. Others argue that this variation in quality is a side or inherent effect of other processes. These types of explanations range from the success of influential production companies in getting their films into prestigious festivals and competitions despite mediocrity, to an effect of trying to attain other types of diversity, such as regional inclusion or commercial considerations. In elaborating on the varying quality of the films in competition, and why this is perceived as a somewhat acceptable 'part of the game,' one comment was that there simply are so many festivals, so many prizes – all assessing diverse qualities – that there are not enough good films to go around. It was also noted that often the final versions of films are not always seen by the selectors, who then go on the reputation or previous work of directors or production companies, or 'promotional material' for the film. It was argued that creating films is an expensive, complex, and long process where lots can go wrong to bring down overall quality. Almost all jury members remark that it is extremely difficult to make a good film and that even at the 'A' festivals there are a lot of bad films as well. As one interviewee stated: 'If you look at theater, the reason why the same twenty-five pieces get played again and again everywhere is that it is incredibly hard to write good drama. In film we have this folly that we do not reuse things, we produce new things each time.' In other words, truly good films are very rare, and even the best festivals are hard pressed to fill a competition field with only good and great films. This may be why awards are given to 'best' rather than 'great' films, as even in a field of mediocrity, one film or performance can be elevated over others.

Another insightful comment concerned the unintended effect that the selection of a rather uniform slate of films reflecting an individual's or committee's tastes or sentiments can have. As we will see below, novelty is one of the central evaluative criteria used by film juries, and a high degree of novelty and distinctiveness is valued. If a programmer or committee selects several films that are novel in a wider population, but resemble each other in some manner, the juxtaposition of these possibly otherwise novel or innovative works against each other can lead to a diminished impression of novelty and creativity. Though each jury member brings their own wider points of reference, in evaluating a common pool of films, the composition of this pool will create its own proximate references and comparative impressions. Thus what might otherwise be a fairly mundane film may in the company of a group of similar innovative products stand out as unique.

Another group of comments focused on the sequence in which the films are shown at the festival and to the jurors. One respondent stated: 'A lot of people have theories about this ... whether it is best to be early, in the middle, or at the end.' The jurors also seem to have many different ideas. Some argue that the programmers actually place films of different quality in different positions, and that, while this may not influence the outcomes at a given film festival, on aggregate and over time it may lead to the impression of certain sequential positions being more advantageous than others. Other informants believe that positioning has an impact on sales and reviews, but not on jurors as they have such sophisticated judgment and have seen so many films that they are not impacted by the order in which they view the works. Still others again claim that sequential ordering does impact jurors because at certain positions in the sequential flow the jurors have contextually relevant reference points. If one position must be put forward as beneficial, it is toward, but not at, the end of the competition.

A further group of comments focuses on the public nature of the viewing process. Several commentators stated in various ways that seeing films is a social process. One experiences a film with one's personal senses, but sitting in a theater with other people and being able to see, hear, and sense their reactions undeniably impacts one's own reactions, experiences, and opinions about the film concerned. This may be connected with the contagion of emotion (Parkinson and Simons 2009) or more conscious processes. Some interviewees mentioned noticing and paying attention to their fellow jury members' reactions, as they often sit together as a group, while others also mentioned general audience reactions, and even the presence of the team behind the film, as affecting their experience of watching the film (as we saw in the vignette above).

Finally, and possibly the most profound comments on the process of viewing films has to do with the corporeal dimension of this process. All respondents mention physical and emotional dimensions of viewing or experiencing films. The phrases vary, but the basic analogies are of 'taking in' a film, of being 'moved' or 'left cold' or 'indifferent,' of being 'hit' or 'impacted,' or not. These emotional and embodied reactions connote very individual and personal experiences. As one respondent put it, it's all about 'I feel, I experienced, I believe.' The challenge, then, in most cases, is translating this personal, emotional, and embodied experience into interpersonally communicable language – first initially intelligible to oneself, then subsequently to a group whose mother tongues are often heterogeneous. This is similar to Ana Alačovska's account in Chapter 6 of how the travel guidebook writer in a bodily manner takes in and experiences a place through 'feeling the place in the feet,' or 'developing a nose,' and then attempts to articulate and convey the intangible quality and meaning of that place to readers.

This process of externalizing feelings and translating the corporeal aspect of the cinematic experience is naturally difficult, but according to many informants made easier by two factors. The first is that many of the emotions felt in viewing films are 'universal' emotions and reactions, meaning that though experienced individually, such feelings and reactions are not unique. As a result, there is a vocabulary in most languages to capture, discuss, and convey such experiences. Thus it's a matter of translating into one's own linguistic equivalents. Films then can be discussed in terms of whether or not, and the degrees to which, they evoked a given emotion, feeling or sensation at a given point, as well as the 'authenticity' of the experience: did the viewer feel natural or manipulated into experiencing the feeling or emotion? Was the experience 'contrived' or 'true?' The second factor is that among those experienced in film production and viewing, there is a technical, occupational vocabulary or jargon that is widespread across the industry and so supports cinematic dialog internationally and inter-culturally. Finally, in the trade-off between precision and basic comprehension, there is always recourse to metaphor, which was commonly invoked.

## *Recording, sounding, and registering opinions*

An important link between the viewing and deliberation process is the time and activities that take place between viewing and plenum discussions. This liminal time is probably the most extensive, unregulated, and discretionary expanse in all jury work. It is likely that just as highly significant as it is, it is also easily overlooked. It is here that initial perceptions and opinions can be affirmed, disputed, or disconfirmed in initial social contacts with other jury members (akin to water cooler or coffee room conversations and casual chat at workplaces), and several informants revealed that such informal conversations profoundly impact their thinking and subsequent actions in plenum deliberations.

Many of our respondents also reported writing notes both during and after screenings in order to remember what they saw, what they felt, and to prepare their comments for further conversations, both in and outside plenum deliberations. While this may be a particular Danish or Scandinavian trait, it was reported as not uncommon, and quite indispensable in defending one's opinions and arguments in subsequent discussions. Being able to give specific examples and exact references to nuances in the films was reported to weigh heavily in the deliberation processes and heighten one's credibility.

While writing notes is an individual process, the period of time between seeing the films and group-wide discussions is filled with dyadic and larger constellation discussions about the films. This time is generally unstructured and leaves to chance who engages whom in dialog and about what. However, there is agreement that it is taboo to discuss one's own and the opinions of the rest of the jury with outsiders during on-going jury work – something that is also respected by outsiders, even if they are very interested parties. As one informant noted: 'People are courteous enough not to contact the jury during the process.' Discussions during moving in and out of the theaters, in hotel lobbies and hotel rooms, at receptions and dinners all form and disperse impressions and ideas among the jury members, and formal and informal 'alliances' or common understandings begin to emerge in these unmanaged social spaces. Some respondents report seeing or engaging in internal 'lobbying' during these periods, whereas others hop over these periods or spaces in their accounts of jury work, and/or simply describe such lobbying as being frowned upon or just unsporting.

Collateral processes, incidental and significant to the ways in which the jury work takes place, are also reported as transpiring during these periods, where personal and career ambitions are discussed and pursued among jury members. The jury members, just like the fashion designers at HUGO BOSS depicted in Chapter 2, attempt to convince the rest of the group of their particular take on good film (or good design) because a positive confirmation from the group will feed back into the person's social position within, in this case, the jury group itself and possibly the film industry as a whole. A similar process is found by Godart and Mears (2009) in their work on the model-scouting process in the fashion industry, where one's opinions and decisions always factor in whether who or what one selects and backs will win acclaim among significant members of the field. As there are no formal procedural rules for how the jury work is to take place, there are consequently no rules for the nature of interpersonal conduct among jury members with regard to pursuing personal gain in addition to, or at the cost of, 'objectivity' in one's jury work. It seems to be a matter of individual discretion and group or cultural norms. Many informants reported being contacted and even subsequently working with persons whom they met or solidified relations with during jury work. However, overt career promoting by building deferential alliances was frowned upon, with scorn poured on those jury members who sold out their integrity and all too obviously sucked up to potential employers, collaborators, or celebrities.

## The plenum deliberation and awarding process

As noted above, deliberation is usually divided up into *étapes* in order to break up the total amount of films and information to be processed. For feature films it was often reported that after three to five feature films a meeting is held to discuss them, usually resulting in a consensus about which films should be accorded further consideration and why, and which films should be dropped from further consideration, at least provisionally. Several interviewees noted that they had experienced an even more decisive, and some might claim more brutal, approach, where the films not mentioned by anyone in the group as being in their top list would simply not be discussed further, and were thereby definitively out of the race. This process of quarter- or semi-finals would be repeated until the entire field was initially treated. After this, the final round at which the ultimate decisions are made would take place. At this stage evaluative criteria and evaluative processes explicitly come to the fore.

The following vignette illustrates such evaluative criteria and processes and revolves around three of the most common evaluative criteria discussed by our informants: novelty and subtlety; genre hierarchies; and individual versus collective performances, as well as the desire to make an authoritative recommendation to the film world. Outstanding individual performances or contributions – from, for example, editors, cinematographers, or composers – are attributed to the members of the cast and crew directly, whereas outstanding collective performances from the cast and crew members, as well as the overall novelty and impression from the film, are attributed to the director and rewarded with best film or director awards. In the vignette, how these evaluative criteria are deployed in broader evaluative processes can also be seen.

*'Okay, what we're discussing here is whether to reward a great, nervy, and original work of superior craftsmanship, or a rather mainstream production which is well told but technically is far from perfect,' said the cinematographer looking around the table.*

*'I just think,' the producer said sitting up in her seat, 'that it's worth rewarding the smoother experience, and quite a sophisticated comedy. Sure, it's familiar, but that's also why it's not such a struggle to sit through it, and it is entertaining. Great sophisticated comedy is 100 times more difficult to make than just another over-intellectualized drama, where you think, well yes, those are beautiful pictures and uhhh … that's an interesting angle to shoot from, or what do I know, but different genres require a different touch.' She pauses, and realizes that her peers are unconvinced. 'I can spot a great success among the real audience, and I don't see the point in rewarding a film that nobody will see. Sometimes boring people to death seems like a bloody winning criterion in itself.'*

*The director leans in. 'This is exactly why we should honor this film. People need to see this. We need to call attention to it, or it will be lost* and forgotten. It's a hell of a picture, a hell of a picture!' He shakes his head, as if he's struggling to comprehend the greatness of the work.

'I agree,' the writer adds, 'the way it elegantly opens the door, but leaves the decision to enter up to me. It doesn't tell me what to expect, but invites me to explore how far I dare to enter – into the space, which is already inside me. Pure magic!'

'I'm not sure I got your lyrical message, but I think I agree,' says the actress at the end of the table who has been quiet up until now. She takes a sip of her coffee, slowly puts down the cup, and pauses for dramatic effect. 'Watching this film was torture. The characters are ugly and horrible! This is – by far – the least audience-friendly film of the bunch. BUT I also think this is a ground-breaking merciless play with the art of film making. That death scene! I felt I was the one dying! I can't explain why, because it's just the way I feel, but this is the one that should get the award for Best Film.'

The producer sits back, sighs, and is about to recognize defeat. But then the film critic weighs in. 'I won't say that this is a remake, but the story is pretty similar to [film XXXXX]. It really isn't as original as you might imagine. And frankly, I think it was too sentimental in its language. I felt almost violated by the attempt to manipulate me into crying.'

The producer sees her chance to put her favorite back in the chase. 'Okay, so the tragic drama is less original than we might have assumed. I can see the qualities that you [others] are talking about, but in my opinion those things are more attributable to the director than the whole production, and it would make sense to award the film in the best director category, and save the best picture award for [her favorite film].'

They all lean a bit back in their comfortable conference room chairs. Then there's silence, and a realization that this is going to be a long evening of piecing together the awards puzzle.

Let us now analyze this vignette and break it down analytically into two discussions: the first on evaluative criteria, and the second on evaluative processes in group deliberation.

One of the most significant evaluative criteria reported universally by the jury members is novelty or originality. As Karpik (2010) notes, all films are at one level unique or singular objects. At more sophisticated levels this criterion is expressed in several different ways. One differentiation based on novelty has to do with topic or theme. As one interviewee expressed it: 'Have we seen this issue dealt with in film before?' The second aspect of novelty has to do with how topics or issues seen before are dealt with in a different manner or from a novel vantage point. Both of these can be termed types of *topical* novelty. A different form of novelty has to do with *expressive* novelty and can be broken down into two types. The first is an overall or holistic novelty that has to do with a style or telling the story in a novel way, visually or in terms of unfolding the plot or characters or other means of overall presentation. The second is in how specific, known situations, problems, attitudes, or emotions are conveyed. Many informants spoke in terms of clichés and conventions in film – accepted and known symbols and codes for conveying, especially visually, complex or strong emotions. This becomes part of the communicative language of film, its standard vocabulary. Where innovation comes in, and is appreciated, is in finding an alternative manner to express these common emotions, experiences, and events in a novel manner that at one and the same time makes the point, but does so in a different manner, avoiding cliché, yet remaining intelligible. This becomes appreciated by those with sufficient 'domain knowledge' to know what is conventional and what is innovative, what is on the edge but not beyond the pale, and thereby expands cinematic language and vocabulary.

On this issue of novelty, one interviewee related the following incident which is partially encapsulated in the vignette above. The jury had seen a film that was initially discussed as highly novel and innovative. During the discussion, a film critic[4] remarked: 'I won't say that this is a remake, but the story is much like this or that film that was released this or that many years ago. So it isn't as original as you might imagine.' The critic could say this because of an enormous knowledge of the field, due to the volume of films seen in an occupational capacity. This example illustrates how novelty, which by its nature is a comparative evaluation, can be approached by extensive knowledge and an ability to discern and argue for how and to what extent similarities can be drawn. Assessments of novelty, therefore, can be made by encyclopedic knowledge and/or sophisticated aesthetic discernment.

---

[4] An occupation where one sees an inordinate number of films as that is one's job, as opposed to spending most of one's time making a far more limited number of films and seeing a moderate number of films as audience or for professional reasons. People in purchasing and distribution also see many more films than film workers in production roles.

Coupled with this is an often appreciated use of subtlety. This may be a Scandinavian or northern European taste, but it was often described in terms of sophistication and trusting, or expecting, a sophisticated viewer or audience. This moves into a more general territory than the above-mentioned conceptions of novelty, which is premised more on comprehensive knowledge to be able to discern novelty comparatively (across films), and entails an ability to read and interpret cinematic expression in terms of fine gradations in life experiences, and possibly also other artistic and aesthetic expressions.

Another common criterion of evaluation for dramatic feature films (as opposed to documentaries, which are not discussed here) has to do with whether the cast performs well. Are these great dramatic presentations? And is this because of, or in spite of, a good screenplay?[5] Here it is both the performances of the actors and the role of the director that are under evaluation, as the latter has ultimate artistic responsibility for the project and one of his or her primary focuses is on the actors' performances. In part this evaluation criterion is given by the nature of the prizes to be awarded – best actor and actress, as well as best director – but it also plays a significant role in assessing the films in terms of the grand prize, the best film award.

Genre hierarchies were also touched on as structuring evaluation, with tragedy ranked above comedy, heavy and serious over light or farce. These were spoken of as common values, though some respondents reported being very much opposed to this hierarchy, while many others implicitly or explicitly supported this hierarchy in terms of preferring films that have 'something to say,' 'something at heart,' or 'something at stake.' One of the interviewees most sympathetic to comedy expressed this distinction in the following terms, 'Okay, this wasn't great art, but I was entertained,' revealing an appreciation of entertainment value while simultaneously affirming the art–entertainment distinction. Coupled with the general observation and assertion that festivals are about cinematic art (though an awful lot of commerce takes place at festivals), at least in the competition and selection process, art is the paramount value. As noted in Chapter 1, genre is a way to keep order or systematize the field of competing films horizontally, but also

---

[5] Here 'degrees of difficulty' similar to judging ice skaters, gymnasts, and divers are weighed: is it an inherently difficult role, or cast? Do the actors overcome handicaps of story or script and so on in their performances?

assumes vertical or hierarchizing dimensions in functioning as a criterion upon which films are evaluated from the two divergent but intertwined perspectives of artistic and commercial value.

Finally, there is a frequently used evaluative criterion that may *prima facie* appear quite banal but it is recurrently invoked and important. This has to do with whether a film is 'good' or not. Almost all jury members remark that it is extremely difficult to make a good film, and that even at the 'A' festivals there are a lot of bad films as well. This is encapsulated in the earlier quote contrasting theater, where canonical works are continuously replayed, and film, where remakes occur, but the overwhelming majority are original productions, though possibly based on stories from other media. Thus in film the orientation is toward novelty and original stories, and as also noted above 'it is incredibly hard to write good drama.'

On this issue an interesting set of analogies arises in discussing what a good film is. On the one hand, analogies revolving around 'comparing apples and oranges' or 'coffee, tea, and hot chocolate' are given to make the point that to a certain extent films are unique but can also be sorted into categories, but that, after a certain point, the uniqueness of films and their general types or characteristics (comedy, drama, tragedy, melo-drama, fantasy, political, and so on) are a matter of basic tastes or preferences. On the other hand, there doesn't seem to be a great deal of difficulty in separating the 'chaff from the grain,' that is, separating the comparatively superior from the inferior. Most informants indicate that 'reducing the field' or separating the films worthy of further consideration from those not worthy is a normal and generally unproblematic process. Or, to take the fruit analogy further, it seems that a differentiation between immature, ripe, and rotten fruit is possible across the board even before preferences for apples and oranges come into play, suggesting a common degree of evaluative criteria or intuitive insight at this level.

Being able to award multiple prizes in different categories can give rise to 'compensatory' and 'distributional' awarding, where awards are not given strictly categorically but sometimes in a descending process of compensating worthy films that did not get a higher award. A film may be given a 'lower' award in another category to demonstrate support for the film rather than the prize going to the categorically best performance. Just about all interviewees had examples of compensatory distribution being a vital tool for the group to eventually agree on a final set of winners, where members of the jury felt they had had a say – through, for example, agreeing to give a film one award in exchange for another film receiving another award. The awarding process was sometimes referred to as resembling a type of kaleidoscopic puzzle, where laying one piece alters where the other pieces can fall. Some interviewees mentioned a strong negative opinion toward this type of negotiation, especially when it entailed compensating for events outside the specific competition (such as giving a type of 'lifetime achievement award' to a particular film maker, or making up for a 'wrong' decision in previous years).

In connection with the distribution of the awards, most interviewees reported the jury starting out 'from the top' – first coming to an agreement on the most prestigious awards, usually 'best film' and 'best director', followed by the less overall prestigious awards for particular occupational contributions. Thus, the best film award is usually the centerpiece around which the other awards are arrayed, again giving support to the above-mentioned fact that awards are not always given strictly categorically but in relation to prior, more prestigious decisions, in a compensatory or 'fair' distributional manner.

In contrast to the possible impression given above that finding a winner is largely 'horse trading,' it was forcefully emphasized by the vast majority of our respondents that the plenum deliberation is also a process in which preferences and opinions are dynamically developed and altered. As collegial discussion is so highly valued, the interviewees declare that they truly listen to, attempt to persuade, and be persuaded by what their esteemed colleagues from other professional backgrounds have to say. It is these discussions that many describe as the real payoff or reward in film jury work. In this sense, despite many stating that they have favorites that they feel and fight strongly for, the process is deliberative and frequently characterized by discovery of new perspectives and dynamic opinion formation, rather than by mere wrangling, which by all accounts also goes on. This process of dynamic opinion formation is also impacted by the fact that dialog among jury members, as mentioned above, often takes place informally and constantly, rather than just in the plenum sessions.

## Conclusion

The aim of this chapter has been to provide a rich sense of the factors that play into the awarding process in film festival prize juries, and the interaction among their members. Relatively great emphasis was placed on outlining the contextual factors that facilitate, constrain, and impact the prize deliberation and awarding process. What can be rendered from this initial inquiry into the operation of film festival prize juries is not so much a theory as a framework of factors that impinges on prize juries. We have identified two sets of compositional factors, both governed by festival leadership. The first has to do with the composition of the juries themselves. Here we see central concerns of the festival leadership: most prominently the legitimacy of the jury in terms of securing the requisite breadth of backgrounds of its members and the PR value of the jury; and operational considerations in terms of securing a jury that can collaborate and deliver its decision on time. The diversity that is usually attained in juries creates challenges in terms of intercultural and inter-occupational differences in assessments and linguistic communication, as well as at least an initial balkanization of presumed national and occupational dispositions and preferences. The second central compositional arena in the hands of the festival leadership is the slate of films chosen for competition, which can send signals to the jury as well as create intended and unintended, overt and subliminal, proximate and comparative juxtapositions that may impact jury deliberations and decisions.

Moving to temporal issues, and keeping the focus on the role of the festival leadership, the sequence in which films are viewed by the jury is discussed as a matter that many on the festival scene have ideas or speculate about, but most of our informants tend to believe that sequential placement is not decisive. Other central temporal factors identified are the necessity of reaching a decision in a compressed timeframe, the existence of unstructured periods for discrete interaction outside of the plenum, and the temporal-socio-spatial dimension of seeing films together as a group. The main criteria involved in evaluating and awarding are left open to the given jury, but tend to revolve around identifying different types of novelty, as well as coherence to a certain extent. Central to the process is the corporeal dimension of individual evaluation, and how this experience is excavated and translated into something that is intelligible and intersubjectively communicable. In part this is possible because jurors tend to evaluate and experience film in a similar manner, so that even imprecise formulations can bring 'I know what you mean and I agree or disagree' responses. Likewise, the corporeal experience is significantly 'intellectualized' and couched in field or professional terms which are also shared within the community.

One of the most intriguing things about film festival prize jury work is that it seems to flagrantly contradict the famous Latin dictum: *de gustibus non disputandum est*. These juries trade and revel in taste and opinion, and it is the core of their deliberative activities. It would be too easy – and in our estimation misleading – to posit that decisions are made by recourse to other factors, such as interests or power. Though it is difficult or impossible to unequivocally point to *the* process or *the* means by which jury decisions are made, with apologies to Pickering (1995), the *mangle* of deliberation which leads to decisions includes large measures of subjective, qualitative, esthetic taste and opinion, expressed in an intersubjectively intelligible way, all being part of a process of social exchange and individual learning and discovery, that usually renders if not agreement at least acceptance of, or acquiescence to, collective decisions.

# References

Bohman, James. 1996. *Public Deliberation: Pluralism, complexity, and democracy*. Cambridge, MA: MIT Press.

Bohman, James and William Rehg, eds. 1997. *Deliberative Democracy: Essays on reason and politics*. Cambridge, MA: MIT Press.

de Valck, Marijke. 2007. *Film Festivals: From European geopolitics to global cinephilia*. Amsterdam University Press.

de Valck, Marijke and Mimi Soetman. 2010. 'And the winner is . . .' What happens behind the scenes of film festival competitions. *International Journal of Cultural Studies* 13 (3): 290–307.

Dodds, John and Morris Holbrook. 1988. What's an Oscar worth? An empirical estimation of the effects of nominations and awards on movie distribution and revenues. In *Current Research in Film: Audiences, Economics, and Law*, Vol. 4, ed. B. Austin, pp. 72–88. Norwood, NJ: Ablex.

Dryzek, John S. 2002. *Deliberative Democracy and Beyond: Liberals, critics, contestations*. Oxford University Press.

English, James. 2005. *The Economy of Prestige*. Cambridge, MA: Harvard University Press.

Gastil, John, Burkhalter, Stephanie and Black, Laura. 2007. Do juries deliberate? A study of deliberation, individual difference, and group member satisfaction at a municipal courthouse. *Small Group Research* 38 (3): 337–359.

Godart, Frédéric C. and Ashley Mears. 2009. How do cultural producers make creative decisions? Lessons from the catwalk. *Social Forces* 88 (2): 671–692.

Gutmann, Amy and Dennis Thompson. 1996. *Democracy and Disagreement.* Cambridge, MA: Harvard University Press.

Habermas, Jürgen. 1990. Discourse ethics: Notes on a program of philosophical justification. *Moral Consciousness and Communicative Action.* Translated by Christian Lenhart and Shierry Weber Nicholson. Cambridge, MA: MIT Press.

  2008. *Between Naturalism and Religion.* Translated by Ciaran Cronin. Cambridge: Polity.

Iordinova, Dina and Ragan Rhyne. 2009. *Film Festival Yearbook 1: The festival circuit.* St Andrews: Film Studies, St Andrews.

Karpik, Lucien. 2010. *Valuing the Unique: The economics of singularities.* Princeton University Press.

Lamont, Michele. 2009. *How Professors Think. Inside the curious world of academic judgment.* Cambridge, MA: Harvard University Press.

Lincoln, Anne E. and Michael P. Allen. 2012. Oscar et César: deep consecration in French and American film acting careers. In *Careers in Creative Industries*, ed. Chris Mathieu, pp. 107–127. New York: Routledge.

Mezias, Stephan, Jesper Strandgaard Pedersen, Ji-Hyun Kim, Silviya Svejenova and Carmelo Mazza. 2011. Transforming film product identities: The status effects of European premier film festivals, 1996–2005. In *Negotiating Values in the Creative Industries: Fairs, festivals and competitive events*, ed. Brian Moeran and Jesper Strandgaard Pedersen, pp. 169–196. Cambridge University Press.

Neilson, William and Harold Winter. 2008. Votes based on protracted deliberations. *Journal of Economic Behavior & Organization* 67 (1): 308–321.

Parkinson, Brian and Gwenda Simons. 2009. Affecting others: social appraisal and emotion contagion in everyday decision making. *Personality and Social Psychology Bulletin* 35 (8): 1071–1084.

Pickering, Andrew. 1995. *The Mangle of Practice: Time, agency and science.* University of Chicago Press.

Tindale, R. Scott, Janice Nadler, Andrea Krebel and James H. Davis. 2002. Procedural mechanisms in jury behavior. In *Blackwell Handbook of Social Psychology: Group process*, ed. Michael A. Hogg and Scott Tindale, pp. 574–602. Oxford: Blackwell Publishing.

York, Erin and Benjamin Cornwell. 2006. Status on trial: social characteristics and influence in the jury room. *Social Forces* 85 (1): 455–477.

# 9 | Restaurant rankings in the culinary field

BO T. CHRISTENSEN AND JESPER
STRANDGAARD PEDERSEN

What constitutes a good meal and how do you evaluate a restaurant? This chapter is concerned with evaluative practices within the culinary field, in particular those performed by two restaurant ranking systems: the *Michelin Red Guide* system handled by the French tire manufacturer Michelin, and the San Pellegrino World's 50 Best Restaurants list organized by the English-based *Restaurant Magazine*. Both ranking systems evaluate and rate restaurants (judging their food, service, physical setting, and so forth) through different sets of practices and means, and with somewhat different results (for other studies of external evaluative practices see Chapters 7, 8, and 10). The *Michelin Guide* system, established in 1900, is based on a standardized system of fixed criteria (Bouty *et al.* 2012). Restaurant evaluations are carried out by a group of trained inspectors who judge restaurants, quality (value for money) and award them star(s) or other symbols indicating their rated quality. The San Pellegrino World's 50 Best Restaurants list, established in 2002, is not based on any explicit criteria for evaluation but has the alleged implicit criteria of 'novelty' and 'innovation.' It is constructed on an elaborate voting system performed by a group of international gastro-experts and resulting in a ranking list of the 'World's Best' restaurants. In order to compare the two ranking systems and study their effects on restaurants in general, we have situated our analysis around the acclaimed Danish gourmet restaurant NOMA.

The authors would like to thank Howard Becker, Keith Sawyer, Timothy Malefyt, and other participants from the two Creative Encounters workshops on 'Evaluative Practices' for their insightful comments on earlier versions of the paper. The chapter has also benefitted from comments provided by Susanne Boch Waldorff and Lærke Højgaard Christensen. Finally, we would like to thank Kirstine Zinck Pedersen for her work on the database media search.

## Evaluative systems as institutionalized practices

How can we understand and theorize evaluative practices such as the ratings and rankings performed by the *Michelin Guide* and the San Pellegrino list? They seem in some way to stand in between, or mediate between, the system of production and the system of consumption in ways similar to those of other intermediaries in other culture-creative fields like, for example, film reviews and music critics. An economist's perspective on this would be to view this situation as an asymmetry of knowledge between the system of production and the system of consumption (or between 'sellers and buyers'), since the quality of aesthetic goods, such as 'fine dining' restaurant food, is not signaled by price alone but needs to be experienced and tested by a qualified analyst (Lane 2010, 2011). Hence such markets are not self-regulating and need some kind of mechanism or instrument to mediate and remedy the imbalance and asymmetry of knowledge. Remedying this asymmetry seems to be one of the roles of intermediaries and gatekeepers such as critics, rating and ranking systems, and so forth.

A sociological view would share the above-mentioned economist's point of view but add to this that the work performed by such intermediaries is not just about rectifying asymmetries of knowledge between producer and consumer; rather, by informing consumers about cultural goods, the work of intermediaries also entails a process of creation and construction of taste. And in today's world, in which the overwhelming number of products and services on offer results in an information overload concerning the numerous options and choices made available, the consumer searches for help and directions about what to choose and how to distinguish quality from inferior goods. Bourdieu (1984) has reminded us that distinctions are made in various ways through deployment of different forms of capital and symbols in society at large, as well as in the field of cultural production (Bourdieu 1993). Following from this, cultural sociologists such as DiMaggio (1987) have argued that distinctions are created through the use of systems of classification, often taking place as a tournament ritual, as in the case of the emergence of new artistic genres. Examples of this are studies of the Grammy awards by Anand and Watson (2004) and of how the Booker Prize and its associated ritual has configured the field of contemporary English literature and the distinctive category of post-colonial fiction

(Anand and Jones 2008).[1] In a study of another tournament ritual, Anand (2011) has shown how a wine contest, 'The Judgement of Paris,' changed the wine industry, while Croidieu (2011), in his study of the French appellation classification system, has demonstrated the stability of that classificatory system.

Institutional sociologists have also argued that rating and ranking systems are other examples of means that create distinctions and that these systems operate as standard-setting devices (Brunsson and Jacobsson 2002) or as a 'categorical imperative' (Zuckerman 1999) for the field in question. A distinction between two types of standard-setting agencies has been made: on one hand, 'self' or 'peer' administered evaluation and accreditation and, on the other, 'external' evaluation and accreditation (Brunsson and Jacobsson 2002; Hedmo *et al.* 2006). Wedlin (2010) argues further that rankings function as rhetorical devices to construct legitimacy within a field, in her case, international rankings in the field of management education. She suggests that European business schools use the rankings as an attempt to alter perceptions of the field and their own position within it (Wedlin 2010). In their study of the field of international business education and the role of an accreditation agency, AACSB (Association to Advance Collegiate Schools of Business), Durand and McGuire (2005) find that such agencies operate as standard-setters and legitimating bodies of the field.[2] This type of accrediting organization and rating system, like the *Michelin Guide* and the San Pellegrino list, operates to award or bestow legitimacy on other organizations. 'By attesting that associated organizations meet specified standards, these institutional agencies provide legitimation to organizations,' (Durand and McGuire 2005: 165). In order to be able to do so they themselves have to be considered legitimate players within their field. Thus, Durand and McGuire (2005) find that such accreditation organizations themselves are facing two types of pressures: a legitimacy pressure in relation to their constituents and a pressure to expand the domain of their activities. While standard-setting and awarding legitimacy to an organization or product is often portrayed

[1] For a separate account of a publishing genre, see Chapter 1 in this volume.
[2] For other studies of business education and the effects of rankings, see Boutaiba and Strandgaard Pedersen 2003; Hedmo 2003.

as a positive action, Zuckerman (1999), in his study of securities analysts, examines the penalties produced for illegitimate role performance. In particular, he argues that the failure to gain reviews by the 'expert' critics who have specialized in the product in question creates confusion about the product category and illegitimacy, which in turn depresses demand. As NOMA represents an attempt to create a new type of kitchen (New Nordic), the extent to which the restaurant lives up to existing expectations and criteria for evaluation embedded in the two ranking systems examined is central to this study.

Thus evaluative processes carried out in the accreditation of organizations, the evaluation of programs, the ranking of a restaurant or rating of a meal are not straightforward processes, but infused with issues of legitimacy and strategic action, as we will see in the following study of restaurant rankings.

While there are many forms of evaluative systems in cuisine (Zagat, Gault–Millau, food critics, and websites with consumer reviews and ratings), two of the most important ones are currently the *Michelin Guide* and the San Pellegrino World's 50 Best Restaurants list. Both the San Pellegrino list and the Michelin system aim at estimating quality and value among restaurants, and the resulting ratings have an enormous impact on the restaurants in terms of bookings, publicity, and reputation, which seem ever more central in what has been termed the 'name economy' (Moeran 2003). These two systems can be said to be competing, insofar as they propose two different ways of estimating restaurant quality, hold different standards, and result in distinct evaluations. Whereas some evaluative systems value change, others avoid it, thus producing somewhat different points of departure for evaluating a restaurant. Furthermore, the two institutionalized evaluative practices described here also differ in their openness to changes in the evaluative system itself. In some systems it is acknowledged that standards and criteria change over time and between contexts, whereas the internal logic of other systems suggests that the system should produce stable and reliable results across time and place. The claim made here is essentially that the institutional logic of evaluative systems, as seen in their internal organization and practice, can be said to lie along a continuum of 'change allowance.' In order to back up this claim, we will first introduce the gourmet restaurant NOMA and then take a look at the internal organization of two competing evaluative systems in cuisine.

## A brief history of NOMA

In December 2002, gastronomic entrepreneur Claus Meyer approached chef René Redzepi. He had been offered the opportunity to operate a restaurant at the North Atlantic House, a former eighteenth-century warehouse, which was being turned into a cultural center for the North Atlantic region and located in the Copenhagen harbour area. The building is situated by the Greenlandic Trading Square (*Grønlandske Handels Plads*) at the North Atlantic Wharf (*Nordatlantens Brygge*), which from 1767 was a center for trade to and from the Faroe Islands, Iceland, Greenland, and the Danish capital. Meyer asked Redzepi to become chef and partner, along with himself and entrepreneur Kristian Byrge, in this new venture. The restaurant came with one requirement: it was to reflect 'Nordicity,' especially North Atlantic Cuisine. 'There was no alternative, given its location and the history of the building,' (Skyum-Nielsen 2010: 11). This constraint on 'Nordicity' turned out to be an initiator of the culinary venture. As a result, in August 2003, in preparation, a trio consisting of the chefs René Redzepi and Mads Refslund, together with Claus Meyer, set out on a study tour of the North Atlantic – a seventeen-day mission to the Faroe Islands, Greenland, and Iceland, to 'absorb gastronomic inspiration and meet possible suppliers of raw materials and décor for what was, as far as we know, the first restaurant with a modern, North Atlantic menu' (Skyum-Nielsen 2010: 11).

In November 2004, the founders of NOMA organized what came to be known as the 'New Nordic Cuisine Symposium.' For the symposium they brought together a number of leading gastronomists and chefs from the Nordic countries in an attempt to extend the idea from being a local Danish to a Nordic venture. During the two-day symposium the twelve participating chefs created, agreed upon, and signed a 'Manifesto for the New Nordic Kitchen.' Inspired by the Dogma95 film manifesto, according to Meyer, the Manifesto was an attempt to define the New Nordic Kitchen according to ten rules. Core values in the Manifesto associate the New Nordic Cuisine with 'purity,' 'freshness,' and 'simplicity,' based on 'local, seasonal ingredients' ('Nordic terroir') and with a 'healthy, green, and environmentally friendly profile.'[3] The New Nordic Cuisine has been summarized as follows:

---

[3] See also Chapter 4 concerning Nordic values as reflected in the faience tableware created by Ursula Munch-Petersen.

Whereas French cuisine has been acclaimed all over the world thanks to the hedonist qualities of the food, and whereas the impressive quality of Spanish cuisine is its technical level, Nordic cuisine represents the dream of recreating a sort of link with nature once again. (Wolff 2011)

The gourmet restaurant NOMA opened in Copenhagen in November 2003, but was by no means seen as an immediate success. Much of the Danish restaurant scene laughed at NOMA's gastronomic concept, providing it with nicknames like 'The Whale Belly,' 'The Seal Humper,' 'Restaurant Lard Thrasher,' and 'The Golden Harpoon' (Skyum-Nielsen 2010: 11).

However, over the next few years NOMA's acclaim by external evaluative systems would rise considerably. Some were more appreciative than others. The San Pellegrino list of the World's 50 Best Restaurants would eventually (2010 and 2011) place NOMA at the top of its list, while the *Michelin Red Guide* has settled on awarding NOMA two Michelin stars. With the case of NOMA in mind, this chapter studies how these two evaluative systems are organized internally, how they are perceived by the domain of cuisine, and what impact their evaluations have had on the restaurants being rated.

## *Internal organization of the San Pellegrino list*

The San Pellegrino list is organized by *Restaurant Magazine*, and was first awarded in 2002. The list is created from The World's 50 Best Restaurants Academy, a group of more than 800 international leaders in the restaurant industry, selected for their expert opinion of the international restaurant scene. Over the years the Academy and its rules have changed slightly, but in 2011 it comprised twenty-seven separate regions around the world. Each region had its own panel of thirty-one members, including a chairperson, made up of food critics, chefs, restaurateurs, food journalists, and highly regarded 'gastronomes' with a high frequency of international travel. Each of them had seven votes to cast. At least ten panelists from each region change each year.

The list is generated on the basis of votes from the Academy according to the following rules: voting is confidential, and panelists may vote for up to four restaurants within their region, while at least three votes must be cast outside their region. Voters must have eaten in the restaurants they nominate within the past eighteen months. There is no way of checking this, however, and of course it does not mean that all 800 panelists eat at all top restaurants every year. Since the results remain confidential, it is unknown whether the restaurant voted No. 1 received 500 votes, or 100 votes, or even fewer. Voters are not permitted to vote for restaurants they own or have an interest in. Nominations must be made for the restaurant, not for the restaurateur or the chef. Panelists submit their seven choices in order of preference (this information is used to decide on positions in the event of a tie). The restaurants are then ranked according to how many votes are cast for them.

As such, it is not possible for a restaurant to be nominated to the list, or apply to be accepted on the list, and it also means that any restaurant in the world is eligible (unless closed at the time of the award). Every year in April, an award ceremony is held in London, where the staff of the top fifty restaurants are invited and a countdown from fiftieth to first place ensues.

## NOMA's history with the San Pellegrino list

In 2006, three years after opening, NOMA entered at No. 33 on the list. The following year the restaurant was voted highest climber on the list at No. 15. In 2008, it was ranked tenth, and jumped to No. 3 in 2009. In 2010, it was voted the No. 1 restaurant in the world, a position it maintained in the 2011 rankings.

This fast climb up the list to the top spot is quite unusual, but not unprecedented in San Pellegrino's (short) history. While the history of the list shows that the top spot for a number of years was dominated by restaurants such as El Bulli (Spain) and The French Laundry (California), The Fat Duck (Bray, UK), run by Heston Blumenthal, entered the list in 2004 in the first runner-up position, and moved to the top position the following year. El Bulli maintained its position at the top of the list for a number of years, being No. 2 in 2010, and has since closed down in order to reinvent itself (thus not appearing on the 2011 list). The French Laundry has dropped down the list over recent years to its current position of No. 56 in 2011.

In ascribing causes to NOMA's fast rise to the top, its managing director, Peter Kreiner, explains:

Luck has played a part. But I also think that we are hitting something typical of the times, and that is what is needed in gastronomy now. Of course there are several waves of gastronomy, so to speak, with one wave hitting after the other. But the natural and local, or what some would call the 'wild kitchen,' that is what we stand for at NOMA. And that is what many others are looking toward at the moment. There is no question that we are … today enjoying the attention of what you could call the substantial part of the food press and the food intelligentsia around the world who come here and think we have an interesting and different take on things.

Lars Peter Hedberg, who is academic chair for the Scandinavian region of the San Pellegrino list, explains it in these terms:

The two keywords, innovation and authenticity, are the explanation for the fast rise at NOMA. I mean they were offering something dramatically different from what the Spanish restaurants have offered over many years. I mean the Spanish have gone for … not the authentic but for the opposite … molecular cooking. I mean transgressing, transforming, scientific but not natural. And then the Scandinavian … not only NOMA, but NOMA for sure most prominently … no, we want to show you what nature can offer. And on top of that we have a new nature to show you that has not been showcased for many years. And it is just as interesting as the Mediterranean world or any other.

## Formal and informal criteria

In the San Pellegrino system, there are no explicit criteria set beyond the above rules – it is the opinion and experience of the panelists, not fixed criteria, that ideally lead them to vote for a particular restaurant. The absence of criteria has been discussed among the twenty-seven Academy chairs, as Hedberg explains:

And they have said … we have been discussing this a lot in the Academy, and we have had a big discussion about this. Why are they not more specific about the criteria? And they said that, no that is our whole idea, we want every restaurant to be able to appear on the list. If a restaurant serves the best possible fish just taken out of the water and just put on the charcoal grill … and a very simple but perfect sauce to go with it, it should be possible for that restaurant to make the list. So they have an answer to that question. But I think that gives some of the strange effects that you see on the list; that everyone can have his own evaluation system, and uses of an evaluation system. And it is a very unstructured sort of approach. And that, of course, has kept many of the three [Michelin] star restaurants out of this list.

The absence of formal criteria, however, does not preclude informal ones, Hedberg explains:

There is a sort of understanding among these chairs that we should promote change, that we should promote evolution in the industry. And not promote historical performances like the Michelin is doing. So . . . I think that is very outspoken, so that is it not only allowed to promote new phenomena coming up or new entries on the list – it is applauded when that happens. Because we want to reach the avant garde of the industry. So I think that is a very good thing about it. It is a very trendy list.

He continues:

Stability and innovation are sort of . . . they are a bit in controversy or conflict, right? I would prefer innovation over stability. And that is sort of the World's 50 best culture. That is . . . what is the interesting new thing, that is what . . . Of course it has to be sustainable innovation, it cannot just be a flash in the pan, that is not the thing, but it must be able to stay innovative, or stay on its own course at least for quite some time. But I mean sometimes you can stay too long on your course, like El Bulli.

## What impact have San Pellegrino evaluations had on NOMA?

The managing director at NOMA, Peter Kreiner, explains that the impact of the San Pellegrino rankings has been extremely important for NOMA, and in recent years the move to the top position on the list he would characterize as the single most important event among all the types of evaluation NOMA is constantly experiencing. The impact is not so much financial in terms of growing turnover. NOMA has maintained a rather small number of tables, so that increasing demand thus does not correspond to more bookings. The restaurant was completely booked even before reaching the No. 1 spot. That being said, the move to the top rank in 2010 had a huge impact on the restaurant's exposure, the public vision of New Nordic Cuisine, and booking attempts made at NOMA. The very next day after reaching the top ranking, NOMA had 100,000 online booking attempts in its reservation system, an interest that has remained. Media coverage can be further quantified by looking at how many times NOMA has been mentioned in Danish newspapers. From 2003 until 2010, NOMA's name appeared in 5,848 Danish newspaper articles. The year after it opened, in 2004, 102 newspaper articles mentioned NOMA. Succeeding years saw the following development: 128 (2005), 241 (2006), 381 (2007), 698 (2008), 1,024 (2009, when NOMA reached the third position on the San Pellegrino list). And then in 2010, when NOMA reached the top position on the list, the restaurant was mentioned 3,259 times in Danish newspaper articles -- more than three times as many as the year before.

## Perceptions of the San Pellegrino list

When glancing through the rankings of the San Pellegrino list, we might ask, what are the terms best describing the list? Besides its focus on innovation and authenticity, Hedberg mentions volatility. The list changes quite a lot from year to year, with more than 150 restaurants having appeared on the list in the ten years of its existence, and a history of rapid and substantial changes in the rankings. Part of the reason may be the rules of having to exchange one-third of the Academy each year. Furthermore, how many votes each restaurant actually attracts remains a secret. In principle, the votes of the '800 Academy' could be distributed over 5,000 restaurants around the globe, with very limited agreement, and few votes would therefore be required to reach the top. But as Hedberg states:

I think for the top five there are very substantial numbers behind them. Or maybe even the top ten. But then I think it gets more wobbly the further down you get. And on the 51–100 list, I think that anything could really happen.

When asked what kind of restaurants are positioned at the high end of the list, Kreiner says he believes that restaurants that emphasize continuous development are rewarded – that is, restaurants that show novelty, want to move and reinvent themselves, and not stand still, together with restaurants that challenge the existing ways of doing things. Kreiner mentions that El Bulli, which held the No. 1 ranking four years in a row (before NOMA took over), is certainly not a conventional place to dine – a huge number of servings, combined with being challenged as a guest: on texture, on taste, on ingredients, and so forth. While Kreiner believes many differences exist between El Bulli and NOMA, he also finds that top positions are not held by classical luxury restaurants. The Fat Duck is another prime example of an innovative restaurant for molecular cooking that has held the top position in the San Pellegrino list.

## Serving the Academy

Since the San Pellegrino list is made up of votes from the '800 Academy' gastronomes (of whom two-thirds are identifiable the following year), it is in principle possible to give these individuals special attention, and Hedberg confirms that it is common for Academy members to receive invitations to particular restaurants. Although most Academy members are said not to respond to such invitations, they do have the effect of putting the restaurant on the map, creating awareness among a very large sample of restaurants that could potentially get their vote. Another way of handling the relationship is to attempt to give Academy members special treatment at the restaurant itself. Kreiner acknowledges that if NOMA knows that someone from the Academy is in town, it would likely be attentive to that individual – but not in the sense of ensuring a table at the restaurant, since it is not possible to circumvent the booking procedure that way. However, frequently these individuals are very focused on getting a table, and keep trying, and then in the end most of them will manage to get one. If they are flexible in terms of times and dates, it is possible to get in and eat.

## Internal organization of the *Michelin Guide* system

The *Michelin Guide* is a series of annual guidebooks published by the French tire manufacturer, Michelin, and has existed for more than 100 years. The oldest and best-known Michelin guide is the *Red Guide* – a European hotel and restaurant guide that briefly describes and evaluates, as well as awards stars to, restaurants included in it.

The *Guide* was first published by André Michelin in 1900, in the very early years of motoring, to help drivers find gasoline distributors, mechanics, and tire dealers, together with places for decent lodging and to eat well while touring France. Jean-François Mesplede, former editor of the *Michelin Guide* in France, still emphasizes the importance of the link to the Michelin tire factories, in that they ensure complete financial independence from the restaurants, and thus a serious and trustworthy evaluation. The target group is any person traveling on

246 _Bo T. Christensen and Jesper Strandgaard Pedersen_

Michelin tires, and not an elite group of people, which also explains why the _Guide_ places heavy emphasis on 'value for money.'

The _Guide_ was initially distributed for free from 1900 to 1920, after which a charge was made. From 1926 it was further developed and began recognizing outstanding restaurants by marking their listings with a star as a first sign of classification and making distinctions. In the early 1930s the system of stars was expanded to a two- and three-star system to enable readers to further differentiate among the restaurants included in the _Guide_. Over the years, the _Guide_ was extended to cover countries other than France, and later on also to encompass guides for selected major cities worldwide (Bouty _et al._ 2012). Today the _Michelin Guide_ collection comprises twenty-five guides covering twenty-three countries and more than 45,000 establishments, but the close link to the tire manufacturer is still evident in that the expansion of the _Michelin Guide_ closely follows market development for where Michelin tires are sold. As such, although it has developed a life of its own over the years, the _Michelin Guide_ remains a marketing tool for a tire manufacturer.[4] This regional interest in tire markets probably explains why there is no Nordic Guidebook, and as such no chance for Danish restaurants outside Copenhagen or Fyn to get any Michelin stars.[5]

The _Michelin Guide_ operates according to a system based on anonymous, professionally trained inspectors, who are assigned the task of visiting restaurants and evaluating them according to a range of criteria in order to make an impartial assessment. The evaluations are done very much according to fixed criteria and precise instructions, by highly trained inspectors frequently with experience in the cuisine field. These inspectors are required to work solely for the _Michelin Guide_ (with no other source of income), and have to undergo intensive training for 3–6 months at the hands of already experienced inspectors. Michelin claims that its inspectors revisit all 4,000 reviewed restaurants in France every eighteen months, and all starred restaurants several times a year. There are approximately 100 inspectors worldwide.

Restaurants are ranked into three stars (exceptional cuisine, worth a special journey), two stars (excellent cuisine, worth a detour), one star

---

[4] Interview with Mesplede.
[5] Copenhagen and Fyn are listed as 'main cities of Europe,' but the rest of Denmark is not included in the guidebooks.

(very good cuisine in its category), or no stars. Since 1955, the *Guide* has also listed restaurants offering 'good food at moderate prices,' a feature now called 'Bib Gourmand,' named after the company logo, the Michelin Man, also known as 'Bibendum.'

All restaurants found worthy to be included in the *Guide*, regardless of their star or Bib Gourmand status, also receive a 'fork and spoon' designation, ranking from one fork and spoon (a comfortable restaurant) to five forks and spoons (a luxurious restaurant) in an attempt to reflect the overall comfort and quality of the restaurant.

Over the years various types of criticism have been raised in relation to the *Michelin Guide* system. These have included the alleged facts that they play favorites and that some three-star chefs are untouchable (for example Paul Bocuse and his Lyon restaurant l'Auberge du Pont de Collonges), that the inspectors are actually fewer in number than claimed by Michelin, and that they therefore cannot visit restaurants every eighteen months, but rather with a frequency of three and a half years (Rémy 2004). Other types of criticism have been associated with chefs having committed suicide after stars were taken away from the restaurant, or that Michelin reviewed restaurants that were not yet open.

## The inspector sits down, and ...

The evaluation criteria are not public and this is, according to Mesplede, derived from the Michelin industrial logic of trade secrets, giving the *Guide* a somewhat mysterious and secretive feel. When an inspector visits an establishment, several things are evaluated and reported.

The first page of the report concerns the evaluative criteria for the 'fork and spoon' and the 'pavillion.' These include an external impression of the restaurant, phone service, reception, general impression of the place, quality of service, visits to kitchen/rooms, and so forth. These criteria do not count toward the star ratings, however. On the second page of the report, an *'essai de table'* (sample of the table) is filled out evaluating only the food (and also the wine, although it is sometimes evaluated on the first page, by ticking the 'grape' if the wine list is good). Each course – appetizer, main course, cheese, and dessert – receives its own rating, from very bad, to bad, average, or one, two, or three stars. As Mesplede explains: 'Our only criteria are the content of the course, the quality of the food, and the bill. Value for money is very important. It is not crystal glass that determines a star.'

These criteria are the same from country to country, and decade to decade. The star ratings, however, are not decided upon a single inspector visit. When an establishment changes star status, typically two or sometimes three (or even more, in the case of ratings of more than one star) different inspectors visit an establishment in order to ensure reliability. In Mesplede's words:

It could be that the inspector on a given day is less receptive, which explains why we make repeated visits. The inspector, of course, has to argue why he thinks a restaurant is extraordinary. But it is clear that if you get a poor reception, you do not appreciate the food the same way. If it is a male inspector being served by a smiling female waiter with a breast size of 95D, it is inevitable that it affects his impression. We would like to avoid these external factors, though.

From September each region holds two monthly meetings, involving the inspectors and the directors discussing each restaurant. Mesplede explains the procedure:

We have what is called a 'star session' during these meetings, which is when we go over the restaurants where a star modification could be made, that is if the restaurant deserves to keep its star, or whether another one should get one, and so on. There may be some inspectors who are not in agreement about the particular restaurant, whether it should have a star or not. Then we discuss things. If you get to a situation where we are unanimous, then there is usually no problem, but you can end up estimating that it is too early for a restaurant to get its star and that it should wait until next year ... But giving a star is always discussed, because if you have been at a restaurant and the first two courses were extraordinary but the dessert was not as good, perhaps the crust was over-baked, but still good, then you would evaluate it as 'really good' with an arrow pointing upwards. But if another inspector who has eaten there at another point in time and estimated it at three stars, then we will not punish the restaurant for one minor flaw on the day. No, there really has to have been a disaster if the restaurant is recommended for stars and does not get it/them. That is why we have different inspectors, at different times, lunch and dinner, taking turns eating either '*a la carte*' or menu, visiting the place in order to get the full picture.

## NOMA's history with the *Michelin Guide*

The *Michelin Guide* (main cities of Europe) of 2004 was published in March, and did not include NOMA, which had recently opened, in November 2003. However, in the next edition (March 2005) it was included and awarded a single Michelin star. The following year, it maintained its one-star status, and received a 'rising star' label on top. Finally, in 2007, NOMA was awarded two Michelin stars, an evaluation it has maintained until this day (2012). The *Michelin Guide* system is very influential on today's culinary scene, and Kreiner, NOMA's managing director, acknowledges that both the early awarding of a single star in 2005 and the shift to two stars in 2007 had a big impact on the restaurant. However, since then, the question remains why NOMA has not yet been awarded three stars. This question has puzzled the Danish culinary scene, food critics, and even bookmakers, who all anticipated a shift to three stars in either 2010, 2011, or 2012. Since the criteria for evaluating restaurants in the *Michelin Guidebooks* are secret, nobody knows why NOMA is not yet a three-star restaurant. As Kreiner puts it: 'What we know is that the *Michelin Guidebook* series operates from fixed criteria, and therefore NOMA must not be meeting some of these criteria.'

## Perceptions of the Michelin system

When characterizing Michelin, Kreiner calls it 'classical' in its evaluation, emphasizing 'classical virtues.' By way of clarification, he adds that his impression is that three-star restaurants worldwide are rather classical and luxury oriented, with thick cloths on the tables, perhaps thick carpets, and gold or silver utensils. However, it is also possible to find a few three-star restaurants with simple and even spartan decorations, so perhaps the exceptions confirm the rule.

Even though reviewers are supposed to arrive anonymously, talk on the local culinary scene ensures that frequently Copenhagen restaurants know when a Michelin inspector is in town (Skov 2008). However, this does not mean NOMA provides anything special for those occasions, other than being aware of the inspector's presence. Speculation on the restaurant scene about what constitutes the Michelin criteria abounds. According to Kreiner, rumors claim that the *Michelin Guidebook* series includes in its star ratings criteria for context, such as tablecloth, waiter, door service, and quality of utensils (although this has been denied by the Michelin system). However, he also clearly states that NOMA is not in any way trying to develop the restaurant to become more in accordance with what rumor has it the *Michelin Guidebook* might have a set of criteria for. For example, NOMA has no tablecloths, and that is not going to change. But Kreiner acknowledges that the nature of the criteria is subject to much speculation and discussion among colleagues in the business, both in Denmark and internationally. The secrecy of the criteria seems to be a big part of the Michelin myth.

## Why does the world's best restaurant have 'only' two Michelin stars?

When comparing the criteria-based Michelin system to the voting system of San Pellegrino, it is interesting to note that the world's currently top-ranked restaurant (according to San Pellegrino) has only two Michelin stars. Several Danish newspaper articles addressed this topic in 2011, following the surprise of NOMA not receiving a third star. For instance, Danish restaurant reviewer Søren Frank complained that the Michelin system by its decision had lost its credibility (Lohse 2011), and Danish top chef Bo Bech interpreted the lack of a third star as the French wanting to punish New Nordic Cuisine, and went on to call the Michelin and the San Pellegrino systems the 'new arch enemies' on the culinary scene (Surrugue and Peitersen 2011). Kreiner diplomatically gave a statement to the press, saying that he was not disappointed about NOMA receiving two Michelin stars but that he had hoped for a third star since it would have been a nice pat on the shoulder for the restaurant staff (Ritzau 2011). In 2012, the controversy was repeated, as the Danish culinary scene was again surprised that NOMA received only two Michelin stars. Rebecca Burr, editor of the *Michelin Guide – Great Cities of Europe*, gave a statement saying that she believed the *Michelin Guide* 'has judged the world's best restaurant "by the book."' Scandinavian region chair Hedberg offered this interpretation:

It is the one million dollar question ... I think they will get their third star, but it will be when NOMA has passed its peak. Then they will be mature for a third star. Because it is just too trendy and too 'revolutionary' and too 'different' from what the Michelin usually promotes. And again, it would be sort of a defeat for them to say 'Okay, World's 50 Best list were right, it is a three star, they are one of the best in the world.' They have to keep NOMA back just for the sake of it ... But they will get their three stars.

When asked whether Mesplede had any idea as to the reason for NOMA not receiving a third star, the former editor of the French guide answered:

Well, the inspectors have probably evaluated this as beautiful and interesting cooking, but maybe it lacks the 'spark' that can be found at other three-star restaurants.

In general Mesplede was also very skeptical about classifying a meal or a restaurant, for that matter, as 'the world's best,' and had the following opinion about the San Pellegrino list:

It is like this list, San Pellegrino, how in the world could you classify the fifty best restaurants? ... They compare something which cannot be compared ... I think these lists are a 'fashion craze' and it is a magazine, which lives from making such lists, everybody earns money from this and I very much doubt the objectivity of the judgment.

When asked about the difference between criteria-based and voting-based evaluations, Kreiner gave the example of how in 2007 *Børsen*, a Danish newspaper, had a criteria-based food review scheme, with four criteria (food, wine, service, comfort). Here NOMA received top marks on food, wine, and service, but not on comfort, thus putting it below other Copenhagen restaurants (Troelsø 2007). Kreiner readily mentioned other examples of restaurants that do not fit 'typical' evaluation criteria for restaurants but nonetheless rank high on the San Pellegrino list, such as Momofuku by David Chang. In some of these restaurants it is only possible to book a table online in a one-week window, where everybody is then trying to click their way to one of the few seats available, and if you are fifteen minutes late, you lose your table. Such constraints put on the guests is a novelty in modern gastronomy, but hardly one you would appreciate if evaluating 'classical virtues.'

## Discussion

Although a century has passed since its first edition, the *Michelin Guide* remains the dominant standard of restaurant evaluation. Until recently the internal organization of the Michelin system was – like film jurying discussed by Mathieu and Bertelsen in Chapter 8 – a black box, making the foundation of restaurant ratings all but a mystery. However, with the current case study and other recent writings (Rémy 2004) some light has been shed on the ways the system seeks to evaluate restaurants, which criteria are used, and how these criteria are translated into stars.

Key features of the two ranking systems are summarized and compared in Table 9.1.

Table 9.1 *Two ranking systems:* Michelin Guide *versus San Pellegrino*

|             | Michelin                    | San Pellegrino             |
|-------------|-----------------------------|----------------------------|
|             | 'Local guide'               | Global ranking system      |
| Age         | 100 years old               | 10 years old               |
| Model       | 'External' review           | 'Peer' review              |
|             | Evaluation standard         | Voting system              |
| Legitimacy  | Trained inspectors          | Global gastro 'experts'    |
|             | Objectivity                 | Subjective experience      |
|             | Fixed criteria              | No (explicit) criteria     |
| Target      | All kinds of 'quality'      | Avant garde                |
|             | Absolute rating             | Relative ranking           |
| Logic       | Consistency and reliability | Novelty and innovation     |
|             | Tradition (modernity)       | Post-modernity             |

The vision behind the ratings was to help travelers make dining decisions (Karpik 2010) when driving around Europe on their Michelin tires. Some indication of the (lack of) evaluation of creativity and innovation in the guide is evident even in the early formulations of its purpose: 'to help vacationers have a *less risky, more practical* journey.' The internal organization of restaurant rankings is basically a set of regionally employed (and highly trained) inspectors who visit restaurants anonymously, in order to make ratings along fixed criteria (food, context, service, and so on). Innovation and creativity are not explicit criteria. A restaurant may receive multiple visits by different inspectors. The inspector subsequently makes a report that is then used in yearly regional meetings held in order to establish which restaurants are to be given a number of Michelin stars. The translation from report to number of stars takes place through group discussion and ultimately voting among the inspectors. As such, the system values consistency in quality dining, security for the individual traveler in making local dining decisions among the restaurants in a particular area, and reliability of ratings over time and among inspectors. Acknowledging that 'everyone can have a bad night,' the system is set up to check for consistency in the level of performance of a restaurant. Such a system does not seem to leave much room for creativity or innovation. Indeed, creativity, change, and innovation are not used as explicit criteria in the Michelin system. This does not mean that they cannot have a positive influence on the restaurant ratings, however.

As research has shown, producing variation in the product range is valued positively in the Michelin system (Durand *et al.* 2007), but introducing more variation than competing restaurants in the product range across disciplinary boundaries (Durand *et al.* 2007) or introducing cooking methods from other disciplines (Rao *et al.* 2004) are valued negatively. As such, although innovation is valued in the Michelin system in an absolute sense, only code-preserving innovation (similar to 'drift' (Becker 1984)) is valued in a relative sense (comparing with other restaurants).

In Michelin, standards and criteria remain constant over time, even though the translation from criteria ratings to stars is not a straightforward calculation. Indeed, the translation and weighing of criteria seek to promote a holistic view of a particular restaurant across criteria, while also considering cultural context. Nonetheless, by maintaining the same standards and criteria for restaurant ratings over time, the internal logic of the system is one of evaluative stability rather than of evolving trends. Code-violating innovation is punished in such a system as it creates confusion about the identity of the product (Zuckerman 1999). The internal structure of the Michelin system thus corresponds to a system wary of innovation, although it acknowledges innovation of the code-preserving kind. Built upon a notion of stable and fixed criteria across time when making evaluations, it assumes stable domain standards, and so is not a system looking to revitalize itself and shift criteria to the taste of the times. Given this need for consistency, stability, and reliability, the resulting list of ratings and restaurants develops rather slowly. Although the *Guide* is published every year, much of its content (up to 75 percent) remains constant. The clear focus is on what the *Michelin Guide* considers the highest 'quality' in gastronomy over time, while not paying much attention to fads and trends in cuisine.

The system seeks to gain legitimacy in the industry in several ways. Unlike awards given by film festival juries, the ratings are always made anonymously by trained inspectors, who must have no interest in the restaurants they rate. The Michelin system in this sense maintains a separation from the restaurant industry, and thus gets much of its credibility from this seeming disconnectedness and independence, like other types of 'external' evaluation (Brunsson and Jacobsson 2002; Hedmo *et al.* 2006). Evaluative systems, like Michelin, as noted by Durand and McGuire (2005), have to legitimate themselves toward their constituents (restaurants and other gastro-experts) but also meet a demand to expand their domain, in the way that Michelin has done successfully over the years with the introduction of guides to new territories (Bouty *et al.* 2012). Nonetheless, criticism has been voiced about how the fixed criteria seem to favor certain kinds of cuisine (notably French cuisine), and about notions of what a high-quality restaurant and a meal might be. Such criticisms impact on Michelin's legitimacy and its claim to 'objectivity.'

Turning to the San Pellegrino list, we find that its ten-year history has been one of increased popularity and the list is now an important evaluative system (as evidenced, for example, in the impact on the publicity and bookings of NOMA upon reaching the top position). However, as noted by English (2005: 53), the competitive character of cultural life, which prizes themselves crudely emblematize, is reflected not just in the individual prizes but also in the nature of their relationships to each other. New prizes (San Pellegrino) may emerge to compete with established systems of evaluation (Michelin), and would (as prizes do) struggle to defend or improve their position in the field of cultural production. While perhaps less so officially, but certainly unofficially, the newcomer (San Pellegrino) attempts to pinpoint the shortcomings of the existing giant in cuisine ranking (Michelin) in making claims as to the importance of its existence. But in doing so, it runs the risk of being seen as a second-order ranking system merely living off the reputation of the Michelin system. The San Pellegrino voting system is based on an academy of 800 well-traveled food enthusiasts, who vote for the restaurants they consider the 'best in the world.' It is thus consensus driven, and aimed at the avant garde in the global 'field' of gastronomy. Contrary to the Michelin system, the San Pellegrino system appears as a self- or peer-administered evaluation (Brunsson and Jacobsson 2002; Hedmo *et al.* 2006) and gains its legitimacy from its Academy of gastronomy experts and 'peers.'

Besides the claim to be rating the 'best' restaurants, there are no official criteria to apply when casting votes. Informally, however, some Academy members seem to share criteria such as 'innovation' and 'authenticity.' While the former criterion in itself encourages change, the latter can be seen as essentially demarking a conceptual change in gastronomy, away from molecular cooking (where innovation lies in novel cooking techniques, exemplified by the Spanish restaurant, El Bulli) to the use of local and in-season ingredients (frequently foraged by the restaurant staff themselves) that may be uncommon in cuisine, and prepared according to reinvented techniques that borrow their inspiration from ancient, and perhaps forgotten, ways of making food.

'Originality' constitutes one of the most widespread and important criteria in the evaluation of cultural production. As seen elsewhere in this book, originality is considered of utmost importance in determining whether a cultural product in essence is moving or changing a domain in valued directions. This we have already seen in Chapter 7 about advertising awards and Chapter 8 about film juries, and was even discernible in the evaluation of oriental carpets, despite its equal obsession with patina and history (see Chapter 10). In her studies of academic funding panels, Lamont (2009) also found that across domains, 'originality' was one of the top two criteria mentioned and valued among panel members (the other being 'significance'). This is important to note, given that 'originality' rarely appears as an overt official criterion in academic funding bodies' instruction to panel members. All the same, this does not preclude members from applying the 'originality' criterion to their ratings in such juried panels. Lamont's work also shows that 'originality' may mean many different things to different people: 'originality' in the social sciences is not necessarily the same as 'originality' in the humanities. As such, it is one thing for the Michelin system not to evaluate or use the criterion of originality officially in its '*essai de table*' report. But what is perhaps even more important in ensuring that the Michelin system does not value originality is its strict training, and system of attempting to ensure an 'objective' evaluation of the meal, without regard to each inspector's personal idiosyncrasies, by means of repeat evaluations by different inspectors. By taking the inspectors' idiosyncrasies out of the Michelin equation, the system is in effect ensuring that originality does not creep into the ratings anyway (as Lamont's work suggests might happen). Yet, Michelin did discover NOMA in 2005 and positively evaluated the restaurant's gastronomic venture (a year *before* NOMA entered the top fifty of the San Pellegrino list).

While the San Pellegrino list does not hold originality, change, and innovation as formal criteria, they seem to be informal ones (at least for the moment). This does not mean, though, that 'innovation' and 'authenticity' will remain the criteria of choice for the Academy. The system explicitly resists specific criteria, and in addition replaces one-third of the Academy members each year, thereby ensuring that a continuous shift of standards and criteria seeps into the system. It is not clear how new Academy members are found and selected, but it seems likely that they are recommended by existing members and recruited through their networks, thus creating a 'club-like' Academy. The internal logic seems to be not only to acknowledge and allow change in standards and criteria over time but in fact to encourage them. The resulting ranking is a list with a multitude of changes occurring each year and with multiple placement changes. Such an organization allows changes in industry standards and criteria to be quickly mapped onto the list. A 'trendy' restaurant may enter and move up the list in a very short time span (as exemplified by NOMA). However, the voting rules also make the list volatile, in that the entry of new Academy members may cause multiple unexplainable shifts on the list from one year to the next. In essence, the list appears to be quickly capturing the shifting trends of cuisine, perhaps at the expense of more stable and enduring values (if such exist).

The San Pellegrino system gains its legitimacy in gastronomy primarily through the selection of a long list of cuisine gatekeepers (individuals in high standing in the industry), as well as the 'democratic' and somewhat 'transparent' voting system established. The choice of explicitly abolishing fixed criteria in the casting of votes further underscores the aim to make a list that captures the consensual opinion of the global community rather than the standards of any particular discipline. In this respect, the list appears to be acknowledging and encouraging domain change. Such a system may capture non-durable innovations that quickly fade away (the 'flash in the pan' or 'flavor of the month'), but may also more easily and more quickly capture and acknowledge change that moves the domain of cuisine in novel directions, crossing boundaries, extending categories, and breaking rules. Basically, it results in a shortening of 'standard life cycles', capturing fashions and trends in shorter temporal increments, while abolishing the hunt for timeless quality.

It should be noted, though, that a system acknowledging shifting domain standards does not necessarily imply placing value on restaurant innovation. In principle, it is quite possible for a voting system to be conservative and stable, and to disregard innovation. Therefore, it is not a given that San Pellegrino will maintain its high turnover of restaurants on the list; this would depend on whether or not 'restaurant innovation' remains an important informal criterion among the raters.

In conclusion, the internal logic and structure of the Michelin and San Pellegrino evaluative systems differ in their interpretations of how they seek 'consensus' through the application of 'standards.' Hedberg explains it as follows:

So I would say volatility is a bit too high on the 'World's 50 best' list, whereas it is too low on the Michelin list. I mean, some of the three-star restaurants in France have been three-star restaurants for forty years, and should have been taken down to two or one or zero perhaps fifteen years ago. So it is a very conservative and a very stagnant list.

In short, while the Michelin system looks toward fixed criteria and consistent quality (gaining legitimacy through independence and anonymity), the San Pellegrino system encourages both restaurant innovation and shortened standard life cycles (gaining legitimacy through novelty and votes among a panel of gatekeepers). The Michelin evaluative system produces an absolute rating of the single restaurant, whereas the San Pellegrino evaluative system produces a relative ranking list comparing and ranking several dozen restaurants, of which one is nominated as the 'best.' In this way, it provides high visibility and media interest aligning with the 'name economy' (Moeran 2003) and contemporary society's quest for 'winners' through an endless series of 'competitions' in almost all aspects of life.

# References

Anand, N. 2011. The retrospective use of tournament rituals in field configuration: the case of the 1976 'Judgement of Paris' wine tasting. In *Negotiating Values in the Creative Industries*, ed. Brian Moeran and Jesper Strandgaard Pedersen, pp. 321–333. Cambridge University Press.

Anand, N. and Brittany C. Jones. 2008. Tournament rituals, category dynamics, and field configuration: the case of the Booker prize. *Journal of Management Studies* 45 (1): 36–60.

Anand, N. and Mary R. Watson. 2004. Tournament rituals in the evolution of fields: the case of the Grammy awards. *Academy of Management Journal* 47 (1): 59–80.

Becker, Howard S. 1984. *Art Worlds*. Berkeley and Los Angeles: University of California Press.

Bourdieu, Pierre. 1984. *Distinction: A social critique of the judgement of taste*. Cambridge, MA: Harvard University Press.

1993. *The Field of Cultural Production*. Cambridge: Polity Press.

Boutaiba, Sami and Jesper Strandgaard Pedersen. 2003. Creating an MBA identity – between field and organization. In *Inside the Business Schools – The content of European business education*, ed. Rolv P. Amdam, Ragnhild Kvalshaugen and Eirinn. Larsen, pp. 197–218. Frederiksberg: Copenhagen Business School Press.

Bouty, Isabelle, Marie-Leandre Gomez and Carole Drucker-Godard. 2012. Maintaining an institution: the institutional work of Michelin in haute cuisine around the world. *Paper presented at the 8th New Institutionalism Workshop in Barcelona*, March.

Brunsson, Nils and Bengt Jacobsson. 2002. *A World of Standards*. Oxford University Press.

Croidieu, Gregoire. 2011. An inconvenient truce: the 1855 Medoc wine event. In *Negotiating Values in the Creative Industries*, ed. Brian Moeran and Jesper Strandgaard Pedersen, pp. 294–320. Cambridge University Press.

DiMaggio, Paul. 1987. Classification in art. *American Sociological Review* 52 (4): 440–455.

Durand, Rodolphe and Jean McGuire. 2005. Legitimating agencies in the face of seduction: the case of AACSB. *Organization Studies* 26 (2): 165–196.

Durand, Rodolphe, Hayagreeva Rao and Philippe Monin. 2007. Code and conduct in French cuisine: impact of code changes on external evaluations. *Strategic Management Journal* 28 (5): 455–472.

English, James F. 2005. *The Economy of Prestige: Prizes, awards, and the circulation of cultural value*. Cambridge, MA: Harvard University Press.

Hedmo, Tina. 2003. The Europeanisation of Business Education. In *Inside the Business Schools – The content of European business education*, ed. Rolv P. Amdam, Ragnhild Kvalshaugen and Eirinn Larsen, pp. 247–266. Frederiksberg: Copenhagen Business School Press.

Hedmo, Tina, Kerstin Sahlin-Anderson and Linda Wedlin. 2006. The emergence of a European regulatory field in management education. In *Transnational Governance*, ed. Marie-Laure Djelic and Kerstin Sahlin-Anderson, pp. 308–332. Cambridge University Press.

Karpik, Lucien. 2010. *Valuing the Unique: The economics of singularies*. Princeton University Press.

Lamont, Michele. 2009. *How Professors Think. Inside the curious world of academic judgment*. Cambridge, MA: Harvard University Press.

Lane, Christel. 2010. The Michelin-starred restaurant sector as a cultural industry: a cross-national comparison of restaurants in Britain and Germany. *Food, Culture and Society* 13 (4): 493–519.

2011. Taste makers in the 'fine dining' restaurant industry: the attribution of aesthetic and economic value by gastronomic guides. *Paper presented at the SASE Conference in July 2011 in Madrid*, in the network on Creative Industries.

Lohse, G. 2011. Michelin-guiden har mistet sin troværdighed [The Michelin Guide has lost its credibility]. *DR Nyheder* April 16.

Moeran, Brian. 2003. Celebrities and the name economy. In *Anthropological Perspectives on Economic Development and Integration. Research in economic anthropology*, Vol. 22, ed. Norbert Dannhaeuser and Cynthia Werner, pp. 299–321. Oxford: Emerald Publishing Group.

Rao, Hayagreeva, Philippe Monin and Rodolphe Durand. 2004. Crossing enemy lines: culinary categories as constraints in French gastronomy. *Paper presented at the Organizational Ecology and Strategy Conference, Washington University in St Louis*, April 23–24.

Rémy, Pascal. 2004. *L'inspecteur se met à table*. Paris: Equateur.

Ritzau. 2011. Vi er ikke skuffede over to stjerner [We are not disappointed over two stars], *Politiken* April 16.

Skov, O. R. 2008. Stjernekrigen [Star Wars], Magasinet. *Politiken* March 16.

Skyum-Nielsen, Rune. 2010. The perfect storm. In *NOMA: Time and place in Nordic cuisine*, ed. Rene Redzepi. London: Phaidon Press.

Surrugue, Stephanie and Nina Peitersen. 2011. Var Franskmændene sure? [Were the French angry?]. *Politiken* April 17.

Troelsø, O. 2007. Danmarks verdensberømte restaurant [Denmark's world famous restaurant]. *Børsen* April 27.

Wedlin, Linda. 2010. Going global: rankings as rhetorical devices to construct an international field of management education. *Management Learning* 42 (2): 199–218.

Wolff, M. R. 2011. From idea to transformation. *Food & Design Denmark* Special Issue 9: 10–11.

Zuckerman, Ezra W. 1999. The categorical imperative: securities analysts and the illegitimacy discount. *American Journal of Sociology* 104 (5): 1398–1438.

# 10 Patina meets fashion: on the evaluation and devaluation of oriental carpets

FABIAN FAURHOLT CSABA AND GÜLIZ GER

This chapter examines how different actors account for the quality and value of oriental carpets. It introduces the subject matter through three case examples: how an auction house expert approaches establishing the market value of carpets; how a dedicated rug collector accounts for his tastes and tactics; and how a quality controller goes about rating the season's work of a village weaving cooperative dedicated to the revival of craft traditions. The evaluative practices of the actors reflect a field that values age and tradition, rather than novelty and creativity, but also a field in decline. In this sense ours is a special case of the evaluation of creativity.

The chapter reconsiders and applies Grant McCracken's (1988) concept of patina in the analysis of how, why, and the ways in which signs of age are valued in oriental carpets. We examine closely how the material properties, processes, and affordances of oriental carpets lend themselves to symbolic uses and judgments of value. Acknowledging that material properties reflecting wear, tear, and care are judged differently, we present a matrix that discerns four approaches to the perception and appreciation of oriental carpets. While sharing some common ground, each approach appraises carpets according to a particular set of criteria and techniques, and privileges certain names, categories, or genres of oriental textiles, while devaluing others. Actors apply such schemes in identifying, appreciating, and evaluating the combinations of the physical properties – patina and others – of carpets.

Although the devaluation of oriental carpets appears to confirm McCracken's claim that patina all but lost its significance with the rise of fashion in the modern era, we seek to demonstrate that the concept of patina might still inform analyses of contemporary cultural markets and products. Not only does the analysis of patina provide a lens through which to explore the connections between material and symbolic properties of cultural objects which are vital for understanding and determining their value, we also suggest that rethinking the relationship between patina and fashion offers new perspectives on how signs and concepts of age and novelty factor into judgments of the appreciation of creative and cultural products.

## 'What is it worth?' An exceptional carpet under the hammer

On September 7, 2007, an antique Persian carpet reached a hammer price of €135,000 at the leading auction house in Denmark. The amount not only set a new record for an oriental carpet in Denmark, it was a staggering fourteen times the estimated sales price. The auction houses carpet specialist, Frederik, who is also on the board of the Danish Rug Association, recounts his experience with the fine rug:

It was strange … it came from some estate in Jutland. One of my colleagues got it from this estate and he sent me a picture of it and I told him, 'You know what, send it over to me! It ought to be sold over here.' And when I rolled it out, I could see it was of a real fine quality. It was quite out of the ordinary. Then I showed it to one of my colleagues – a former carpet dealer with many years of experience in the business. And he was also almost bowled over. Then, I realized as the day of the auction approached and inquiries were made about it … and those making the inquiries … When you know some of the real big names are asking about it, you know it has the potential for going really high.

The item was a pictorial rug from Kerman in Iran measuring 270 × 164 cm. With a knot count of about 700,000 knots per square meter, this means that it is made up of some 3 million knots. Its design depicts fruit trees with a variety of birds on the field and animals and portraits of male figures of different nationalities on its main border. Woven inscriptions identify who ordered, designed, and executed the carpet and date it to 1336 AH, which corresponds to 1908. The auction catalog identified the carpet in detail, described it as a 'unique masterpiece,' and estimated it at €10,000. Auction houses may deliberately set the estimated price attractively (low) in order to encourage more buyers to attend in the hope of making a good deal, and thereby help spark a bidding contest. But the auction house expert readily concedes that the estimated price was set too low. Later he discovered that a similar carpet had been sold a couple of years earlier at Christie's for about £120,000, and even if the prime Danish auction house is 'not Christie's' and cannot attract quite the same clientele of top international buyers, the expert feels he ought to have factored previous international auction prices into his estimate. He still marvels at the carpet's details when asked to explain its qualities and value:

Exceptionally fine quality: excellent condition, then the overall impression, and when you went in and looked at the birds ... really, when you saw how nuances had been knotted into the fruits, if you imagine, it was as if there was an inflow of light from one side. That was the impression one got looking at that apple, you know. The inflow of light was almost knotted into it, you see. And like, unique and rare ... that's a big part of it. So there were four or five factors that in combination made it so attractive.

While attesting to the enduring appreciation of oriental carpets in the West, the recent record price does not signal a healthy market for fine hand-woven carpets in Western Europe. Indeed, the interest in traditional home furnishings and antiques in general, and oriental carpets in particular, has been diminishing. This, and the discrepancy between the pre-auction estimate and the hammer price, seems to confirm widespread notions about the opaque and erratic nature of the market for oriental carpets. It is not only novice buyers who find themselves bewildered, even experts at times have difficulty determining the monetary value of rugs.

The record bid in Denmark came from an American dealer, who believed that he would be able to resell the carpet at a profit to a customer after a few years. But what might possess a private collector, not necessarily a very wealthy one, to spend extraordinary sums on old floor coverings? How are such inclinations developed? Consider the account of an avid American collector, who has built a world-class collection in his special field of interest, on how his passion and addiction developed.

## Developing a passion and addiction

Harry is a naturalized American of British origin and an accomplished academic who travels frequently. He was introduced to oriental carpets through his wife-to-be's carpets – which he now considers to be 'junk' – that she received as gifts while working in Turkey in the late 1960s. Harry now has a collection of 200 exquisite pieces, bought across the US and Europe.

He recalls with pride his first steps to becoming a collector and explains how he started pursuing his newly realized passion for color:

One of my first two pieces I bought from a picker in Chicago, in the 1970s. Not in good shape. A Malayir medallion, corroded celadon green, earth colored apricot. I was more interested in color, I was a color person. I loved the Malayir: the colors, design of the field was medallion, like the Kuran, simple border. I loved the elegance of the simple border on the earth colored apricot. The green was lower than the rest; the 3D texture was wonderful.

After reading about carpets, he decided to collect 'narrowly': only from a very small part of Iran – Fars, nomadic, Quasghai (a Turkic tribe) – and a certain era, 1870–1910. He collects carpets and any textile from that era, 'when rugs were being made and exported to Europe in great quantities from Iran,' and when all wool was handspun and all dyes natural. The introduction and rapid spread of synthetic dyes and machine-spun yarn in the late nineteenth century, even to the most remote regions, carried the seeds of decline of the oriental carpet in terms of aesthetic and technical quality, as well as 'authenticity.' While this development was instrumental in the producers' attempts to meet increased Western demand, it obstructed the art of oriental carpets since these carpets entailed less variation, known as 'abrash' and 'variegation' in the colors (Eiland and Eiland 1998: 51) and the resultant regularity of structure, surface, and color left discerning buyers disenchanted. Moreover, these dyes faded unsatisfactorily and the fade is an important aesthetic dimension of oriental carpets. Eiland and Eiland (1998: 60) note that synthetic dyes 'represent one of the rare examples in which modern science has, at least so far, failed to match traditional standards.' Carpet connoisseurs like Harry gradually turned their interest exclusively toward older, naturally dyed carpets, which as time passed became more and more rare and expensive. Hence, rugs produced in the past are idealized and narratives of declining standards underpin judgments of their cultural and market value.

The depth (and price) of Harry's passion became evident to himself and his wife in the late 1970s.

One decision that was truly momentous in retrospect: an exhibition in London, I think it was 1978, of late nineteenth-century Quasghai rugs, for sale in relation to the book *Woven Treasures*. I heard about the book, then went to London, and bought the cover rug from the book. Which knocked my socks off. So did fifteen other carpets from the show. I paid one third of a year's salary. Huge amount of money, my darling wife let me know it. The place was sky high. Dollar was weak, 2.4 to the pound. 7,000 pounds – 17,000 USD. Too high a price! But I loved the rug. I was making a commitment to myself as a collector. Then I knew that I was willing to pay fortunes for carpets. I realized my commitment. Next day there was an auction. I bought another carpet, same quality, for 30 percent cheaper. I started thinking about the price differential. After that day, I never overpaid for any carpet. On my way back from London I thought, I am the owner of two world-class carpets.

To his disappointment, his wife reacted 'not very positively,' yet she tolerated his passion. Harry laments that 'she has been interested in rugs on the floor, not as art' and that, unlike other collectors' wives who are interested and go to conventions and exhibitions with their husbands, his wife does not: 'I feel very sad about that. That we could not participate as couples. I am known as a quiet outsider, not an insider.'

Harry is also disheartened by the diminishing interest in fine oriental carpets, experienced by Frederik. 'It breaks the heart of the collector to look at *Architectural Digest*,' he laments, suggesting that now maybe one of twenty of homes represented have rugs. Ten years ago, he reckons the ratio was eight out of twenty, fifteen years ago sixteen out of twenty. Harry also points to the adverse influence of interior design:

The interior decorator business likes sleek, modern lines. Marble and wooden floors for which you pay a fortune – you want the floor to be seen. Carpets are regarded as fussy, not sleek and modern. Now people want expensive furniture and paintings to dominate a room rather than carpets. . . . Young people are socialized to a different taste. No one under 40–45 buys rugs any more.

The carpet trade has responded in ways that disturb the admirer of oriental craft traditions. 'So in many countries carpet producers turned over backwards and are making carpets that are oriental in structure but not in design – monochromatic or few colors.' The growing influence of contemporary design and interior decoration trends, in other words, plays a key role in eroding demand at least in the general or decorative market as opposed to the collectors'.

## Just like the old

In response to the realization of the adverse effects of compromises in the craft, there have been initiatives aimed at keeping alive and reviving local carpet production and craft traditions. One of them involves the

Turkish-based German chemist Harold Böhmer, who has applied modern spectrographic analysis to rediscover natural dyes and helped spark a series of initiatives in Turkey (Csaba and Ger 2000; Eiland 1993; Ger and Csaba 2000; Opie 1998). Together with Marmara University, Böhmer co-founded the DOBAG project, a cooperative in Western Anatolia. DOBAG reproduces the designs of the region around Çanakkale, Ezine, Bergama, and Manisa. According to Böhmer:

We do the designs of the last 100 years. This is a work that lives here, continuation of living traditions. Besides, these designs that weavers have always made, we have them make in different colors. The only difference (from the 100-year-old carpets) is the difference in colors.

Serife Atlihan, the university professor in charge of quality control and general supervision, gives examples of how she and Böhmer seek to guide the weavers in the cooperative:

We say, use white sparingly. White does not look beautiful, the gaze is captured by the white, too bright. The customers say so, too. We say, don't put yellow and green next to each other. Yellow is used after the indigo to make green. When they are adjacent, yellow appears too strong.... We did research on aesthetics, the color combinations of old carpets. They never used yellow and green next to each other.

Böhmer and Atlihan's evaluation criteria emphasize the technical qualities and the neatness of the weave and the cut. Atlihan grades each carpet by examining the front and the back carefully. She gives three grades: super, 1, and 2, but gives 2 rarely. On one occasion when we were accompanying her, she rated eighteen of the thirty-five carpets as 'super.' The earnings of the weavers depend on these ratings. Explaining what 'neat' is, Atlihan shows us a rug:

Look, the back is dirty. Threads are hanging. The weaver did not cut them out properly. We tell them 100 times. They do it in a hurry and leave it (without properly finishing it).... That one, the sides are too tight, makes the carpet look like lettuce leaves. Have to knot the tassels twice.... Not using the scissors properly, putting in an extra thread, the ends pulling, wavy ends and sides, lettuce, that's bad. The worst is when there is a fold, like lettuce. Then it ages badly. Inserting one thread loosely, one tightly makes a lettuce. Have to feed in at the same tightness.... This one, the trimming is good, the cut is good, the technique is good, this is 'super.' But the side is a bit crooked, not a big problem. When the whole is very beautiful, little errors can be tolerated.

In addition to the neatness of the work, the designs are important. Responding to our inquiry about aesthetics, she says:

The top border on this one is too narrow.... That one, the patterns in the middle are too intertwined. When there are three large patterns in the middle, it is better to have tiny designs around it; the medium-size designs are too much. Small ones make it more spacious, open.

She also checks the proportion of the length and the width: 'Too short or too narrow is not suitable for living rooms. People want to place carpets in the middle of a room, not under the furniture.'

DOBAG carpets are sold internationally, but demand is declining. While some customers adore DOBAG carpets, others are less enthusiastic. An American scholar of Turkish folk art suggested: 'In Çanakkale, Balıkesir, Manisa women were weaving, hand spinning and making natural dyes before Böhmer. Very beautiful carpets too. Now with Böhmer and Atlihan's strict control, some DOBAG carpets are becoming stale, stiff, boring.' A Turkish dealer concurs: 'DOBAG was an exciting project. But they lacked something. They could not achieve the same researcher-scholar-creative dynamism they showed in dyes and colors in creating a variety in designs and sizes. Hundreds of look-alike small carpets.' So, producing carpets 'just like the old' may not always work well, at least not in this case, even though the once-lost techniques are reinvented.

## Signs of age and value: beyond patina?

For the mass of society, the notion of patina is itself hopelessly antique, a charming notion that has passed from fashion. Patina, if it lives on, does so in tiny social enclaves where it keeps the gate with all its former perspicuity but precious little of its former glory. (McCracken 1988: 43)

Why are older carpets highly valued, but less so than in the past? Which material properties in rugs are appreciated and why?

McCracken's theory of patina (1988) seems like a pertinent framework in which to address issues of evaluation and devaluation raised in our case of the market for oriental textiles. His analysis accounts for the physical properties or processes of aging and explains their symbolic significance and social function. For McCracken, patina reflects conditions under which value and status are represented by things that are old, rather than new. Such conditions prevailed in medieval and early modern Europe, where the 'patina' system of consumption and status representation enjoyed its heyday, before being eclipsed by fashion, without entirely disappearing in the modern world.

Some of the material processes and properties that are valued in judgments of oriental textiles – such as the softening of colors, natural corrosion of pile, and integrity of structure, material, and design – can be understood as patina. Arguably, the golden age of oriental carpets was in the medieval and early modern period. In this era, rugs were among the most potent symbols of power and status (as evidenced in the display of oriental carpet in portraits of Europe's ecclesiastical and aristocratic elites) and the craft reached its highest level of acclaim and sophistication. Despite periodical and regional revival, the oriental carpet art and market has been in decline ever since and now, as patina, shows little of its former glory. So apparently McCracken's theory of patina is applicable to oriental carpets and offers explanations for the valuation, as well as the long-term devaluation, of these cultural artifacts. In the following section, we will first review the main elements in McCracken's theory of patina and address the limitations of interpreting oriental carpets solely in terms of patina. Then we suggest ways to extend and revise McCracken's analysis of patina – in ways that inform evaluative practices in cultural and creative industries.

## Patina and the representation of status

In his essay 'Even dearer in our thoughts – Patina and the Representation of Status before and after the Eighteenth Century, consumer anthropologist McCracken (1988) advances the concept of patina as a key to understanding strategies of status display and historical shifts in systems of consumption. Patina is a material property – the small signs of aging such as dents, chips, oxidization, or being worn away that accumulate on the surfaces of objects of human manufacture over time, due to exposure to the elements or other aspects. He describes poetically how a thing's 'original surface takes on a surface of its own' (1988: 32), capturing how objects in the process of patination are singularized and develop an identity. But these alterations of surfaces have symbolic significance, serving as evidence of the status of the owner. Patina does not communicate status directly but – more subtly – authenticates it. By suggesting how long the object has been in the possession of the owner's family, patina enables distinctions between old and new wealth. In early modern

England, wealth might have been able to buy individuals all the trappings of the nobility, but escaping the stigma of commonness took time, a long time – several generations, in fact. The accumulation of patina was an effective public indicator of how far along the long path to gentle standing a family was.

McCracken argues that patina was an effective vehicle for communicating social distinction. Since it reproduces some of the qualities of the thing it signifies, patina represents an iconic sign (in Charles Sanders Peirce's scheme). The accumulation of this sign of age on family possessions, in other words, signifies the duration of that family's claims to wealth. Obviously, patina's communication of status depends on a string of assumptions and inferences observers make about the individuals' status claims: patina expresses the age of an object; the object's age reflects the duration it has been in a family's possession; the possession of the object indicates a considerable discretionary income, which in turn suggests an elevated social status (McCracken 1988: 36). The iconic relationship between the signifier and the signified facilitates the inference of patina as a measure of true status. The connection is natural and motivated, rather than arbitrary. Appadurai (1996: 73–74) calls this transfer 'the subtle shift of patina from the object to its owner or neighbor,' and notes that this process can be fully accomplished only in a context of felicitous conditions.

McCracken considers patina strategies in relation to three other systems of status display and verification: sumptuary laws regulating consumption practices according to class status; possession of closely guarded insignia and seals as proof of class status; and 'invisible ink' strategies – the cultivation of certain kinds of knowledge, which serve as the primary indicators of group affiliation. The patina system has the advantage (over the former two) of not requiring a central authority to issue and reinforce rules or official signs of rank. Every social actor is able to approximate status and immediately tell apart legitimate from fraudulent status claims. However, since patina's status symbolism is better understood by those in established, elevated positions of status, it has the same advantage as the 'invisible ink' strategy in operating as a 'hidden code immediately intelligible to those of genuine standing and well concealed from all but the most sophisticated pretenders' (McCracken 1988: 35). Patina, though, is more robust than the 'invisible ink' strategy, which, according to McCracken, works best in confined, static social environments.

The patina system was eroded by the acceleration of fashion and its expansion to a range of product categories (including houses and home furnishings) with the consumer revolution in eighteenth-century England. As new products and tastes emerged and became status markers, patina offered no protection for high-standing social groups. This set in motion a dynamic of constant superordinate innovation, rapid trickle-down, and subordinate emulation. Since then, fashion has reigned as the dominant system of status representation, and patina has played an ever more marginal role.

For McCracken real patina objects are non-exchangeable: they lose their power if they are acquired. In other words, they are inalienable 'extensions of the family,' to paraphrase Belk (1988). Patina shifts from object to owner, from material property to status marker, only as long as it stays in the possession of the family. However, this comes across as a very narrow conception of patina, which forecloses further exploration of patina strategies in the modern era. McCracken does not go into any detailed investigations of cases of patina, neither their materiality in particular products nor of detailed studies of how 'subtle shift of patina from the object to its owner' worked in practice.

So, how might the analysis of patina be applied in studying the physical and symbolic properties and evaluation of oriental carpets? Rather than assuming that patina objects are inalienable, or at least lose their value as status markers outside the family, we suggest that patina on objects might have a sign value for others and that patina objects do have (independent) cultural and economic value. Ultimately this will lead us to question whether patina has been eclipsed by fashion and is of negligible significance today. We believe that a more open conception of patina might lead to the reconsideration of what impact patina and similar material properties have on the meaning and value of objects, beyond their ability to (in)validate status claims in hierarchical societies of the past. Drawing on and moving beyond McCracken's inquiry, we now return to the case of oriental carpets.

## Patina and oriental carpets

We have seen that while the market for oriental carpets has been in decline, higher prices for top-range carpets, as well as trends favoring certain types, suggest a more complicated picture. As the production of non-industrial-quality carpets has dwindled, supply has depended on older carpets re-entering the market. Since the older carpets grad-ually wear out beyond repair and restoration, the stock of old carpets constantly shrinks. As the number of fine carpets in good condition gets scarcer, prices increase. Periodically, the market is revitalized by the (re)discovery of previously neglected types of oriental textiles. Such trends tend to change tastes and patterns of demand. It also makes oriental carpets more susceptible to fashion and design trends. Nevertheless, oriental rugs are no longer among the primary markers of taste and status, and consequently have lost much of their appeal as objects of trade and investment. While a community of dedicated collectors, scholars, and dealers continues to share members' knowl-edge and passion for rugs, the interest and appreciative skills in the field are not being adopted by younger generations enough to repro-duce market demand. However, markets are dynamic and demand is based on the fashions and trends that define the desirability of a good, as much as the features of that good. Oriental carpets are no excep-tion. It is not unreasonable to expect that when home-decoration fashions change, the oriental carpet market will also change.

Regardless of levels of demand, we believe that the analysis of patina needs to deal more closely with the material properties of cultural goods and explore their connection to the symbolic meanings and values of these goods. McCracken implies that patina can occur naturally, or can be a result of human use, and assumes patina to be a fairly accurate and transparent indicator of the age of objects, which enables it to act as evidence of duration of ownership. But his lack of engagement with material properties leaves a number of questions unanswered: do all signs of age constitute patina? Does patina signify things other than age? What if signs of age result from human efforts to advance, delay, or restore patina? Does patina refer only to the desirable signs of age? If so, which signs of age are desirable, and, as Appadurai (1996: 75) puts it, how might we distinguish wear from tear?

The material properties of oriental carpets help illustrate some of these issues. We have seen how color is a key factor in the evaluation (and devaluation) of oriental carpets. As Eiland and Eiland (1998: 50) point out, 'the rug's appearance and manner in which it ages are to a large extent dependent on the dyes that have been used' and, when carpet making relied on complicated methods of natural dyeing, the cost of dyes is likely to have matched that of the wool. Dyes differ in their color fastness and the long-term effect their application has on the wool. Colors tend to fade or otherwise change with exposure to light or abrasion. Colors may bleed when exposed to moisture and the dyestuff or processes required to achieve certain hues weaken the fibers of the wool. Some of these effects are regarded as detrimental to the carpet, some are found desirable, and some are a matter of degree, debate, or taste. The bleeding of colors and rapid fading are undesirable, since they are found to upset the harmony of the colors or obscure design through loss of contrast. The aging processes through which colors settle, mellow, or soften are generally highly sought-after aesthetic effects. Dyes that produce dark colors tend to weaken the wool and erode the pile quicker than other dyes. This can create a so-called relief effect, where the darker areas in the design have lower pile than the lighter areas. At a certain point, the darker pile disappears altogether, disrupting the structure of the rug. The relief effect (normally) attests to a certain age and is considered natural and interesting. In fact, it is sometimes imitated by cutting the pile of darker wool more than the surround pile. It might indicate either the use of natural dyes (and traditional craftsmanship) or early synthetic dyes. Both attest to a certain age, but are usually judged differently.

Another physical property of carpets relating to color – but not directly, at least, a sign of age – is abrash: variations in color. A field of yellow in a design may have slight variations in the shade of yellows in horizontal lines. This effect is usually found on so-called tribal or village carpets, which rely on small-scale production. In rural settings yarn is dyed in small batches and each batch tends to vary slightly in colors because the dyeing process is difficult to control and replicate, especially with natural dyes. Abrash might be perceived as either an imperfection, resulting from sloppiness, or a hallmark of traditional folk arts, which gives the rug uniqueness, charm, and spirit. Abrash might be an indication of age, since most recent carpet production is based on larger-scale, centralized dyeing using more standardized and controllable synthetic dyes. But here we find that the effect can also be produced deliberately to imitate more primitive and older rugs for commercial purposes.

There are many indicators of the age of carpets other than those pertaining to color. Some are clearly related to natural processes of wear and decomposition (sheen, thickness of pile, integrity of structure); others depend on accumulated knowledge about the craft and design traditions of different regions and eras. Certain combinations of spinning, knotting, or weaving techniques, sizes, stylistic elements, or other properties are known to be characteristic for a given region and era of production. We might ask whether such combinations can be considered patina as a physical property. They are not 'direct' and 'natural' signs of age, but still evidence of a rug's origin in time and space. They represent a more indirect connection between object and age than the patina discussed by McCracken.

This points to the difficulty in distinguishing physical properties from symbolic properties of cultural goods. And it also brings us back to McCracken's notion of 'invisible ink,' the 'hidden' codes of status symbolism that enable distinction and social exclusion.

Anyone entering the world of oriental carpets will feel at a loss as to how to make sense of the variety and value of carpets. Unable to make such distinctions, the novice has little idea of what the carpet (or the way the owner talks about or displays it) might reveal about its owner (their wealth, knowledge, or taste). An expert, however, may know more than the owner about the carpet's age, origin, or value and will have a clear idea of how this reflects back on the owner. It is in this sense that we might talk about 'invisible ink' and 'hidden' codes. Bourdieu refers to the 'explicit or implicit schemes of perception and appreciation' in the consumption of cultural goods (1984: 2). It is such schemes, which are not necessarily entirely invisible, that actors apply in investing cultural goods with meaning, value, and capacity for sensory or aesthetic enjoyment.

We discern different approaches to, or (sub)schemes of, perception and appreciation in oriental carpets. Veteran collector Sam Gordon, in a critique of rug scholarship, proposed a distinction between what he calls 'anthropological' or 'ethnological,' 'art-historical,' 'structural,' and 'aesthetic' or 'socio-psychological' approaches to carpets (Gordon 2001). He finds that rug scholars, for whom he expresses great disdain, tend to view carpets through any one of the first three lenses. They neglect the aesthetic gaze, which for him represents genuine appreciation of oriental carpets. While Gordon's classification is sketchy, it does provide a rough framework through which our analysis of modes of perception and appreciation, material and symbolic properties, and evaluative criteria can be further developed.

The 'art-historical' approach goes back to the nineteenth century, when museum curators started to acquire and display classical sixteenth- and seventeenth-century carpets. They used knowledge about European paintings displaying oriental carpets with distinctive patterns to approximate the date and origins of fine items in European collections. The ties forged to European fine art and nobility (and perhaps their oriental counterparts) contributed to canonize Safavid, Ottoman, and Mughal carpets.

The so-called 'anthropological' or 'ethnological' approach, meanwhile, valorizes nomad and peasant carpets as authentic representations of the traditional crafts and ways of life of tribal communities. In this view, the simpler and more spontaneous designs embody the folkloristic, primitive, or primordial. Brian Spooner has analyzed the quest for and negotiation of authenticity in the carpet trade, which is most pronounced within this approach. He defines authenticity as a 'conceptualization of elusive, inadequately defined, other cultural, socially ordered genuineness' (Spooner 1986: 225) and argues that, 'because of social expansion recently we have been needing more and more of it' (ibid.). In order to satisfy our need for authenticity, we have altered our criteria for it. The devaluation we have described perhaps suggests criteria of authenticity have reached their lower limit for oriental carpets, or that we have turned to other sources of authenticity.

Referring to the structure and construction of carpets, the 'structural' approach focuses on material properties. Its condition, knot count, regularity, and other more technical qualities are key parameters in appraising its value. It tends, as does the art-historical approach, toward the ideal of classical carpets, favoring products of royal and urban workshops rather than village or tribal arts. However, it is less concerned with provenance and cultural canons.

The 'aesthetic' approach shares the focus of the structural approach on the material qualities of carpets. Or, perhaps more accurately, it is predicated on the capacity of carpets to evoke strong, immediate sensory and emotional gratification in the observer. Rather than the structural aspects, it is the color, texture, and design of the carpet that matter in this approach. While, like the 'anthropological' approach, it values the qualities of more 'primitive' folk art, the aesthetic gaze is less concerned with the carpet's communities of origin, context of production, and ritual uses.

Harry can, like Sam Gordon, be identified with the 'aesthetic' approach:

To most collectors the physical condition is everything. I am a collector who does not care about condition. I never counted knots.... What excites me is the color contrasts – how colors set each other off. The field, background black, makes colors shine. I like dark colored fields, unlike rookies who like lighter colored fields. I am taken also by elegant simplicity. Bolder splashes of color, a lot of color on an open field.... Well-balanced designs. I also like the tactile aspect. Resilience of the carpet – has to do with good wool.... The thrill is about the beauty of a piece. The skill of the young woman who made it. A piece by a Khamseh woman: she took a three-medallion design, worked in the tradition; but she knew how to make the colors sing; she knew how to work in open space; she did it in muted colors, put in chickens, peacocks.

Consider also an American collector from New York:

I am a visually oriented person. I get rug catalogs from all over the world.... I buy on aesthetics.... I look and buy, more than read. Of course, knowing what they are improves their aesthetics. I don't care for the technical stuff. I am only interested in tribal arts.... Color is important.... I buy fragments too; some fragments are exquisite.... I find the devotion, the naiveté in Christ paintings of the Renaissance charming. You find that in carpets! If I could collect cave paintings that's what I'd do.... Primal. Simple, yet so beautiful.

As these collectors' words imply, the four approaches do not represent independent modes of perception and appreciation. All of Gordon's four approaches, with more or less insistence, disavow industrial and mass production methods, direct influence of consumer demand, and trends in interior design and decorative arts. But the approaches vary in terms of which forms of patina they recognize and value higher than others. The aesthetic approach, for instance, values abrash more than the structural approach, and for slightly different reasons than the anthropological approach (visual effect vs. authentic representation of nomadic or village traditions).

   The quotes also indicate that the division of material and symbolical (properties) may well be flawed. The provenance and the history of a region or a village or an ethnic group shape not only the symbolic but also the material properties of oriental carpets. Then, the primitive, primal, primordial aspects that collectors and experts value may well offer an extension of McCracken's patina. Perhaps only those carpets which remain unadulterated by (Western) commercial influences and thereby retain a high degree of artistic integrity produce the visual and tactile effects in which the somewhat romantic aesthetic gaze delights.

## Patina meets fashion

We have used the analysis of patina to explore how material properties, processes, and affordances are connected to the symbolic meaning and evaluations of carpets. This leads us to question the notion of patina as 'natural,' 'material' signs of age, and patina strategies as outmoded ways of employing patina (on) objects to validate status claims.

As stated, McCracken suggests that patina was replaced by fashion as a dominant system of status representation, and plays a marginal role in modern society. The general decline in interest in oriental carpets, as a result of modern styles and ever-changing trends in interior design, seems to confirm this hypothesis. New, fashionable objects have no patina. Patina objects, prestige goods that age gracefully, or goods that become prestigious because they age gracefully, are not in fashion. Yet, our case has presented evidence that fashion and patina, cults of newness and age, mix in odd ways. We saw that there are also fashion trends in old carpets. Periodically, new types of oriental textiles are discovered or rediscovered and become the subject of a periodic surge in collector and market interest. Of course, this may be seen as evidence of the fashion system's hegemony. However, we might view the phenomenon as a special case of Caves' (2000) 'Ars Longa' property of creative industries, which addresses the durability of certain cultural products. The value of fine oriental carpets is expected to increase (amid fluctuations) over an extended time period. We can also find creativity and innovation in old carpets. The accumulation of patina on objects means that they, in a sense, live. Since carpets undergo gradual transformation over time, the aesthetic consequences of choices in materials and design may become fully evident only decades after carpets are finished. Also, as the schemes of perception and appreciation develop over time, or collectors or experts with an eye for finer details come across forgotten items, innovative breaks from tradition, or creative executions that push traditions, are discovered in the old. Harry imagines the Khamseh woman who wove one of his carpets, as he revels in her innovations and extensions of traditions:

The best ladies go one step beyond tradition but are still embedded in tradition. There is a limited repertoire of designs. I actually place a lot of value on novelty. The Khamseh lady I mentioned – the major overall Gestalt is set by tradition – she copies a design, then incorporates in her own other stuff. Nothing is made from nothing. Innovation is limited, within genre.

But we may argue that it is not only fashion and innovation that are found in markets for patina objects; patina also imposes itself in the fashion system. We suggested that the notion of patina could be extended to signs of age or allusions to past forms and styles that are arbitrary (symbolic) rather than 'natural' or 'direct' (iconic). If we think of patina even more broadly, we might think of concerns of modern corporations (in not only luxury and fashion) with authenticity, nostalgia, heritage, and retro styles as a kind of patina effect. Chapters 4 and 5 in this volume hint at this.

What is the appeal of patina today, then? Patina objects, as McCracken suggests, probably play a marginal role in status representation in contemporary society. As noted with Appadurai (1996: 76), we doubt whether the subtle shift of patina from object to owner ever worked as smoothly in practice as in theory.

However, the complex and subtle shifts certain objects undergo over the course of time inspire actors to engage with them. These actors assign symbolic meaning and value to things and their aging processes. Or, put differently, the material properties and processes lend themselves particularly well to, or afford, various symbolic uses. The symbolic properties and value of patina objects include identity value (expressing self-concept and social position) and linking value (facilitating or communicating social communion and group membership), apart from, of course, economic (market price) and cultural value (cultural and historical significance). We have stressed the role of more or less 'invisible ink' or schemes of perception and appreciation in mediating between objects and actors and between actors. We might ask how central these schemes are for the appreciation of oriental carpets. Finer, old pieces seem to be capable of inspiring a powerful sense of delight and even awe. One of the expressions of patina in carpets is sheen, which brings associations of aura. And it is perhaps an auratic effect that patina brings to objects. Patina objects evoke direct and immediate responses, perhaps not by virtue of the material properties themselves but because patina validates a whole set of associations between carpets and scarcity, singularity and uniqueness, ritual uses, heritage, history, and myths. Moreover, just as the material and the symbolic are embedded in each other, the new and the old, fashion and patina can also be in dialog with each other – in carpets, music, fashion clothing, and so on. Not only oriental carpets but many other cultural and artistic objects of the Other, such as African masks

(Torgovnick 1990), provide contemporary consumers with the means to enact their modern tastes and their search for authenticity. Such objects become status markers as objects of another time and space, as well as being objects of fashion. Patina and fashion, the past and the present, interact.

# References

Appadurai, Arjun. 1996. *Modernity at Large: Cultural dimensions of globalization.* Minneapolis: Minnesota University Press.

Belk, Russell W. 1988. Possessions and the extended self. *Journal of Consumer Research* 15 (2): 139–168.

Bourdieu, Pierre. 1984. *Distinction. A social critique of the judgment of taste.* Cambridge, MA: Harvard University Press.

Caves, R. E. 2000. *Creative Industries: Contracts between art and commerce.* Cambridge, MA: Harvard University Press.

Csaba, Fabian F. and Güliz Ger. 2000. Global village carpets: marketing, tradition and the oriental carpet renaissance. In *Marketing Contributions to Democratization and Socioeconomic Developments*, ed. Clifford J. Schultz and Brune Grbac, pp. 138–152. Arizona State University.

Eiland, Murray L. III. 1993. The past re-made: the case of oriental carpets. *Antiquity* 67 (257): 859–863.

Eiland, Murray L. III and Murray Eiland, Jr. 1998. *Oriental Carpets. A Complete Guide*, 4th Edition. New York: Bulfinch Press.

Ger, Güliz and Fabian F. Csaba. 2000. Flying carpets: the production and consumption of tradition and mystique. In *Advances in Consumer Research*, Vol. XXVII, ed. Stephen J. Hoch and Roben J. Meyer, pp. 132–137. Provo, UT: Association for Consumer Research.

Gordon, Sam. 2001. Collector and literature. *Ruglore*. Online at: http://home. earthlink.net/~gordsa/page11.html, retrieved 2011–05–12.

McCracken, Grant. 1988. *Culture and Consumption. New approaches to the symbolic character of consumer goods and activities.* Bloomington and Indianapolis: Indiana University Press.

Opie, James. 1998. Starting over: the 1990s rug revival. *Hali* 100 (20): 199–203.

Spooner, Brian. 1986. Weavers and dealers: the authenticity of an oriental carpet. In *The Social Life of Things*, ed. Arjun Appadurai. Cambridge: Cambridge University Press.

Torgovnick, Marianna. 1990. *Gone Primitive: Savage intellects, modern lives.* University of Chicago Press.

# Afterword

# Evaluative practices in the creative industries

KEITH SAWYER

In 2003, I published a chapter in an edited volume titled *Critical Creative Processes*. The volume contained chapters by psychologists that focused on the mental processes underlying individual decision making (Runco 2003). In the psychology of creativity, there has been a long tradition of contrasting idea generation – sometimes called 'divergent thinking' – with idea evaluation, sometimes called 'convergent thinking.' Many people believe that evaluation and judgment are detrimental to creativity. After all, one of the best-known rules in brainstorming is 'suspend judgment.' And yet, the editor of the 2003 book concluded that 'evaluative processes are necessary for good creative work' (p. x).

The book you hold in your hands reinforces this finding: evaluative practices are an essential and necessary part of good creative work. This book is a valuable complement to psychological studies of creative evaluation, because it provides a deep examination of social practices and organizational cultures. These chapters provide ample evidence that creativity is not the result of an isolated genius, working without constraints, separated from all concerns for convention and audience, detached from social systems (Becker 1982; Sawyer 2012). These chapters analyze the evaluative processes of creators, teams, managers, organizations, juries, and committees. And as I argue toward the end of this afterword, the ultimate evaluation is done by the market and the customers. Creative evaluation is always collective and distributed through social systems.

In these concluding comments, I focus on three themes that run through these chapters:

1. *When* are evaluative decisions made? What are the types of situations that evaluative decisions are made in?

2. *What* practices are involved in the making of each decision? What are the evaluative criteria used in evaluative practices?
3. *Who* makes them – what person, group, or organizational unit?

## 1. When are evaluative decisions made?

Moeran and Christensen's introduction to this volume notes an important distinction between evaluative practices that occur continuously during the process of the work and evaluative practices applied at the end to the completed product. I propose terms from educational assessment research, which distinguishes between *summative assessment* – a test given at the end of a learning process to determine how well the learner has mastered the material – and *formative assessment* – frequent and continuous evaluations, during the learning, that are meant to guide a more effective learning process (Carver 2006). By analogy, I will use the terms 'summative evaluation' and 'formative evaluation.'

Formative evaluations occur during the work: at every moment, the creator applies tacit understandings that guide each act. These are generally implicit and embedded in creative work practices. Summative evaluations occur at the very end and are evaluations of a completed product that is ready to go to market. These evaluations tend to be guided by explicitly stated criteria, and often use highly articulated metrics (such as net present value calculations based on judgments of risk, anticipated market size, and production costs). For example, San Pellegrino's restaurant review process is extremely explicit – the elaborate voting system of 800 experts, each region's 31-member panel, etc.

At a midpoint between formative and summative evaluation, many organizations evaluate projects at predetermined moments in the product development process, to determine whether to continue, to modify, or to terminate a project. Several of the chapters show that these innovation processes are often explicitly articulated, with multiple moments of evaluation along the way.

- Two chapters analyze formative evaluations by creators during the creative process: O'Donnell on chamber quartets (Chapter 3) and Alačovska on travel guidebook entries (Chapter 6).
- Four chapters analyze formative evaluations by both the creator and the organization: Childress on book publishing (Chapter 1);

Vangkilde on HUGO BOSS (Chapter 2); Moeran on Royal Copenhagen (Chapter 4); Krause-Jensen on Bang & Olufsen (Chapter 5).

- Three chapters analyze summative evaluations: Mathieu and Bertelsen (film festivals – Chapter 8); Christensen and Strandgaard Pedersen (restaurants – Chapter 9); Csaba and Ger (carpets – Chapter 10).
- Two chapters analyze both formative and summative evaluations: Malefyt's chapter (7) analyzes both formative and summative evaluations during the creation of and reception to an advertising campaign, and Moeran's chapter (4) analyzes formative evaluations of *Ursula* during the creative process, and also summative evaluations during its reception.

Perhaps the most elaborate description of an articulated process is Chapter 5 on Bang & Olufsen. The chapter describes *Idealand*, which has traditionally mediated engineering and contract designers, and uses the TOP development process which is a version of the traditional product development 'funnel' (at B&O referred to as a 'tube'). In the *Idealand* process, design is first done by an external designer, and then engineering starts, with no interaction between them. The influential designer David Lewis views his goal as designing a television that looks good when it is turned off.

Chapter 5's case study of *Beosound 5* describes a challenge to the linear TOP methodology represented by *Idealand*. *Beosound 5* emerged from a parallel development process, *Idealab*, which had been created to respond to the digital revolution and the importance of software and user interface design. *Idealab* worked outside the TOP process, and this led to frequent competition between *Idealab* and *Idealand*. *Idealab* emphasized the end user, the user interface, and the software, instead of the external form. *Beosound 5* was the first product to emerge from *Idealab*, and it was not compatible with the TOP process – particularly because the linear nature of that process could not adequately address user interface design.

## 2. What practices are involved?

The primary focus of these chapters is what evaluative practices are used, and what evaluative criteria are involved in these practices. When evaluative criteria are organized into a shared symbolic system, I call that system an *evaluative regime*. An evaluative regime is an implicit or explicit shared cognitive and cultural model that contains a set of criteria and forms of grounding for backing evaluative claims.[1]

I identified the following evaluative regimes in these chapters. Each evaluative regime is associated with a distinct set of practices for backing evaluative claims.[2]

- The *aesthetic* evaluative regime: is it a new and interesting design?
  Sources of backing evaluative claims: appeals to aesthetic taste and to design history and tradition.
- The *craft/professional* evaluative regime: does it conform to professional standards of the worker? Is it well crafted?
  Sources of backing evaluative claims: workers' personal experience with materials and with their profession.
- The *manufacturing* evaluative regime: can we make it, reliably and dependably, at a cost that customers can/will pay?
  Sources of backing evaluative claims: knowledge of large-scale factory processes and manufacturing costs.
- The *brand/genre* evaluative regime: does it align with the brand's image and what it stands for? Is it truly an example of the genre that it is represented as?
  Sources of backing evaluative claims: experience, market expertise.

Note that none of the sources of backing for evaluative claims is objective; rather, evaluative claims are backed by experience and knowledge. This corresponds to an old observation in sociology, generally first attributed to Simmel's criticism of Marx, that value is never inherent in an object but emerges from subjective and social processes (1978; also see Appadurai 1986; Moeran and Strandgaard Pedersen 2011). This is why issues of power and authority are critical; these are discussed in section 3 below. This is also why argumentation practices are of central importance, and I discuss argumentation after I describe these four evaluative regimes.

---

[1] Compare with Appadurai's concept of *regime of value* (1986: 15). Chapter 10 on carpets proposes four 'schemes' that are similar to what I mean by evaluative regimes: art-historical, structural, anthropological, and aesthetic (p. 1).

[2] Compare with Moeran and Strandgaard Pedersen's (2011) taxonomy of values, in an analysis of fairs and festivals: appreciative (corresponding to 'aesthetic'), technical/material (corresponding to 'craft/professional'), social, situational, and utility values.

## The aesthetic evaluative regime

In Vangkilde's account of the HUGO BOSS designer trip to Milan (Chapter 2), the designers make evaluative decisions about what is inspiring. They can't describe it; they say 'it is just a feeling.' Likewise, the Creative Director can only say, 'I just have a feeling.' The junior designer Louise tries to explain what results in this feeling: an 'unusual and surprising combination,' 'something you have not seen or thought of before.' They like designs that are 'surprising and quite exceptional;' 'surprising, unusual, exceptional, wild, crazy or the like.'

Of all four evaluative regimes that I consider here, the aesthetic regime is the least explicitly articulated, the one where evaluative claims are most grounded in subjective judgments. These chapters provide many examples of professionals making aesthetic statements and claims, and appeals to domain history, but these are not codified and articulated into a standardized and intersubjectively shared system. As such, evaluative claims within this regime are likely to depend most heavily on role and status (see section 3 below).

## The craft/professionalism evaluative regime

Alačovska's study of a travel book writer in Chapter 6 contrasts the corporate evaluative regime presented by the publisher's guidelines with the craft evaluative regime of the author, the 'craft standards or inner criteria of excellence by which they judge good or bad performance.' These internal evaluations derive from an internalization of the rules of the practice and an awareness of the community of other practitioners.

In Moeran's study of Royal Copenhagen in Chapter 4, the craft regime is paramount. Ursula, the famous designer, says it's important to know why one should make a new product – it must be for the 'right reason' and be 'something that consisted of human and functional values.' Poulsen's metaphor, 'you learn through your fingertips in this job,' is a wonderful insight into the craft regime. The author calls this 'an aesthetics of production.'

Csaba and Ger's study of carpets in Chapter 10 often speaks of craft, although in this case the concern is judgments of craftsmanship many years after the work is complete. 'Patina' is the most desirable quality in a carpet, but patina is not immediately obvious; it requires expertise to determine which signs of aging are truly indications of status. One of their many examples is that dark dyes cause the pile to age and thin faster than light dyes, so on old carpets the darker areas are a bit lower, resulting in a bas relief effect. And yet, some new carpet makers or merchants actually will trim the pile in the darker areas to emulate this aging effect. Only an expert can tell the difference.

## The manufacturing/business evaluative regime

This evaluative regime judges the extent to which an idea can be successfully manufactured, and at a cost that will allow the product to be priced at what the market will bear. In contrast to the craft regime, which focuses primarily on creative work by a creative professional, this regime focuses on large-scale manufacturing and marketing. We generally don't associate this evaluative regime with creativity per se. But in some of these chapters, it plays an important role in creative industry evaluative practices.

This evaluative regime is most prominent in Moeran's chapter on the *Ursula* line of pottery (Chapter 4). Ursula's design was evaluated highly by the craft regime (the former Bing & Grøndahl managers admired it) and the aesthetic regime (it is now in design museums in Copenhagen), but to be manufactured it nonetheless had to 'fit the faience clay body used by Royal Copenhagen' and certain chemicals couldn't be used in the glaze because they were known to be poisonous. Some designs were simply 'too difficult to carry out in production.' Another production issue was consistency, because after glazing, finished pots are sorted into firsts (high quality) and seconds (lesser quality). Ursula wanted to use a glaze that was designed to vary in color across the pot. But if the glaze didn't look the same every time, the sorters would be confused and unable to determine which pot was a first and which a second.

Ultimately, although the *Ursula* line won design awards, and is in the collection of the Danish Museum of Art & Design, it cost too much to make given the retail pricing the market would bear, and it was discontinued in 2011. In a sense, all the above evaluative regimes were correct, even though they came to different conclusions.

## The brand and genre evaluative regime

This fourth evaluative regime is the one that receives the most attention in these chapters. Many issues surrounding brand and genre are presented in terms of a tension between tradition and novelty. For example, Christensen and Strandgarrd Pedersen's analysis of restaurant rankings in Chapter 9 contrasts the evaluative regimes used by San Pellegrino and Michelin: the San Pellegrino evaluations tend to reward novelty and change, whereas Michelin emphasizes tradition and continuity. In general, strong brand identity is associated with pressures toward tradition and stability; Michelin is a venerated strong brand, whereas San Pellegrino is a more recent player.

We see similar contrasts between tradition and novelty in the case studies of Bang & Olufsen, HUGO BOSS, and Royal Copenhagen – all companies with strong brand identities. Krause-Jensen (Chapter 5) observes that some designs are said to have a 'Bang & Olufsen DNA' that senior management chooses for in design competitions – an implicit evaluative criterion. At Bang & Olufsen, new products are expected to live up to the Bang & Olufsen reputation for great design, and senior management makes these decisions.

In Chapter 4 on Royal Copenhagen, the brand evaluative regime looms equally large. Designer Finn Naess says, 'We had a lot of work to do to develop [Ursula] into something that could be sold as a Royal Copenhagen product,' implying an evaluation of 'what is consistent with the brand.' The style of the *Ursula* series did not align with Royal Copenhagen's 'classical tradition.' The Royal Copenhagen brand stands for 'luxury;' Ursula's faience style was 'simple luxury' or 'unluxury' (Ole Jensen).

In general, a brand represents a constraining element. New creative products must not be too new; they must represent an instantiation of the brand. However, it seems that our contemporary trend is toward more rapid change in a brand's identity. Csaba and Ger, in discussing the carpet market, cite Grant McCracken's theory of 'patina' which proposes that, until quite recently in Europe, value and status inhered in things that were old. Patina authenticates wealth, in part, because it takes a few generations to develop in an object. In the modern era of consumption, the 'fashion system' is opposed to, and increasingly replaces, the patina system.

Genre plays the same functional and symbolic role as the brand – a creative product can make sense, in the broader market and system of other existing products, only if locatable in an identifiable category (brand or genre). Childress's chapter is about 'the genre conventions through which *Jarrettsville* was made sense of during the processes of creation, production, and reviewing.' The novel *Jarrettsville* had to be placed in a genre, due to the imperatives of publishing and book selling, and yet it could be interpreted as belonging to many different genres. Different people at the publisher associated it with different genres. The publicity staff at the publisher and the regional sales reps had the final word: it would be sold as literary fiction, and specifically as Civil War fiction, in an attempt to benefit from the success of the recent novel *Cold Mountain*, which had been adapted as a successful movie.

Alačovska describes a similar genre/brand focus in travel guidebook publishing (Chapter 6). Alačovska doesn't state this explicitly, but it appears that the reason why the publisher's editorial brief exists is that many different writers contribute to a single book, and the editors need to enforce a common 'editorial voice' throughout the volume for the reader, and also convince the reader that common standards have been applied regardless of which reviewer has written a particular review: 'In travel publishing the authorial voice is inundated by the publishing brand.'

## The position of the product in a system

New product development managers are trained to think about a portfolio of investments in new innovations, knowing that only a few of them will ultimately be profitable and most of them will fail. A standard portfolio management strategy is to categorize each new product by its degree of risk and the degree of potential reward if it succeeds. Low-risk and low-reward products are usually the bulk of the portfolio; they are fairly certain to succeed, but the likely revenue and profit margin are relatively low. High-risk products should be potentially high-reward to be pursued; these tend to form a relatively small percentage of a portfolio. Within this framework, each new idea is always evaluated in the context of the complete portfolio.

Mathieu and Bertelsen report that the jurors watch all of the films, then evaluate them relative to each other – because they have to rank the best. Thus evaluative decisions are always contextualized against a field of alternatives. They describe an important aspect of evaluations in this context: they are often focused on 'compensatory distribution' as a result of a necessary process of negotiation, when different jury members have different opinions about the best film, one person may be placated by giving their choice a lesser award. In some cases, a prize is awarded to a director or actor to make up for a perceived wrong decision in a previous year, although several of those interviewed expressed disdain for this practice.

In the case studies of HUGO BOSS, Bang & Olufsen, and Royal Copenhagen, evaluative decisions are embedded in a system of multiple products, brands, and lines. For example, a key criterion for the BOSS Orange designer team is that the new funky-formal collection cannot intrude on the brand identity of BOSS Black, another BOSS brand that is the formal wear brand. At the presentation of the mood boards, the Creative Director says, 'It's not anymore about a single item ... it is a combination of all of the products together.' Most of the discussion among designers is about whether a given concept is too narrow, or whether it can 'be reinterpreted and evolved continuously.' The criteria used for evaluation are that a concept must be new, must fit with the brand, must be fixed and yet flexible (to extend with variation over multiple seasons), must balance concreteness and abstraction, and must be realizable.

The same is true when editors evaluate book manuscripts. Childress quotes from a rejection letter in which an editor says that they already have a similar title being published and they can't have two books that are too similar.

## Argumentation

In these four evaluative regimes, the backing for evaluative claims is always subjective. Many of the tensions described in these case studies result when people make different evaluative judgments, often because they work within different evaluative regimes. In several of the chapters, we see an analysis of the deliberations that take place when different people have made different evaluations. The contested cases generally result when two or more different communities or evaluative regimes are interacting; this is when argumentation becomes necessary.

Moeran quotes designer Finn Naess describing a contrast between two evaluative regimes that resulted from a corporate merger of two dinnerware companies that formed Royal Copenhagen. Naess tells an interesting story about the different relationship between artists and senior management at the two companies prior to the merger. The Royal Porcelain Factory would have the artists do a show every three months, and they would walk through and choose what they liked.

Senior management didn't provide comments directly to the artists; they were mediated through Naess. In contrast, at Bing & Grøndahl, management would walk through the artists' work a couple of times each week. Regarding the *Ursula* design, Naess said: 'And, of course, they had totally different opinions about what was "good" and what was "bad," about what was worth developing further and what wasn't. And Ursula's work was something they *really* disagreed on.' The Bing & Grøndahl people found it 'exciting and imaginative;' RPF said it was primitive and would never sell.

Ursula's own explanation of this clash was to say that marketing liked designs that would sell, whereas her judgments were based on 'design history.' Ursula argued that her tableware line was grounded in design history and tradition, and also appealed to traditional craftwork processes. Thus we see that the backing for one's evaluative decisions tends to be taken from the corresponding evaluative regime. And they were both right: the Ursula line won design awards and is in museum collections, *and* it could not be sold at a profit.

With many of the chapters, there are confidentiality issues and other concerns that make it difficult to gain access to actual moments of argumentation, so the authors indirectly approach this topic through interviews. In the analysis of restaurant reviews, the researchers were not able to observe actual arguments – for example, discussions among the multiple inspectors at Michelin about a given restaurant – because of the complete secrecy of the system. In Chapter 8 on film juries, the data were interviews after the fact, rather than actual observations. These particular conversations will perhaps always remain private and inaccessible to researchers, but future research with less secretive organizations might involve the ability to videotape and analyze processes of evaluative argumentation.

Vangkilde reports on contrasting evaluations in the final meeting at HUGO BOSS. The new concept can't be something that's already been done, and it has to be workable as the basis for several collections. And yet, there was disagreement on whether specific ideas meet these criteria.

Foucault (1969/1972) criticized the focus on propositional statements associated with Chomskian linguistics and structuralism, and argued for a shift in focus to practice. This was also the motivation behind Bourdieu's book published a few years later: *Outline of a Theory of Practice* (Bourdieu 1972/1977). These French theorists heavily influenced a later strand of Anglo-American theoretical exploration of the structure-agency dialectic (e.g. Archer 1995; Giddens 1984).

The data presented in these chapters are primarily interview materials, and as such the chapters tend to focus on the propositional content – the explicitly statable beliefs. But of course, 'practices' are not a set of beliefs that can be described in an interview; they are observable, contextualized, social, communicative, collective behaviors. They are often unstatable, tacit, implicit, taken for granted. By relying heavily on interview material, the chapters end up saying less about practices. In future work, it would be interesting to learn more about the unstated, implicit, tacit practices that were observed in these ethnographies, perhaps by using methods of interaction analysis (Sawyer 2006) to directly observe practices in action.

## The dialogism of evaluative regimes

Many chapters describe situations where a single person simultaneously considers multiple evaluative regimes:

- Christensen and Strandgaard Pedersen referred to 'the dual nature of flexibility and stability.'
- Malefyt used similar language to talk about innovation within a brand identity.
- Vangkilde writes that HUGO BOSS is 'continuously balancing continuity and newness' and 'the evaluative practices concerned precisely, I think, this effort to enter a space betwixt and between continuity and newness.'

Simultaneously inhabiting multiple evaluative regimes is similar to the phenomenon Bakhtin (1981: 330) called *dialogism*: 'the problem of the double-voiced, internally dialogized word.' Although Bakhtin's primary purpose was to analyze discourse in the novel, his concepts of dialogism and voicing are helpful to characterize the ways that creative industry players occupy distinct evaluative regimes. Because creative organizations are made up of individuals inhabiting a variety of evaluative regimes, participants may strategically switch voice – speak within a distinct evaluative regime – when they move between organizational groups (management, marketing, or production). Each individual is capable of speaking from a variety of voices, determined by his own location in the organization, and his strategic intent in a given encounter; consequently, each person's speech contains what Bakhtin called 'heteroglot voices.'

Bakhtin (1981) argued that in situations of heteroglossia, there always remain tensions between the discourses. I suspect that the professionals interviewed for these chapters are capable of inhabiting multiple discourses – multiple evaluative regimes – and that in face-to-face encounters, creative professionals are quite strategic in their dialogic invocation of a range of evaluative regimes. But this would become apparent only upon rigorous analysis of naturally occurring conversations within an organizational context.

## Explicit and implicit

Creative evaluations are applied at all moments in the innovation process. In the formative evaluation that occurs throughout the creative process, individuals evaluate and select their own ideas and ways of proceeding. In the summative evaluations that occur at various endpoints and intermediary moments, collaborative groups collectively decide that some ideas are more worth pursuing than others. The criteria applied in formative evaluations tend to be relatively implicit; they often are not codified or written down, although many creators are capable of describing and explaining their evaluative decisions when asked. And yet also with most cultural models, there are components of the model that participants are not fully aware of – they can be discerned only by observing actual practices.

The chapters on HUGO BOSS and Royal Copenhagen describe some explicit components of evaluative regimes that are primarily used in formative evaluations. The designers at HUGO BOSS say they look for 'unusual and surprising combination'; ideas that 'disturb the designers' existing perspectives'; things that 'break with the common or the ordinary'; ideas that can 'be reinterpreted and evolved continuously.' The formerly Bing & Grøndahl staff at Royal Copenhagen valued a look that was 'primitive,' not 'properly finished,' 'exciting and imaginative.' And yet, note that these terms remain quite vague – probably difficult to codify in an objective system of evaluation.

In summative evaluation, the criteria and processes tend to be codified and made explicit. Most creative organizations have in place explicit and codified criteria, and also well-articulated product development processes that specify exactly when those criteria are to be applied. But in these chapters, there is relatively little examination of formalized and codified evaluative criteria. One exception is Christensen and Strandgaard Pedersen's chapter, which presents a fascinating contrast between the explicit evaluative regime of Michelin and the lack of such a system with San Pellegrino – both of them examples of summative evaluation.

On film festival juries, the criteria are not explicitly specified but rather 'are usually up to the actual jury itself to formally or informally establish and administer' (Mathieu and Bertelsen). They list some of the criteria used by film juries: novelty or originality (vs. cliché and convention): topic, theme, vantage point, how situations are conveyed; quality of acting performances and the direction; genre hierarchy (films are evaluated against other films in the same genre, e.g. comedy or drama, and yet some genres are considered better, with drama the most prestigious), global judgment about whether it is 'good' or not; emotional impact.

I suggest three potential explanations for why evaluative practices are more likely to be explicit during the organizational, collaborative, summative moments: (1) group deliberations take place and decisions must be explained and justified (see 'argumentation' above); (2) organizations tend to explicitly codify procedures that have a history of success at a macro level (sales figures, profit margins, total shareholder return, etc.); (3) the accounting procedures associated with the traditional new product development process require explicit quantification of risk, uncertainty, potential market size, etc.

Overall, the majority of the chapters do not report the explicit evaluative terms actually used in creative industries. Perhaps that is because these chapters are ethnographies of creative practice rather than organizational studies of business decisions. And as such, most of the chapters focus on the formative evaluative moments that occur during the process, those moments during which evaluative criteria are most implicit.

## Where do evaluative regimes come from?

A few of the chapters speak to how new evaluative regimes originate. O'Donnell's analysis of a completely new type of music performance – four string quartets performing simultaneously – is a study of how the players collectively develop a new evaluative regime. Their primary goal is 'togetherness,' 'listening deeply to and responding to one another's musical choices in the moment ... to improvise in relation to the score, the collective pulse, and the emerging choices they are all making.' The new spatial format seemed to make this desired state impossible. What O'Donnell calls 'ensembling' – 'a collective flow-like state that happens when group members think "towards a central point" (citing Blum 1986: 14), and collective action and awareness merge into one' – is what I have called 'group flow' (Sawyer 2003, 2007). O'Donnell argues that this is the quartet players' most important criterion, and that their evaluative decisions were all oriented toward making ensembling happen. The desire for ensembling resulted in the use of a click-track, even though it felt 'military' and it was foreign to their usual aesthetic.

NOMA's creators have a higher ambition than simply to create a restaurant; they are attempting to create a new evaluative regime. The NOMA founders organized a symposium on New Nordic Cuisine in 2004; a 'manifesto' was signed by twelve chefs; a book was published. Managing director Peter Kreiner situates NOMA in a broader historical trend, 'the natural and local, or what some would call the "wild kitchen," that is what we stand for at NOMA. And that is what many others are looking towards at the moment.' The origin of the natural and local movement is generally considered to be Alice Waters' restaurant Chez Penisse, in Berkeley, California, in 1971. A more direct and recent precursor of NOMA is the widely acclaimed restaurant Aquavit in New York City, where star chef Marcus Samuelsson began serving Scandinavian-inspired cuisine in the early 1990s. The authors mention that there was a 2003 TV show 'Scandinavian cooking' on American PBS, the same year NOMA opened, but which must have been conceived and produced two or three years prior to this. But this historical trajectory is not discussed in the chapter, giving the impression that NOMA appeared de novo, and that the founders came up with the idea for natural, local, and Scandinavian cuisine on their own.

In general, the chapters do not provide a historical and situated context for the evaluative practices observed. As with NOMA, for all of these chapters, the evaluative practices analyzed have a history and have already been engaged in previously by other individuals and organizations. How does an evaluative regime originate? How does it change over time? How was it applied last year, or at a different company, and what was the result? What reason is there to believe that it will result in successful creative products?

A related set of questions includes: how do people acquire an evaluative regime? How do they master the evaluative practices, and the associated decisions, actions, and ways of speaking? Perhaps because of my own academic home in learning sciences and developmental psychology, I am particularly interested in how members of professional communities acquire evaluative practices that are implicit, tacit, and taken for granted. This process involves socialization into a community of practice, and these socialization processes have been studied extensively by education researchers. There is a long tradition of studies of the acquisition of professional expertise and the novice–expert transition (Ericsson *et al.* 2006), and an equally rich tradition of studying how individuals are socialized into communities of practice (Rogoff 1990; Wenger 1999). One of the chapters describes such moments: Vangkilde's chapter on HUGO BOSS describes meetings at which the senior Creative Director seems to be attempting to socialize the five young designers into how to think like a professional designer.

## Theorizing the evaluative regime

The above discussion of evaluative regimes assumes that there exists a shared set of evaluative criteria and practices. What is the nature of this shared cultural system of ideas?

One potential theorization of the evaluative regime is the *cultural model*. A cultural model is 'a cognitive schema that is intersubjectively shared by a social group' (D'Andrade 1987: 112). Beginning in the late 1970s, cognitive anthropologists began to elaborate a cognitive view of culture, in which culture is seen as residing in part within the heads of its members. These scholars proposed the notion of 'cultural models,' which are schemas that are intersubjectively shared among members of a social group (Cole 1996; Shore 1996).

However, such approaches have been criticized as being overly structural, and for neglecting how cultural models originate, clash, and change over time. The first such sustained critique is associated with Foucault's *Archeology of Knowledge* (1969/1972). 'Archeology' is Foucault's term for the study of how ideas (and ways of talking about ideas) originate, disseminate, propagate, and form into coherent systems. Archeology was Foucault's attempt to replace Thomas Kuhn's (1962) concept of the *paradigm*, which Foucault believed was overly structural, neglected the strategic practices of participants, and neglected how shared bodies of knowledge originate, clash, and change. The technical terms he proposed to replace structuralist notions like Kuhn's paradigm were 'archive,' 'discursive formation,' and 'discursive practice' (Sawyer 2002). Some such theoretical account of the history of ideas would be useful in the analysis of evaluative practices, as a way of explaining how evaluative practices originate, disseminate, and propagate.

After the publication of *The Archeology of Knowledge*, Foucault was criticized for having neglected the role of power and authority in discursive practices. This led to his late-career shift to studies of power and knowledge (e.g., Foucault 1975/1977). This is the topic of my third and final section – how the invocation of evaluative regimes is related to role, status, and authority.

## 3.  Who engages in evaluative practices?

In the medieval era, when artists and musicians were supported by royal patrons, the only evaluations that mattered were those of the patron and a few trusted advisors. Evaluative practices were not institutionalized and collective; rather, they inhered in powerful individuals. In the modern era this is no longer the case; evaluative practices are shared, collective, and distributed. In these chapters, the agentive group engaged in the evaluative practice varies in size. Most of the cases describe situations in which evaluative power is concentrated among a small number of people (Royal Copenhagen, Bang & Olufsen, HUGO BOSS, Jarrettsville). These cases tend to analyze formative evaluations. In some of these cases, most evaluative power is held by a single individual (the creative director at HUGO BOSS); in others, evaluative practices are collective and collaborative, involving negotiation and argumentation (Royal Copenhagen, Bang & Olufsen). In contrast, a few chapters describe situations in which evaluative power is distributed across many people (restaurant reviews, movie juries); these cases tend to analyze summative evaluation.

Csikszentmihalyi (1988) called the collective community of experts in a domain 'the field.' Becker (1982) identified several distinct members of the field, distinguished by their level of expertise and their influence:

- intermediaries
- connoisseurs
- amateurs
- the public.

When creative professionals engage in evaluative practices, they are quite frequently imagining the future evaluative decisions of the field. Childress reports his informants mentioning Kakutani, the book reviewer at *The New York Times*. Book editors must always be thinking, 'Would Kakutani like this book?' The publisher considers which US national public radio shows the author might go on, naming the popular Diane Rehm show. Many creative industries have people with such power and influence, and they play prominent roles in the evaluative practices of everyone in the industry.

The introduction refers to the 'name economy': the status that attaches to a name with a reputation and history. In highbrow design industries, 'the name' is essential; the designer is valorized. The charisma of the name has a monetary value that is commonly referred to in business as 'brand equity.' Because of this value, marketing can use the name to charge more, resulting in higher profit margins. 'Name' can attach to a person, an organization, or a brand. San Pellegrino's legitimacy comes from the fact that the 800 individuals have a 'high standing in the industry': 'food critics, chefs, restaurateurs, food journalists, and highly regarded "gastronomes" with a high frequency of international travel.' The legitimacy comes from the individual reviewers. Michelin's legitimacy comes from 'independence and autonomy' and from the brand and the brand's history. The reviewers remain anonymous.

The designer David Lewis looms large at Bang & Olufsen. His forty-year string of successes gives him the power to act in a way that a young new untested designer could not. His 'authority in matters of design is absolute and his autonomy is protected.'

Vangkilde's analysis of HUGO BOSS shows the absolute authority of the creative director. When he responds to the final presentation (described at the beginning of the chapter), he says: 'What you have done here is highly remarkable. It is really exciting. It is very close to what I had in mind, and you have done a remarkable job in interpreting and realizing my vision.' The creative director at HUGO BOSS justifies his evaluative decisions by saying 'I just have a feeling.' This form of justification is effective only for someone in authority.

Mathieu and Bertelsen indirectly raise another extra-aesthetic factor involved in aesthetic judgments: a junior person may tend to agree with a senior person with more power, in hopes of creating an alliance that might further his career. Mathieu and Bertelsen's conclusion refers to alliance building, strategic concessions, and selecting what is worth fighting for. Those who have lesser status need to provide additional justifications (see above section on argumentation). When a person with status is receiving a negative evaluation, additional interactional and organizational work needs to be done (see 'Successes versus failures' below). The Creative Director at HUGO BOSS does not need to expend so much energy rejecting the young Talent Pool designs because they do not have a very high status: 'I have to be honest . . . it is, indeed, not what I am looking for … you still need to work hard.' Moeran and Strandgaard Pedersen (2011: 12–13) refer to this as a 'social value,' a valuation influenced by social relations.

Individuals in creative industries tend to inhabit one particular evaluative regime, although of course they are fluid and overlapping (see 'dialogism' above). In these chapters, we see some description of the culturally defined roles and expectations for each position in an organization. For example, in an advertising firm (Malefyt) creatives and account executives have a long tradition of stereotyped roles. In Royal Copenhagen, the case study indicates at least three different roles (designers, mediators, and executives) but we don't read much about how they are perceived and stereotyped. What public performance or 'face' (Goffman 1959) is expected and considered appropriate for each role? Role expectations would influence evaluative practices, if not the explicit beliefs themselves, to the extent that a particular evaluative regime is perceived to be consistent with the performative nature of the role. Workers at Royal Copenhagen expect Ursula to appeal to design tradition and craft; if, instead, she presented a PowerPoint with customer research data, it would be out of character. Earlier, I suggested that these professionals are capable of strategically inhabiting multiple regimes through dialogism; but engaging too enthusiastically in an evaluative practice that is out of type for one's role might raise suspicions, or at least would require additional interactional work for everyone.

## Why do people participate in evaluative practices?

The certainty of an eventual evaluation is likely to influence the creative process, as shown in studies by Teresa Amabile (1996) and others on the negative effects of rewards on creativity. In creative industries, workers are motivated by a combination of intrinsic and extrinsic rewards. They identify themselves as creatives, and yet they are not pure artists, doing 'art for art's sake' – they want their ideas to be produced. As it is a job, they want the financial remuneration that comes with success. And if they fail, they risk losing their job. Consequently, in the creative industries, evaluative practices are always deeply embedded in the creative process; the creator constantly applies formative evaluations to determine how to revise and move forward, with the goal of generating a product that will receive a positive summative evaluation and therefore will be produced and sold. Given the ever-present role of career and financial imperatives in the creative industries, and in the daily work lives of creative professionals, it is surprising that very little discussion of motivation appears in these chapters.

Of course, it is not only creatives who are motivated to make effective creative evaluations. If managers and creative directors make effective summative evaluations, the products that are released will sell well, the business will thrive, and their compensation will increase. Those who make good summative evaluations gain enhanced prestige; they develop a reputation for being able to make good evaluative decisions.

Some of the chapters discuss who gets the credit for a successful creation. In advertising, creatives get the awards, but the account side doesn't have a mechanism to be rewarded (Malefyt). In book publishing, the editor doesn't get any credit, although there are famous cases of them later claiming they deserve credit (e.g., author Raymond Carver and editor Gordon Lish [Sawyer 2012]). In movies, the director usually gets the credit (however, the distribution of credit is always negotiated and codified in the contracts).

Mathieu and Bertelsen's chapter explains why film experts agree to serve on juries: it is because the names of jurors are publicly known and being chosen enhances the prestige of the judge (see English 2005, on the prestige economy). The chapter reports that the more famous members of the jury are often paid and that everyone is treated like a VIP with the 'luxury' that the festival can provide. Regarding restaurant reviews, the San Pellegrino 800 derive prestige from having their names publicly known.

Malefyt argues that for the advertising firm to gain a business benefit from an advertising award, the award must be explicitly attached to the creatives at the firm. This leads them to claim sole credit for the creativity and deny collaborative credit to outside vendors or partners. There is a business need, given the dynamics of the industry, to exaggerate the role of the individual genius; and yet, in reality, each ad campaign is a collective and institutional product, involving outside vendors and partners.

## Topics for future study

In this final section, I discuss three potential topics for future research.

### *Successes versus failures*

Many of the chapters are studies of ideas that received positive summative evaluations and eventually made it to market. And yet we know from studies of new product development that 90 percent or more of initially funded ideas never make it to market. The innovation process involves many dead-ends (Sawyer 2007). So it is possible that the understanding of evaluative practices that emerges from these case studies is biased; perhaps evaluative practices are somehow different when the result is a *negative* decision, and a project is terminated and never released to the market.

There are reasons to believe that evaluative practices would be different when they lead to a negative decision. Saying 'no' is harder than saying 'yes' because someone's feelings might be hurt, and because there are likely to be at least some people invested in the idea who believe it should have received a positive evaluation. An employee's end-of-year review may be negative; those involved may lose their jobs. Justifying a negative decision should thus require a higher degree of argumentative backing. This presents an opportunity for future research: a study of the differences in evaluative practices involved in selecting an idea that is eventually released to the market, versus those involved in rejecting an idea and terminating a project.

### *Highbrow versus lowbrow*

In this book, all of the chapters analyze expensive 'highbrow' status products, except for Alačovska (travel guides) and advertising (Malefyt). This raises an interesting question: are evaluative practices likely to be different with highbrow and lowbrow products? I think so, because in lowbrow industries, the evaluative decisions of the broad public become paramount. In highbrow industries, there are 'experts' and 'connoisseurs' whose evaluative judgments have authority. In a highbrow domain, even if the general public doesn't like it, the elite and educated wealthy customer may still like it. In a highbrow domain, a work may be judged to be important, even if the larger public does not like it; that cannot happen in a lowbrow domain.

The buyer of a highbrow product makes a decision in part on how the object will reflect his/her status, good taste, and elevated position in life. The companies studied here depend on this; HUGO BOSS and Bang & Olufsen want their products to look recognizably like their brand exactly because their brand carries symbolic status value, and that is a large part of what the customer is buying.

If evaluative practices are different in highbrow and lowbrow creative industries, then it would be productive to ask whether the practices documented in these chapters would be found in similar form in low-brow industries, such as:

- TV sitcoms
- Hollywood movies (blockbusters)
- pop artists (Justin Bieber)
- computer software
- video games
- mobile phone applications.

There is a risk that a focus on highbrow industries might result in a greater emphasis on the creator as a solitary, visionary figure: the famous designers at Bang & Olufsen, for example, or at Royal Copenhagen. Both David Lewis and Ursula Munch-Petersen have their designs on display at the Danish Museum of Design, thus receiving the full 'art world' treatment described by Becker (1982) in his analysis of the social processes whereby 'craft' is transformed into 'art.' Many of the lowbrow products on the above list are generated by large teams and organizational processes, rather than single creators. Lowbrow products are more likely to be generated in response to what the public wants, rather than in response to the internal vision of a brilliant designer. Consequently, the evaluative practices would be different, and the relative authority of the different evaluative regimes would be different. For example, the 'design history' regime would decline in authority, and the 'marketing' regime would increase. Argumentation practices would be different as well.

## The market as evaluator

How do evaluative regimes originate and then disseminate? A simple first hypothesis would be that evaluative practices originate with those who are more expert, and then disseminate to those with less and less knowledge. (See the above list of Becker's nested audiences.) The intermediaries and connoisseurs are the source of the evaluative practices, in other words, and then the general public learns from them. These case studies implicitly accept a linear model of dissemination.

But in the Internet era, this sort of top-down model risks seeming out of date. At the workshop, Childress argued that these experts are becoming 'disintermediated' – this is a term that has been coined to describe the participatory nature of Web 2.0, in which everyone is both a producer and a consumer. In all cases, the future success of any creative industry firm depends on the perceived legitimacy of the evaluations. This is particularly true in highly educated, market-driven societies, where each person is free to make their own consumption choices. With film festivals, the evaluative decisions 'build or erode legitimacy and publicity.' The jury must 'live up to the public's, the media's and the film industries' perceptions of what is fair, balanced and representative.' Film festivals will lose credibility if they are perceived to make bad/incorrect decisions (film makers will stop submitting, people will stop coming).

Christensen and Strandgaard Pedersen report that Michelin lost some credibility by its decision not to give NOMA three stars. Surely these considerations would influence any evaluative practices engaged in by gatekeepers and intermediaries who depend on perceived legitimacy (among the broad audience) for their power. Michelin would eventually experience a drop in sales and status if their evaluations were increasingly perceived to be incorrect.

Creative firms know this, of course, although it rarely comes up in these chapters. (One exception is Krause-Jensen, who notes that at Bang & Olufsen, two key criteria for evaluation are that it must appeal to consumers, and it must be affordable). In all of these case studies, those participating in the evaluative practices have to answer to an ultimate arbiter, the larger community. And as such, these evaluative practices are always business decisions as well as aesthetic decisions. Experts often have different taste from the masses, but in creative industries, experts are paid to make things the customers will like. Successful evaluative regimes are always those that internalize the perceived collective judgments of the market.

Regarding Alačovska's travel writer, I found myself thinking of the average tourist who would be carrying and reading the book. The tourist, visiting a city for the first and perhaps only time, is likely to value different criteria than the experienced traveler. Alačovska describes an incident where the writer wanted to include an entry on a

strange wig museum, and the editor rejected it as not being interesting
enough for their readers. And yet, the author says she is always thinking
about the audience, as for example in how she will write a story about
smoking marijuana in Amsterdam, in such a way that young people
won't find it too attractive and older people won't be offended. She can
describe her reader: 'I need to cater to an audience that is youngish,
cultured, and smart; that lives in a big metropolis, is probably childless,
and can afford to spend a day or two, or a long weekend, somewhere
nearby, and not be particularly bothered with the prices.'

Markets are mechanisms that assign a collectively determined value to
a product through the interaction of supply and demand. The value of a
stock in a company emerges from a collective and distributed evaluative
process; is this not an evaluative practice? Likewise, Apple can charge
substantially more for its computers than Windows PC computers with
similar technical specifications. But Apple can do that only because
customers will continue to buy at that higher price. Each time a consumer makes a purchasing decision, is this not an evaluative practice?

Mass evaluations (markets, open source communities, crowdsourcing) are absent from these case studies. There are several occasions
when the customer is mentioned, but these stories are always told
from the point of view of the creative professional. For example, when
Moeran describes how the *Ursula* line eventually made it to market, he
tells the story as reported by Ursula. After management decided not to
produce it, they agreed to let her show it in one of their stores for a
month. It sold out and got rave reviews. The positive evaluative judgments made by the public and by an influential newspaper critic led
management to change its mind. And yet, the story is told by Ursula to
justify her belief in the strength of her design; it is not an analysis of the
public's response in its own right. (Why did the newspaper critic like it?
What did he say? Why did consumers purchase it – for what use? What
did they intend the use of *Ursula* to signify to their dinner guests about
their own identity and taste?)

Csaba and Ger report that contemporary carpet making responds to
market demand and Western taste, and true collectors don't like that.
The authors don't say why, but imply that it's because it results in
carpets that are less authentic. And yet, authenticity itself is a socially
constructed concept, and represents its own evaluative regime – one that
is otherwise not addressed in these chapters. They report that young
people don't buy carpets, that tastes in interior design have changed

toward sleeker lines, and carpet sales have declined. So carpet makers are making more modern and contemporary designs (which, it is implied, are not authentic).

In some online communities, the evaluations of the larger market have become more important than those of experts. This trend is likely to continue – restaurant reviews on TripAdvisor potentially could replace Michelin; hotel reviews on hotels.com could replace Lonely Planet. Many consumers choose to use the emergent evaluation of the online community rather than read reviews by experts.

To the extent that the evaluations of the broad public begin to replace the evaluations of an inner circle of connoisseurs and experts, the case studies in this book may be focused on a creative industry model that is fading in importance – case studies of an older model that is more top down. Perhaps the intermediated model of evaluation is more appropriate for highbrow products, whereas a crowdsourcing model is more appropriate for lowbrow products. After all, the definition of lowbrow is that which appeals to the masses, thus the evaluative practices of the masses becomes the most relevant explanatory factor. Then, a study of evaluative practices becomes a branch of market research – interviewing consumers about why they chose a particular brand of toothpaste, or a brand of tableware.

A focus on customers is particularly appropriate for today's globalized markets, because each country forms a distinct market, and different evaluative decisions may be found in each market. Surely, professionals in creative industries, in today's globalizing world, are always taking into account the global reception of a new idea, as they engage in evaluative practices? Surely, discussions occur like: yes, they will love it in France, but the Chinese don't buy that sort of thing, and we can't afford to write off the Chinese market. There is an exciting opportunity for future study of the evaluative practices involved in developing products for the global market.

## Summary

There has been surprisingly little ethnographic study of creative practices in the creative industries. The neglect is even more surprising given the increasing importance of the creative and cultural industries to many economies. These chapters are an important step forward in our understanding of creativity and innovation.

I am grateful to the editors and the authors for providing such stimulating and important case studies. These chapters are filled with rich ethnographic detail, and they helped me to think about creativity in a very different way. My early drafts of this conclusion chapter were nearly twice as long; these chapters stimulated a broad range of thoughts for me, and I believe that is the greatest measure of important scholarly work.

I close on a reflective note. All of the authors are academic staff at a university, and consequently they also participate in evaluative practices as scientists and scholars. A few studies of academic evaluative practices have been done, but these studies aren't mentioned in these chapters. We rank our own institutions, via THE and Q rankings which are largely reputational, also via the Shanghai method which does not use reputational attributions. We sit on grant review panels to determine which research proposals are worthy of funding (Brenneis 1994; Lamont 2009). We engage in anonymous peer review of journal manuscripts several times each year.

I suggest that we might become more reflective about the role that evaluative practices play in our own lives: evaluating journal quality as we decide where to submit an exciting new study; evaluating a colleague's scholarship as we decide whether to hire or to promote them; evaluating which research topics are interesting and show promise; choosing which research site to study; posting a comment on a blog, or a review on Amazon.com. In a sense, my entire chapter is an extended evaluation, and I have raised many questions I might apply to myself. What evaluative regime have I applied in writing this chapter? Where did this regime originate, and how did I come to inhabit it? Why was I granted the honor of writing the concluding chapter? What was my motivation for agreeing to undertake this responsibility? How will you, the reader, respond to this chapter, and how will that influence me (and others) in the future? As we study creative practices at famous companies, we may learn something about ourselves. We all inhabit evaluative regimes, and we all participate in argumentation during which we appeal to status and authority. Our scholarly lives are filled with evaluative practices.

## References

Amabile, Teresa. 1996. *Creativity in Context: Update to the social psychology of creativity*. Boulder, CO: Westview Press.

Appadurai, Arjun. 1986. Commodities and the politics of value. In *The Social Life of Things: Commodities in cultural perspective*, ed. Arjun Appadurai, pp. 3–63. New York: Cambridge University Press.

Archer, Margaret S. 1995. *Realist Social Theory: The morphogenetic approach*. New York: Cambridge University Press.

Bakhtin, Mikhail M. 1981. Discourse in the novel. In *The Dialogic Imagination*, pp. 259–422. Austin, TX: University of Texas Press.

Becker, Howard. 1982. *Art Worlds*. Berkeley and Los Angeles: University of California Press.

Blum, David. 1986. *The Art of Quartet Playing: The Guarheri Quartet in Conversation with David Blum*. New York: Cornell University Press.

Bourdieu, Pierre. 1972/1977. *Outline of a Theory of Practice*. New York: Press Syndicate of the University of Cambridge. Originally published as *Esquisse d'une théorie de la pratique* (Geneva: Droz, 1972).

Brenneis, Donald. 1994. Discourse and discipline at the National Research Council: a bureaucratic Bildungsroman. *Cultural Anthropology* 9 (1): 23–36.

Carver, Sharon M. 2006. Assessing for deep understanding. In *The Cambridge Handbook of the Learning Sciences*, ed. R. Keith Sawyer, pp. 205–221. New York: Cambridge University Press.

Cole, Michael. 1996. *Cultural Psychology: A once and future discipline*. Cambridge, MA: Harvard University Press.

Csikszentmihalyi, Mihalyi. 1988. Society, culture, and person: a systems view of creativity. In *The Nature of Creativity*, ed. Robert J. Sternberg, pp. 325–339. New York: Cambridge University Press.

D'Andrade, Roy. 1987. A folk model of the mind. In *Cultural Models in Language and Thought*, ed. Dorothy Holland, and Naomi Quinn, pp. 112–148. New York: Cambridge University Press.

English, James F. 2005. *The Economy of Prestige: Prizes, awards, and the circulation of cultural value*. Boston, MA: Harvard University Press.

Ericsson, K. Anders, Neil Charness, Robert R. Hoffman, and Paul J. Feltovich, eds. 2006. *The Cambridge Handbook of Expertise and Expert Performance*. New York: Cambridge University Press.

Foucault, Michel. 1969/1972. *The Archeology of Knowledge and the Discourse on Language*. New York: Pantheon Books. Originally published as *L'Archéologie du Savoir* (Paris: Editions Gallimard, 1969).

1975/1977. *Discipline and Punish*. New York: Vintage Books. Originally published as *Surveiller et Punir: Naissance de la Prison* (Paris: Editions Gallimard, 1975).

Giddens, Anthony. 1984. *The Constitution of Society: Outline of the theory of structuration*. Berkeley, CA: University of California Press.

Goffman, E. 1959. *The Presentation of Self in Everyday Life.* New York: Anchor Books.

Kuhn, Thomas S. 1962. *The Structure of Scientific Revolutions.* Cambridge, MA: MIT Press.

Lamont, Michele. 2009. *How Professors Think: Inside the curious world of academic judgment.* Cambridge, MA: Harvard University Press.

Moeran, Brian and Jesper Strandgaard Pedersen. 2011. Introduction. In *Negotiating Values in the Creative Industries,* ed. Brian Moeran and Jesper Strandgaard Pedersen, pp. 1–35. Cambridge University Press.

Rogoff, Barbara. 1990. *Apprenticeship in Thinking: Cognitive development in social context.* New York: Oxford University Press.

Runco, Mark A., ed. 2003. *Critical Creative Processes.* Cresskill, NJ: Hampton Press.

Sawyer, R. Keith 2002. A discourse on discourse: An archeological history of an intellectual concept. *Cultural Studies* 16 (3): 433–456.

    2003. *Group Creativity: Music, theater, collaboration.* Mahwah, NJ: Erlbaum.

    2006. Analyzing collaborative discourse. In *The Cambridge Handbook of the Learning Sciences,* ed. R. Keith Sawyer, pp. 187–204. Cambridge University Press.

    2007. *Group Genius: The creative power of collaboration.* New York: Basic Books.

    2012. *Explaining Creativity: The science of human innovation* (2nd edition). New York: Oxford.

Shore, Bradd. 1996. *Culture in Mind: Cognition, culture, and the problem of meaning.* New York: Oxford University Press.

Simmel, Georg. 1978. *The Philosophy of Money.* London: Routledge & Kegan Paul.

Wenger, Etienne. 1999. *Communities of Practice: Learning, meaning, and identity.* New York: Cambridge University Press.

# Index

CPSIA information can be obtained at www.ICGtesting.com
Printed in the USA
LVOW12*0958170614

390404LV00001B/1/P